THE SHAKESPEAREAN INTERNATIONAL YEARBOOK

1: WHERE ARE WE NOW IN SHAKESPEAREAN STUDIES?

The Shakespearean International Yearbook

1: Where are we now in Shakespearean studies?

Edited by
W.R. Elton and John M. Mucciolo

Ashgate

Aldershot • Brookfield USA • Singapore • Sydney

Published by
Ashgate Publishing Limited
Gower House
Croft Road
Aldershot
Hants GU11 3HR
England

Ashgate Publishing Company
Old Post Road
Brookfield
Vermont 05036–9704
USA

British Library Cataloguing-in-Publication data

The Shakespearean International Yearbook
   Vol. 1: Where are we now in Shakespearean studies?
   1. Shakespeare, William, 1564–1616 – Criticism and interpretation
   I. Elton, W.R. (William R.)   II. Mucciolo, John M.
   822.3'3

ISBN 1 85928 353 5

ISSN 1465-5098

Typeset in Sabon by Manton Typesetters, 5–7 Eastfield Road, Louth, Lincs, LN11 7AJ and printed on acid-free paper and bound in Great Britain

Contents

Acknowledgements

The editors wish to acknowledge the encouragement of the late Professor Kenneth Muir; and to thank Rachel Lynch of Ashgate Publishing, S.F. Johnson, John M. Steadman, and Provost William P. Kelly of the Graduate School, City University of New York.

Foreword

Angus Fletcher

It has been said that we do not possess Shakespeare – he possesses us. Yet this power and right of possession do not persist unchanged over the centuries. Through and beyond the English-speaking world, Shakespeare has taken on the great originating role, and he addresses each age anew. His interpreters, staging or reading him, continue to re-invent him anew and it is their invigorating search for 'new approaches' that gives us the illusion that we own Shakespeare. Even Samuel Johnson shared the belief: 'What mankind have long possessed they have often examined and compared, and if they persist to value the possession, it is because frequent comparisons have confirmed opinion in its favour'. Johnson's *Preface* of 1765 held that 'what is most considered is best understood', and on this view, just before the new millennium, there should be little new to be understood about Shakespeare. But if, which seems equally likely, Shakespeare is the possessor, owning every new generation, then (rather oddly) the poetry is coming to understand *us* better and better, and not the other way round. Accordingly, the present *Yearbook* demonstrates underneath all technicalities the fervour of a hidden process by which our amplest and least explicable poet continues to determine us – in the deepest layers of our being, to quote Pope, Shakespeare is 'an instrument of nature'. We, as readers at least, are Shakespeare's creatures, and in that degree Keats was surely close to the truth when he wrote that Shakespeare's works are the commentary on a 'life of allegory', (according to the strict analogy Keats drew between such a worthwhile life and the Hebrew scriptures, whose 'figurative' character cries out that we must respond with commentary, with interpretation). The question then arises whether these readings can, or should, seek to transcend their own era. Such a transcendence would seem to account for the canonical universality of this art. Yet interpreters may belong unavoidably to their own culture.

By and large, the present collection addresses the mood and movement of Shakespearean interpretation at the present time. Some twenty chapters cover a wide range of engagements with the poet, and yet not even an extensive coverage can be schematically complete. This first volume of the

Shakespearean International Yearbook is merely a beginning, however extensive its purview. As the galloping powers of media take an ever greater toll – eroding or altering literacy? – there will need to be further commentary on these changes of Shakespeare's position for the field of popular culture. In its inaugural volume the *Yearbook* seeks rather to address certain issues fundamental to the interpretive encounter. The scene of this encounter is always the play – we hold Hamlet's view, that the play will catch us, inwardly. The reader here will find commentary on current views of several particular works, from *Julius Caesar* to *The Tempest*. If the former tragedy continues, as John Velz suggests, to raise questions of imperial style and the rhetoric of dictatorship, Shakespeare's last comedy has newly seemed a post-colonial document, a reading which, John Mucciolo observes, can shift awareness away from the central concern of that play, with Prospero's wisdom and his 'beating mind'.

King Lear has recently dramatized the question of textuality itself, and Knowles addresses current thinking on that major topic. One registers delight in the fact that Kennedy and Donno both show how the *Comedies* speak to the changes of culture in our time. While we find detailed interest in Malvolio the malcontent, we also find, with Donno and Kennedy, an index to larger post-modern explorations, in which gender studies do indeed clarify the Elizabethan drama. For *The Tempest* Mucciolo's bibliography indexes a whole field of critical discourse. Mainly this involves a matter of poetics, namely, is the play itself an entertainment, or a quasi-political commentary? Is *The Tempest* to be experienced or construed? Can the play possess us, at once, in both ways? Or, in other terms, how are we to adjudicate between the 'timeless' claims of the poem and the time-dependent claims of our interpretive encounter? If *The Tempest* is both poem and text, then surely there will be tension between the two states of expressive being.

Nowhere are such adjudications more apparent than with readings of the *Sonnets*. Dubrow reminds us that a new edition, Duncan-Jones's Arden *Sonnets*, shows 'that formal analysis is hardly an exhausted mode of inquiry', while Helen Vendler has now emphatically re-established an approach to the poems as 'art', as exemplifying a craft of composition – a view long held, but in our times sorely needing to be updated. Of course, the poetics of sonnet form cannot acquire value without those poems possessing our consciousness, and defining our needs. Dubrow gathers commentary upon perhaps the liveliest of such concerns – the question of gender in the *Sonnets*, as scholars like Orgel have posed a theatrical context for our study of Elizabethan sexuality and its public rendering.

While the lyrics express, the plays present, and fittingly more than one chapter here explore conditions of that enactment. Much excitement, popular (one might say touristic) as well as scholarly, surrounds the construction of the new Globe Theatre, and both Demaray and King address the current state of staging the plays. To materialize an Elizabethan or Jacobean theatrical space, by actually constructing a late-twentieth-century house, however lucky or unlucky the replica, is today to engage directly with the post-modern condition, that is, with the production of what Baudrillard has called simulacra. To 'rebuild' the theatre is one way, by reverting to origin, of trying to possess its chief playwright. At present there is also the iconic millennarian value of the reconstructed Globe. But underneath all such questions lies the abiding issue of acting. Again, Hamlet to the players, or Hamlet speaking to *himself*! John Russell Brown addresses the current state of performances, which, as he observes, continues to develop under the aegis of 'performance studies'. This dramaturgic approach to the canon is inherently a process of immediate encounter, following 'new and less impressionistic ways of studying any play in performance'. Performance will always remain central to Shakespeare, for any actual production is always a court of appeal, even when its judgements may later be overturned. In this light it becomes critically important to understand the reader's 'performance' of the text-as-read, in the manner of Harry Berger's two books, *Making Trifles of Terrors* and *Imaginary Audition: Shakespeare on Stage and Page*, since indeed Shakespeare exists for most of us as a silently read, silently consumed commodity. One notes that in an earlier essay on 'history and ideology', Jonathan Dollimore and Alan Sinfield had called Shakespeare's audience his *readers*: 'It is easy for us to assume, reading *Henry V*, that foreign war was a straightforward ground upon which to establish or celebrate national unity'. We read, we do not go to the play. On the other hand, Sinfield dealt with production practices and audience reception, in his 'Royal Shakespeare: Theatre and the Making of Ideology' in *Alternative Shakespeare* of 1985, where we are reminded that acting is a kind of reading. By the same token John Barton's book of 1984 about the Royal Shakespeare Company (RSC), *Playing Shakespeare*, deals continuously and intensely with the relations between drama and its scripts as read. In a sense all reading of texts, as texts, tends toward interpretation, so that we inevitably want the sort of discussion occurring in the *Yearbook*. We want to hear about our approaches and methods of encounter, but we continue to need a reminder of the Renaissance 'ideas' which subtend the text at its point of origin, before interpreters got into the act.

All the chapters in Part 3 deal with critical domains of historical research: the monarchy, the language, the religious tensions, the value-system of heroic honour, the law, and the English-Continental link to Italy. These are traditional fields, and no less important for all that; but our reviews indicate that all are being re-examined. Sommerville indicates that D.H. Willson's antipathetic account of James I has been recently rebalanced, along with much other historical revision that will clarify the Jacobean political scene for Shakespearean scholars. The 'history' work described by Sommerville needs to be a basis of literary interpretation. The law and its constituting principles remain fundamental to our sense of the social orders in the plays, as R.J. Schoeck's chapter reminds us. The history of influence remains always a field of conflict which here, in the chapter 'Shakespeare and the Italians', Frances Barasch relates to recent research on the *commedia dell'arte* and other elements of Italian dramatic practice. While the New Historicism has provided a much needed climate of scepticism about conformist opinions regarding historical fact, now that diminished post-modern anxieties call for a less 'subversive' Renaissance, we may return to contextual studies not quite so sharply flavoured by anecdote. To give but one important example: in his forthcoming book on *Troilus and Cressida*,[1] W.R. Elton makes ground-breaking use of theatrical history, to illuminate the play's relation to the Inns of Court revels. This archivally informed approach steers us away from the standard reading – *Troilus* as problem play – and shifts to a new paradigm, *Troilus* as the intensely clever, complex and erudite *dramma giocosa*, a combination of comedic elements suitable to an unusual, and uniquely word-conscious audience, the lawyers. The Inns of Court hypothesis is not new, but the rigour and scope of Elton's study set a new standard. In a similar fashion, it may be that a restless Machiavellian version of the heroic character suits our own time, but we still profitably return, with John M. Steadman, to the rich ancient philosophical roots of heroic magnanimity. Perhaps no topic is of deeper import than the poet's relation to religion, and we get an overview of current controversy and research from Donna B. Hamilton. Philological forays into the history of Shakespeare's language are as important now as they were in the nineteenth century – hence we need N.F. Blake's account. If language changes, so do ideas – but how do these latter get transformed? The same historical imperatives apply to all our excursions into the history of ideas as these inform the drama.

The broadly extensive view taken here allows the *Yearbook*'s commentators to convey, yet once more, that Shakespeare could give his audience what it wanted, while giving that audience 'what it never dreamed of'. Charles Lamb was surely right when he questioned our over-simplistic conclusion that Shakespeare is natural, and hence 'everybody can understand him'. Natural indeed, but as Lamb noted, this deep grounding 'lies out of the reach of most of us'. Hence we are never surprised to discover new slants on older Shakespearean questions, despite the troubling fact that academia and its popular offshoots continue to perpetuate the Shakespeare industry. This industry has some of the properties of original sin.

The 1980s and '90s have seen deeper explorations into Shakespeare's presentations of erotic ambiguity, as observed in Bruce R. Smith's chapter on 'Homoeroticism and Shakespeare'. Richard Levin, with accustomed clarity, chronicles the current wave of research into the poetry and cultural materialism. In the same controversial climate, as John Jowett indicates, the establishment and the 'deconstruction' of the canonical texts belong to a period in which, as he puts it, no single texts (or editorial decisions, one might add) can 'set themselves out as monumental and definitive'. All the more reason to get analytic surveys of what is being done in the contested field of textual instability – with *King Lear* as the archetypal recent case. Instability indeed is our watchword, perhaps, as Levin implies, intensified by the differences between an 'old' politically committed materialism and the 'new' materialism which in his view has 'no discernible political purpose'. Levin and the other contributors to this volume testify to the fact that, like the century itself, this is a transitional time for Shakespearean studies.

Fundamentals of critical practice must at the least reckon with this instability as the non-place where art and reality meet. For it is now clear that art and society cannot be reduced to a crude bilateral symmetry. Historians of literature have for long pretended that art and society interact, but perhaps only through a late twentieth-century view of culture does this interaction become adequately complex. In an 'Afterword' to Dollimore and Sinfield's volume, *Political Shakespeare*, Raymond Williams said that 'certain inherent features of these plays, accentuating certain permanent features of any drama, alter from the beginning the assumptions on which many traditional kinds of analysis have been based'. The plays do not give us an essential Shakespeare, despite Dover Wilson's 1937 'biographical adventure' under that title. But if there is no essential poet here, there is also no perfectly neutral 'multivocal form' we can ascribe to the plays. Raymond Williams held to the belief that we should treat 'the texts themselves as history', implying a sophisticated scheme for research. Such a programme requires probing inquiry into the nature of textuality itself, so that a broader horizon is needed here than is usually given. Aesthetics needs to be historicised. When, as Claus Uhlig here observes from a European perspective, the aesthetic domain puts politics into historical question, it follows that we need some rather sharp rethinking of latterday Marxist theory. Robert Weimann's work on theatre and medieval popular culture occupies a central historiographic place here. Uhlig calls for a reinstatement of Hegel's *Aesthetics*, which would provoke a broad inquiry into an aesthetic that evades regression to Romantic organicism, an aesthetic that might historicise the notion of character, carrying it beyond Bradley's magisterial account. Bradley, who lectured on Hegel's notions of tragedy, nevertheless left the Hegelian field undeveloped. One can still ask fundamental questions about the relation between art and the various faces of history.

While there is every reason to praise the intensity of 'ideological positions', when these, as with some recent cultural materialists, demonstrate that Shakespeare was not an unthinking conservative, there is also need to question when that very same scepticism hardens into a conformist vision. There are many shades to the politically correct. Such is one target of Graham Bradshaw's partial polemic, 'State of Play'. Bradshaw wants to limit the drab and destructive effects of 'group think' – attitudes Harold Rosenberg wryly was wont to associate with what he called 'the herd of independent minds'. Bradshaw writes further of one particular test for his perspectival Shakespeare, namely the method of delivering soliloquies, since this particular speech-type reveals both a subjectivity (an I) and a special mode of contact with audiences (an eye). A perspectival Shakespeare was probably always one sense in which generations have appreciated Shakespeare. Kenneth Burke explored many ways in which this was so, but earlier on in the 1904 lecture 'Shakespeare the Man', Bradley clearly expressed one basis for the perspectival approach. While noting the poet's general acceptance of the principle of 'degree' and the performance of hierarchically imposed rules, Bradley went on to say that 'there appear to be no further absolute principles than these: beyond them all is relative to the particular case and its particular conditions'. Relativity of action is matched by relativity of character. Such, in part, but centrally, is the critical mission of Harold Bloom's monumental study, *Shakespeare: The Invention of the Human*. To give but one example of the poet's character-making plenitude: imagine the invention of Falstaff. Maurice Morgann had said that Shakespeare 'scatters the seeds of things', and when modern critics show how each play argues with itself, attacking or defending its own meanings, they are, in fact, showing how it is that these plays come to seem natural to us. Our understanding of this dramatic self-regulation depends largely on our awareness that nature is an ecological order of things. In this context, one benefit of Bradshaw's comments on the 'romantic' readings given by Jonathan Bate is the idea that, before Romanticism could reintroduce the phenomenology of self and other, there had developed an older and deeper tradition of *natura naturans*, the Renaissance conception that the self is (if anything) a variable entity whose transactions in the world can only share in the variability. Shakespeare's twice-used phrase, 'prophetic soul', suggests an instability at the heart of man, since prophecy is never sure, though always intense. Bradshaw praises John Lee's insistence on the humanism of Montaigne, who remains a model of variability within order. We are left, by this chapter, as by others in the *Yearbook*, with an ever deeper sense that the poet stretches our intellectual and spiritual capacity, for there is no doubt we have recently seen, and will see, wars of conformity against the free reader. There is much of value in all current inquiries, Bradshaw and others would say, and in this pursuit there is revealed a desire to let each play speak, as such, and hence to allow interpretation to proceed from a critical canon established, as it were, from within. This 'within' is the poet's own. No amount of well-intentioned post-modern piety will permit a *Shakespearean* expression its free rein. Without returning to genteel repressions, our contributors seem to say, we need to preserve the love of art and artistry these plays and poems start from, and end with.

It might be tempting to assume that 'political Shakespeare' or 'alternative Shakespeare' or even a 'global Shakespeare' is now permanently enthroned, as computers give wider access to more information if not a more deeply informed knowledge. But the Reading Room of the British Museum has closed, and that closing marks a profound change. Granted that the differences between interpretation and criticism, and their overlap, are not much understood, but it seems that for some time interpretation has replaced criticism and its normal emphasis upon poetics. Rhetoric has overcome poetics. A belief in *meaning for our time* has replaced the original understanding Ben Jonson expressed, when he said of Shakespeare: 'he was not of an age, but for all time'. This may seem to post-modernists a naïve critical opinion, but Jonson actually knew the poet's ways of working and knew his local fame. Jonson was here the generous critic. He does not pretend to stand above the plays of the First Folio. The same Jonsonian refusal of interpretive superiority appears in Milton's first published poem, in which he called Shakespeare 'Delphick', that is, monumentally incising and conveying a 'deep impression' – exactly what is *not* subject to any temporary fashions of reading. We cannot avoid our own standpoint, but there is among earlier authors – maybe even the jealous Greene – a belief that there is in the plays something oddly *alone* about Shakespeare. We might want to understand this 'Shakescene', but we certainly cannot do so, if we fail to examine what these plays are – as plays, not sociological indices or political documents. If there has always been a tendency to study, and appreciate, the development of character in the plays, this follows from the play-aspect, the *action*, of the drama. ('For they are actions that a man might play'.) To be involved with such matters today will appear not merely naïve, but contrary to the advancement (to use Bacon's term) of recent commentary and fact-finding. But to the critic, who judges form and artistic effect, the concern will not appear nostalgic or naïve. Criticism is the essential demand, no less so in an age unwilling to take the problem of essences seriously. For criticism asks, in the case of Shakespeare, why indeed his poetry still speaks to its audience with such universal power. It is time to replace suspicious commentaries with ambiguous readings, perhaps in Empson's seventh sense.

   A continued, and legitimate, fascination with Shakespeare is not a fact that needs apology – he is clearly one of the most entertaining dramatists who ever wrote. We are as fascinated by 'character' as he was. The nimble, percipient, humane attitude underlying these plays needs now, as before, no special pleading. Yet surely there is something politically suggestive about his success: he wrote for a world fully involved with, and for a long time to come, fully committed to aristocratic values. Democratic Shakespeare may be a contradiction, and in the present media-driven 'culture' of democracy one wonders what can *truthfully* be said about him. His counterpoints will yield access to partial truths, to be sure. But it seems we need to reconsider the positive as well as negative values associated with aristocracy, with privilege, with empire even. If we fail *fully* to contrast the poet's age with our own, we shall fail in appreciating the poet's art. The chapters in this volume survey certain conditions of this art, and in future volumes scholars will be dealing with the way these plays exist in a world approaching, finally, the status of his theatre, that is, global status. In the title of this *Yearbook* the term 'international' is perhaps no longer what it was for Allardyce Nicoll, Philip Edwards, and other advisors to the *Shakespeare Survey*. The late Kenneth Muir, remembered here by Edwards, not least for his distinguished editorship of the *Survey*, would doubtless note our changing situation. The 1950 *Survey* listed correspondents from twenty-eight separate countries and included articles from Bulgaria, Germany, Belgium, and Denmark. The same dispersion of commentary could be matched today, perhaps, but now a unitary metaphor has supervened to cover what is called a global order of things. 'All the world's a stage', but now the stage is the whole world, a global construct. It remains to be seen whether this commerce-driven worldview is, in fact, destroying (rather than preserving) the multiplicity of differences so clearly present in the works of Shakespeare.

REFERENCE

1. Elton, W.R. (1999), *Shakespeare's 'Troilus and Cressida' and the Inns of Court Revels*, Aldershot: Ashgate.

PART 1

Methodologies and Controversies

1   State of Play

Graham Bradshaw

My brief, or invitation, was to comment on 'where we are now' in our view of Shakespeare's tragedies. A short answer might be, all over the place, yet I feel more hopeful about our present situation than I did a few years ago, when writing *Misrepresentations*.[1] It is hard to tell whether the climate is changing, or just the weather, and publishers continue to assemble and market their offerings under different, divisive 'ismic' labels (feminist, New Historist, cultural materialist, etc.), but there does seem to be more traffic across the frontiers of what Robert Alter calls 'groupthink'.

Since it's difficult to collect and organise responses to such diverse activity, I should explain the changes of direction in this chapter's four sections. I begin in the 'main theatre' which, like its Stratford equivalent, attracts nearly all of the tourists and publicity but is less hospitable to Shakespeare or audiences than the smaller theatres. Here politically correct critics call for the 'democratization' of a canon dominated by Dead White European Males, new historicists reverse Ben Jonson's critical verdict by concentrating on a Shakespeare who is decidedly of his age, not for all time, and the more aggressive cultural materialists see the teaching of Shakespeare as an 'instrument of domination' in an ongoing cultural conspiracy;[2] my chief concern is that the 'climate' in this theatre is too politicized and quarrelsome to allow any real engagement with the intricacy and subtlety of a Shakespeare play. The second section examines what I take to be a significant difference in our ways of staging tragic soliloquies, and the third section then goes on to ask whether and how these changes in modern acting style reflect different contemporary ways of considering Renaissance conceptions of 'self' or 'subjectivity'. These changes of direction are selective but not arbitrary, since I am suggesting that some very influential contemporary accounts of 'subjectivity' are anachronistic, and that in this case 'where we are now' shows that where we are going may be quite unlike where we have been. The final section expresses my belief, or hope, that we will be engaging more directly with Shakespeare's perspectivism. Both our present situation and the history of Shakespearean criticism repeatedly demonstrate the effects of this perspectivism while all

3

too rarely addressing the cause. So much by way of summary; let us enter the main theatre . . . .

MOTES, BEAMS AND FAULTLINES

Robert Alter's worries about 'groupthink' appeared in his response to the *Partisan Review* questionnaire for its 1993 Special Issue on 'The Politics of Political Correctness'; he was depressed by that 'ideologically driven' climate in which 'some departments of English . . . have made Toni Morrison more important than Shakespeare' (510).[3] Since it's easier to sell to groups than individuals, so-called 'identity politics' is part of the same late-capitalist package, with which professed anti-capitalists cannily or thoughtlessly collude. Doubtless, more eyebrows would have been raised if Adrienne Rich had said 'I' not 'we' when pronouncing, in her richly confident fashion, that 'We know more than Jane Austen because our lives are more complex, more than Shakespeare because we know more about the lives of women'.[4] But, as Peter Erickson approvingly declared in 1991, literary merit and 'individual talent' count for little in Rich's fundamental 're-vision' of Shakespeare and the whole 'concept of canon', since 'it is the artistic production of the group as a whole that merits inclusion'.[5] If we are looking ahead to what I take to be the central issue of what we make of Shakespeare's perspectivism, we should notice how Erickson endorses Rich's and Harold Bloom's view that *The Merchant of Venice* is 'an anti-Semitic text' since 'there is no reason to doubt that the historical Shakespeare would have agreed with his Portia' (104). The justifying arguments for this view, or the similar view that *Othello* is 'racist', flout one of the few basic principles in Shakespearean criticism: unless we can produce strong contrary evidence, there is no excuse for presuming that the attitudes and responses of an Elizabethan or Jacobean audience, or Shakespeare, were more fixed and narrow than the range or spectrum of attitudes represented within the play.

In his 'autobiographical preface' to *Returning to Shakespeare* Brian Vickers was as pessimistic as Alter, when contrasting the critical situation in 1989 with that he had known two decades earlier:

> In Cambridge, in the 1960s, it was unquestioned that a writer's language was of major importance: that awareness is becoming increasingly rare. In recent years critics have brought an ever-smaller range of approaches to bear on Shakespeare. In this age of fragmentation and specialism, it seems to be enough to use just feminism, or ideology, or psychoanalysis, in none of which does Shakespeare's language – seen in appropriate historical and analytical terms – play any particular role. Many critics today wish to acquire status and identity by belonging to a clearly defined and separate school, with its own methodology and values; few of them seem to ask themselves, 'What else do I need to know?' The range of questions asked – and hence of answers – gets progressively narrower, critical writing more repetitive, easily identifi-

able in terms of a group style, while our understanding of Shakespeare is diminished in the process.

As if to vindicate this gloomy view, the 1980s finished with the Modern Language Association's December 1989 Special Session to debate the case of Richard Levin. In 1988 Levin had published an essay on 'Feminist Thematics and Shakespearean Tragedy'[7] which extended his ongoing critique of 'thematic' criticism to critics like Coppélia Kahn, Marilyn French, Marianne Novy and Madelon Gohlke, while carefully and specifically exempting non-thematic feminist critics like Linda Bamber, Catherine Belsey, Lisa Jardine and Katherine McLuskie. Nonetheless, twenty-four feminists (including some Levin had exempted or praised) wrote a furious joint letter of protest to the PMLA, and the controversy raged on until the Special Session. What made all this depressingly symptomatic was the nickel-nosed indifference to any concept of critical debate, or what was once (it seems so long ago) called 'the common pursuit of true judgement'; criticism was something one dished out, but never expected to receive.

In his customarily provocative way Levin had isolated various important Shakespearean issues. He questioned the 'location of the cause of the tragic outcome in "masculinity" or "patriarchy", operating through the individuals and the society as a whole' (127), asked what implications the 'denigration' of the 'tragic hero' had for the tragic effect (131), discussed specific instances where 'the concrete facts of the play never really fit the abstract theme of the critic' (129), and maintained that 'the tragedies are not criticizing their own gender assumption but just assuming them, along with other conditions underlying the dramatized action, which is their real subject' (134). Levin's argument was sharply focused but not always compelling; for example, many critics think *Othello* and *Coriolanus* do explore gender assumptions. Yet the replies to Levin seldom addressed the Shakespearean issues he had raised, and some participants even wanted to deny his right to make points they agreed with. When Carol Cook admitted that she too disagreed with some of the readings Levin had criticized this could have led into a critical discussion of the plays in question but didn't, because Cook was more concerned to explain that what her group, including critics like Jardine, McLuskie and Karen Newman, objected to was the 'humanist' orientation of earlier feminist criticism, whereas Levin was (allegedly) engaged in a 'power struggle' that 'entails the targeting of feminism'.[8] Such retreats into 'groupthink' treat the Shakespearean issues as merely ancillary or instrumental.

We are constantly told that discussing Shakespeare inevitably involves other, wider issues, and of course that is true; yet the extraordinary quarrelsomeness of so much recent criticism has also shown how frequently the other, usually politicized issues deflect or divert us from discussing Shakespeare's plays. Whether that happens not only depends on, but shows, what we think more important. When British cultural materialists found the concept of 'containment' in Stephen Greenblatt's 'Invisible Bullets' politically defeatist, and the Marxist Walter Cohen protested that Greenblatt's Foucauldian belief that 'any apparent site of resistance ulti-mately serves the interests of power' showed New Historicism's 'liberal disillusionment',[9] they were objecting to Greenblatt's political stance, not to his account of Shakespeare's. In his reply Greenblatt addressed this political issue by insisting that he wasn't saying, and indeed didn't believe, that all sites of resistance are 'ultimately co-opted': 'Some are, some aren't'.[10] But since Greenblatt saw no need to return to, or modify, his own argu-ment that Shakespeare's second tetralogy constantly shows 'subversion contained', the reply was in effect saying, 'Please sir, I didn't say that, Shakespeare said it.'

The first Greenblatt essay I ever read was 'Murdering Peasants', and I vividly remember my excitement. Since Greenblatt is so concerned with what he calls the 'margins', and since his 'margins' tend to be more interesting than almost anybody else's 'centre', it would be absurd to expect him to 'go through' a play in some scene-by-scene fashion. Yet the appeal of his very influential discussion of *Othello* may very well owe more to the fascination of the 'other issues' *Renaissance Self-Fashioning* addresses; despite the vivacity of Greenblatt's account of Iago, he cannot produce any convincing textual evidence for this extraordinary idea that the 'dark essence of Iago's whole enterprise' is to 'play upon Othello's buried perception of his own sexual relations with Desdemona as adulter-ous'.[11] Since I discussed this at some length in *Misrepresentations*, taking it as an example of the way in which so much contemporary criticism raids Shakespeare to 'instantiate' a theory without allowing the play to test the theory (190–201), I was naturally interested to see many of the same objections appearing, quite independently, in James Cunningham's recent, admirably non-partisan *Shakespeare's Tragedies and Modern Critical Theory*.[12] One conclusion might be that discussion of Shakespeare's trag-edies is in a bad state if basic textual objections are discounted as narrowly textual; another, less depressing and perhaps more realistic conclusion might be that many very influential readings of Shakespeare have also been textually strained, like Ernest Jones's or even Wilson Knight's read-ings of *Hamlet* and that Greenblatt was managing, like a contemporary Montaigne, to combine his concern with the 'self' (on which more in a moment) with other, related anxieties – male anxiety, sexual anxiety – that touched contemporary nerves. Critical dialogue remained a possibility, not least because Greenblatt himself allows that 'sustained, scrupulous atten-tion to formal and linguistic design will remain at the centre of literary teaching and study'.[13]

British cultural materialist critics like Alan Sinfield and Jonathan Dollimore certainly wouldn't agree with that, since they always associate 'traditional critical activity' with reactionary politics and 'a social order that exploits people on grounds of race, gender, sexuality and class'.[14] In this critical (or anti-critical) climate any specifically Shakespearean disagreement is likely to be translated into politicized, 'groupthink' terms. To take a personal example, when Alan Sinfield reviewed *Misrepresentations* he couldn't say much about my book or Shakespeare since his one-and-a-half *TLS* pages were largely devoted to providing an indignantly corrective, heroic-nostalgic account of the rise of British cultural materialism.[15] I was chiefly struck by the contrast between his old-fashioned narrative of continuity and my own somewhat clinical or diagnostic attempt to isolate (and list in my subject index) those coercive dualisms and either/or binarisms that provide the assumptive basis for so many 'materialist' readings; I confess, I still think that what I was doing and what Sinfield disliked so much he couldn't bring himself to mention it was closer to what anybody seriously committed to 'cultural materialism' or 'cultural poetics' or historicizing our present ought to be doing. Any 'materialist' who believes that values are culturally and historically specific should see that this applies to his or her own values. Greenblatt is intensely aware of this, but Sinfield isn't, so that one obvious 'faultline' in Sinfield's *Faultlines* is that it is concerned only with those 'faultlines and breaking points' which 'enable dissident reading' (9). In this book, as in Dollimore's *Radical Tragedy*,[16] the relentlessly adversarial contrasts between 'the liberal reading' and 'the dissident reading' cannot but seem contrived, when decades of pluralism have made it impossible to isolate 'the' liberal or 'humanist' reading of any Shakespeare play, and when any 'dissident perspective' is presented as not only always superior but transhistorically, transculturally true. A politicized (and 'mystified') agenda then shapes the response to any play and its characters; so, for Sinfield, the 'easiest way to make *Othello* plausible in Britain is to rely on the lurking racism, sexism, and superstition in British culture' (5), but Emilia 'takes notable steps towards a dissident perception' (46). Since I was arguing that to privilege the 'dissident perspective' in this too predictable way 'short-circuits' the far more subtle and intricate way in which Shakespeare's plays organize different, and dissident, 'perspectives', I hoped it would be apparent to some readers that my own critical quarrel with British 'cultural materialist' readings was different from that in Brian Vickers's *Appropriating Shakespeare*[17] – less learned, alas, but also less negative, and less proprietorial in its view of Shakespeare. But of course it was no surprise, and amusing to my friends, to see Sinfield's review bracketing Bradshaw and Vickers as 'political reactionaries, who are happy to celebrate Shakespeare's allegiance to the state propaganda of his time' (4).

Since most of the literature we read and value is rooted in beliefs and assumptions we no longer share, we are the losers if we cannot be interested in different habits of thought and modes of feeling, in other cultures and other periods of our own culture; something like this is also true of criticism. I find myself interested by and (I think) learning from, say, Coppélia Kahn, Janet Adelman and Valerie Traub's discussions of 'masculine identity' in *Macbeth* and *Coriolanus* even though I don't share their psychoanalytical assumption and draw a rather firm line when William Kerrigan thinks *Hamlet* shows when little Shakespeare was weaned.[18] On the other hand, the intolerance and exclusivity of much contemporary criticism has been fuelled by the habit of carrying out magpie-like raids on whatever glitters in other disciplines, without waiting to see why these disciplines are more divided or sceptical in their views of, say, Derrida, Foucault, Freud, or Lawrence Stone. In *Appropriating Shakespeare* Brian Vickers wants to demolish the different approaches he criticizes; I doubt that the book will succeed in that, and suspect its lasting value will be prophylactic – as an awesomely well-documented warning to would-be believers and magpies that all that glisters is not gold, and that their authorities are not sacred texts.

Precisely because the approaches Vickers attacks have now been around for a long time, familiarity (and predictability) has encouraged a more diffused scepticism. As Anthony B. Dawson observes, 'There is by now a strong sense of *déjà entendu* in the very sound of words like "gender" and "class", and the ideologically pure concepts such terms represent tend to incite resistance, even when one shares the leftish assumptions of those who utter them' (30).[19] Dawson also refers to 'a resurgence of interest in subjectivity and a broadening insistence on heterogeneity of response to cultural phenomena' (30). I hope both these points are true and want next to consider, as a kind of test case, how one seemingly limited issue can invite us to cross the frontiers of 'groupthink'. My 'test case' involves a change in acting style which began a few years before J.L. Styan's *The Shakespeare Revolution*[20] claimed that contemporary actors and directors were recovering the authentic 'Shakespeare experience'. Pressing the example a little harder also suggests how some very influential arguments about 'subjectivity' may be tendentiously cohesive and historically anachronistic.

EYE-CONTACT

In the theatre, eye-contact may be of two kinds. It may be unfocused and generalized, looking out to the audience as a collective presence, or it may involve gazing directly at individual members of the audience in a more intimate or searching way. In Peter Hall's famous 1965 *Hamlet* David Warner addressed the audience in this deliberately direct way and was thrilled by the consequences. One evening, when he peered into the stalls and asked, 'Am I a Coward?', somebody shouted 'Yes!' and the delighted Warner found Shakespeare's script offering the appropriate responses. When he replied, 'Who calles me Villaine? . . . Who does me this?', and a name was shouted back, Hamlet's next, vehemently self-critical but seemingly spontaneous response was already written in: 'I should take it: for it cannot be, / But I am Pigeon-Liver'd . . . ' Warner remembers this as one of the most exhilarating nights of his acting career, and in her useful study of *Modern Hamlets and their Soliloquies* Mary Maher explains:

> He was stunned with the rightness of feeling and the naturalness of speaking these soliloquy lines directly to the theatre audience. The text supported him absolutely. No adjustments in timing, motivation, or thought needed to be made. He was still making discoveries inside the act of performance, and it filled him with a sense of awe about Shakespeare's dramaturgy.[21]

Well, maybe, but 'rightness of feeling' and ideas of 'naturalness' always have a historical and cultural location, and since the effect of eye-contact is also inevitably social and cultural the theatrical interaction that thrilled Warner and many members of his largely youthful 1960s audience wouldn't have been possible in other contexts. In her entry for 'Eye-Contact' in the *Oxford Companion to the Mind* Mary Argyle records that 'During conversation, two people seated 2 metres apart will each look at each other for about 60 per cent of the time (with wide individual differences), and there will be eye-contact for about 30 per cent of the time'.[22] But in Japan, where I live, any prolonged eye-contact is likely to cause discomfort among the older generation, and the possibility of eye-contact with an audience barely exists in traditional Japanese theatre: the puppets in Bunraku can't look at anyone, Noh actors are masked and should be looking at a pillar, and on the rare occasions when a Kabuki actor looks into the audience from the stage it's understood and enjoyed as a theatrical signal that his mistress is present. In North America direct eye-contact is accepted and even expected, so that dropping the eyes, which in South America might signal respect, may be construed as shiftiness.

Maher herself notes that Sir Henry Irving and Johnston Forbes-Robertson never made eye-contact with their audiences when speaking Hamlet's soliloquies, and that one reason we know this is that 'observers complained only when actors spoke too much to the audience' (xxii). Yet by 1984 John Barton was telling his RSC actors, 'There are very few absolute rules with Shakespeare, but I personally believe that it's right ninety-nine times out of a hundred to share the speech with an audience and a grave distortion of Shakespeare's intention to do it oneself'.[23] That slide from personal belief into speculation on Shakespeare's intention shows how, as Harry Berger warns in *Imaginary Audition*, stage-centred critics 'often ignore the influence of particular styles or traditions of acting on what counts as an actable interpretation'.[24] To reapply a point W.B. Worthen makes about Styan's 'paradigmatic text', Barton is 'correlating three moments where an author-effect is produced: in the author's original intention, in a mode of stage production understood to recover that authority, and in the response of the audience, whose "experience" of the stage reproduces that intention' (13).[25] Gielgud, whose Hamlet was for so long regarded as a touchstone, would certainly have disagreed with Barton. His delivery of the soliloquies was always internalised; the audience overheard an intense self-communing that 'never once acknowledged their presence' (16).[26] When

Richard Burton was rehearsing the third soliloquy in the 1964 production Gielgud directed – just a year before the Hall–Warner *Hamlet* – Burton's own strong impulse to 'speak it to them' met with Gielgud's sharp disapproval: 'It's such a phony technique to come out on the apron in a proscenium theatre. It seems to me it's more realistic to keep it within the scene'.[27] Making eye-contact in a proscenium theatre is certainly difficult since the audience is largely invisible beyond front stage lights, but Gielgud's wish to be 'realistic' and 'keep it within the scene' wasn't merely dictated by practical exigencies. Alec Guinness told Maher that when he played Hamlet the soliloquies were all 'delivered in the conventional way – as introspective speeches, as if the character was thinking aloud to himself and not explaining his situation to an audience, as is sometimes now the case', and confirmed that 'Certainly Gielgud and all actors I had seen either before him or around that time, did the same': 'In fact, I suppose one could say that the soliloquies were treated as *part of the play* and not [as a] comment on it. But right or wrong I don't see it makes a great deal of difference' (20).

Right or wrong, there is a great deal of difference between what these earlier actors did and what contemporary actors now find 'natural', or 'realistic'. What Gielgud had discouraged Burton from doing in 1964 and what Hall encouraged Warner to do in 1965 was being followed by Nicol Williamson in 1969 and Albert Finney in 1975 and Michael Pennington in 1980, and is now favoured by most of the contemporary Hamlets Maher interviews. Anton Lesser kept to the older tradition in Jonathan Miller's 1982 production 'even though it was first performed on a three-quarter thrust stage, the kind of stage historically associated with direct-address soliloquies', and when the production was transferred to a larger, proscenium arch theatre, 'the soliloquies became even more inward' (132).[28] Randall Duk Kim went in the opposite direction, explaining that 'although there are no set rules about performance, only options', his own experience of the 'thrust stage' made him 'believe that Shakespeare would have taken full advantage of the special actor-audience spatial relationship that operates in such a theatre' (164). Derek Jacobi and David Rintoul used direct address very selectively. In the third soliloquy they both used internalized delivery until that point where Hamlet is at his most external, howling and cursing like Laertes or any other conventional revenger; and then, at the suddenly implosive moment when Hamlet becomes self-conscious and in that sense more *inward* ('Why, what an Asse am I!') the delivery was externalised, or shared with the audience. On the other hand, both Jacobi and Rintoul saw the final Q2 soliloquy ('How all occasions') as, in Rintoul's words, 'very very much directed to the audience, with definite eye contact' (112, 141).

Kevin Kline chose not to make direct eye contact in his 1990 production, but recalled that when he first played Hamlet in 1986 he had 'thought all the soliloquies should be done to the audience' and his director, Liviu

Ciulei, 'was always against this': 'You see, Liviu felt that Hamlet was *feigning* madness throughout.' The logic in that 'You see' was intelligent, since Kline himself was seeing that any immediate theatrical pay-off in directly addressing the audience has further consequences: 'It can let you off the hook, can take you off the spot as Hamlet, and thus keep you away from madness'. Four years later, Kline's preference for 'inner-directed soliloquy' was consistent with this view that Hamlet 'attained a kind of madness at times' (185). Randall Duk Kim chose direct address but similarly recognized that his own preferred 'option' had interpretative consequences, or conditions: 'You see, I don't think Hamlet goes mad, and I don't think the audience thinks he goes mad. If anything, he's *too* sane. The direct-address soliloquy has a way of confirming his sanity' (165).

The notion of 'sharing' is complicated, not least because direct address may *reduce* the audience's sense of Hamlet's onstage isolation. Kline recalls that the 'one time' he did 'do direct address' (in the fourth soliloquy) it 'got didactic and preachy' since 'it took the onus off Hamlet, off me, and let me share it with [the audience], diffusing the moment entirely, making it a general moment instead of "so particular with me" '; Kline similarly notes that if the third soliloquy is delivered 'into their eyes' (in Warner's fashion), 'then I am explaining it to them and I'm not going *through* it as I should be' (185). 'Sharing it' is one of John Barton's key notions, but few actors playing Hamlet want to forfeit an audience's sympathy, and Gielgud's 'self-communing' clearly didn't have that effect on his audiences. The nearest cinematic equivalent to direct address and eye-contact in the theatre is so-called 'in-camera' delivery, and in his 1948 film Olivier's Prince *never* looks into the camera in soliloquies. His 'To be or not to be' is a touchstone, with its initial shots of the back of Hamlet's dyed blonde head, followed by the subliminal shot of a human brain.

But Olivier's use of direct, in-camera address in *Richard III* is different, and that difference is suggestive. Although there is no direct evidence of what Burbage and other Globe players did in soliloquies – or in monologues, or in the so-called 'asides' that multiply like rabbits in modern editions, as if in promiscuous response to our sublunary notions of 'realism' – Olivier, Gielgud, and at least two previous generations of actors had allowed direct address and eye-contact to an Edmund but *not* to Lear, to an Iago but *not* to Othello. This implies a coherent, though not necessarily historical or 'authentic', view of what tragic protagonists can and can't do. When an actor playing Richard III, or Edmund, or Iago, comes closer to the audience he is simultaneously distancing himself *and* the audience from the drama which suddenly seems to be taking place *behind* him. In such cases, the rather paradoxically distancing effect of 'sharing it' emphasis these characters' confidence that they are smarter than anybody else, and also emphasises their sense of themselves as surrogate dramatists who certainly don't regard the plays they think they are producing as 'tragic'. Conversely, there seems to be some idea (or less articulate instinct) that the tragic protagonist shouldn't address the audience directly because he shouldn't distance himself from his own tragedy. But when a highly intelligent contemporary actor like Ian McKellen uses direct address when playing Macbeth as well as Richard III, he clearly doesn't feel constrained by any such idea, or implied rationale.

Of course it would be wonderful to know whether Burbage felt any such constraint, but we don't. If we did, that would have profound implications, not only in relation to the post-1965 shift in acting style, but also in relation to Stephen Orgel's pregnant observation that modern ideas of genre are exclusive, whereas Renaissance notions of genre were inclusive.[29] Too often, the distinction between comedy and tragedy seems to turn on endings, as though tragedy ends in death whereas comedy ends with marriage (before the tragedy starts). To have some distinction that manifested itself in acting styles, from scene to scene, would indeed be something. Yet it wouldn't tell us what would work now, for us; even if we could attend an 'authentic' Globe performance – with boy actors playing women, and without that concern for the visual aspects of performance which distinguishes modern directors like Peter Brook or Ninagawa – this could not guarantee an 'authentic' response. Indeed, Styan's argument that non-realistic performance styles recover the authentic 'Shakespeare experience' implodes, unless we can imagine spectators at the Globe thinking, 'At last! what a relief to get away from realism'.

Shakespeare's perspectivism and his preference for what the eighteenth century nervously called 'mixed' drama work against any exclusive conception of the 'tragic'. Of course *Othello* is decidedly tragic from Othello's point of view, but from Iago's or even Emilia's point of view it is a horrible farce in which the protagonist is not someone who 'loved not wisely, but too well' (a phrase that might be reserved for Desdemona), but a filthy 'gull'. Since all these, and other, perspectives are available within the drama, it's all the more difficult to guess what did nor should happen, for instance in 4.1, where the 'tragic' protagonist is successively degraded. Othello's verbal collapse into incoherent prose – '(pish) Noses, Eares. and Lippes' – is followed by the physical collapse; when he comes to he is babbling in untragic fashion of horns, and is soon locked into even more degrading prose throughout the eavesdropping, which, as the theatrically experienced Harley Granville Barker observed, brings him 'to the very depth of indignity':

> Collapsed at Iago's feet, there was still at least a touch of the tragic in him, much of the pitiful. But to recover from that only to turn eavesdropper, to be craning his neck, straining his ears, dodging his black face back and forth like a figure in a farce – was ever tragic hero treated thus?[30]

Modern actors, including Olivier, often cut Othello's exclamations in this appallingly degrading climax to the scene. But if the blackened Burbage addressed the audience directly, for example in exclaiming 'Looke how he laughs already!' or 'So, so, so, so: they laugh, that winne', that would merely have emphasized the way in which what Othello is locked into is already dramatically and generically more complicated and painful than any un-'mixed' tragedy. And for the audience, any sense that Othello is a 'tragic hero', while Angelo and Leontes are characters in 'comedy', is tested against the alarmingly tragi-comic exploration of what all these characters have it in them to become – which raises other important questions about 'character' and the 'self'.

I-CONTACT

The contrast between Olivier and McKellen's use of eye-contact shouldn't obscure the similarity in their post-Freudian, post-Stanislavskian ways of thinking about 'character' and the 'self'. As is well known, Olivier's sense of Hamlet was modelled on Ernest Jones's development of Freud's theory about an 'Oedipal complex'; *Hamlet* becomes 'the tragedy of a man who could not make up his mind' because of the way his mind was made up before he was a man. Similarly, McKellen makes actorly sense of Richard III as somebody who, long before the play starts, became what he now just is: 'Richard's wickedness is an outcome of other people's disaffection with his physique. His mother's cursing outburst . . . exemplifies the verbal and emotional abuse which from infancy has formed her youngest son's character and behaviour'.[31]

These psychologised, post-Freudian views see the 'self' as something already 'formed' and in that sense knowable. So far as Hamlet is concerned, they can be assimilated to the post-Romantic idea that Hamlet's own appeal to an authenticating inner self – 'that within, which passes show' – announces something distinctively new, and modern. But they conflict with that post-Marxist, anti-essentialist view of the 'self' that made Christopher Norris scoff when Leavis refers to Othello's 'essential make-up'[32] and led cultural materialist critics like Francis Barker[33] and Catherine Belsey[34] to argue that Hamlet's 'that within' is a gap, or 'essentialist-humanist' illusion. Two examples I discussed in *Misrepresentations* (9–10)[35] show how this argument turns on theory-driven dualisms and a coercively arbitrary 'not-but': Jonathan Dollimore's claim that identity is 'constituted not essentially but socially' obviously owes less to Shakespeare, or Renaissance conceptions of 'self', than to Marx's insistence that 'it is not the consciousness of men that determines their being, but, on the contrary, their social being that determines their consciousness', just as Dollimore's claim that '*virtus* is shown to be not innate but the effect – and thus the vehicle – of court power' dutifully echoes Foucault's argument that 'the individual is an effect of power, and at the same time, or precisely to the extent to which it is that effect, it is . . . its vehicle'.

Since these conflicting, post-Freudian and post-Marxist views are both modern, they may both be misleadingly anachronistic. As Jonathan Sawday warns, in a thoughtful essay on 'Self and Selfhood in the Seventeenth Century', 'The rich, post-Freudian vocabulary of self-reflection upon which we now draw is, by definition, of relatively recent origin' (29).[36] As for the cultural materialist and New Historicist tendency to regard the self as a 'product', it's worth noticing how these critics constantly appeal to Foucault, but very selectively, ignoring those late lectures in which Foucault observed, 'Perhaps I've insisted too much on the technology of power and dominion', and confessed to being 'more and more interested' in what he called the 'technologies of self'.[37] In offering a 'genealogy of subjectivity' as something other and more than a history of discipline and subjection, the dying Foucault was moving away from the position adopted by those critics who repeatedly cite his earlier work to support their view of the 'self' as a social or externally produced 'product'; in tracing a line from Plato and Augustine through the Renaissance, he was moving towards a position more like that taken by Katharine Eisaman Maus in *Inwardness and Theater in the English Renaissance*. Maus starts from Hamlet's 'that within' as a would-be authenticating appeal to 'the difference between an unexpressed interior and a theatricalised exterior'.[38] In acknowledging that her 'program' may 'seem, to some, regressive or misconceived', she cites Barker and Belsey and numerous other 'new-historicist and cultural-materialist attempts to "write the history of the subject"', but insists on the historical difficulty of supposing that 'Hamlet's boast of "that within" is anachronistic, as though Shakespeare has mysteriously managed to jump forward in time and expropriate the conceptual equipment of a later era' (2–3).

The danger of anachronism is perhaps best illuminated by Charles Taylor in *Sources of the Self: The Making of the Modern Identity*, since this actually provides the kind of Geertzian 'thick description' that New Historicists keep promising but seldom deliver. So, for example, Taylor warns against ascribing modern senses to the words inscribed above the oracle at Delphi, since the meaning of 'Know thyself' depends on the historically located vocabulary of meanings available at the time, and the Greeks 'didn't normally speak of the human agent as "ho autos", or use the term in a context which we would translate with the indefinite article'.[39] Similarly, when Polonius tells Laertes, 'This above all; to thine owne self be true', and when he rebukes Ophelia by telling her, 'You doe not understand our selfe so cleerely, / As it behooves my Daughter, and your Honour', his own notion of knowing or understanding the self is – as the OED notes – equivalent to 'knowing one's place'. Polonius is *not* invoking that substantive sense of 'self' for which the OED entry reads: '3. Chiefly Philos. That which in a person is really and intrinsically he (in contradistinction to what is adventitious); the ego (often identified with the soul or mind as opposed to the body): a permanent subject of successive and various states of consciousness'.

Sawday sensibly warns that 'we cannot trust dictionaries, not even the *Oxford English Dictionary*, to establish the currency of an idea' (29).[40] To which we might reply, like Shakespeare's perplexed Gloucester, 'And that's true too' – since a vexingly elusive version of the 'Which came first, the chicken or the egg?' problem appears as soon as we ask whether the appearance or sudden proliferation of new concepts and meanings is not only starting something but *answering to* something. Sawday himself remarks on the proliferation of terms with the prefix 'self-' in the later seventeenth century, and quotes the OED's comment on this prefix formation:

> *Self*-first appears as a living formative element about the middle of the sixteenth century ... The number of *self*-compounds was greatly augmented towards the middle of the seventeenth century, when many new words appeared in theological and philosophical writing, some of which had a restricted currency of about fifty years (e.g. 1645–1690).

Still, those warnings the OED provides also need to be considered. For example, words like 'individual' and 'identity' existed in Elizabethan English, but 'identity' meant something more like 'identical' and wasn't applied to people before 1638, while the modern sense of 'individual', with its now dominant sense of interiority, wasn't present (in writing) before 1646, and 'interiority' only entered the language in 1701. The earlier senses of 'personality' discriminated between persons and things, and that word didn't gain the sense of 'that quality or assemblage of qualities that makes a person what he is, as distinct from other persons; distinctive or individual character' (2.a) before 1795. Although Anne Ferry agreed that Hamlet possessed a modern inwardness, her valuable study *The 'Inward' Language*[41] acknowledged that words like 'inward', 'introspection', 'consciousness' and 'awareness' were either not present or lacked their later, interior meanings. In other words, many words or meanings which were available when the endless discussions of Hamlet's 'character' began weren't available when Shakespeare wrote *Hamlet*. 'Character' referred to handwriting ('Tis Hamlets Character') and to social types (as in the character sketches of Hall, Overbury and Earle), without being bound up with any notion of interiority. Yet Catherine Belsey uses the 'self', 'human nature' and the 'individual' interchangeably with the 'subject', while agreeing with Francis Barker to dismiss Hamlet's 'that within' as an ideologically insupportable gap; on the other side of the Atlantic, Greenblatt collapses 'selves' into 'human identity' and that term into the 'human subject', even though – as John Lee protests in an important, as yet unpublished thesis – 'Each of these terms involves complex notions and should be distinct, and distinct in important ways, from each other'.[42]

Lee's own survey of British Cultural Materialist discussions concludes, very severely, that the repetitive cohesiveness of their argument turns out to be 'either a quasi-religious polemic, disguised in a confusion of terms, or a poor use of out-of-date histories, or of out-of-date structuralist theories of cognitive development' (184). As for the New Historicist, Greenblattian argument that identity is an expression of authority, embodying the product of the intersection of authority with an alien, Lee observes that this 'rigidly formulaic' approach to identity is not only ahistorical but acritical: differentiation becomes impossible since 'all identities are profoundly similar, and all literacy depictions simply judged on their ability to disclose the underlying economy of the identity' (185). So, for Greenblatt, the depiction of Prince Hal's identity illuminates every other, in becoming the 'cultural key illuminating the circulation of power', while for Karen S. Coddon, Hamlet's possible madness turns out to be the 'paradigmatic case' of madness, whose 'crisis of subjectivity' is Hamlet's 'crisis of authority', which is the crisis of authority of Elizabethan culture – and so on (185). The really worthwhile, Geertzian part of Greenblatt's 'cultural poetics' is inevitably defeated if we keep reading in what only came later, and if accounts of cultural difference are so entangled with politicized agendas and other forms of modern wishful thinking. As Lee observes, the most important reason why a vocabulary of essentialist interiority cannot be found in *Hamlet* is that it did not exist outside it: 'its absence in *Hamlet* is a reflection of its absence from the wider culture' (191).

So how can we make textual and historical sense of Hamlet's 'that within'? Lee's own answer makes three important moves, which all suggest how 'where we are now' may be changing. Lee's first suggestion, that we should examine what is characteristic and characterising in Hamlet's metaphors, is promising and very timely: apart from the pioneering efforts of a few critics like Ann Thompson, contemporary Shakespeare criticism has been too preoccupied with theories of 'race, gender, and class' to take account of the revolutionary development in theories of metaphor. Unfortunately Lee doesn't take this far, but his next move is fascinatingly unexpected: he applies the 'REP-tests' in George A. Kelly's 'fixed-role therapy' to Hamlet's soliloquies. This is shrewd and instructive, since Kelly sees 'personality as an active process which is self-built, and not as a quasi-concrete unchanging and yet unrecoverable antecedent substance' (212),[43] and Lee himself wants to show how Hamlet's 'that within' is not, as Barker and Belsey would have it, an essentialist–humanist fantasy, but is textually produced as 'a central area created through a web of relationships' (222). Since this allows a view of the 'self' that is quite different from Greenblatt's 'self-fashioning', but is also 'flat' or unhistoricised, Lee develops Charles Taylor's contrast between the two opposed 'facets of modern individuality' represented by Montaigne and Descartes. As Taylor puts it, the Cartesian quest for an 'order of science, of clear and distinct knowledge in universal terms' is at odds with Montaigne's call for 'a deeper engagement in our particularity', where the 'Montaignean aspiration is always to loosen the hold of such general categories of "normal" operation and gradually prise our self-understanding free of the monumental weight of the universal interpretations, so that the shape of our originality can come to view': where Descartes 'calls for a radical disengagement from ordinary experience' and wants 'to find an intellectual order by which things in general can be surveyed', Montaigne wants 'to find the modes of expression which will allow the particular not to be overlooked' (182).[44] For Lee, the 'Montaignesque' shape of Shakespeare's conception of 'self' appears when Hamlet discusses what 'denotes' him in terms of an inner–outer construct which is both more modern and rhetorically more vulnerable than Claudius's and Gertrude's conventional use of the common–particular construct; here we might notice how, in a play so much concerned with acting, reflexivity inevitably increases that vulnerability: the actor playing Hamlet pretends to have and show an authenticating inwardness which passes show. Montaigne famously declared that if he could locate a 'settled' self he wouldn't need to write, or 'essay'; in Lee's account, *Hamlet* represents and explores different conceptions of 'self', and Lee concludes, daringly, by arguing that many of the Folio revisions show Shakespeare changing his mind about what ideas of 'self' Hamlet should express, and when.

This comparison with Montaigne helps to explain the way in which Shakespeare's characters so often speak of the 'self' at moments when its stability or reality is perplexingly in doubt. 'Does any heere know me?' asks Lear, 'Who is it that can tell me who I am?' 'Eros, thou yet behold'st me?' asks Mark Anthony, 'Heere I am Anthony, / Yet cannot hold this visible shape.' Where Anthony can no longer 'hold' the 'shape' others 'behold', and feels it 'dislimn' (a unique and astonishing word), Coriolanus cannot reconstruct a self that could 'stand', and the 'never . . . but . . . as if' sequence hollows out his desperate affirmation that he will 'never'

> Be such a Gosling to obey instinct: but stand
> As if a man were Author of himself, & knew no other kin.

If we are given to discussing the 'appearance and reality' topos in Shakespearean tragedy it is too easy to read in modern notions of a 'real' self without noticing whether the Shakespearean text resists it – for example, if we assume that when King Duncan mournfully reflects that 'There's no Art / To finde the Mindes construction in the Face' Duncan himself is assuming that there is a fixed or essential self behind the appearance. 'Construction' allows for a more temporary or provisional arrangement of different, competing elements. When Shakespeare's characters are more confident, his plays tend to expose or refute them. We can't take Malcolm's confidently summary view of the Macbeths as 'this dead Butcher, and his Fiend-like Queene' because we already know that Macbeth's construction' was more complicated than that, and also know that fiends don't commit suicide. Similarly, when the youthfully confident Desdemona affirms, 'I saw Othello's visage in his mind', she speaks as though she has the 'Art' which Duncan says does not exist; she hasn't, of course, or she would see the mind of her murderer, and this suggests how *Othello* gives a tragic inflexion to the romantic comedies' preoccupation with the constructive or delusive role of the imagination, especially lovers' imagination. I observed earlier that Othello, like Angelo and Leontes, does not know what he has it in him to become; Macbeth watches his own inner transformations with a mesmerised, courageously attentive horror. In all these cases Shakespeare's own 'Art' presents the 'self' as an alarmingly dynamic and unstable ensemble of possible selves, or matrix of everything we have it in us to become. Whatever emerges from this matrix of potentialities is established through and in a 'web' of social and rhetorical relationships, and is in that inescapable sense socially and linguistically constituted. But this view of the 'self' as constituted allows more room for agency than Greenblatt's conception of 'self-fashioning', and makes the British cultural–materialists' marxoid assaults on 'essentialist–humanist' conceptions of the 'self' seem simplistic and distractingly anachronistic.

I have dwelt on Lee's thesis as an example of the way in which 'where we are' now is beginning to look different from where we have been, and a similar point might be made about Maus's book. Her argument is unlike Lee's in placing more emphasis on religious concepts of an inner self, but of course these approaches are not mutually exclusive. For example, both seem fruitful at that moment when we first see Othello struggling to control or 'govern' himself after the riot in 2.2, and regarding the 'self' in question as an arena of conflicting potentialities ('Now by Heaven, / My blood begins my safer Guides to rule . . . '). What is Christian, or post-Augustinian, in this stratified, vertiginous view of the 'self' is a source of terror, not reassurance, and doesn't open the door to the kind of 'Christian humanism' that Sinfield claims was dominant until the 1970s: 'a genial, moderate (except when under threat), gentlemanly/ladylike attachment to something not too specific, but involving a loose respect for Jesus' Sermon on the Mount and an assumption that "redemption" will come to people of goodwill' (144–45).[45] I myself think that the specifically Christian elements in *Macbeth* or *Hamlet* or *King Lear* always increase, without relieving, the sense of terror.

Sinfield mentions Kenneth Muir and Theodore Spencer without discussing those 'humanist' critics who, like W.R. Elton and Wilbur Sanders, challenge the allegedly 'dominant' attempts to provide a blandly consoling, 'Christian' view of Shakespeare's tragedies. Such characteristic distortions and suppressions may explain why that 1960s argument is now reviving in a different form, and it seems depressing to have to fight over the same ground, like the 'Thistles' in Ted Hughes's poem, just because the best work of an earlier period is being ignored. In *The Rest is Silence*,[46] an absorbing study of the fear of 'death as annihilation' in the Renaissance, Robert N. Watson is no less determined than Sanders was, in *The Dramatist and the Received Idea*[47] to reckon with – instead of diluting – the terrors of *Macbeth*. But Watson doesn't mention Sanders. Indeed, his study also shows in a more unfortunate way how necessary it is to cross frontiers and, on occasion, the Atlantic: he seems unaware of the large body of

work by British critics and historians which would support his own arguments – not least when he, like Maus(11),[48] feels compelled to take issue
with Greenblatt's no less all-American argument that atheism, in the Renaissance, was 'almost unthinkable' (22).[49] Certainly, we need to distinguish
between the 'unthinkable' and the 'unprintable', if we are to explain why
the flood of anti-atheistic tracts began some two centuries before the first
direct avowal of intellectual atheism was published in England, in 1782;
moreover, since Renaissance science offered no alternative account of
creation, 'atheistical' views could be and were attacked as irrational (83–
84, 298–89).[50] Yet what Sir Thomas Browne called 'secondary atheism' –
allowing for God's existence, but denying his providential concern with
sublunary affairs – was certainly a familiar position in Shakespeare's lifetime, and is copiously documented in Elton's King Lear and the Gods –
which Watson also ignores, and which brings me back to the issue of
perspectivism.

'PERSPECTIVES BEGIN TO TELL TALES'

Elton's magisterial study showed how King Lear represents a range of
contemporary religious and irreligious attitudes in a multivocal way, without privileging any particular view or voice. In sharp contrast, Dollimore's
argument that 'In fact,' King Lear 'repudiates the essentialism which the
humanist reading of it presupposes' (190–91)[52] privileges and amplifies
those voices which accord with the critic's 'radical' position. To represent
this contrast in political or ideological terms, as a clash between 'humanist' and 'radical' approaches to Shakespeare, would be to ignore the way in
which Elton was himself challenging the loosely 'Christian' readings which
Sinfield characterises as 'humanist'. Rather, the contrast is critical, and
procedural: Elton doesn't think it possible to detach the play's or Shakespeare's view from the intricate and complex interplay of voices and
perspectives, whereas Dollimore doesn't hesitate to ascribe to 'the play'
those views (and intentions) which most accord with his own. In this
respect Dollimore's own procedure is ironically much closer to that of the
'Christian' readings Elton criticises. Here I am wanting to make the kind
of point Albert Tricomi makes when, after worrying about the selective
but totalising effect of anecdotes in New Historicist criticism, he observes
that the 'cultural historicist must still survey the multiple, competing discourses within a culture'.[53] It is no less necessary to attend to the multiple,
competing perspectives in a Shakespeare play. Put baldly, my own assumption, which makes me think Elton is right about something Dollimore gets
wrong, is that a Shakespearean play is a complex, highly perspectival
design.

Because the plays excite us so much, we constantly debate different views
of Hamlet or Othello, or Caliban and Henry V, as though there were some

right or single view; but we seldom ask whether the plays excite us so much because their conflicting perspectives anticipate, and even orchestrate, our critical debates. A philosopher, I think it was John Searle, once remarked that when we don't know the word for 'key' we can't ask whether there is a key in the drawer, but once we know the word and can ask the question the answer is not in the word but in the drawer. For some influential contemporary critics there is nothing in the Shakespearean drawer. So, for Terence Hawkes, Shakespeare's plays are not complex designs but 'chaotic sites', which can be 'made to support' quite different 'causes' and have no meaning 'beyond the various readings to which they may be subjected'.[54]

Hawkes's deconstructionist view might seem to receive support from the increasing number of recent studies of 'foreign Shakespeare'. In early nineteenth-century Germany, for example, as in Verdi's Italy, Shakespeare was not (in Sinfield's ugly phrase and sense) an 'instrument of domination' but an instrument of liberation, above all from French classicism and cultural dominance; but by the 1830s the revolutionary authors of the 'Young Germany' movement were, as Werner Habicht puts it, disparaging 'both Hamlet's dreamy and soliloquizing failure to act efficiently and the German introspection he was seen as personifying'.[55] A century later – in 1934, the year in which the Nazis first controlled the choice of plays which were to be performed in Germany – 235 German theatres opened their seasons with new productions of Shakespeare plays; by 1937 that figure had actually risen to 320, the Hitler Youth had been regaled with a special Shakespeare festival attended by Rudolf Hess, and one spokesman for Nazi *Kulturpolitik* had claimed – proudly, but also plausibly – that there had been more productions of Shakespeare in Germany than in the rest of the world put together.[56] This fascination with Shakespeare isn't as easy to explain as the notoriously anti-Semitic production of *The Merchant of Venice* in which Goebbels personally selected Werner Krauss to play Shylock, and in that last case we also need to understand why the same play is now 'the most performed Shakespearian play' in Israel (145)[57] (12–13).[58]

Of course, as Hawkes would insist, these German responses were all 'appropriations' that were historically located in different cultural and political circumstances. So were the English responses, including those of the first Globe audiences (or Hawkes and Bradshaw), and as much is true of all responses to any writer. That should not surprise or disturb us, unless we believe there are purely literary values. But the Hawkesean view doesn't begin to explain why the Germans were so enthralled by Shakespeare, not some other dramatist. I began this chapter by saying that our present, admittedly chaotic or confusing, critical situation made me more hopeful. One reason for this hopefulness is that the recent, often enthralling, spate of studies of how Shakespeare was received and assimilated not only in Europe and Russia, but in countries like Japan, China or South Africa, make it more than ever difficult to evade the question: why, after four centuries, is Shakespeare the world's most performed dramatist?

Jonathan Bate put this crucial question in *The Genius of Shakespeare*,[59] and takes different examples – involving Chartist and West Indian 'appropriations' – to show how Shakespeare could be and was harnessed to radical, rather than conservative or reactionary, political causes (214–216, 240–244). But Bate thinks this a sufficient reason to dismiss what he scornfully calls the 'New Iconoclast argument' of critics like Greenblatt, Dollimore, Sinfield, Michael Bristol, and Hugh Grady (190–91, 358), and is no less condescending to their opponents, whom he calls the 'Anti-PC Vigilantes' (317–19). The point I'm wanting to make here is not merely that Bate cheerfully supposes that 'appropriating' Shakespeare is what other, lesser critics do, but that his discussion of what he calls Shakespeare's 'aspectualism' derives from Romantic criticism, and presents a correspondingly limited view of Shakespeare's perspectivism.

The Romantic, character-centred nature of Bate's approach appears when he observes, '*Hamlet, Othello, Macbeth, Lear*: think of these titles and one thinks first of a character, then of other characters and a story' (278). Do we really think of Othello before thinking of Iago and 'a story'? It is startling to find 'our finest Shakespeare critic' (to quote the dust-jacket) or indeed any contemporary critic writing like this: 'Do you believe that there is some essence to human being that can be known in itself – call it conscience, call it consciousness? You do? Then your icon is Hamlet. Or do you believe that we are nothing but the roles we play, that the only form of being is *action*? Yours is Iago' (293). Nor does it help to be told, later, that 'being and acting are indivisible' (332). Earlier, Bate explains that Hamlet 'has become a universal dramatic character because he is an icon of human consciousness': 'he seems to embody the very nature of human *being*; it is consciousness that forms his sense of self, his "character" ... ' (257). Just before that, Bate was explaining that an 'iconic moment' is iconic because it 'means the same thing in 1600, in 1800, in 2000' (254).

Such remarks, and Bate's use of terms like 'essence', 'self', and 'character', show a breathtaking indifference to the concerns – not merely the procedures, or interpretative conclusions – of much or most contemporary criticism, not only of Shakespeare. They also show how – despite his assorted references to Wittgenstein, Heisenberg and the 'aspectuality of truth', which suggests that he needs to read Thomas Nagel – Bate's concept of Shakespeare's aspectuality' doesn't really advance beyond Keats's concept of 'negative capability'. He tells us (recycling Norman Rabkin's duck-rabbit argument) that 'Both the Hal aspect (call it the rule of providence) and the Falstaff aspect (call it the rule of the body) are truths of the Henry plays, but you cannot see them both at one and the same time' (328). As I argued in a book Bate reviewed, Rabkin's own version of the 'duck-rabbit' presents grave difficulties (77–80);[60] but Rabkin was at least discussing what he takes to be mutually exclusive, either/or views of Henry V. When Bate extends and reapplies Rabkin's duck-rabbit argument to the

'Hal aspect' and the 'Falstaff aspect' in 'the *Henry* plays' he produces a far more extensive and tendentious 'either-or'. His argument assumes that these plays present only two significantly opposed 'aspects', or points of view, or perspectives, and 'that you cannot see them both at one and the same time'. If we correct Bate's 'both' by allowing that these multivocal plays present more than two perspectives – including those of Henry IV or Michael Williams, or the King of France or the Yorkist conspirators – Bate's argument becomes all the more untenable: if we can't even 'see' two opposed 'aspects' at the same time, how could be make sense of more? Undeterred, Bate goes on to maintain that 'Both the Prospero aspect and the Caliban aspect are truths of *The Tempest* but you cannot see them both at once and the same time' (328). Once again we should ask why these two, and only two, 'aspects' are privileged: why exclude the 'Miranda aspect' or 'the Ariel aspect'? Although Bate evidently thinks that his own 'aspectual' either-or justifies his condescending view of Greenblatt's anti-colonial reading, which allows for 'the Caliban aspect' but not for the 'Prospero aspect', that won't do either: how could it, if we cannot 'see' one 'aspect' without blocking out the other?

The crucial point, I take it, is that Shakespeare's perspectivism doesn't only involve representing the irreducibly different ways in which different characters see and feel their own situations – Keats' 'negative capability', Blake's 'As a man is, so he sees'. It is also structural, in ways that never concerned Keats. Here Bate's recycling of the idea that 'the invention of plot was not our dramatist's greatest strength' (139) is all too revealing: it shows how his concept of 'aspectuality' is character-centred and barely connects with what he no less revealingly calls the 'story'. In this old-fashioned view, what matters is not that something like the 'story' of the bond in *The Merchant of Venice* is taken from somebody else's 'story', but that Shakespeare shows his 'genius' by presenting 'the Shylock aspect'. But if we are seriously concerned with Shakespeare's perspectivism, we should also be asking why Shakespeare chose to harness that unoriginal 'story' of the bond to the (unoriginal, and originally quite separate) 'story' of the caskets and the final ring-imbroglio, when fashioning his own intricately complex design.

A similar point may be made about all those readings of *Hamlet* which take a critical view of the prince as though this were something the play simply provoked, and not something which the play's perspectivism helps to explain. Although Shakespeare's prince so obviously dominates Shake-speare's play, one difference between them is that Hamlet is hardly ever concerned to imagine what anybody else thinks and feels, whereas *Hamlet* is almost promiscuous in its creatively compulsive fascination with how differently other characters think and feel. Because Shakespeare's play is so much more concerned to explore these perspectival differences by going 'inside' Claudius, Ophelia, Laertes, Polonius, and even Rosencrantz and Guildenstern, it constantly complicates our view of Hamlet's view of his various victims. Similarly, when the play establishes dramatically pointed contrasts between the responses of three sons and a daughter to the death of a father, or shows how indifferent Hamlet is to the fate of his country (which he considers a 'prison', but which Claudius, in his own unheroic but capable way, protects), *Hamlet* invites us to take a larger or more complicated view than Hamlet's. Yet the history of *Hamlet* criticism, and more generally of Shakespearean criticism, shows how regularly that invitation, or challenge, is either declined or taken up in a more piecemeal, character-centred way. In other words, this history repeatedly illustrates the *effects* of Shakespeare's perspectivism, and a critically alarming reluctance to examine the *cause* of those effects. Everybody reading this essay will be familiar with that Shakespearean metaphor, 'All the world's a stage', but our best way forward may be to think about how profoundly that metaphor reflects Shakespeare's way of staging a world.

REFERENCES

1. Bradshaw, Graham (1993), *Misrepresentations: Shakespeare and the Materialists*, Ithaca: Cornell University Press.
2. Sinfield, Alan (1992), *Faultlines: Cultural Materialism and the Politics of Dissident Reading*, Oxford: Clarendon Press, 261–9.
3. Alter, Robert (1993), 'The Persistence of Reading', *Partisan Review*, LX, 4, 510–516.
4. Rich, Adrienne (1986), *One Lies, Secrets, Silence: Selected Prose 1979–1985*, New York: Norton, 49.
5. Erickson, Peter (1991), *Rewriting Shakespeare, Rewriting Ourselves*, Berkeley: University of California Press, 105.
6. Vickers, Brian (1989), *Returning to Shakespeare*, New York and London: Routledge, 1989.
7. Levin, Richard (1988), 'Feminist Thematics and Shakespearean Tragedy', *PMLA*, 103, (2), 125–38.
8. Kamps, Ivo, (ed.) (1991), *Shakespeare Left and Right*, New York and London: Routledge, 74.
9. Cohen, Walter (1987), 'Political Criticism of Shakespeare', in Jean E. Howard and Marion F. O'Connor, (eds.), *Shakespeare Reproduced: The Text in History and Ideology*, London and New York: Methuen, 33, 18–46.
10. Greenblatt, Stephen (1990), *Learning to Curse: Essays in Early Modern Culture*, New York and London: Routledge, 165–66, 233, 190–201.
11. Greenblatt, Stephen (1980), *Renaissance Self-Fashioning: From More to Shakespeare*, Chicago: University of Chicago Press.
12. Cunningham, James (1997), *Shakespeare's Tragedies and Modern Critical Theory*, London and New Cranbury, N.J: Associated University Presses, 66–70.
13. Greenblatt, Stephen (1988), *Shakespearean Negotiations: The Circulation of Social Energy in Renaissance England*, Oxford: Clarendon Press, 4.
14. Dollimore, Jonathan and Sinfield, Alan, (eds.) (1985), *Political Shakespeare: New Essays in Cultural Materialism*, Manchester: Manchester University Press, vii–viii.

15. Sinfield, Alan (1994), 'Untune That String: Shakespeare and the Scope for Dissidence', *Times Literary Supplement*, 22 April, 4–5.
16. Dollimore, Jonathan (1984), *Radical Tragedy: Religion, Ideology, and Power in the Drama of Shakespeare and his Contemporaries*, Chicago: University of Chicago Press.
17. Vickers, Brian (1993), *Appropriating Shakespeare: Contemporary Critical Quarrels*, New Haven: Yale University Press, 6–7.
18. Kerrigan, William (1994), *Hamlet's Perfection*, Baltimore and London: Johns Hopkins University Press, 77–8.
19. Dawson, Anthony B. (1996), 'Performance and Participation', in James C. Bulman, (ed.), *Shakespeare, Theory, and Performance*, London and New York: Routledge, 29–45.
20. Styan, J.L. (1979), *The Shakespeare Revolution*, Cambridge: Cambridge University Press.
21. Maher, Mary Z. (1992), *Modern Hamlets and their Soliloquies*, Iowa: Iowa University Press, 41, 16.
22. Argyle, Mary (1987), 'Eye-Contact', in R.L. Gregory, (ed.), *The Oxford Companion to the Mind*, Oxford: Oxford University Press.
23. Barton, John (1984), *Playing Shakespeare*, London and New York: Methuen, 94.
24. Berger, Harry T. (1989), *Imaginary Audition: Shakespeare on Stage and Page*, Berkeley: University of California Press, 13.
25. Worthen, W.B. (1996), 'Staging Shakespeare: Acting, Authority, and the Rhetoric of Performance', in James C. Bulman, *Shakespeare, Theory, and Performance*, London and New York: Routledge, 12–28.
26. Maher, Mary Z. See n. 21.
27. Sterne, Richard (1967), *John Gielgud Directs Richard Burton in 'Hamlet': A Journal of Rehearsals*, New York: Random, 36.
28. Maher, Mary Z. See n. 21.
29. Orgel, Stephen, (ed.) (1987), *The Tempest*, Oxford: Oxford University Press, 4.
30. Granville Barker, Harley (1958), *Preface to 'Othello'*, Princeton: Princeton University Press, 54.
31. McKellen, Ian (1996), *William Shakespeare's 'Richard III': A Screenplay*, London and New York: Doubleday, 22.
32. Norris, Christopher (1988) *Deconstruction and the Interests of Theory*, London: Pinter Publishers, 1988, and Norman: University of Oklahoma Press, 1989, 123.
33. Barker, Francis (1984), *The Tremulous Private Body: Essays in Subjection*, London: Methuen.
34. Belsey, Catherine (1985), *The Subject of Tragedy: Identity and Difference in Renaissance Drama*, London: Methuen.
35. Bradshaw, Graham. See n. 1.
36. Sawday, Jonathan (1997), 'Self and Selfhood in the Seventeenth Century', in Roy Porter, (ed.), *Rewriting the Self: Histories from the Renaissance to the Present*, London and New York: Routledge, 29–48.
37. Foucault, Michel (1988), in Luther H. Martin, Huck Gutman and Patrick H. Hutton, (eds.), *Technologies of the Self: A Seminar with Michel Foucault*, London: Tavistock, and Amherst: University of Massachusetts Press, 19.
38. Maus, Katharine Eisaman (1995), *Inwardness and Theater in the English Renaissance*, Chicago: University of Chicago Press, 1–2.
39. Taylor, Charles (1989), *Sources of the Self: The Making of Modern Identity*, Cambridge: Cambridge University Press, 113.
40. Sawday, Jonathan. See n. 36.

41. Ferry, Anne (1983), *The 'Inward' Language: Sonnets of Wyatt, Sidney, Shakespeare, Donne*, Chicago: University of Chicago Press.
42. Lee, John (1995), *Shakespeare's 'Hamlet' and the Controversies of Self*, PhD, University of Bristol, 182.
43. Lee, John. See n. 42.
44. Taylor, Charles. See n. 39.
45. Maus, Katharine Eisaman. See n. 38.
46. Watson, Robert N. (1994), *The Rest is Silence: Death as Annihilation in the English Renaissance*, Berkeley and London: University of California Press, 21–23.
47. Sanders, Wilbur (1968), *The Dramatist and the Received Idea: Studies in the Plays of Marlowe and Shakespeare*, Cambridge: Cambridge University Press.
48. Maus, Katharine Eisaman. See n. 38.
49. Greenblatt, Stephen. See n. 13.
50. Bradshaw, Graham. See n. 1.
51. Elton, W.R. (1966), *'King Lear' and the Gods*, San Marino, Calif.: The Huntington Library.
52. Dollimore, Jonathan. See n. 16.
53. Tricomi, Albert (1996), *Reading Tudor-Stuart Texts Through Cultural Historicism*, Gainsville: University Press of Florida, 83.
54. Hawkes, Terence (1988), 'Wittgenstein's Shakespeare', in Maurice Charney, (ed.), *'Bad' Shakespeare: Revaluations of the Shakespeare Canon*, London: Associated University Presses, and Rutherford, N.J.: Farleigh Dickenson University Press, 55–60.
55. Habicht, Werner (1994), *Shakespeare and the German Imagination*, Occasional Paper no. 5, Hertford: International Shakespeare Association, 8.
56. Strobl, Gerwin (1997), 'Shakespeare and the Nazis', *History Today*, 16–21, May.
57. Elsom, John, ed. (1990): *Is Shakespeare Still Our Contemporary?* London: Routledge and Kegan Paul.
58. Bradshaw, Graham. See 1.
59. Bate, Jonathan (1997), *The Genius of Shakespeare*, London: Picador.
60. Bradshaw, Graham. See n. 1.

2   Shakespeare between Politics and Aesthetics

Claus Uhlig

Much as I would like to 'hasten into the midst of things' and to tackle my subject directly, I cannot do so. For too many voices have by now begun to swell the choir of Shakespearean criticism so that one fails to hear a dominant note that could provide orientation. What is more, the two poles of our theme, politics and aesthetics, are not evenly distributed nowadays, since over the last two decades the aesthetic has lost ground against the political element in discourse, nay, even has had to suffer being exposed as yet one more form of ideology.[1] Especially on the part of an openly political mode of literary criticism there has been and still is in evidence a tendency to place theory and works of literature on the same level and with that to privilege cultural and social contexts over texts proper. And with projects like these, the aesthetic is bound to be a nuisance.

It is therefore no surprise that the anti-hierarchical impulse just indicated could not but affect the study of Shakespeare, the central figure of the Western canon.[2] Thus any topic devoted to him cannot be discussed without a prior, albeit brief, account of the main forms of discourse obtaining in today's levelling Shakespearean criticism. For according to a commonplace hermeneutic insight familiar by now, any conceivable scholarly result one might be confronted with is, after all, more or less directly conditioned by the approach chosen. With this in mind, I should like to start by reviewing four major trends in recent Shakespearean criticism. They belong to the era of post-structuralism and can be subdivided into deconstruction, psychoanalysis, New Historicism together with cultural materialism, and feminism.[3] After this brief survey, the impact of these approaches on Shakespeare's conception of politics would call for attention, finally leading up to a search for criteria that, despite all appearances to the contrary, would still permit us to regard a literary text – or a play by Shakespeare for that matter – as a work of art.

I

To begin, then, with perhaps the most prominent project in today's efforts to undermine traditional critical securities, deconstruction. Mainly inspired by Derrida, deconstruction in its radical linguistic scepticism has come to question all hitherto valid assumptions which even up to structuralism assured the coherence of Western culture. Above all, deconstruction denies the one-to-one relation between signifier and signified; instead it postulates the free play of signifiers that lack a transcendental plane of reference, being as they are dissolved into mere self-referentiality. Owing to this obvious circularity of signifier and signified, deconstruction radiates instability and negates the very possibility of meaning; the latter is always absent, dispersed in a chain of signifiers. Taking, furthermore, the world of human experience to be structured in analogy with the model of language, deconstruction at the same time insinuates that neither autonomous individuals nor self-evident truths – precisely those transcendental signifiers that could guarantee meaning – actually exist.[4] To be sure, deconstruction thus conceived does not conceal its subversive qualities, seeing that its critical procedures are apt to destroy notions such as textual autonomy, mimesis, authorial intention, or textual coherence into the bargain.[5] In view of all this, it is of course not surprising to find deconstructionist criticism yielding results that are predetermined by its very assumptions – yet one more instance of hermeneutic circularity. And exactly a volume such as that edited by Atkins and Bergeron under the title *Shakespeare and Deconstruction* bears sufficient witness to this.

Not unlike deconstruction, psychoanalytic criticism, especially in the style of Lacan and his school, has by now developed its own, self-vindicating strategies. In 'rewriting' Freudian psychoanalysis, Lacan's theories are clearly indebted to the post-structuralist theorem of the fundamental impossibility of ever realizing presence, coherence, or meaning. This linguistic assumption structures his account of the nature of human identity. Accordingly, for Lacan a human being's sense of self is formed not autonomously but by a process of identification with other objects or subjects in the world. Through the father's entry into its life and the parallel discovery of sexuality, every child must learn that identity depends on difference and absence. At the same stage of development language is discovered, which is likewise grounded in the principles of difference and absence. But contrary to pure deconstructionism, language for Lacan has a symbolic function: it stands in for the object that is not present. All that is available indeed is merely symbolic substitution in a world of language where meaning is always dispersed. To a greater extent than with Freud, the autonomy and coherence of the self are thus undermined in Lacan's radically linguistic conception of the human psyche. In the end, human identity for him is formed through social processes and definable only in opposition against an 'other'.[6] These and similar assumptions have now begun to take hold of American psychoanalytic criticism in particular, as is evidenced above all in the collective volume *Representing Shakespeare*, edited by Schwartz and Kahn, a volume for whose contributors the poet's texts re-enact central aspects of the process of individualization in terms of dramatic action.[7]

Now, to those scholars and critics impatient with deconstructionist wordplay or psychoanalytical ingenuity, American New Historicism or, alternatively, British cultural materialism might, at least at first sight, have seemed a more rewarding approach to Renaissance literature in general and to Shakespeare's texts in particular. Endeavouring still to maintain a more or less stable relationship between signifier and signified, new historicists and cultural materialists, in their uncompromising contextualization of literary texts, strongly rely on a Marxist notion of ideology, albeit extended and redefined along the lines of Althusser for example. Accordingly, ideology is understood not only as a form of political propaganda but also, and above all, as the dominant discourse in a society that consists of a set of practices, ways of conduct, current ideas, and views of the world, pervading everyday life and being perpetuated by institutions such as education, family, religion, culture, and law, in short, by those 'ideological state apparatuses' that subdue the subject of its own accord already.[8] Owing to such an internalized, as it were, concept of ideology, new historicists as well as cultural materialists exclude beforehand any autonomous, let alone aesthetic, status for literature. Instead, they see it deeply implicated in the social process of a given period and are eagerly bent on analysing the interplay of dominant ideology and marginal discourse in literary texts or cultural institutions such as the theatre – especially the theatre of Shakespeare and his time – and that more often than not in terms of class, race, and gender.[9]

Seeing that literature is thus more or less reduced to a site of ideological struggle on the part of new historicism and cultural materialism, it does not fare better at the hands of feminism either, the last of the four critical trends to be discussed initially. For, while methodically drawing from sources that extend from liberal humanist positions to deconstructionist practices, feminism's thematic focus is always the issue of gender. Examining most of the time the ways women are represented in literary texts, feminist critics are as attentive to ideologies as their new historicist or materialist counterparts. And not least owing to this awareness, the overall impact of feminist criticism on literary studies has been to undermine the male-centred viewpoint of traditional criticism.[10] What is more, with regard to Shakespeare, feminist criticism has by now generated quite a variety of different, if sometimes mutually antagonistic, approaches to his work. On the one hand, there are those who stress the poet's indebtedness to medieval misogyny, whereas, on the other, we find feminists of a more apologetic cast of mind, who are inclined to regard Shakespeare as a kind of proto-feminist, already pointing ahead to a modern image of women and being fully aware of the problems of patriarchy. Surely one would have to differentiate among more than just two groupings on this score, but one thing should be absolutely clear: namely, that feminist criticism, far from merely being one more theory among others, is rooted in a definite political movement that started back in the 1960s and '70s, and began to invade Shakespeare studies during the early 1980s.[11]

II

Thus we would seem to have arrived already at the first catchword of the paper's title, politics, although it is, for the sake of clarity, advisable in the present context to distinguish from the start between politics in the sense of Shakespeare and the themes of his age and politicization in the contemporary manner aforesaid. For, if touched upon ever so briefly, the four critical trends of our present as discussed just now will have put beyond doubt one thing: they have radically changed our conception of both the poet and the Elizabethan era, and that precisely on account of the obvious politicization of Shakespeare studies. What was once taken for granted, i.e., the comfortable reliance upon well-ordered 'Elizabethan world pictures'[12] or well balanced 'Elizabethan compromises'[13] – and it happened half a century ago – is no longer valid now. And it is especially with regard to the treatment of Shakespeare's history plays, which exemplify political thematics along Elizabethan lines most conspiciously, that this change of paradigm in the study of literature can best be illustrated.

As is known, among the major chronicle sources of the sixteenth century for this particular group of works, pride of place belongs to Edward Hall's monumental *Vnion of the Two Noble and Illustre Famelies of Lancastre and York*, inspired by Polydore Vergil and published posthumously by Richard Grafton in 1584. According to the testimony of his programmatic title, Hall subordinates his historical material to a general theme, i.e., he sees the history of England as a continuous chain of events, reaching from the late Middle Ages, more exactly, from the enforced abdication of Richard II (1399), to the final expiation for this usurpation through the death of Richard III on the battlefield (1485), nay, actually into the Renaissance-present of the 'triumphant reign of King Henry the Eighth'. This causal nexus, established through guilt and atonement in both a religious and political sense, is at the same time more than just a formula of historiographic explanation: exalted to the height of events willed by God, the political rivalries between the houses of Lancaster and York, happily ended by the golden age of the Tudors, gain with Hall the status of a myth which could not but please the Tudors, newly risen to power at the close of the Wars of the Roses, and that for both ideological and propagandistic purposes.

As is further known, Tillyard extrapolated the said 'Tudor myth', adumbrated in Polydore Vergil and elaborated by Edward Hall, from the history writing of the English Renaissance and used it as a foil for his interpretation of Shakespeare's histories.[14] Subsequent research, it is true, brought forth many reservations in this respect, differentiating for instance between Shakespeare's handling of history in the earlier York and the later Lancaster tetralogy, but in questions of method it did not really leave the ground of his indeed influential work.[15] And as regards the poet's personal political opinions – provided such a topic is still relevant in a post-structuralist age of dead authors who hide behind the figures of their texts anyway[16] – we may be assured that Shakespeare as a loyal subject shared the basic assumptions of his epoch and, in the histories especially, brought to bear a conservative perspective upon rebellion, civil war, and all levelling tendencies, thus helping to stabilize the 'Law-and-Order' ideology of the Tudors.[17]

Yet this attitude was bound to give way roughly with the change of power from the Tudors to the Stuarts in 1603, because since then the poet, leaving behind his former Tudor orthodoxy, tends toward a scepticism of stoical and pessimistic persuasion that, while not fatalistically negating any involvement in the politics of the day, 'sublates' it in the dramatic pursuit of those issues transcending time and ideology which characterize his great tragedies up to the present moment.[18] These will not be subject to debate in their entirety here, but only in so far as they touch upon one or the other political thematic complex which now, in his tragic period, still harks back to the histories. Thus *Hamlet* (c. 1600), for instance, does not only revolve round the problem of revenge, endlessly delayed in its execution, but also round the theme of the usurpation of a throne by a murderer.[19] While *Othello* (c. 1604) is commonly regarded as a 'domestic tragedy', we again encounter the political element in *King Lear* (c. 1605), and this time in the folly of disburdening oneself and dividing one's realm: a king is either a king or else nothing, as the hoary Lear must experience to his great dismay.[20] And in *Macbeth* (c. 1606), finally, the political element manifests itself once more in the form of murder, usurpation, and tyranny, not without, of course, at the same time flattering James I, the new patron of Shakespeare's company of players, through the motif of the witches, that of genealogical continuity, or the evocation of 'king-becoming graces'.[21] To glance briefly at the Roman plays, in which Shakespeare locates the political theme safely distanced in time from the Elizabethan age, while still unambiguously harping – although this certainly holds true more for *Julius Caesar* (c. 1599) than for *Antony and Cleopatra* (c. 1607) – on the anxieties and worries of his own day. It goes without saying that in these plays, as in the more mature histories already and then above all in the great tragedies, concepts such as authority, power, honour, freedom, or order are never broached in isolation from their human, more exactly, interhuman frame of reference.[22] The most political play of the whole series, *Coriolanus* (1607), bears particular witness to this, even if, or precisely because, the relationships mentioned have been seriously disturbed in this case, seeing that the hero, in his aristocratic disdain and proud want of moderation, not least *vis-à-vis* the populace, is at heart lonely and isolated – a circumstance certainly not enhancing his appeal to our democratic age any more than to Shakespeare's.[23] So far on politics.

In the above summary characterization of Shakespeare's histories, I had already observed that the critique of Tillyard – and his name has remained linked up to the present with the study of the dramatic sequence in question – did not at first really break new ground in respect of method. This was, however, to be altered radically with the shift of theoretical paradigm during the 1970s and '80s, as illustrated in my introduction with reference to four exemplary critical trends. Now not only Tillyard's own nationalistically circumscribed outlook was pounced upon, but also and above all his monistic approach in its apparent naïvety.[24] Yet, once we realize, as was already adumbrated before, that the critical perspective which has achieved hegemony of discourse today, directed as it is against all forms of scholarly or institutional establishment, is in its own turn determined ideologically – and that holds true especially for contributions from the camp of new historicism as well as cultural materialism[25] – then we might likewise not be willing to surrender to it completely. Scholarly monism, whether urged from the left or the right – as I said, Shakespeare studies have meanwhile become so politicized that one cannot but phrase it in this way – must never be the last word; and that above all for one reason, namely, because such an attitude, if apparently ever so sophisticated in its modes of argumentation, ultimately leads to reductionism and strives, in the interest of this or that socio-political concern, toward appropriation of Shakespeare's texts which have suffered degradation to mere pretexts in the process. But simply to complain is to no avail here.[26] In other words, has the literary or even political and ideological appropriation of Shakespeare not always been a cultural phenomenon throughout history?[27] Consequently, the study of the past should be seen as liable to the shifting grounds of scholarly and critical fashion. In a certain sense, the Renaissance itself has paved the way to such a view of things, seeing that it left behind the primarily analogical patterns of thought of the Middle Ages and moved on to the more relativistic positions and dialectical methods of Early Modernity, thus providing us with multiple hermeneutics.[28] And any meaning we might generate with this help, is thus always already both culturally and historically conditioned – more often than not leading up to a hermeneutic act in which the creative discourse of the past and the critical discourse of the present tend to interact, even to become fused.

Still, it is precisely in this connection that a word of warning would be in order. It applies above all to New Historicists as well as cultural materialists, and that more exactly to their respective concept of history. For with them, history is no longer understood in universalistic or holistic terms as with Hall and Tillyard, but rather as particularistic and fragmented in character, moreover comprising the most divergent forms of discourse at a given time, i.e., the dominant ones just as well as the marginalized ones.

Even if remaining on the whole within the confines of the Renaissance, they nevertheless tend to move around freely in space and time, preferring to argue by sometimes rather speculative 'analogies' or 'homologies' between disparate phenomena, since any principle of causality, however defined, is ruled out beforehand. Along with post-structuralist historical methods like these, both schools, when analysing literature in relation to history, conceive the latter on the model of the former and indiscriminately treat historical documents like texts and these in turn like those. In this manner of discourse levelling, they try to penetrate into the heart of an epoch's everyday life, always intent on overturning conventional hierarchies or effacing customary distinctions between élite and popular culture.[29]

It cannot be denied offhand that exactly a poet of the theatre like Shakespeare is, for a start, fully noted in the everyday life of his age. Not only does he share in the production of Elizabethan ideology, as is borne out sufficiently through the highly patriotic history play *Henry V* (*c.* 1598),[30] but he must also comply with it as royal subject.[31] Witness for instance the problem of censorship he encountered with *Richard II* (1595), especially with regard to the abdication scene (IV. i): Queen Elizabeth I saw herself potentially threatened thereby, and the scene in question was not allowed to be printed in the early editions of the play.[32] Yet regardless, there is no warrant to focus too exclusively on literary texts as battlegrounds for ideologies in conflict or political struggles for power,[33] although it is to be expected that from now on especially British and Anglo-American studies in the Renaissance will continue with the project of politicization.[34] The crux of the matter, however, is that the aesthetic element thus falls by the wayside. In this particular respect, both New Historicists and cultural materialists would seem to align themselves with deconstructionists, who are likewise concerned with the undermining of hierarchical structures in literary texts, whose former constituents are then permitted to be dispersed into a series of equally underprivileged 'differences'. And with procedures like these, what once again no longer counts is the aesthetic to whose precarious status in today's Shakespeare studies we must now turn.

III

Judging alone by the number of publications devoted to it of late, the aesthetic would appear to enjoy a boom, but appearances are deceptive, for behind them there lurks something like a fundamental crisis. Trying at first to account for its possible reasons in what follows, we shall then ascertain whether the aesthetic could not, in the teeth of opposition, be rehabilitated for the study of literature in general and the plays of Shakespeare in particular, and that with reference to a central text used for purposes of illustration.

In this connection, it should be clear from the start that the egalitarian tendencies of today's post-structuralist literary criticism, as discussed in the foregoing, can, of their own accord, not avoid levelling literary texts – let alone an author possibly of genius and hence troublesome – to the ground of their contexts, thus subsuming them under that 'classless democracy of texts'[35] that corresponds to the articulation of their more or less radical, if at times hidden, political persuasions. Furthermore, since they detect concealed ideological motives everywhere, the aesthetic in its turn has likewise had to suffer the charge of ideology. It is, on the one hand, brought forward by Marxism and, on the other, by deconstruction. A Marxist is bound to regard the aesthetic with mistrust, even hostility, because he holds it mainly responsible for, or at least implicated in, the 'construction of the dominant ideological forms of modern class-society', whose characteristic division of labour he, on account of his nostalgia for an earlier, supposedly organic social totality, hates from the bottom of his heart.[36] Hence one can well understand the materialist programme of 'dissident reading', aimed as it is at revealing any text as a 'site of cultural contest', denying self-sufficiency to literature, and maligning coherence as a 'chimera'.[37] To be sure, I myself am now not nostalgic for Romantic organicism, which would not be in order for a contemporary of postmodernism, but what I absolutely deem worthy of criticism in the Marxist approach is its too frequent and too unmediated equation of art on the one hand with life on the other. Put differently, contrary to what Marxists wish to assert, 'essential asymmetry between art and life' must rather be assumed to be the first principle of aesthetics, as is affirmed by today's analytical philosophy of art when stressing the fact that works of art are, first and foremost, about art and therefore require something like a concept of art allowing for this circumstance.[38] That way, the branch of philosophy in question is able to avoid a mistake typical of Marxists, namely, to identify art with the content of works of art or to interpret mere juxtapositions of social and artistic phenomena as correlations (ibid. 150); (280–287)[39] – the best method, by the way, to miss the 'duplicitous ontology' of literary works of art, vacillating as they are between mimesis and autonomy.[40]

Surely all this is ideological now in its turn and would not do justice to the opinions on aesthetics of, say, a Marcuse,[41] seeing indeed with surprise that the concept of ideology has become so ubiquitous nowadays. Thus equally, as already mentioned, with deconstruction which views the aesthetic with suspicion, it seems, because it has tended, and that especially through the reception of Kant by Schiller, in the direction of a globalized conglomerate of concepts whose totalitarian implications provide grounds for political concern to a Paul de Man for example.[42] Therefore the charge of ideology on his part. If, however, we were to 'deconstruct' his own notion of ideology, we would soon realize that it is characterized by a radical linguistic scepticism in the wake of which the label of ideology is attached precisely to 'the confusion of linguistic with natural reality, of reference with phenomenalism'.[43] Let us leave such a position, which ultimately would lead to hermeneutic nihilism,[44] to its own devices for the moment, especially as it does not move us further forward with regard to Shakespeare the dramatist.

For more serious than the charge of ideology in the present context is the fact that aesthetics meanwhile seems to have lost its object, i.e., the work of art itself. This is first of all to be understood in the general sense that, in the development of art from modernism to post-modernism, the traditional unity of the work of art has been dissolved more and more. Both in theoretical pronouncement on the arts and in their practical execution, one could witness a kind of 'eclipse of the work of art',[45] whose former closure and organic disposition of all its parts became negated programmatically; coherence and autonomy of the work of art were said and shown no longer to exist, nay, they were often even being destroyed systematically.[46] The 'crisis of the concept of the artwork' thus specified can now, more particularly in relation to our poet, also be discovered in contemporary Shakespearen studies, and that with regard, first, to textual criticism and, second, to theatrical practice. Thus, in contrast to earlier generations of editors, the so-called 'new' bibliography now operating contextually, is concerned to confront us, instead of the formerly stable, yet basically hybrid text of a given Shakespearean play, with the plurality of textual versions that have come down to us through history – an endeavour not only disintegrating the single work that on principle will never be finished, but also making the act of interpretation more difficult.[46A] In quite similar fashion, today's practice of staging Shakespeare's plays, while rejecting only slightly older historical attempts at theatrical reconstruction[46B] as 'essentialist' and having in its turn – I am talking especially of 'performance theory' as the basis of this practice – received its inspiration from the literary theories of poststructuralism as previously discussed, teaches us that a Shakespearean text can never be stable or authoritative, but must be conceived as the collective product of all those participating in the act of creating meaning in the theatre.[47] And with this remark enough might, for the time being, have been said on the crisis of the concept of the artwork, having become completely pluralistic by now and, in addition to that, undergone frequent debasement from text to mere pretext.

Now, what are the consequences of all this for the role of aesthetics in the study of literature? One will have to stand back and think afresh. In this respect, and that much should be clear from the start, any simple recourse to those older monolithic notions of the aesthetic that had evolved systematically between the eighteenth and twentieth century[48] is to be ruled out. (In a similar vein the argument was conducted in my earlier discussion of the change in historiography from universalistic to particularistic notions.) Instead, post-modern thought, mistrustful as it is of globalizing or holistic concepts, rather tends to give credence to those fragmented individual aesthetic insights that are derived from the empirical data of actual artistic practice.[49] Accordingly, two strands of thought now converge here, both of them quite decidedly urging us to return to the presystematic stage of aesthetics. The pluralistic or disintegrated category of the artwork shifts the emphasis within aesthetic discourse from the pole of the object to that of the subject, whereby the subject in its turn now sees itself first of all thrown back on its own sensuous experience.[50] Thus it appears only logical to have recently attempted to repristinate the aesthetic by falling back on the time-honoured and broad sense of Greek *aisthesis* (sense perception). Whether conceived right away in conjunction with ethics again[51] or even in interaction with *poiesis* and *katharsis* as similarly basic aesthetic experiences[52] – not to mention the efforts of Lyotard and others to move art 'aisthetically' beyond the limits of representation by stressing its material qualities[53] – it must be admitted that *aisthesis*, the receptive aspect of the aesthetic process, has regained a prominent place in today's discourse on philosophy and literature. Its newly acquired dignity is above all indebted to Kant's *Critique of Judgment*,[54] where it has been analysed with strict reference to the sensuous impact of aesthetic phenomena that bring 'art' to consciousness in the first place. The fact that Kant asserts the superiority of the natural beautiful over the artistic beautiful and thereby renounces the hypostasis of the artwork[55] cannot but highlight the timeliness of his third critique in a time like ours that has come to apprehend precisely the latter category as a problem.[56] Thus Kant obviously stands behind Dufrenne, the most impressive exponent of today's phenomenological school of aesthetics. According to him, no object of art, be it a painting, a sculpture or, as in our context, a Shakespearean play, gains the status of an 'aesthetic object', as he calls it, unless perceived by a given subject, i.e., subject and object must be joined in interaction to create the 'aesthetic object' whose being is not 'the being of an abstract signification' but rather 'the being of a sensuous thing which is realized only in perception'.[57] It almost amounts to a compensation for the lost unity and totality of any work of the imagination, if it thus depends on the aesthetic experience or the reflective participation of a spectator to make such a work into a work of art in the first place.[58]

Be this active engagement in the work of art itself ever so difficult to achieve, it is not downright impossible. To return to Shakespearean studies: focusing his attention on *Hamlet* and *Lear*, R.A. Foakes recently tried, in spite of the equalizing tendencies of the contemporary critical fashions this paper has also had to contend with, to reclaim both tragedies as aesthetic experiences. To achieve this purpose, he re-activated, however selectively, Coleridge's theoretical concept of 'inward illusion', or temporary half-faith, through which the reader or spectator, filling out in an activity of the imagination the incompleteness of a given play's theatrical representation, contributes on his or her part to the recreation of an imaginary world. And in view of the fact that we as readers and spectators have at once an objective as well as a subjective relation to a text, each of us completing its 'meaning' on the basis of its perceived 'design', we at the same time become aware of an author's – in our case, Shakespeare's – artistry.[59]

Such an emphasis on the dialogic, if not even dialectic, nature of the aesthetic process now might indeed be full of potential for the future. All the same, the aesthetic experience, which at times may make too heavy demands on the subject, appears to me like a rather empty category, seeing that a similar exception could be taken to phenomenology at large on account of its rigorous epistemological reticence. It accords nicely with this observation that especially Kant's aesthetic critique would seem to have been buttressed 'only to a slight degree by a living knowledge and concrete reminiscence of important works of art'.[60] As is well known, Hegel's monumental *Aesthetics* (given as lectures between 1817 and 1829) now provides an alternative to this, and not alone for the reason that it is, by contrast, extremely rich in actual aesthetic perception but also for privileging again, in overturning the priorities of Kant, the artistic beautiful against the natural beautiful, thereby according its ancient right to the concept of the artwork.[61] Thus it will not be taken amiss, I trust, if a student of literature in the end resorts to Hegel's *Aesthetics*, and that with regard to a particular play of Shakespeare's.

IV

The selective repristination of certain particularized theorems or insights one could carve out, like fragments, from the systematic block of Hegelian aesthetics bears, in our context, above all on Hegel's appreciation of Shakespeare's art of representing character. This theme is broached throughout his lectures on the philosophy of fine art: in the first part which treats of the beautiful as such and the ideal, where he discusses the definiteness of the ideal according to action and character; in the second part which traces the ideal in its evolution through the symbolic, classical, and romantic forms of art, whereby the latter, for serving as the transition to modern times, is accorded independence and individuality; and, finally, in the third part devoted to the several types of art where, in addition to the development of dramatic poetry, he depicts the art of characterization in modern drama. In this connection, the same three traits are constantly stressed by Hegel with regard to Shakespeare's dramatic figures: firstly, 'their total individuality', whereby the English dramatist, to his great advantage, does not only differ from the Greeks but also from the French, Italians, and Spaniards whose characters are said by Hegel mostly to be stereotyped through one single pathos. Such a totality of the human representing the ideal aspect of Shakespearean figures, must, however, secondly, be associated with the real one, since it is only by connecting the ideal with the real that the poet, thirdly, achieves that complete liveliness and concrete determinateness which distinguishes his characters above all others. This determinateness and firmness of character elicits Hegel's highest praise, as the following passage may prove:[62]

> The more Shakespeare on the infinite embrace of his world-stage proceeds to develop the extreme limits of evil and folly, to that extent [. . .] he concentrates these characters in their limitations. While doing so, however, he confers on them intelligence and imagination; and by means of the image in which they, by virtue of that intelligence, contemplate themselves objectively, as a work of art, he makes them free artists of themselves, and is fully able, through the complete virility and truth of his characterization, to awaken our interest in criminals, no less than in the most vulgar and weak-witted lubbers and fools.
> (trans. F.P.B. Osmaston [1920], Bloom, 1995, 70)[63]

In this complex, sheer unfathomable passage from his *Aesthetics*, we can see the culminating point of Hegel's lifelong study of, and familiarity with, Shakespeare.[64] Besides, the passage quoted has quite recently been drawn upon again, and that by Harold Bloom in a voluminous defence of the 'Western Canon', whose central star Shakespeare also is to him. Especially with reference to Hegel's talk of 'free artists of themselves', Bloom is also concerned with opposing today's current socio-political theories of literature, oblivious as they are of art – their representatives are aptly labelled by him as the 'School of Resentment' – and to establish the validity of the aesthetic in the analysis of Shakespeare's dramatic figures.[65] Such a project would have been quite unthinkable until recently, seeing that the analysis of character was scorned by the modernistic representatives of the 'new criticism', who succeeded in dominating discourse immediately after World War II. According to them, a play had to be viewed primarily as a poetic structure, organized with the help of recurrent motifs and metaphors, to whose 'texture' dramatic figures would have to be subordinated. Needless to say, post-modern critics now welcome the study of character, whose revision is on the agenda again today, not in the sense of a naïve return to, say, the Shakespeare critic A.C. Bradley, who in his day had already been inspired by Hegel,[66] but rather with a sharpened awareness of the psychic fragility, conventional constitution[67], as well as contradictory construction of any dramatic figure, briefly, in the spirit of that pluralistic fragmentation which in so many other respects would appear as our epoch's signature.[68]

However, it is high time by now to adduce the promised example of Shakespeare's work in order to attempt, by way of conclusion, something like a reconciliation of politics and aesthetics. The piece in question, since we started by looking at the histories, is *Richard II* (1595), the play which to all intents and purposes represents the prehistory of the whole historical process dramatized in the two tetralogies. What is more, this play, with regard to its protagonist, admits of ideal 'inscription' into the passage quoted from Hegel's *Aesthetics*, to put it in post-structuralist terms.

In short, the history play *Richard II* dramatizes political failure not least as the result of a disturbed relation to time that in the world of politics always asks to be filled with action. This political thematic strand is then, toward the end of the drama, treated aesthetically in that the now powerless king, in his prison monologue (v.v.1–66)[69] actually presenting himself as 'free artist of himself', painfully becomes aware of his squandering of time and opportunity by producing a series of similes. Having finished with the opening of his monologue, the captive Richard hears music (v.v.41), whereupon he breaks into the following lament (41–49):

> Music do I hear?
> Ha, ha! keep time – how sour sweet music is
> When time is broke and no proportion kept!
> So is it in the music of men's lives.
> And here have I the daintiness of ear
> To check time broke in a disordered string;
> But for the concord of my state and time,
> Had not an ear to hear my true time broke:
> I wasted time, and now doth time waste me.

Subsequent to this, the dethroned king compares his person to the parts of a clock (50–58), reaching to the conclusion (58–60): 'But my time / Runs posting on in Bolingbroke's proud joy, / While I stand fooling here, his Jack of the clock'.

As in a focus, the lines of monologue quoted gather motifs pursued by Shakespeare throughout the play. That way Richard's confrontation with himself fulfills the function of a summary retrospect, finally bringing home to him his failure as a politician. Since the young king had from the very beginning not 'accorded' his actions to the demands of his high office (II.i.17–30, 100–103, 241–245), the analogy of musical 'discord' to personal and thus at the same time political disharmony carries a profound sense. The same holds true for the closely linked motif of wasting time the dethroned Richard himself now bewails in gaol. Not without reason, considering how carelessly Richard treated time when banishing Bolingbroke, his later adversary (I.iii.208–215, 226–232), and how high-handedly he discarded customary rights, as guaranteed by the normal course of time, in disinheriting his exiled enemy (II.i.195–199), thus indirectly adumbrating his own fall in advance (II.i.213–214). What is more, in the further onward movement of the history play, political thematics are articulated with recourse to manifold deployments of the motif of time (III.iv.54–66; v.i.24–25), whose most inexorable aspect consists in the irreversability of lost opportunities (III.ii.67–74, 80–81).[70] Thus it is only consequent when Richard, having, politically speaking, in the end become a helpless victim of time, compares himself, in the aesthetically felt self-accusations of the prison monologue, to a clock, conceiving the expressions of his grief as indications of time (v.v.57–58): '[...] so sighs, and tears, and groans, / Show minutes, times, and hours [...]'. This identification basically marks the disgraceful reduction of the deposed king to a mere instrument of measurement; he can no longer shape time actively but only register it passively, and that as Bolingbroke's 'Jack of the clock' (v.v.60).

In addition to that, the uniformity of the course of time, as registered in prison, becomes for Richard an emblem of the monotony of his grief. The consciousness of time's pitiless passing here in gaol constitutes the last variation of the theme of suffering running through the play not only since the politically explosive abdication scene, in which Richard, excellent actor that he is, had ritualistically exalted himself into a kingship of grief (IV.i.191–199). And thanks to this reversal, i.e., the exchange of his earthly crown for an almost Christian kingship of care (III.ii.210), Richard the man might have gained sympathies necessarily denied to Richard the politician. As regards the development of the dramatist himself during the work on his histories, one has therefore felt entitled to note 'that the historical element properly speaking interested Shakespeare less and less from drama to drama and the free creation of human beings (culminating in *Henry IV*) more and more'.[71] In this sense Hugo von Hofmannsthal was able to characterize King Richard II as 'elder brother of Hamlet'[72] – which brings us back full circle to Hegel's *Aesthetics*.

It is to be hoped that the above attempt at reconciling the political with the aesthetic element by interpreting, if ever so sketchily, a selected Shakespearean history play, which already tended in the direction of tragedy, could demonstrate that a respect for both realms would seem to be necessary for something like an ethics of discourse in the study of literature. To be sure, nothing speaks against working in the inter- or indeed multidisciplinary manner called for nowadays, but political or ideological appropriations of literary texts, especially when confusing concerns of the present with themes of the past in a speculative and anachronistic way, are to be rejected. And that not least of all for depriving us of the pleasure Shakespeare's plays, understood as works of art, can still give to us.

REFERENCES

1. Carroll, David (ed.) (1990), *The States of 'Theory': History, Art, and Critical Discourse*, New York: Columbia University Press, 1–2. Hartman, Geoffrey H. (1991), *Minor Prophecies: The Literary Essay in the Culture Wars*, Cambridge, Mass./London: Harvard University Press, 2. Grabes, Herbert (1995), 'Errant Specialisms. The Recent Historicist Turn Away From Aesthetics', *REAL*, 11, 159–172.

2. Taylor, Gary (1990), *Reinventing Shakespeare. A Cultural History from the Restoration to the Present*, London: The Hogarth Press, 298–372; Grady, Hugh (1991), *The Modernist Shakespeare: Critical Texts in a Material World*, Oxford: Clarendon Press, 190–246.

3. Erickson, Peter (1991), *Rewriting Shakespeare, Rewriting Ourselves*, Berkeley/Los Angeles/Oxford: University of California Press, 8.

4. Eagleton, Terry (1983), *Literary Theory: An Introduction*, Oxford: Blackwell,

127–150; Horstmann, Ulrich (1983), *Parakritik und Dekonstruktion: Eine Einführung in den amerikanischen Poststrukturalismus*, Würzburg: Königshausen und Neumann, 15–19; Felperin, Howard (1985), *Beyond Deconstruction: The Uses and Abuses of Literary Theory*, Oxford: Clarendon Press; Atkins, G. Douglas/Bergeron, David M. (eds) (1988), *Shakespeare and Deconstruction*, New York/Bern: Lang.

5. Parker, Patricia/Hartman, Geoffrey (eds) (1985), *Shakespeare and the Question of Theory*, New York/London: Methuen; Norris, Christopher (1985), 'Post-structuralist Shakespeare. Text and Ideology', in Drakakis, 47–66.

6. Eagleton, Terry (1983), *Literary Theory: An Introduction*, Oxford: Blackwell, 151–193; McCanles, Michael (1988), 'Shakespeare, Intertextuality, and the Decentered Self', in Atkins/Bergeron, 193–211.

7. Schwartz, Murray M./Kahn, Coppélia (eds) (1980), *Representing Shakespeare: New Psychoanalytic Essays*, Baltimore/London: The Johns Hopkins University Press, xii–xiv.

8. Althusser, Louis (1971), *Lenin and Philosophy and Other Essays*, trans. Ben Brewster, London: New Left Books, 169; Dollimore, Jonathan/Sinfield, Alan (1985), 'History and Ideology: The Instance of *Henry V*', in Drakakis, 206–227; Howard, Jean E. and O'Connor, Marion F. (eds) (1987), *Shakespeare Reproduced: The Text in History and Ideology*, New York/London: Routledge; Eagleton, Terry (1991), *Ideology: An Introduction*, London/New York: Verso, 146–153; Freadman, Richard/Miller, Seumas (1992), *Re-Thinking Theory: A Critique of Contemporary Literary Theory and an Alternative Account*, Cambridge: Cambridge University Press, 72–114; Hawkes, David (1996), *Ideology*, London/New York: Routledge, 121–30.

9. Dollimore, Jonathan (1984), *Radical Tragedy. Religion, Ideology and Power in the Drama of Shakespeare and His Contemporaries*, Brighton: Harvester; Cohen, Walter (1987), 'Political Criticism of Shakespeare', in Howard/O'Connor, 18–46; Wayne, Don E. (1987), 'Power, Politics, and the Shakespearean Text. Recent Criticism in England and the United States', in Howard and O'Connor, 47–67 (see note 8); Greenblatt, Stephen (1988), *Shakespearean Negotiations. The Circulation of Social Energy in Renaissance England*, Berkeley: University of California Press; Holderness, Graham (ed.) (1988), *The Shakespeare Myth*, Manchester: Manchester University Press; Sinfield, Alan (1992), *Faultlines: Cultural Materialism and the Politics of Dissident Reading*, Oxford: Clarendon Press; Wilson, Scott (1995), *Cultural Materialism. Theory and Practice*, Oxford/Cambridge, Mass.: Blackwell.

10. Thompson, Ann (1988), '"The Warrant of Womanhood". Shakespeare and Feminist Criticism', in Holderness, 74–88; Callaghan, Dympna (1989), *Woman and Gender in Renaissance Tragedy: A Study of 'King Lear', 'Othello', 'The Duchess of Malfi', and 'The White Devil'*, New York/London: Harvester Wheatsheaf; Wayne, Valerie (ed.) (1991), *The Matter of Difference: Materialist Feminist Criticism of Shakespeare*, New York/London: Harvester Wheatsheaf; Harvey, Elizabeth D. (1992), *Ventriloquized Voices: Feminist Theory and English Renaissance Texts*, London/New York: Routledge.

11. Cohen, Walter (1987), 'Political Criticism of Shakespeare', in Howard/O'Connor, 18–46; Grady, Hugh (1991), *The Modernist Shakespeare: Critical Texts in a Material World*, Oxford: Clarendon Press, 235–245.

12. Tillyard, E.M.W. (1943), *The Elizabethan World Picture*, London: Chatto and Windus.

13. Siegel, Paul N. (1957), *Shakespearean Tragedy and the Elizabethan Compromise*, New York: New York University Press.

14. Tillyard, E.M.W. (1944), *Shakespeare's History Plays*, London: Chatto and Windus.

15. Sanders, Wilbur (1968), *The Dramatist and the Received Idea: Studies in the Plays of Marlowe and Shakespeare*, Cambridge: Cambridge University Press, 79; Kelly, Henry Ansgar (1970), *Divine Providence in the England of Shakespeare's Histories*, Cambridge, Mass.: Harvard University Press; Frey, David L. (1976), *The First Tetralogy: Shakespeare's Scrutiny of the Tudor Myth. A Dramatic Exploration of Divine Providence*, The Hague/Paris: Mouton.

16. Felperin, Howard (1985), *Beyond Deconstruction: The Uses and Abuses of Literary Theory*, Oxford: Clarendon Press, 200–204.

17. Oppel, Horst (1963), *Shakespeare: Studien zum Werk und zur Welt des Dichters*, Heidelberg: Carl Winter Universitätsverlag, 299–300; Levin, Harry (1976), *Shakespeare and the Revolution of the Times: Perspectives and Commentaries*, New York: Oxford University Press, 35–36.

18. Shanker, Sidney (1975), *Shakespeare and the Uses of Ideology*, The Hague/Paris: Mouton, vii–x, 220–224.

19. Wilson, J. Dover (1951), *What Happens in 'Hamlet'*, Cambridge: Cambridge University Press, third edn, 30–38; Honigmann, E.A.J. (1963), 'The Politics in *Hamlet* and "The World of the Play"', in Brown, John Russell and Harris, Bernard (eds), *Hamlet*, London: Arnold, 129–47.

20. Leimberg, Inge (1961), *Untersuchungen zu Shakespeares Zeitvorstellung als ein Beitrag zur Interpretation der Tragödien*, Köln: Kölner Universitätsverlag, 65–68, 82–85.

21. Paul, Henry N. (1950), *The Royal Play of 'Macbeth': When, Why, and How It Was Written by Shakespeare*, New York: Macmillan, IV, iii, 91–94.

22. Knights, L.C. (1979), *'Hamlet' and Other Shakespearean Essays*, Cambridge: Cambridge University Press, 150–71.

23. Stirling, Brents (1949), *The Populace in Shakespeare*, New York: Columbia University Press, 35–45; Patterson, Annabel (1989), *Shakespeare and the Popular Voice*, Oxford/Cambridge, Mass.: Blackwell, 120–153; Baumann, Uwe (1996), *Vorausdeutung und Tod im englischen Römerdrama der Renaissance (1564–1642)*, Tübingen/Basel: Francke, 79–83.

24. Lindenberger, Herbert (1975), *Historical Drama: The Relation of Literature and Reality*, Chicago/London: The University of Chicago Press, 12–14; Grady, Hugh (1991), *The Modernist Shakespeare: Critical Texts in a Material World*, Oxford: Clarendon Press, 158–89; Hawley, William M. (1992), *Critical Hermeneutics and Shakespeare's History Plays*, New York/Bern: Lang, 11–14.

25. Dollimore, Jonathan/Sinfield, Alan (eds) (1985), *Political Shakespeare. New Essays in Cultural Materialism*, Manchester: Manchester University Press; Holderness, Graham (1985), *Shakespeare's History*, Dublin: Gill and Macmillan/New York: St. Martin's Press, 21–32; Wilson, Richard/Dutton, Richard (eds) (1992), *New Historicism and Renaissance Drama*, London/New York: Longman; Holderness, Graham (1992), *Shakespeare Recycled: The Making of Historical Drama*, New York/London: Harvester Wheatsheaf.

26. Vickers, Brian (1993), *Appropriating Shakespeare: Contemporary Critical Quarrels*, New Haven/London: Yale University Press.

27. Taylor, Gary (1990), *Reinventing Shakespeare: A Cultural History from the Restoration to the Present*, London: The Hogarth Press; Marsden, Jean I. (ed.) (1991), *The Appropriation of Shakespeare. Post-Renaissance Reconstructions of the Works and the Myth*, New York/London: Harvester Wheatsheaf.

28. Elton, W.R. (1971), 'Shakespeare and the Thought of His Age', in Muir, Kenneth/Schoenbaum, S. (eds), *A New Companion to Shakespeare Studies*, Cambridge: Cambridge University Press, 180–198, 192.

29. Veeser, H. Aram (ed.) (1989), *The New Historicism*, New York/London:

Routledge; Thomas, Brook (1991), *The New Historicism and Other Old-Fashioned Topics*, Princeton, N.J.: Princeton University Press; Healy, Thomas (1992), *New Latitudes: Theory and English Renaissance Literature*, London: Arnold, 57–83; Cantor, Paul A. (1993), 'Stephen Greenblatt's New Historicist Vision', *Academic Questions*, 6 (4), 21–36.

30. Dollimore, Jonathan/Sinfield, Alan (1985), 'History and Ideology: The Instance of *Henry V*', in Drakakis, 206–27.

31. Kavanagh, James H. (1985), 'Shakespeare in Ideology', in Drakakis, 144–165; Wells, Robin Headlam (1986), *Shakespeare: Politics and the State*, London: Macmillan.

32. Shakespeare, William (1961), *King Richard II*, ed. Peter Ure, The Arden Shakespeare, London: Methuen, fifth edn, lviii–lx; Levin, Harry (1976), *Shakespeare and the Revolution of the Times, Perspectives and Commentaries*, New York: Oxford University Press, 35–6; Saccio, Peter (1977), *Shakespeare's English Kings: History, Chronicle, and Drama*, New York: Oxford University Press, 32.

33. Bradshaw, Graham (1993), *Misrepresentations. Shakespeare and the Materialists*, Ithaca, New York/London: Cornell University Press.

34. Kamps, Ivo (ed.) (1991), *Shakespeare Left and Right*, New York/London: Routledge.

35. Krieger, Murray (1981), *Arts on the Level: The Fall of the Elite Object*, Knoxville, Tenn.: University of Tennessee Press, 44.

36. Eagleton, Terry (1990), *The Ideology of the Aesthetic*, Oxford: Blackwell, 3, 373.

37. Sinfield, Alan (1992), *Faultlines, Cultural Materialism and the Politics of Dissident Reading*, Oxford: Clarendon Press, 47–51.

38. Wollheim, Richard (1980), *Art and its Objects*, Cambridge: Cambridge University Press, second edn, 99; Danto, Arthur C. (1981), *The Transfiguration of the Commonplace: A Philosophy of Art*, Cambridge, Mass.: Harvard University Press, 149.

39. Savile, Anthony (1982), *The Test of Time: An Essay in Philosophical Aesthetics*, Oxford: Clarendon Press, 280–87.

40. Krieger, Murray (1981), *Arts on the Level: The Fall of the Elite Object*, Knoxville: Tenn.: University of Tennessee Press, 19.

41. Marcuse, Herbert (1978), *The Aesthetic Dimension: Toward a Critique of Marxist Aesthetics*, Boston: Beacon Press, 8, 23.

42. de Man, Paul (1984), *The Rhetoric of Romanticism*, New York: Columbia University Press, 263–66; de Man, Paul (1996), *Aesthetic Ideology*, ed. Andrzej Warminski, Minneapolis: University of Minnesota Press, 1–11, 129–62; Norris, Christopher (1988), *Paul de Man: Deconstruction and the Critique of Aesthetic Ideology*, New York/London: Routledge, 53–64, 114–123; Harpham, Geoffrey Galt (1994), 'Aesthetics and the Fundamentals of Modernity', in Levine, George (ed.), *Aesthetics and Ideology*, New Brunswick, N.J.: Rutgers University Press, 124–149.

43. de Man, Paul (1986), *The Resistance to Theory*, Minneapolis: University of Minnesota Press, 11.

44. Etlin, Richard A. (1996), *In Defense of Humanism. Value in the Arts and Letters*, Cambridge: Cambridge University Press, 136–42.

45. Klein, Robert (1981), *Form and Meaning: Essays on the Renaissance and Modern Art*, trans. Jay, Madeline/Wieseltier, Leon, Princeton, N.J.: Princeton University Press, 176–83.

46. Bubner, Rüdiger (1989), *Ästhetische Erfahrung*, Frankfurt am Main: Suhrkamp, 19–20, 30–4.; Taylor, Gary (1990), *Reinventing Shakespeare: A Cultural History from the Restoration to the Present*, London: The Hogarth

Press, 344–47, 356–62; Styan, J.L. (1977), *The Shakespeare Revolution: Criticism and Performance in the Twentieth Century*, Cambridge: Cambridge University Press; Dessen, Alan C. (1995), *Recovering Shakespeare's Theatrical Vocabulary*, Cambridge: Cambridge University Press.

47. Taylor, Gary (1990), *Reinventing Shakespeare: A Cultural History from the Restoration to the Present*, London: The Hogarth Press, 304–11, 336–7; Bulman, James C. (ed.) (1996), *Shakespeare, Theory, and Performance*, London/New York: Routledge, 1–11; Worthen, W.B. (1996), 'Staging "Shakespeare". Acting, Authority, and the Rhetoric of Performance', in Bulman, 12–28.

48. Cassirer, Ernst (1944), *An Essay on Man: An Introduction to a Philosophy of Human Culture*, New Haven/London: Yale University Press, 137–70; Beardsley, Monroe C. (1966), *Aesthetics. From Classical Greece to the Present. A Short History*, New York: Macmillan; Osborne, Harold (ed.) (1972), *Aesthetics*, Oxford: Oxford University Press, 1–24; Schneider, Norbert (1996), *Geschichte der Ästhetik von der Aufklärung bis zur Postmoderne. Eine paradigmatische Einführung*, Stuttgart: Reclam.

49. Henrich, Dieter/Iser, Wolfgang (eds) (1984), *Theorien der Kunst*, Frankfurt am Main: Suhrkamp, second edn, 14, 34.

50. Bowie, Andrew (1990), *Aesthetics and Subjectivity: From Kant to Nietzsche*, Manchester: Manchester University Press.

51. Nussbaum, Martha C. (1990), *Love's Knowledge: Essays on Philosophy and Literature*, New York: Oxford University Press, 148–67, 168–94; Grabes, Herbert (1996), 'Ethics, Aesthetics, and Alterity', in Hoffmann, Gerhard/Hornung, Alfred (eds), *Aesthetics and Ethics: The Moral Turn of Postmodernism*, Heidelberg: Universitätsverlag C. Winter, 13–28.

52. Jauss, Hans Robert (1984), *Ästhetische Erfahrung und literarische Hermeneutik*, Frankfurt am Main: Suhrkamp, fourth edn, 71–90, 125–65.

53. Lyotard, Jean-François (1990), 'After the Sublime. The State of Aesthetics', in Carroll, pp. 297–304; Welsch, Wolfgang/Pries, Christine (eds) (1991), *Ästhetik im Widerstreit: Interventionen zum Werk von Jean-François Lyotard*, Weinheim: VCH, Acta Humaniora, 9–10; Barck, Karlheinz, et al. (eds) (1991), *Aisthesis. Wahrnehmung heute oder Perspektiven einer anderen Ästhetik. Essais*, Leipzig: Reclam, third edn, 445–68.

54. Kant, Immanuel (1790), *Critique of Judgment*.

55. Kant, Immanuel (1924), *Kritik der Urteilskraft*, ed. Karl Vorländer, Hamburg: Meiner, sixth edn, 151, §42; 159–60, §45.

56. Bubner, Rüdiger (1989), *Ästhetische Erfahrung*, Frankfurt am Main, Suhrkamp, 34–8; Esser, Andrea (ed.) (1995), *Autonomie der Kunst? Zur Aktualität von Kants Ästhetik*, Berlin: Akademie Verlag.

57. Dufrenne, Mikel (1973), *The Phenomenology of Aesthetic Experience*, trans. Casey, Edward S., et al., Evanston, Ill.: Northwestern University Press, 218.

58. Bubner, Rüdiger (1989), *Ästhetische Erfahrung*, Frankfurt am Main, Suhrkamp, 52–69; Etlin, Richard (1996), *In Defense of Humanism: Value in the Arts and Letters*, Cambridge: Cambridge University Press, 17–18.

59. Foakes, R.A. (1993), *Hamlet versus Lear. Cultural Politics and Shakespeare's Art*, Cambridge: Cambridge University Press, 132–37, 220–24.

60. Kant, Immanuel (1924), *Kritik der Urteilskraft*, ed. Karl Vörlander, Hamburg: Meiner, sixth edn, xv.

61. Bubner, Rüdiger (1989), *Ästhetische Erfahrung*, Frankfurt am Main, Suhrkamp, 35; Ferry, Luc (1993), *Homo Aestheticus: The Invention of Taste in the Democratic Age*, trans. de Loaiza, Robert, Chicago/London: The University of Chicago Press, 122–28.

62. Hegel, Georg Wilhelm Friedrich [1955], *Ästhetik*, ed. Friedrich Bassenge, Frankfurt am Main: Europäische Verlagsanstalt, 2 vols, second edn, II, 577.
63. Bloom, Harold (1995), *The Western Canon: The Books and School of the Ages*, London: Macmillan, 70.
64. Wundt, Max (1934), 'Shakespeare in der deutschen Philosophie', *Shakespeare-Jahrbuch*, 19–26, 70, 9–36; Wolff, Emil (1949), 'Hegel und Shakespeare', in Martini, Fritz (ed.), *Vom Geist der Dichtung. Gedächtnisschrift für Robert Petsch*, Hamburg: Hoffmann und Campe, 120–179; Lukacher, Ned (1986), *Primal Scenes: Literature, Philosophy, Psychoanalysis*, Ithaca, N.Y./London: Cornell University Press, 178–235.
65. Bloom, Harold (1995), *The Western Canon: The Books and School of the Ages*, London: Macmillan, 20, 69–73.
66. Bradley, A.C. (1905), *Shakespearean Tragedy*, London: Macmillan, second edn, 16, 348.
67. Bradley, A.C. (1909), *Oxford Lectures on Poetry*, London: Macmillan, second edn, 69–95.
68. Taylor, Gary (1990), *Reinventing Shakespeare: A Cultural History from the Restoration to the Present*, London: The Hogarth Press, 334–35.
69. All quotations from *Richard II* are from the Arden Shakespeare edition of 1961 (see n. 31).
70. Stürzl, Erwin (1965), *Der Zeitbegriff in der elisabethanischen Literatur. The Lackey of Eternity*, Wien/Stuttgart: W. Braumüller, 215–18; Uhlig, Claus (1967), *Traditionelle Denkformen in Shakespeares tragischer Kunst*, Hamburg: Cram, de Gruyter, 107–10; Schamp, Jutta (1996), *Repräsentation von Zeit bei Shakespeare. Richard II, 1,2 Henry IV, Macbeth*, Marburg: unpub. diss., 170–86.
71. Schirmer, Walter F. (1954), *Glück und Ende der Könige in Shakespeares Historien*, Köln/Opladen: Westdeutscher Verlag, 10.
72. Hofmannsthal, Hugo von (1957), *Ausgewählte Werke*, ed. Rudolf Hirsch, Frankfurt am Main: S. Fischer, 2 vols, II, 397.

3   What! *You*, Will? Shakespeare and Homoeroticism

Bruce R. Smith

Implicitly at least, a connection between Shakespeare and homoeroticism goes back to 1640, when John Benson edited *Poems written by Wil. Shakespeare Gent.* and quietly removed evidence that the sonnets had ever been addressed to a fair young man. For fifty years before that, however, the likes of Philip Stubbes and John Rainolds had been railing against stage plays, partly on grounds that boy actors aroused homoerotic desires in spectators. Stubbes and Rainolds can be written off as cranks, of course, but once again Shakespeare's name may be implicated: in the words of sonnet 111 'subdued/ To what it works in, like the dyer's hand'.[1] More recently, and more insistently, questions about Shakespeare and homoeroticism have come to the fore in a series of books and essays that began to appear in the mid-1980s: Eve Sedgwick's *Between Men*,[2] Joseph Pequigney's *Such Is My Love*,[3] a special issue of *South Atlantic Quarterly*, 88 (1) devoted to 'Displacing Homophobia' (1989), Gregory Bredbeck's *Sodomy and Interpretation*,[4] Jonathan Dollimore's *Sexual Dissidence*,[5] Sedgwick's *Epistemology of the Closet*,[6] my *Homosexual Desire in Shakespeare's England*,[7] Valerie Traub's *Desire and Anxiety*,[8] the papers collected in Claude J. Summers and Ted-Larry Pebworth's *Homosexuality in Renaissance and Enlightenment England*,[9] Jonathan Goldberg's *Sodometries*,[10] the papers collected in Susan Zimmerman's *Erotic Politics*,[11] and the papers collected in Jonathan Goldberg's *Queering the Renaissance*[12] and *Reclaiming Sodom*.[13] In one way or another all of these books and essays are indebted to Michel Foucault's *History of Sexuality*[14] for the fundamental proposition that sexuality has a history, to Stephen Greenblatt and Jacques Derrida for strategies of analysis, and to feminist criticism for examples of politically engaged reading that is nonetheless attentive to problems of ontology and historical difference. On the subject of male homoeroticism, a critically powerful paradigm already existed in Alan Bray's *Homosexuality in Renaissance England*, later supplemented by an essay on 'Homosexuality and the Signs of Male Friendship in Elizabethan England'.[15]

The later 1990s have witnessed a second wave that includes Stephen Orgel's *Impersonations: The Performance of Gender in Shakespeare's England*,[16] Mario DiGangi's *The Homoerotics of Early Modern Drama*,[17] and Jeffrey Masten's *Textual Intercourse: Collaboration, Authorship, and Sexualities in Renaissance Drama*,[18] as well as important contributions to the issues in Mark Breitenberg's *Anxious Masculinity in Early Modern England*,[19] in Patricia Parker's *Shakespeare from the Margins: Language, Culture, Context*,[20] and in a range of essays, several of which are collected in Valerie Traub, M. Lindsay Kaplan, and Dympna Callaghan's *Feminist Readings of Early Modern Culture: Emerging Subjects*,[21] in Louise Fradenburg and Carla Freccero's *Premodern Sexualities*,[22] and in David Hillman and Carla Mazzio's *The Body in Parts: Fantasies of Corporeality in Early Modern Europe*.[23] The wave continues. A new volume of essays on Shakespeare's sonnets edited by James Schiffer[24] reopens the question of homoeroticism in three new essays by Joseph Pequigney, Valerie Traub, and me, as well as in reprinted pieces by Peter Stallybrass[25] and Margreta de Grazia.[26] Traub's *The Renaissance of Lesbianism in Early Modern England*[27] promises to consolidate the work on female homoeroticism that Traub has already published in *Desire and Anxiety*[28] and in scattered essays. My purpose here is to survey this recent scholarship. In doing so, I do not intend to give these books and articles the full critical review they deserve but to establish some common ground and relate them to each other. The result, I hope, will be an even wider conversation than the one already in progress.

AGREEMENTS AND DISAGREEMENTS

Out of the work of the 1980s and early 1990s several points of consensus have emerged – points that the more recent books and articles confirm:

1 With respect to early modern culture, 'sexuality' must be used as an heuristic term. According to Foucault, 'sexuality' did not exist as a conceptual category in the sixteenth and seventeenth centuries.
2 Wherever and whenever, sexuality is a cultural construct, not a natural given.
3 In any culture, sexuality is not an independent phenomenon. It exists in complicated relationships to gender, social rank, ideology, and material economy.
4 As inventions of the nineteenth century, 'homosexuality' and 'heterosexuality' are highly dubious as concepts for analysing early modern culture. The gender of one's sexual partners was not the starting point for anyone's self-identity in 1600.
5 On the other hand, the words available in early modern English to describe same-gender sexual relations – 'sodomy', 'filthiness', 'the sin-

not-to-be-named', 'tribadism'– likewise fail to cover the full range of such relations. In Jonathan Goldberg's words, 'sodomy is not homo-sexuality *tout court*, nor are male/female relations of alliance the same as heterosexuality'.

6   Shakespeare's plays and poems, despite their centrality in the canon of English literature, do not exhaust the range of possible ways in which homoeroticism in early modern England could be represented.

Equally clear from the existing scholarship is the fact that there are at least four questions still very much in dispute:

1   What is the relationship between homoeroticism as a state of affections and 'homosex' as a range of physical acts? Work by Bray[30] and Traub[31] points up just how unstable this particular binary is. Medical, ethical, and legal writings condemn genital acts between persons of the same gender, and yet the rhetoric of friendship for both genders points toward those very acts. Recent critics vary in where they place the emphasis. DiGangi, for example, carefully distinguishes 'homosexual-ity' from 'homoeroticism' and prefers the latter term, in part because it covers a much wider range of textual evidence. Traub in *The Renais-sance of Lesbianism in Early Modern England* does the same: 'Erotic attraction and longing need not involve genital contact, though both engage the body as a physical, sensual, pleasurable resource'. Bredbeck and Goldberg, on the other hand, are much more interested in the physical acts encoded in the rhetoric of homeroticism. Goldberg's es-says on '*Romeo and Juliet*'s Open Rs'[32] and 'The Anus in *Coriolanus*'[33] present cases in point.

2   What is the relationship between sexuality as a social construction and gender as a social construction? As we shall consider later, the phe-nomenon of boy actors exposes the problem in a particularly graphic way. Sedgwick[34] takes it as 'axiomatic' that sexuality and gender are two separate things. For critics like Traub and Goldberg it is important to detach sexual relations from heterosexist models, with all the differ-ences in power dynamics and body postures that those models imply. Dympna Callaghan, however, has raised forceful objections to this stratagem, arguing that 'gender always disciplines sexualities, and that this outcome, far from being unforeseeable, has all the banal predict-ability of patriarchal power'.[35]

3   A specific version of the same general question is how female homoeroticism is to be situated *vis-à-vis* male homoeroticism. Three main problems make it difficult to answer such a question: evidence (since writing and publishing in early modern England were activities controlled by men, there are fewer texts that seem to encode female homoeroticism and fewer still that were written by women), ontology (reading female sexual experience alternatively as the same as male experience or else as its binary opposite has the same effect of render-

ing female experience illegible on its own terms), and the sexual politics of the late twentieth century ('gay' and 'lesbian' stand in an uneasy relationship to each other). In her book *Desire and Anxiety* (1992) and in her essay 'The (In)Significance of 'Lesbian' Desire in Early Modern England'[36] Traub has given these issues their most most extensive treatment.

4 The state of contemporary sexual politics poses, finally, an even larger question: what is the relationship between studies of homoeroticism in Shakespeare and the larger academy within which these studies are carried out? I shall conclude by proposing an answer to that question.

The books and articles that have appeared since 1995 map out, it seems to me, five sites for investigation: language, bodies, gender, social order and contemporary sexual politics. I propose that we consider each of these five topics in turn.

LANGUAGE

Sexuality and textuality: how are they related? If in general, metaphor and metonomy represent two alternative thought processes, then sexuality as a particular case may be analysed along the same lines. Common sense would suggest that sexuality and textuality exist as two parallel phenomena. On one side is sexuality as a physical, social, and psychological concern; on the other, the texts that, quite literally, *trans*-scribe those concerns. Textuality is related to sexuality, in this view, as a kind of metaphor. Much of the best recent work on homoeroticism challenges that assumption and demonstrates how sexuality is bound up in the very words that would describe it. Textuality is related to sexuality, in this view, as a kind of metonymy.

Masten's *Textual Intercourse* proceeds from just such an understanding of language: texts in early modern theatre, Masten argues, were generated through homoerotic exchanges among men. The idea that poets produce works of art through acts of conception and birthing – acts that exclude women – goes back to Diotima's disquisition on love in Plato's *Symposium*. 'Now, some people', Diotima told Socrates, 'are pregnant in body, and for this reason turn more to women and pursue love in that way ... while others are pregnant in soul ... with what is fitting for a soul to bear and bring to birth. And what is fitting? Wisdom and the rest of virtue, which all poets beget, as well as all craftsmen who are said to be creative'.[37] Masten demonstrates how Plato's trope controlled early modern ideas of collaborative authorship, evidenced in the rhetoric of dedicatory epistles, printers' prefaces, and congratulatory verses, in the plots of plays like *The Two Gentlemen of Verona* and *The Two Noble Kinsmen*, in the economic organisation of players' companies, and sometimes in the playwrights' living arrangements. Shakespeare is the ideal subject for a book like this one because since the eighteenth century Shakespeare has been constructed as the very paragon of Author. Masten's aim is to demonstrate 'the author as contemporaneous with (not prior to) those texts and their publication'.[38] Under these circumstances, paternity is not just a 'metaphor' for authorship; rather, textual authority is implicated in political and sexual discourses. Early modern ideas of authorship are situated at the conjunction of discourses we now would separate and label as sexual, textual, and political. It was in the course of the seventeenth century, Masten argues, that the textual and the sexual devolved into the separate conceptual categories they remain today.

In *Shakespeare from the Margins* Parker deploys a similar understanding of language, one that she labels 'materialist'. Her argument is that 'Shakespearean wordplay – far from the inconsequentiality to which it has been reduced not only by the influence of neoclassicism but by continuing critical assumptions about the transparency (or unimportance) of the language of the plays – involves a network whose linkages expose (even as the plays themselves may appear simply to iterate or rehearse) the orthodoxies and ideologies of the texts they evoke' (13). In effect, Parker's method combines a new historicist interest in circulations of power with a deconstructive sensitivity to language. With respect to homoeroticism Parker charts all sorts of unexpected connections. Through the very first word she takes up – *preposterous* (literally, 'back-frontward' or, if you will, 'arsyversy') – Parker manages to link royal succession, primogeniture, orthography, sexual orthodoxy, and cultural authority, so that sodomitical acts and the transvestite theatre become, in more ways than one, *pre-post-erous* phenomena. The preposterous in early modern usage is deployed in opposition to the natural and the necessary. But, as Parker observes, 'nature as a category in the early modern period was less a given than a site of contention' (54). A chapter on '"Rude Mechanicals": *A Midsummer Night's Dream* and Shakespearean Joinery' takes up Helena's speech of protest when Hermia abandons her for Lysander (II.ii.195–216) and forges connections, across class and gender, with the mechanicals, opening up the possibility of a specifically female-female 'craft'. Elsewhere Parker sets up affinities among *ingle, angle,* and *English,* with attention not only to the boy actors and the part of the page in *The Merry Wives of Windsor* but to *Henry V* and the 'fault' Henry discovers among the English rebels, especially 'the man that was his bedfellow', Scroop (II.ii.8). Parker's exposé of the sexuality of Henry's textuality confirms Richard Corum's argument[39] that *Henry V* is a 'sado-lethal' text. In a chapter on *Othello* and *Hamlet* Parker fastens on the words *dilate, fault,* and *privy* and via images of unfolding discovers linkages among state intelligence, women's genitals, the monstrous, the beginnings of modern notions of privacy, the 'open secret' of sodomy, and the 'show-and-tell' of transvestite theater.

In his contribution to *The Body in Parts*[40] Masten performs a similar act of recuperative deconstruction on the word *fundament*. Armed with early modern dictionaries like John Florio's *A World of Words*, Masten directs attention to a variety of passages – notably Bottom's description of his dream in *A Midsummer Night's Dream* and Holinshed's account of the execution of Edward II – that suggest the interconnections among *fundament*, *fundamental*, and *foundation*. Instead of being the repository of filth and self-annihilation, Masten proposes, the anus might figure as a point of origin, a site of creativity, the foundation of great projects. In more ways than one, this is a revolutionary proposition. It continues the political work of *Textual Intercourse* in the way it positions male–male eroticism at the very center of cultural production in early modern England. At the same time, it offers a model for attacking the assumption that sexual behaviour of all sorts necessarily involves an 'actor' and a 'patient', a doer and a receiver. 'Queer philology' is Masten's own name for what he does in this project and in *Textual Intercourse*.

In the project of recovering female homoerotic desire language is crucial, for the very reason that the language of desire in early modern culture was dictated by men. That is the case even in the great declarations of female homoerotic passion in Shakespeare's scripts. Emilia in *The Two Noble Kinsmen* may celebrate her friendship with Flavina in graphically physical terms and conclude that 'the true love 'tween maid and maid may be / More than in sex [in]dividual' (I.iii.81–82), but her words were conceived and birthed by male authority, in the persons of William Shakespeare and John Fletcher, and were voiced onstage by a boy actor. Traub confronts this situation head on in her forthcoming book. To look for an authentic 'lesbian' rhetoric in early modern texts, she argues, may be accepting a false dichotomy. Male-authored language might, in fact, provide a rhetoric that could be appropriated by women whose erotic desire is turned toward women: 'The language of chaste bodies and proper conduct exceeds its ideological mandate not only by its compulsive repetition, exhortation, and hyperbole, but by proffering negative exempla which then become available to women for emulation' (1999).

BODIES

To turn from language to the human body would seemingly be to turn from the most obvious of cultural variables to the least. In its visible, tactile, audible, odiferous, even tasteable presence the body seems to be *there*, a 'natural' given, in a way that language is not. In *Making Sex: Body and Gender from the Greeks to Freud*[41] Thomas Laqueur challenged such assumptions by demonstrating the persistence, well into the early modern period, of Galen's idea of one-sexed body sharing the same genitalia: the heat-perfected male body with its extruded genitals and the cooler, imperfect female body with its internal genitals as the obverse of the male's. Greenblatt's essay 'Fiction and Friction'[42] had already given this idea critical currency. With respect to homoeroticism, the Galenic model has proved particularly useful in discussions of the female body. Traub in 'The Psychomorphology of the Clitoris'[43] and, more recently, Katharine Park in 'The Rediscovery of the Clitoris'[44] have both called attention to the way the clitoris, rediscovered from ancient texts and anatomized for the first time in the mid-sixteenth century, was taken by men to be a female substitute for the phallus and hence the very focus of male anxieties that women might indulge in erotic pleasures that did not include *them*. Park argues, indeed, that it was through medical discussions of the clitoris in the sixteenth century (her examples are French) that female homoeroticism first received wide publicity. In medical texts, at least, such notices surpassed those given to male homoeroticism. Enlarged in male imagination to sometimes monstrous proportions, the clitoris functioned as a 'natural' substitute for the dildos that scientific and legal treatises found absolutely necessary in constructing sexual relations between women. A 'medico-satiric discourse of the *tribade*' constitutes, in the typology of Traub's most recent work, one of two schemes for representing female homoeroticism in early modern texts. The other is a 'literary–humanist discourse of idealized friendship', celebrated, for example, in the poetry of Katherine Philips. Where 'the trope of *tribade*' insists on the 'masculinisation' of at least one body in imaginings of female homoeroticism, 'the rhetoric of erotic simili-tude' dwells on the sameness of the two bodies. Helena's image of herself and Hermia as 'like to a double cherry: seeming parted,/ But yet an union in partition' (*MND* 3.2.210–211) is a signal example. It is the second of the models that Traub finds circulated in writings by women themselves.

Concerning the male body, Mark Breitenberg in *Anxious Masculinity in Early Modern England* (1996) uses Burton's *Anatomy of Melancholy* to locate erotic desires of all sorts in the humoural body. In Burton's excursus on 'Love's Tyranny' Breitenberg finds physiological justification for Bray's observation that 'sodomy' in the early modern sense of the term was something to which *anyone*, male or female, could succumb. Women who desire women figure among Burton's examples, but the stakes are higher for men, since ideals of masculine behavior are founded on rationality and control. Lust in Burton's scheme is a physiological given; what varies are the laws and customs that various cultures use – or fail to use – in order to control lust and direct it toward productive ends. Witness the toleration of homosexual acts among 'Asiaticks, Turks, Italians . . . . And terrible to say, in our country, within memory, how much that destestable sin hath raged' (quoted 60). Breitenberg's analysis of homoerotic desire as it figures in Burton's *Anatomy* advances two important points: (1) that early modern ways of understanding erotic desire, whatever the object, begin with the humoural body and (2) that 'the opposition between natural and unnatu-ral sexual practice is . . . not based on the object of one's desire, as it will become by the end of the nineteenth century, but rather upon the extent to which 'love tyrannizeth over men,' in the continual struggle to contain desire with reason and self-control' (62). To such imperatives of reason and self-control the theatre posed a special threat. The body as pleasured by the theatre, in spectacles of homoerotic violence as well as in gestures toward extra-dramatic acts of 'lust in action', is the subject of my own most recent work on homoeroticism: 'Rape, Rap, Rupture, Rapture: R-Rated Futures on the Global Market'[45] and 'L[o]cating the Sexual Subject'.[46] In both essays I attempt to reconstruct the visceral experience of watching and hearing such representations of erotic action. This attempt at reconstruction I call 'historical phenomenology'.

Homoeroticism in the representation of gendered bodies onstage has been investigated by numerous critics since the mid-1980s: essays by Peter Stallybrass[47, 25], Dympna Callaghan[48, 49], and Cynthia Marshall[50] give particular attention to the body's anatomized parts. Where Stallybrass (ibid.) calls attention to the presence of the male body, even beneath the costume that Desdemona proceeds to take off in *Othello* IV.iii, Callaghan insists on the presence of the female body in the very exclusion of female bodies from the stage. Thus in *Twelfth Night* she sees in Malvolio's cross-gartering an act of transvestism just like Viola's assumption of a page's costume. In reading aloud the letter ostensibly left for him by Olivia and remarking aloud on 'her very C's, her U's, ['n'] her T's' Malvolio marks *himself* with the bodily signs of femaleness.[51] The specifically homoerotic implications of such a reading are made explicit in Callaghan's more recent essay 'The Castrator's Song: Female Impersonation on the Early Modern Stage'.[52] All surviving complaints about bad performances by boy actors on the commercial stage, she claims, concern not what they looked like but how they sounded. What was prized was a quality of treble sound best achieved, and certainly more lastingly achieved, by castration. Investigation of genital surgical procedures in early modern medical texts, critical pressure on Viola's decision to have herself presented to Orsino as 'an eunuch' (*TN* 1.2.52) and his analogy between her 'small pipe' and 'the maiden's organ' (I.iv.32–33), and testimonials to boy actors' vulnerability to sexual abuse lead Callaghan to the conclusion that 'The castrato hangs over the English stage as an (in)credible threat. Symbolic yet plausible, the castration embodied by the castrato actualized the articulation of difference on which male mimesis was based' (324). The represented body of Coriolanus is subjected to a similar gendered and sexualized scrutiny in Cynthia Marshall's essay 'Wound-Man: *Coriolanus*, Gender, and the Theatrical Construction of Interiority' (1996). Frequent references to Coriolanus's perforated body, Marshall argues, serve to effeminize him in ways that accord as well with Lacanian psychoanalytical theory as with the early modern contrast between the 'open' female body and the 'closed' male body. The homoerotic implications of Coriolanus's position are established via a quotation from Judith Butler's *Bodies That Matter*:[53] 'The threat of a collapse of the masculine into the abjected feminine threatens to dissolve the heterosexual axis of desire; it carries the fear of occupying a site of homosexual abjection' (quoted 109–110). Such an observation, as Marshall points out, helps to explain the blatant homoeroticizing of Coriolanus's body on the part of Aufidius – and in specifically female terms. But that is to assume that 'homosexual' = 'female' = 'abject'. Butler deploys those terms within a late twentieth-century economy of power. When one of Aufidius's servants says of Coriolanus, 'Our general himself makes a mistress of him', it is not at all clear who is being said to have power over whom. 'Mistress', after all, is the female equivalent of 'master', and the servant goes on to claim that, in his devotion to Coriolanus, 'our general is cut i'th'middle, and but one half of what he was yesterday' (IV.v.199–203). Callaghan would challenge us to give that 'cut' a second thought.

GENDER

'Mistress', however it may be qualified, is the word Aufidius's servant uses to designate Coriolanus – and in that choice raises the most contentious issue in studies of early modern homoeroticism. The question can be stated simply: is homoerotic desire in early modern culture articulated *across* gender, *within* gender, or *outside* gender? Addressing the question is certainly not helped by the fact debate has been focused on two highly conspicuous but highly extraordinary situations: boy actors dressed as women and women who adopted male fashions or actually tried to pass themselves off as men. In both cases gendered appearance does not match anatomical fact, making each a perfect site for demonstrating the social constructedness of gender. To complicate matters, however, each was also the site for a disjunction between appearance and reality with respect to social status (actors frequently played their social betters, cross-dressers adopted fashions that in many cases had begun at court) and even age (boy actors played roles older than their years, maids who cross-dress in ballads often try to act like seasoned soldiers). To gauge the homoerotic component in such transactions one has, then, to take into account variables other than gender – not to mention the very unusualness that attracted hostile notice in the first place. Be that as it may, the debate over gender versus sexuality in the construction of early modern homoeroticism remains obsessed with the bodies of boy actors.

The few surviving comments by early modern observers are contradictory enough to suggest that what one saw (or heard) in boy actors was very much in the eye (or ear) of the beholder (or listener). Against the fulminations of Stubbes and Rainolds are ranged the matter-of-fact acceptance of custom registered by Thomas Platter on seeing *Julius Caesar* at the Globe in 1599 ('When the play was over, they danced very marvellously and gracefully together *as is their wont*, two dressed as men and two as women' [166, emphasis added]),[54] Henry Jackson's unperplexed use of the

Latin feminine to describe the affecting performance of Desdemona in a production of *Othello* by the King's Men at Oxford in 1610, George Sandys's aesthetic complaint in 1615 that the women's roles he observed played by women at Messina were 'too naturally passionated' (247), and Lady Mary Wroth's unillusioned references in the 1620s to 'play boys' who try to portray women.

Boy actors and female cross-dressers loom large in Stephen Orgel's *Impersonations* (see note 16), which studies the performance of gender in a number of situations but with most sustained reference to the theatre. In the course of his analysis Orgel turns a number of received opinions on their head:

1   that the pre-professional drama of England had been exclusively male and that women never performed professionally on London's stages (in addition to women in various guild-sponsored productions and in masques at court, Orgel marshals evidence of women in visiting troupes, as well as a solo performance by Mary Frith [*alias* Moll Cutpurse] at the Fortune in 1611);

2   that boy actors taking the parts of women were erotically appealing only to men (Cressida expresses appreciation of Troilus's boy-like qualities, Rosalind and Celia comment on Orlando's extreme youth, Venus speaks a blazon of Adonis's beauty);

3   that marriage is the telos of Shakespeare's comedies (to be precise, they characteristically end just before marriage, whereas plays that continue beyond marriage 'depict the condition as utterly disastrous: *Romeo and Juliet, Othello*' [17]);

4   that there was widespread anxiety about homoeroticism in early modern English culture ('The love of men for boys is all but axiomatic in the period; and despite fulminations in theological and legal contexts against the abominable crime of sodomy, most of what men and boys could do with each other did not constitute sodomy, and it was . . . a crime that was hardly ever prosecuted' [71]);

5   that, under the rules of early modern culture, women functioned only as producers of offspring and as tokens of exchange among men (counterexamples are provided by the careers of Moll Cutpurse and Bess of Hardwick).

Why, then, did the early modern stage in England 'take men for women'? In part, Orgel says, because they were erotically appealing, just as women were. Indeed, within a patriarchal economy of power, they were substitutable one for the other: 'both are treated as a medium of exchange within the patriarchal structure, and both are (perhaps in consequence) constructed as objects of erotic attraction for adult men. Boys and women are not in competition in this system; they are antithetical not to each other, but to men' (103). Any complete answer to the question, however, has to explain why boy actors appealed, not only to men, but to the female spectators who made up a sizeable portion of the audience. A subset of the question 'Why did the early modern stage in England take men for women?' then becomes 'What did women enjoy about a theatre we find misogynistic?' Orgel's ultimately contradictory answers reflect, in large part, the gender divide of the audience. On the one hand, the transvestite stage negotiates a huge cultural anxiety, 'a manifestation of the audience's, and ultimately of the culture's, desire for a disarmed woman'. On the other hand, it shows women that their sexuality is powerful and attractive and that, in situations like cuckoldry, they can use it to their advantage – at least within the confines of a dramatic fiction. But the reference point, in Orgel's argument, remains male: transvestite theatre is 'a performative construction that both reveals the malleability of the masculine and empowers the feminine, enabling *the potential masculinity of women* to be realized and acknowledged, if safely contained within the theatre's walls' (106, emphasis added). Callaghan's explanation of the theatre's appeal to women is more radical, in more ways than one. If castration looms as a threat in male impersonations of females, then it is more pleasurable *not* to possess the organ that serves as the radical marker of gender difference:

> even though women were excluded from the Renaissance stage, castration referred to docked masculinity rather than female deficiency. Thus, while the production of dramatic representation did not include women, it did not preclude, indeed may have enhanced, their pleasure in a spectacle which, in its production of sexual difference, exempted them from the cultural and symbolic violence of castration (343–344).[49]

The contrast could hardly be sharper with views of the theatre as a site for strictly male homoerotic exchange. (See, for example, Lisa Jardine in *Still Harping on Daughters*.)[55] Callaghan's move provides a new explanation for Traub's argument (1992b: see note 36) that Helena's protestations to Hermia, Viola's flirtations with Olivia, and Emilia's reminiscence of her friendship with Flavina offered representations of homoerotic excitation among women quite as strong as the male homoerotic pleasure in such often cited scenes as Ganymede's dialogue with Orlando.

Across gender, *within* gender, *outside* gender: the most radical possibility of all is the third. To argue that boy actors are sexually appealing to men because they were dressed like women is, in Goldberg's view, to assume heterosexuality as a norm:

> the fact that there is no divide between hetero- and homosexuality does not mean that all sexuality is heterosexual (does not mean that the boy is really a cover for a girl or that homosexuality is a replay of heterosexuality without women). If that is presumed (if it is taken to be the case that cross-dressing reveals that male/male or female/female sexual attractions are really heterosexual, or would be if they could), the homosexuality that is allowed and recognized through cross-dressing is liable to be construed as failed ... or averted ... heterosexuality.[56]

As an instance of the latter possibility he cites Orgel. The difference between the two critics' viewpoints can be witnessed in how they read the ending of *As You Like It*. In the first folio's direction that Hymen tell the Duke 'Thou mightst join *his* hand with *his*/ Whose heart within his bosom is' (I.iv.112–113, emphasis added) Orgel finds an insistence on the male-ness of all parties to the erotic transaction being represented onstage: 'In a society that has an investment in seeing women as imperfect men, the danger points will be those at which women reveal that they have an independent essence, an existence that is not, in fact, under male control, a power and authority that either challenges male authority, or, more dangerously, that is not simply a version or parody of maleness, but is specifically female' (63). Goldberg, by contrast, seizes on the ambiguities of the play's Epilogue as an instance of gender undecidability. After warning that all cross-dressing, even in Shakespeare, is not the same, Goldberg proposes that Rosalind/Ganymede 'sustains a differentiated identity that produces the boy as a sex that is neither male nor female and thus as a site for male/male (those two beardless boys, Orlando and Ganymede), female/ female (those two dark ladies, Phebe and Rosalind), and male/female desires that are not collapsed one into the other'.[57] Gender is very much a part of Orgel's reading; Goldberg's gestures toward no gender at all.

From whatever angle one considers the situation, gender difference seems to me inevitable: two characters of the same biological sex either play out erotic roles that are appropriated *across* gender or else they play out roles *within* gender that depend on the other gender for their very 'within-ness'. Or they do both. Coriolanus plays the 'mistress' to Aufidius's love-struck suitor, but in Aufidius's dreams at least the two have also 'been down together . . . ,/ Unbuckling helms, fisting each other's throat' (IV.v.125–126). Whether sexual roles exist *outside* gender is a nice question, and one that we cannot begin to answer until we 'un-think' gender entirely.

SOCIAL ORDER

DiGangi's reading of *As You Like It*[58] points up the limitations of late twentieth-century presuppositions about 'sexual orientation'. What is at issue in the questions that Rosalind/Ganymede poses to Orlando, he proposes, is not whether Orlando will seek sexual pleasure with other *women* after marriage but with other *men*: 'she simultaneously tries to determine if Orlando will express a homoerotic desire for Ganymede, whom he has just 'married,' or if he will remain constant to the absent Rosalind whom Ganymede portrays' (57). What is more, when Rosalind raises the possibility that Orlando might find his wife 'going to your neighbour's bed' (IV.i.160), she fails to specify the gender of said neighbour, opening up the prospect of homoerotic relationships after marriage for *both* partners. For all that, DiGangi proposes, the play's ending keeps the play safely within orthodox ideas about marriage. Far from celebrating gender indecidability (as Goldberg would have it) or the exclusion of a subjectivity that is gendered female (as Orgel proposes), the ending shapes for DiGangi as a device whereby female homoerotic desire (Celia's for Rosalind) and male homoerotic desire (Orlando's for Ganymede) are both rejected. Ultimately, DiGangi argues, the Epilogue disallows the homoerotic mobility performed in the play itself. The 'ifs' of the Epilogue all presume heteroerotic desire. They have the effect of casting the *theater* as a realm of homoerotic possibility but denying that possibility in real life: 'male homoerotic desire is finally offered as a retrospective theatrical pleasure' (62).

DiGangi's essentially conservative reading of the ending of *As You Like It* stands in especially sharp contrast to Goldberg's semiotic free-fall. Which reading is the more compelling? In part, the issues here are methodological: where deconstruction finds an *aporia*, new historicism is apt to find containment. Although acknowledging his indebtedness to deconstruction, DiGangi defines his own methodology as 'materialist': his interest is not in exposing the emptiness of social and erotic categories but in 'exploring the historical determinants of social and erotic categories' (x). Each chapter of DiGangi's book is therefore focused on a different dramatic genre and on one particular ideological conflict or social practice: the homoerotics of marriage in Ovidian comedy (including *Twelfth Night* and *As You Like It*), the homoerotics of mastery in satiric comedy (a genre in which Shakespeare showed little professional interest), the homoerotics of favoritism in tragedy (*Richard II* contrasted with *Edward II*, *Sejanus*, and Chapman's *Bussy D'Ambois* plays), and the homoerotics of masculinity in tragicomedy (primarily in scripts by Fletcher).

Through it all DiGangi sets out to demonstrate that ' "sodomy' is not the paradigmatic example or master category of Renaissance homoeroticism, but one among many social and ideological determinants that make up the intricate network of same-sex relations in early modern England' (x). In DiGangi's usage, 'sodomy' is always politically freighted; 'homoerotic', politically neutral. DiGangi suggests that Bredbeck and Goldberg, in their focus on sodomy, neglect 'more orderly forms of homoeroticism' (7). Masten in *Textual Intercourse* shares DiGangi's project. With respect to the plot of *The Two Gentlemen of Verona*, for example, he observes that 'Homoeroticism . . . is not always and already a disruptive and unconventional deconstruction of a sex/gender system. In this play, and in the highly class-inflected context of gentlemen's conduct books and essays, homoeroticism functions as part of the network of power; it constitutes and reflects the homogeneity of the gentlemanly subject'(48). Traub's new book similarly refuses to read female/female eroticism as necessarily subversive: she attends instead to 'a range of exprssions existing in comfortable, even companionable, proximity to marital desire and reproductive alliance'.[59]

How do the plays of Shakespeare shape up in this more broadly conceived political context? For a start, as most of the recent critics insist,

Shakespeare's plays were not (and are not) the only game in town. DiGangi is typical in making a conscious attempt to de-centre Shakespeare. First of all, DiGangi argues, an investment in the 'rich language' of Shakespeare's plays has deflected attention from the degree to which the display of male bodies, sometimes in sensational situations, was part of early modern performance. A more important reason has to do with the fact that Shakespeare's representations of eroticism do not exhaust the range of homoerotic practices in his society. Shakespeare barely figures in DiGangi's chapter on master/servant relations in satiric comedy. Finally, Shakespeare's plays may be constitutive of twentieth-century ideas about the family: 'Perhaps Shakespeare's status as the most familial Renaissance playwright depends in part on his status as the most familial: the one who seemingly celebrates the affective heterosexual couple that we 'recognize' as the source, both biologically and historically, of the modern family' (29–30). (One thinks, however, of Catherine Belsey's contention[60] that 'love' and 'lust' in Venus and Adonis exist in a much less oppositional relationship to each other than modern apologists for 'family values' assume.)

Shakespeare's apparent conservatism may in part be a function of his generation. Nicholas Radel[61] has argued that tragicomedy, a genre that Shakespeare began to explore only at the end of his career, provided a means for defining and foregrounding male homoerotic desire in a way markedly different from earlier drama. The emergence in plays by Beaumont and Fletcher of figures whose homoerotic desires are explicitly declared signals, in Radel's analysis, the emergence of a recognizably homoerotic stereotype – a type against which normative heterosexuality could be defined and empowered. The plays of Fletcher and his peers can be situated, Radel proposes, 'between two historical constructions of eroticism in the early modern period, one lacking any clear distinction of a marginalized homoerotic minority and another in which just such a group was emerging' (165). Radel's example is the title character in Fletcher's The Humorous Lieutenant, but one thinks of Palamon and Arcite's hyperbolic friendship in Shakespeare and Fletcher's The Two Noble Kinsmen, as well as Emilia's forthright declaration of her devotion to Flavina.

If male homoeroticism in early modern culture was not coincident with the crime of sodomy, if it could sometimes serve to consolidate male power structures rather than to undermine them, one wonders if female homoeroticism might not need to be repositioned as well. Most writing on female homoeroticism in early modern culture has stressed its supposed marginality: its absence from English laws that criminalize sodomy, the comparative infrequency of references to it elsewhere, the dominance of male tropes in describing it – ultimately, in Traub's apt phrase, its '(in)significance'. Traub's own work is doing much to show that such views all depend on how one views the evidence. Orgel's accounts of the transgressive careers of Moll Cutpurse and Bess of Hardwick demonstrate how two women of widely distant social ranks were able to play the male power system to their own advantage. Bess of Hardwick did it in part through marriage; Moll, by her own account at least, outside of marriage. Jean Howard's account of 'sex and social conflict' in *The Roaring Girl*[62] emphasizes the specifically erotic forms of Moll's rebellion: her line 'I love to lie o' both sides o'th'bed myself' as a possible declaration of her sexual tastes and playing a viol between her legs as a possible emblem of autoeroticism. New work by Howard[63] continues to find in erotic behaviour opportunities for female transgression and locates it specifically in the theatre, in plays like *Westward Ho!* The most original, most exciting aspect of recent studies of early modern homoeroticism is, in my view, the attempt to recover women's erotic experience. To do so requires a strategic balance between new historicist and deconstructive reading strategies.

Contemporary sexual politics

One new development in early modern studies is a growing awareness that reading for sexual difference has a history. The Folger Library has recently acquired the papers of Edward Slocum (1882–1946), a professional engineer who spent much of his private time in the 1920s, 30s, and 40s assembling evidence of homoeroticism in English Renaissance literature – evidence that in many cases anticipates the most recent research and most ingenious re-readings. Awareness of the issues goes much further back, however. Research by Hariette Andreadis,[64] studying the ways in which the poems of Sappho were published, commented upon, and translated in the sixteenth and seventeenth centuries, reveals that anxiety about the poems' sexuality does not appear, in English texts at least, until relatively late, in the 1640s. This is precisely the moment, we might note, when Benson published his 'heterosexualized' edition of Shakespeare's sonnets. Later instances of what amounts to 'homosexual panic' *avant la lettre* have been studied by de Grazia[65] in the editing of Shakespeare's works in the eighteenth century, by Michael Dobson[66] in the institutionalisation of Shakespeare as the national poet of England beginning in the 1660s, and by Stallybrass[67] in the 'sexing' of Shakespeare's sonnets in the nineteenth century.

Interest in homoeroticism in Shakespeare's plays and poems since the 1980s proceeds, however, on grounds that only Slocum begins to anticipate. As Goldberg says of his own work, '*Sodometries* undertakes an investigation of sodomy in the Renaissance on the supposition that such an inquiry, however much it is attentive to the alterity of the past, is not simply a piece of antiquarianism'.[68] Goldberg reiterates the point in *Queering the Renaissance*, which begins with an essay by Janet E. Halley on the case of *Bowers v. Hardwick*,[69] in which the US Supreme Court cites historically unexamined texts going back to the sixteenth century in support of a state's right to pass laws governing the sexual conduct of consenting adults in the privacy of their own homes. Homoeroticism as a subject of inquiry in the academy today is profoundly implicated in the identity politics of the late twentieth century. Orgel explains why reading from such a vantage point requires no apology: 'The demystification, destabilising, deconstruction of the Shakespearean text has increasingly become the business of criticism, and to read the plays through Renaissance documents, rather than through our own, refigures them, often radically. It can be argued that this is a historical claim only in a special sense, and that the plays are thereby being refigured not as Renaissance texts but as modern or post-modern ones; but in fact all claims about the past except the most narrowly archeological are historical in the same sense: they assume – often, to be sure, without acknowledging it – that we are involved in history as much as Shakespeare or Galen or archival documents' (64). What Orgel charts here is not a one-way act of reading in which late-twentieth-century scholars impose postmodern concerns on early modern texts. Quite the contrary. What Orgel describes is a *dialogue* in which early modern texts of all sorts – law books, medical books, conduct books, chapbooks, commonplace books, shipping registers, parish registers, court registers, broadside ballads, inventories of household goods – are read *alongside* fictional texts of the period and *against* the later texts that have dictated our own preconceptions about eroticism and sexuality. As a result of this two-way process, configurations of sexuality and gender in contemporary culture are subjected to destabilization quite as much as the configurations in early modern culture.

That makes it doubly difficult to ground history in identity politics. If sexuality is a cultural variable, if the construction of homoerotic desire in early modern England is different from the construction of homoerotic desire in Europe and America today, then how can one presume to write 'gay' and 'lesbian' history? Several tactics have been tried. At one extreme is Joseph Cady, who in a pair of essays and in a forthcoming book, argues that in early modern England male/male love (and not just male/male acts of anal penetration) was recognized as a phenomenon in its own right and that it had a code name, '*masculus amor*' or 'masculine love'[70] and[71]. It is therefore possible, Cady argues – indeed necessary – to write 'gay' history, since something like the conceptual category of 'gay' did exist in early modern England. Confirmation that 'masculine' was used as an erotic qualifier has been noted by Charles Forker[72] in a reference from the 1650s to '*Masculine conversation* and *intimacy*' as terms for James I's relationship with Robert Carr. In researching documents related to Bridewell Prison, Michael Holmes has likewise found an instance of 'masculine sweetheart'[73] as a description for one male inmate's relationship to another. At the other extreme is queer theory's insistence that all conceptual categories, then and now, are regimes of political control – except, perhaps, for 'queer' – and that what one is writing is the history of *différance*.

The best strategy, I believe, is to be worked out somewhere in between these extremes, in what Traub calls 'a *strategic* historicism' (see note 27) (emphasis added). Feet firmly planted in the political present, one reads texts from the past with a certain set of questions in hand; at the same time, one expects that texts from the past will call into question the very questions with which one began. To interrogate the textualization of homoeroticism in the past is to discover that the contemporary terms 'gay' and 'lesbian' are no less historical constructs, and no more stable, than the early modern terms 'sodomite' and 'tribade'. There is a political lesson in that, an injunction to respect the diversity of self-identifications and erotic practices that the words 'gay' and 'lesbian' purport to cover. The ultimate subject of investigations into early modern homoeroticism may not, however, be 'gay' or 'lesbian' at all. If eroticism in early modern culture defies the constitutive categories of the late twentieth century, implying something much closer to what we would call bi-sexuality or, better still, 'pan-sexuality', then the subject of Shakespeare and homoeroticism is not the history of a special interest group but the history of every body.

REFERENCES

1. Shakespeare, William (1988), *Complete Works*, Oxford: Clarendon Press, 764.
2. Sedgwick, Eve (1985), *Between Men: English Literature and Male Homosocial Desire*. New York: Columbia University Press.
3. Pequigney, Joseph (1985), *Such Is My Love: A Study of Shakespeare's Sonnets*, Chicago: University of Chicago Press.
4. Bredbeck, Gregory (1991), *Sodomy and Interpretation: Marlowe to Milton*, Ithaca: Cornell University Press.
5. Dollimore, Jonathan (1991), *Sexual Dissidence: Augustine to Wilde, Freud to Foucault*, Oxford: Clarendon Press.
6. Sedgwick, Eve (1991), *Epistemology of the Closet*, Berkeley: University of California Press.
7. Smith, Bruce R. (1991), *Homosexual Desire in Shakespeare's England: A Cultural Poetics*, Chicago: University of Chicago Press.
8. Traub, Valerie (1992a), *Desire and Anxiety: Circulations of Sexuality in Shakespearean Drama*, London: Routledge.
9. Summers, Claude J., and Ted-Larry Pebworth (eds) (1992), *Homosexuality in Renaissance and Enlightenment England: Literary Representations in Historical Context*, Binghampton: Harrington Park Press.
10. Goldberg, Jonathan (1992), *Sodometries: Renaissance Texts, Modern Sexualities*, Stanford: Stanford University Press.
11. Zimmerman, Susan (ed.) (1992), *Erotic Politics: Desire on the Renaissance Stage*, London: Routledge.
12. Goldberg, Jonathan (1994a), *Queering the Renaissance*, Durham: Duke University Press.
13. Goldberg, Jonathan (ed.) (1994b), *Reclaiming Sodom*, London: Routledge.
14. Foucault, Michel (1976–84) (English translation 1978–86), *A History of Sexuality*, Robert Hurley (trans.), 3 volumes, New York: Pantheon.
15. Bray, Alan (1982) (reissued 1995), *Homosexuality in Renaissance England*, London: Gay Men's Press; Bray, Alan (1990), 'Homosexuality and the Signs of Male Friendship in Elizabethan England' in Goldberg 1994a (see n. 12).

16. Orgel, Stephen (1996), *Impersonations: The Performance of Gender in Shakespeare's England*, Cambridge: Cambridge University Press.
17. DiGangi, Mario (1997), *The Homoerotics of Early Modern Drama*, Cambridge: Cambridge University Press.
18. Masten, Jeffrey (1997a), *Textual Intercourse: Collaboration, Authorship, and Sexualities in Renaissance Drama*, Cambridge: Cambridge University Press.
19. Breitenberg, Mark (1996), *Anxious Masculinity in Early Modern England*, Cambridge: Cambridge University Press.
20. Parker, Patricia (1996), *Shakespeare from the Margins: Language, Culture, Context*, Chicago: University of Chicago Press.
21. Traub, Valerie, M. Lindsay Kaplan, and Dympna Callaghan (eds) (1996), *Feminist Readings of Early Modern Culture: Emerging Subjects*, Cambridge: Cambridge University Press.
22. Fradenburg, Louise, and Carla Freccero (1996), *Premodern Sexualities*, London: Routledge.
23. Hillman, David, and Carla Mazzio (eds) (1997), *The Body in Parts: Fantasies of Corporeality in Early Modern Europe*, London: Routledge.
24. Schiffer, James (ed) (forthcoming), *Shakespeare's Sonnets: Critical Essays*, New York: Garland.
25. Stallybrass, Peter (1992), 'Transvestism and the 'Body Beneath': Speculating on the Boy Actor' in Zimmerman 1992 (see n. 11).
26. de Grazia, Margreta (1993), 'The Scandal of Shakespeare's Sonnets', *Shakespeare Survey* 46, 35–40.
27. Traub, Valerie (forthcoming 1999), 'Introduction: 'Practising Impossibilities'' in *The Renaissance of Lesbianism in Early Modern England*, Cambridge: Cambridge University Press.
28. Traub, Valerie (1999), *Desire and Anxiety*.
29. Goldberg, Jonathan (1992), *Sodometries*, 129.
30. Bray, Alan (1994), 'Homesexuality and the Signs of Male Friendship'.
31. Traub, Valerie (1992), *Desire and Anxiety*.
32. Goldberg, Jonathan (1994), '*Romeo and Juliet's* Open Rs', in *Queering the Renaissance*, Durham: Duke University Press.
33. Goldberg, Jonathan (1994c), 'The Anus in *Coriolanus*', paper delivered at annual meeting of Shakespeare Association of America.
34. Sedgwick, Eve (1991), *Epistemology of the Closet*.
35. Callaghan, Dympna (1996a), 'The Terms of Gender: "Gay" and "Feminist" in *Edward II*' in Traub, Kaplan, and Callaghan, 280. (See note 21.) (1996).
36. Traub, Valerie (1992b), 'The (In)Significance of "Lesbian" Desire in Early Modern England' in Zimmerman 1992 (see n. 11).
37. Plato (1997), *Complete Works*, John M. Cooper (ed.), Indianapolis: Hackett, 491.
38. Masten, Jeffrey (1997a), *Textual Intercourse*, 10.
39. Corum, Richard (1996), 'Henry's Desires' in Fradenburg and Freccero 1996 (see note 22).
40. Masten, Jeffrey (1997b), 'Is the Fundament a Grave?' in Hillman and Mazzio 1997 (see n. 23).
41. Laqueur, Thomas (1990), *Making Sex: Body and Gender from the Greeks to Freud*, Cambridge: Harvard University Press.
42. Greenblatt, Stephen (1988), *Shakespearean Negotiations: The Circulation of Social Energy in Renaissance England*, Berkeley: University of California Press.
43. Traub, Valerie (1995), 'The Psychomorphology of the Clitoris', *GLQ*, 2, (1–2), 81–113.

44. Park, Katharine (1997), 'The Rediscovery of the Clitoris' in Hillman and Mazzio 1997 (see n. 23).
45. Smith, Bruce R. (1995), 'Rape, Rap, Rupture, Rapture: R-Rated Futures on the Global Market', *Textual Practice* 9, 421–444.
46. Smith, Bruce R. (1996), 'L[o]cating the Sexual Subject' in Terry Hawkes (ed.), *Alternative Shakespeares, Volume 2*, London: Routledge.
47. Stallybrass, Peter (1991), 'Reading the Body and the Jacobean Theater of Consumption' in David Scott Kastan and Peter Stallybrass (eds), *Staging the Renaissance: Reinterpretations of Elizabethan and Jacobean Drama*, London: Routledge.
48. Callaghan, Dympna (1993), '"And All Is Semblative a Woman's Part": Body Politics and *Twelfth Night*', *Textual Practice* 7 (3), 428–452.
49. Callaghan, Dympna (1996b), 'The Castrator's Song: Female Impersonation on the Early Modern Stage', *Journal of Medieval and Early Modern Studies* 26 (2), 321–353.
50. Marshall, Cynthia (1996), 'Wound-Man: *Coriolanus*, Gender, and the Theatrical Construction of Interiority' in Traub, Kaplan, and Callaghan 1996 (see n. 21).
51. Callaghan, Dympna (1993), 'And All Is Semblative a Woman's Part', 436.
52. Callaghan, Dympna (1996b), 'The Castrator's Song', 343–44.
53. Butler, Judith (1993), *Bodies That Matter: On the Discursive Limits of 'Sex'*, London: Routledge.
54. Platter, Thomas (1937), *Travels in England 1599*, Clare Williams (trans.), London: Jonathan Cape.
55. Jardine, Lisa (1983), *Still Harping on Daughters*, Brighton: Harvester.
56. Goldberg, Jonathan (1992), *Sodometries*, 111.
57. Sandys, George (1615), *A Relation of a Journey Begun Anno Domini 1610*, London: W. Barrett.
57. Goldberg, Jonathan (1992), *Sodometries*, 142–143.
58. DiGangi, Mario (1997), *The Homoerotics of Early Modern Drama*.
59. Traub, Valerie (1999), 'Introduction: "Practising Impossibilities"'.
60. Belsey, Catherine (1995), 'Love as Trompe-l'oeil: Taxonomies of Desire in *Venus and Adonis*', *Shakespeare Quarterly* 46 (3), 257–276.
61. Radel, Nicholas F. (1997), 'Homoeroticism, Discursive Change, and Politics: Reading 'Revolution' in Seventeenth-Century English Tragicomedy', *Medieval and Renaissance Drama in England* 9, 162–178.
62. Howard, Jean, 'Sex and Social Conflict: The Erotics of *The Roaring Girl*', in Zimmerman 1992 (see n. 11).
63. Howard, Jean (forthcoming), *Theatre of a City*.
64. Andreadis, Hariette (1997), 'Sappho in Early Modern England' in Greene, Ellen (ed), *Re-Reading Sappho*, Berkeley: University of California Press.
65. de Grazia, Margreta (1991), *Shakespeare Verbatim*, Oxford: Clarendon Press.
66. Dobson, Michael (1992), *The Making of the National Poet*, Oxford: Clarendon Press.
67. Stallybrass, Peter (1993), 'Editing as Cultural Formation: The Sexing of Shakespeare's Sonnets', *Modern Language Quarterly* 54 (1), 91–103.
68. Goldberg, Jonathan (1992), *Sodometrics*, 18.
69. Halley, Janet E. (1994), 'Bowers v. Hardwick in the Renaissance', in Goldberg 1994a (see n. 12).
70. Cady, Joseph (1992), ' "Masculine Love", Renaissance Writing, and the "New Invention" of Homosexuality' in Summers and Pebworth 1992 (see n. 71).
71. Cady, Joseph (1993), 'Renaissance Awareness and Language for Heterosexuality: "Love" and "Feminine Love" ' in Summers, Claudia J. and Ted-Larry

Pebworth (eds) *Renaissance Discourses of Desire*, Columbia: University of Missouri Press.
72. Forker, Charles (1996), ' "Masculine Love", Renaissance Writing, and the "New Invention" of Homosexuality: An Addendum', *Journal of Homosexuality* 31 (3), 85–93.
73. Holmes, Michael (forthcoming), 'Rogue Signs: Gentlemen, Friendship, and Uncivil Seduction'.

4 After Oxford: Recent developments in textual studies

John Jowett

Two decades ago Michael Warren asserted that 'What we as scholars, editors, interpreters, and servants of the theatrical craft have to accept and learn to live by is the knowledge that we have two plays of *King Lear* sufficiently different to require that all further work on the play be based on either Q or F, but not the conflation of both'.[1] Perhaps more than any other single statement, Warren's paper led to the rise of Shakespeare textual studies as they now confront us. What followed in the first place was a highly elaborated account of Shakespeare as a reviser of his own work, presented in a collection of essays entitled *The Division of the Kingdoms*.[2] Here the text of *King Lear* was radically reformulated as a work that can be represented legitimately as either the Quarto-based *History of King Lear* or the Folio-based *Tragedy of King Lear*, but on no account in the conflated text editors had artificially constituted in the eighteenth century. The Oxford Shakespeare of 1986 was the first critical edition to reject the conflation and to present the two versions as separate entities.[3] Though some have sought to modify certain aspects of the hypothesis, no subsequent edition except re-issues of earlier texts has attempted to ignore or refute the view that Shakespeare revised this play. Yet it is far from the case that the revolutionary moment of the 1980s led to a stable new order of things. In the wake of the revision theory, textual studies have become an area of contestation where major issues such as authorial authority or the formation and mediation of literary value are energetically debated. Editing has lost its former mystique; it has come to be seen as a culturally specific and challengeable activity.[4] Even a general editor of the Arden 3 Shakespeare, David Scott Kastan, has referred to the theoretical 'impossibility of editing', notwithstanding 'the inescapability of it'. In that contradiction, he suggests, lies 'the excitement of textual studies today'.[5]

The revolt against the New Bibliography that had dominated textual study for most of the century was perhaps of necessity oppositional, and in the course of it the New Bibliographers have sometimes been reduced to caricature. For example, contrary to what is on occasion implied, the movement's leading scholar W.W. Greg did not insist on binary categorizations of texts. Terms such as 'good' and 'bad' quartos were usually and most properly applied to loose groupings, and Greg recognized the limitations and dangers of the terms in that he himself used the quotation marks that might now sometimes be mistaken for a deconstructive irony of recent innovation. Greg would not have been surprised by Kathleen O. Irace's recent insistence that no two 'bad' or 'short' quartos are alike.[6] He was clear about what could merely be supposed; he was careful to make qualifications such as 'generally'; he spelt out the specific differences between texts within the same general grouping; he acknowledged that there were 'doubtful' quartos; he was well aware that dramatic manuscripts defy effective categorization, inhabiting 'a misty region of Weir, a land of shadowy shapes and melting outlines';[7] he noted that even the conservative R.B. McKerrow disapproved of the notion of a 'definitive' edition, and he himself described the notion as 'silly'.[8]

Still, the sometimes extreme relativism of many recent approaches to editing is far removed from the balmy and industrious optimism of the New Bibliography.[9] The revision theory destabilizes the text in ways that go beyond the theory itself – and it is worth noting that some of the contributors to *The Division of the Kingdoms* such as Randall McLeod and Michael Warren himself, became leading lights of a movement opposed to editing. The revision theory is not simply an initiatory stage in recent thinking about Shakespeare's text; it is an early and vital example of textual studies responding to wider changes of critical climate. Nevertheless, the fact that the only fully re-edited complete works of Shakespeare in recent years brings this change unignorably into public view must have helped to focus many minds on the issues that arise from the disintegration of the conflated *King Lear*. The two-text *King Lear* revealed editing itself as a variable and perhaps even arbitrary activity. The text of Shakespeare could no longer appear a fixed, stable, given thing. Why the Oxford Shakespeare could not be the end of the story needs explaining in more detail.

In its editorial policies and even in its physical make-up, the Oxford Shakespeare manifests a fruitful tension between a centripetal force binding the edition together and a centrifugal force pulling it apart. A price for upholding the complete works as a self-contained entity presented in one volume is exacted in the process of splitting that is manifested both within and around the text itself. Virtually all the edition's most characteristic features can be subsumed under the heading of division. The *Textual Companion*, separately published after the *Complete Works* in 1987, splits the apparatus and documentation away from text. The electronic *Complete Works* was perhaps the first such edition to be brought out alongside a major print edition of a writer's works. Even within the print medium and within the edition proper, the two volumes presenting the text respectively in old and modern spelling formats instruct the reader in the duality of outcomes. Thus the Oxford Shakespeare is strung between the model of a canonical, single-volume, plain-text Complete Works and a highly postmodern edition characterized by fragmentation and multiplicity. Within the edition(s), the apparently stable canon is problematized by a free recognition that a number of the texts are collaborative or of doubtful authorship, and an acceptance that only a narrow margin of doubt determines that the plausibly Shakespearian material in *Edward III* has been excluded. The inclusion for the first time of the minor lyric 'Shall I Die, Shall I Fly' as a poem by Shakespeare has a similar effect.[10]

In the case of the Division of the Kingdoms into two *King Lears*, the effect of the revision theory as a centrifugal force pulling apart the self-contained unitary work is clear for all to see. As de Grazia and Stallybrass have commented, 'The possibility of multiple texts, then, constitutes a radical change indeed: not just an enlargement of Shakespeare's works but a need to reconceptualize the fundamental category of a *work* by Shakespeare' (their emphasis).[11] The point can be shifted to a local level: multiple texts require a reconceptualization of what constitutes a *word* by Shakespeare.[12] The question is of recurrent and unignorable significance to establishing the text, not least because authorial revision could, in principle, occur anywhere.[13]

For there is a practical difficulty in two-text editing that has wider consequences for the stability of the text. Until the revision theory became plausible as a basis on which to act, editorial decision-making was relatively straightforward. In some situations, such as *Othello*, determination of the text might involve careful negotiation between two texts of unequal and different authority, though even here the usual view would be that one reading was right, the other wrong. More usually, editors followed a copy-text except where its reading was in doubt. At first sight it seems as though this procedure can apply to the separate editing of *The History of King Lear* and *The Tragedy of King Lear*. Each has its copy-text; each copy-text is followed except where the editor decides it is in error. The New Bibliography had always recognized the theoretical possibility of revision, and its principles could be adapted to the new situation. Yet two-text editing in practice, if it is to justify itself, has to go forward on a more cautious basis than the eclectic editing recommended by Greg. The Quarto text of *King Lear* by any account has suffered badly through transmission. Its departures from Folio readings are, by the revision hypothesis, authorially rich, but, as anyone who has considered Peter Blayney's magisterial study of its printing will be aware, they are rich in printing-house errors too.[14] Given a Quarto/Folio variant the editor has not simply to decide which is right and which is wrong, but to judge first whether the variant is of the 'either/or' kind or the 'both-and' kind. It is here that the revision theory inserts a new element of instability into textual editing. In the numerous cases where there is no self-evident answer to the 'either/or'/'both-and' dilemma, the editor has to determine where legitimate and inferrably authorial variation ends, where error begins. At what point does the presumption in favour of the copy-text based on the revision hypothesis collapse? Because it cannot be assumed that error is present in one of the two readings, it becomes far more difficult to define what error is.

Gary Taylor, as editor of *King Lear* in the Oxford *Complete Works*, attempts to control the unstable threshold of error by adopting a policy 'as far as possible, to emend Q – where emendation seems desirable – as though F did not exist, seeking in every case the most plausible explanation of the apparent error, and the most economical restoration of sense'.[15] A subtlety of Taylor's editing is that this claim is not applied to the treatment of the Folio, which is therefore in the Oxford edition by a small but significant and deliberated margin a more eclectically edited text. The distinction is necessary simply because the First Quarto indirectly influences the Folio and that influence cannot be disregarded. But both edited texts seek to preserve all that can be explained in terms of authorial variation. A straightforward example of a presumption in favour of revision can be seen in *The History of King Lear* at 2.1.34. Where the Quarto reads 'iniurious' a noun is logically required, and the Oxford *History* text adopts the reading 'injurers' rather than Folio 'Enemies'. The implications are that 'iniurious' is a relatively simple error for 'injurers', and that Shakespeare revised his original reading 'injurers' to 'Enemies'. But there remains an uneasy tension between the objective of preserving and even, through editorial emendation, maximizing the difference between Quarto and Folio on the one hand, and the objective of correcting error on the other. Here is an example of Taylor's guiding principle leading him to presume in favour of a doubtful Quarto reading. Where Lear famously says 'Come, unbutton here' as he slips into insanity (3.4.102–3), the reading is that of the Folio; the Quarto unexpectedly reads 'come on bee true' in its uncorrected state, and merely 'come on' after the press had been stopped and an invented or authoritative correction made. Here an editor must ask whether the reading is at fault in the 'corrected' or 'uncorrected' Quarto reading or both. The mechanics of transmission are obviously complex, but after considering them an editor has to decide whether either or both readings actually make(s) sense and whether that sense is adequate. The criterion here is not whether the Quarto reading, or one of the two readings, is as good as the Folio's. At issue is whether it is good enough to have been written by Shakespeare in the first place. Taylor follows the uncorrected Quarto reading. A critic such as Anne Meyer, finding such a reading incompatible with 'Shakespeare's Art', will accuse him of failing to accept that the relationship between 'on bee true' and 'unbutton' is that of misreading, 'on bee true' being an error.[16] Indeed Jay L. Halio's edition, entitled (it may be thought misleadingly) *The First Quarto of 'King Lear'*, emends to 'Come, unbutton'.[17] This lays Halio open to the opposite accusation, of collapsing textual difference towards the best single reading, though it is surely a persuasive solution if one assumes, as is the case, that F does exist.

Any two-text *King Lear* is vulnerable to similar criticisms pulling in two opposing directions. The upholder of 'unbutton' will suggest that the validation of difference under the heading of revision has the effect of giving validity to error. To some critics, such as E.A.J. Honigmann, who was a pioneer in recognizing the presence of authorial variants in *Othello*, the process that begins in preserving alternative authorial readings ends, at worst, in passing off poor or implausible readings as Shakespeare's. Authorial revision can, with caution, be recognized, but it does not follow that a presumption in favour of revision can be extended to inferior readings and minor variants of doubtful provenance. For Honigmann there can be no presumption. In his full-length study of the texts of *Othello* he argues that Q and F derive from authorial manuscripts that differed to a limited extent in ways that are attributable to revision, but the weight of his argument lies in his demonstration that both texts are heavily contaminated by corruption in various shapes.[18] Q, for example, entirely lacks Desdemona's moving 'Willow Song', which is arguably crucial to the entire episode in which (in F) it is sung. Honigmann suspects theatrical botching, perhaps because the boy actor who played Desdemona in a particular production was incapable of singing. Q is marred in ways such as this to the extent that it could not possibly serve as copy-text for an edition, let alone stand as it was printed with minimal modification as it does in the 'Shakespearean Originals' series.[19] Unfortunately F is also in many respects imperfect, and becomes Honigmann's preferred text only by default. In editing he weaves carefully between the two. *Othello* is a different case from *King Lear*, but Honigmann points out that there has been no systematic attempt to investigate how far the claims for revision in *Lear* need to be modified by a full and due recognition of other causes of textual variation.[20] There have, however, been a number of studies that debate the extent to which the variation might be explained by accounts other than authorial revision, such as censorship, inept theatrical adaptation or bungling in the printing house. They concentrate usefully on some of the most radically variant passages such as the 'mock trial' scene that is omitted in F.[21] R.A. Foakes comes up with an elegant explanation of another passage that falls somewhere between cryptic and unintelligible as it is represented in F. Where the more committed two-text editors justify the lines' cryptic quality as appropriate to the episode in which they stand, Foakes suggests that a valid cut has been accidentally over-extended, with the result that a few lines need retrieving from Q.[22]

Another commentator will say that Halio or even Taylor, in conflict with the objective of preserving the difference between the two texts, has locally engaged in a partial reconflation. In *The Tragedy of King Lear*, where the Folio has Cordelia ask if Lear's was a face 'To be oppos'd against the iarring windes', Taylor reads 'To be opposed against the *warring* winds' (4.6.29). 'Warring' is a Quarto reading, but Q's version of the line has a second variant, and so reads, 'To be *exposd* against the warring winds'. The case for regarding the two texts as simply different at this point is strengthened by Q's provision of three lines after this line that are not in F. There is nothing wrong with Folio 'jarring' in itself, but Taylor has judged it a significantly weaker reading than 'warring', to the extent that Shakespeare is unlikely to have revised in this direction.

Of course reviewers have always been able to seize on details such as these to criticize an editor as a cavalier emender, but sceptical conclusions as to the textual condition itself are also possible. Jonathan Goldberg argues from the revision theory that 'An examination of the textual properties of Shakespearean texts ... will never produce a proper, selfsame Shakespearean text', and indeed that 'we have no originals, only copies. The historicity of the text means that there is no text itself'.[23] Goldberg drives fast from the observation 'we have' to the declaration 'there is', as though what we don't have must be denied existence, but he is right to note an instability in the Shakespearian text that goes beyond dual outcomes.

If the authorial text cannot be given secure single or even dual fixity, it becomes more plausible to argue that the text should be identified with the points of stability that we do have, the Quarto and Folio printings. At this point a claim on behalf of the material document assumes precedence over any claim on behalf of Shakespeare. The principle can be seen at work in the Shakespearean Originals series. One of its general editors Graham Holderness describes Halio's emendation of Quarto Lear's 'first intent' to Folio Lear's 'fast intent' as 'inexplicable'. Some critical editors might agree, but Holderness's statement is in line with his position of principle that 'there is in fact no philosophical justification for emendation'.[24] The philosophy in question is materialism, or at least a version of it. The argument that editors wrongfully replace a historical artefact (their copy-text) with their own approximate conceptualization of something else (the authorial text) has been expressed forcefully by several critics.[25] To a similar effect, the editorial theory of versions as developed with immediate reference to writers other than Shakespeare often defines the term *version* as a discrete extant textualization.[26] Here too emendation can come to be seen as a falsification of a materialized text. It is an undeniable and important consequence of the two-text *King Lear* that it draws attention to the separate integrities of the texts as they are printed, and gives currency within Shakespeare textual studies to the notion of separate textualizations. As compared with the conflated text, the differences between, for instance, an old-spelling edition based on F and the printed document itself might seem relatively slight. Yet the distance between the critical editors who work from the two-text position and the opponents of emendation is very considerable indeed. To the two-text critical editor the *version* is defined, not in the text as printed, but something antecedent to it.[27] Indeed in this usage, as seen in practice in, for example, the Oxford Shakespeare *Complete Works*'s editing of *Richard III*, the version might lie at some considerable remove from either substantive printed text.

It is easy to see the limitations of either point of view. The opponents of emendation fetishize the printed text as an object in itself, and in so doing they occlude both the process whereby it came into being and the very reason why it came into being.[28] Though they claim to adopt a historicist position, they isolate the printed book from all contingency. Its 'identity' lies in its 'self-differentiation from the process of production and exchange'.[29] The proper reading text is accordingly a facsimile or reprint of an early printing that is detached from its authorial and theatrical production. Critical editors, on the other hand, treat the printed text as evidence of something else that came before it. When they refer to manuscripts such as prompt-books (or playbooks) and foul papers (or authorial drafts), they specify documents that probably existed but that cannot be recovered in their full specific detail. William B. Long's work on dramatic manuscripts has shown that we know less than we used to think we knew about the physical features and taxonomy of such documents, and Paul Werstine makes a strong case to the effect that editors have invented overconfident descriptions of the objects towards which they aspire in order to make their endeavours possible.[30] The distinction between a pre-theatrical and a theatrical manuscript is not, however, absurd, nor are editors' attempts to discern the features of a manuscript in the features of a book printed from it. In most respects, once allowance has been made for significant advances in knowledge about dramatic manuscripts and the book trade, many of the traditional 'narratives' remain plausible in themselves and more effective than any competing account. Nevertheless, Werstine and Long offer unignorable reminders that inferences about printers' copy must always be regarded as provisional, and that, by constantly varying one from another, manuscripts defy rigorous categorization.

However, editors often do not conceive of their task as to reconstruct a missing document. G. Thomas Tanselle distinguishes between 'the texts of a work as they existed in the mind where it originated ... the texts the author *intended*' and realized texts involving agents other than the author 'that may in some ways conform to what the author *expected*' (my emphases).[31] Neither approach necessarily refers to a specific manuscript. The intended text that Tanselle prefers resides, problematically, in the author's mind. In the case of the 'expected' text of a play, its realization can be located, again problematically for editors, on the boards of the stage rather than in a document. A specific playbook can have accretions from several stagings; for this and other reasons it can be, to the modern reader, unreliable, misleading, or downright incorrect. On this basis it can become the editor's task to tease out the theatrical coherence of a play with the conditions of the early modern stage fully in mind, and express it according to a more modern semiotics.

Modernization of spelling and regularization of stage directions are two closely related aspects of what has emerged as a single editorial philosophy. Both involve sacrificing textual specificity in order to convey what are regarded as the essential elements of a text's meaning. With respect to modernization, the document, whether an extant printed text or a lost manuscript, is seen as a repository of signs, specifically words. Following Greg's famous distinction in 'The Rationale of Copy-Text',[32] variant spellings, punctuation, initial capitals, italicized proper names, abbreviated speech-prefixes and other such features are seen as 'accidentals' (or in the vocabulary of the Oxford Shakespeare editors and others, 'incidentals'). These are pragmatically separable from matters of substance and capable of being treated differently. Such a distinction is considerably strengthened by the consideration that compositors and other textual transmitters would have considered themselves free to impose their own preferences or house style on the accidentals but obliged to copy the substance accurately.[33] Greg, as an advocate of original-spelling editions, would have preserved such features nonetheless, but the distinction he made enabled others, most notably Stanley Wells, to replace the more haphazard modernization practices of earlier editions with a more systematic approach to the whole process.[34]

Of course the distinction between two words and two spellings of a single word can be arbitrary. In some situations 'wrack' and 'wreck' can be regarded as variants of the same word, in other situations 'wrack' can indicate a range of meanings not available in 'wreck' and the forms need to be regarded as substantively distinct. The OED itself is inconsistent and sometimes evasive in defining whether a form is a spelling variant or a distinct word. As might be expected, early modern practices are still more fluid and variable. If the boundary between words and spellings is intrinsically blurred, comparable difficulties surround the modernization of punctuation. The punctuation in printed texts in most cases probably owes little to what Shakespeare wrote and is repeatedly misleading to the modern eye. The fact remains that punctuation is undeniably constitutive of meaning. Editors have long accepted that punctuation can be 'substantive', or at least 'semi-substantive', but the terms are misleading insofar as the modernizing editor usually remains more concerned with the syntactical relationships conveyed by the pointing than with the literal marks themselves. The distinction between 'accidentals' and 'substantives' that is so crucial in enabling the editor to move away selectively from some of the particularities of the copy-text is here again far from absolute.

Randall McLeod has developed subtle arguments to the effect that matters of so-called accidence are in fact important to the way the reader apprehends the book. He extends his discussions to fine details such as ligatures,[35] and to broader details such as speech-prefixes.[36] McLeod argues that when editors normalize variant speech-prefixes they are imposing an unnecessary rationalization of the text. Alternations between prefixes stipulating Mother, Wife, Lady and Old Lady for the figure editors usually call Lady Capulet (a form not found in their copy-text at all) are, McLeod suggests, of considerable significance to the conceptualization of a dramatic role at a particular moment in the play. Barbara Mowat and Annabel Patterson have made a similar point about the alternations between speech-prefix forms for Shylock and Jew in Q *The Merchant of Venice*.[37] Typically, the editor's position is that these variant names are confusing; speech-prefixes are not in any case part of the dramatic text as it is spoken, and the rule prescribing one name for one dramatic role is simply common sense. Here too editing involves sacrificing a certain kind of nuance in the name of establishing the matter defined, a little arbitrarily, as the matter of substance. In speech-prefixes and stage directions it is theatrical rather than verbal substance that counts. McLeod points out that the stabilization of speech-prefixes stabilizes dramatic identity: 'and voilà, by reductio editionis, a Shakespearean Individual'.[38] This kind of reduction is best understood in terms of theatrical practice rather than what McLeod sees as an inappropriate model of human identity. It is true that the variations can be very telling markers of attitude towards the dramatic role. Yet it can scarcely be assumed that Shylock would have acted more stereotypically when the prefix was for the Jew, or that the actor of Capulet's wife would have added a shake of flour to his wig when called an old lady, even supposing that the variants survived transcription into the playbook and hence into the actors' parts, which is doubtful. What McLeod most usefully emphasizes is that the readers of modern editions lose some interesting and indeed significant features that would have been incidentally available to the readers of the early modern printed book. The compensating gain to the readers of modern editions is that they are saved from practices of naming that are often provisional, cryptic, or self-contradictory, and that were never devised for the reader of print in the first place. By this means they are enabled to imagine something closer, not to a manuscript of the play, but to the play as it would have been performed. The speeches gathered under a standardized prefix correspond to those that would be gathered in the manuscript of an actor's part. Editorial stage directions may never have been written, but, if editors are sufficiently skilful, the stipulated action would have been enacted.

Underlying these editorial practices are assumptions as to why and how today's readers should meet with a Shakespeare play. These amount to what Michael Bristol has called 'a specific sociology of reception'.[39] One large assumption, which is usually seen in a positive light but could alternatively be regarded as coercive, is that we are interested in Shakespeare as a dramatist who wrote for the theatre, and who took relatively little if any interest in seeing his plays in print.[40] This viewpoint is often articulated in general introductions as a matter of historical and critical interest, but it is bound up with editorial practices as well. Though widely accepted, such a perspective on Shakespeare is not fixed and inevitable. Many kinds of critical endeavour are well served by the standard form of editing that is now usually based on it; others are not. It should be added, however, that only a dedicated minority of any critical persuasion is in practice prepared to abandon the seductively usable modern edition and read their Shakespeare in photographic facsimiles of the original quartos and Folio.

Insofar as editing presupposes that the text can be defined with reference to its historical origination, its practices depend on accepting the idea of the author. Yet the author can be figured in various and contested ways. This debate has yet to be followed through to its conclusion, if it has one. Tanselle's discussion of authorial intentions, quoted above, refers to a fundamental principle of author-based editing, one that, in the case of plays, draws a hard line between the author and the theatre. For Greg too the ideal presentation of the text is *'in the form in which we may suppose that it would have stood in a fair copy, made by the author himself, of the work as he finally intended it'*.[41] The position of principle is unequivocal and, for Greg, necessary. He regards readings from 'a playhouse source' (xliii) with deep suspicion, for only authorial alterations in it will be of value, and these will be all too difficult to distinguish from the rest. In contrast, the Oxford Shakespeare accepts those texts that, in Tanselle's phrase, the author expected. Wells's Shakespeare is firmly a 'man of the theatre'.[42] Taylor, in his contributions to the Oxford Shakespeare, draws on Jerome McGann's work on the 'Sociology of the Text' where the text as published takes precedence over the private authorial text; McGann argues that textual authority resides in 'the actual structure of the agreements' between author and publisher as 'two cooperating authorities'.[43] The author writes with an end in view, which is the making public of the text, and the text is significantly incomplete until that happens. In the case of the Shakespearian stage play, the performance on stage stands in for publication in print as the end in view. The author's draft is pre-performance, the printed text is post-performance, and it is performance that counts. This means that a certain measure of authorial authority becomes delegated to the players.[44] Shakespeare anticipated that the text he wrote would undergo theatricalization in ways he would not in every instance control himself. If we cannot be certain whether, for example, it was Shakespeare himself or another member of the company who introduced a theatrical cut, the question is not from this perspective critical, as it would have been to Greg.

The questions that arise are, first, whether the Oxford editors go far enough in qualifying the centrality of the author, and, second, whether one can go much further and still edit in a coherent way.[45] In the Oxford Shakespeare the author is undeposed; indeed he is not even so much the king in parliament but rather the king in council. Yet, according to historians such as G.E. Bentley, the early modern dramatist did not enjoy anything like the degree of authority suggested by this metaphor. The playwright was commissioned by the company to produce a manuscript of a play for a fixed sum; after he had been paid he usually ceased to retain any rights over the text.[46] Masten has gone further by suggesting that, although things were changing, during Shakespeare's working life the dominant model of textual production was not authorship as we now understand it but collaboration; single authorship, though increasingly practiced, was the exception.[47] Masten probably urges his case too strongly, for the discussion by Bentley on which he draws indicates that over half the plays of the period would have been written in the first instance by a single dramatist; moreover the written formulations that reflect how people thought about playmaking lean still further towards the model of single authorship. To some extent too it can be argued that Shakespeare as one of the principal actors in his company *and* dramatist was a special case, though Taylor himself has knocked some holes in this particular assumption.[48] If editors are serious in wishing to find historical validity in the way they invoke Shakespeare as a figure who has some kind of authority over the Shakespearian text, they may need to go further than they have done in responding to the theatre's participation in making the text. A model of author-theatre collaboration that accords independent authority to the theatre as well as the author may be more appropriate.[49] But such a model would not be easy to use. The editorial notion of authority is, after all, a tool to assist in making decisions, and bifold authority could not avoid affording a less decisive instrument.

Though Janette Dillon has perceptively drawn attention to some of the limitations to such an approach,[50] the text in the theatre might hypothetically replace the authorial text as the objective of editorial endeavour.[51] This line of thought has been important to the recent revaluation of the 'bad' quartos. It should be pointed out immediately that there is a logical incompatibility between a theatre-centred approach and an approach that values the printed text in its own right. The search for the play in the theatre leads behind the printed text, treating it as evidence of something other than it. There is, furthermore, sometimes uncertainty as to whether the 'bad' quartos bear any direct witness to performance. This said, a refreshing and positive energy can be found in the criticism that explores the 'bad' quartos as performance versions in their own right.[52] A reading or passage that can only be rejected as an error if considered in relation to what Shakespeare wrote can become valid and even interesting when explored as an alternative script for performance. In this way the question of textual transmission can, for a time at least, be set to one side.

This approach works as long as questions of authorial authority are deemed irrelevant. Correspondingly, it is only by invoking Shakespeare as author that one can securely argue that these texts are textually, as opposed to aesthetically, inferior to their longer counterparts. It may be agreed that Q2 *Romeo and Juliet* is more complex, literary, and refined than its shorter predecessor. The riposte is that Q1 is more compact, dramatically efficient and energetic. Choose your aesthetic perspective, choose your text. No matter how strongly many readers will prefer Q2, a hierarchy based solely on taste will always be vulnerable. But the 'suspect'or 'bad' texts are almost certainly less Shakespearian. Although occasional critics such as Urkowitz still suggest that the short quartos may be early authorial versions, the arguments for regarding them as later and less immediately authorial texts are strong and convincing.[53] This being the case, it would be disingenuous both to put forward these texts as equals to the longer versions in a world without the pre-formed hierarchy of value set in place by authorship, and at the same time to promote their special interest as alternative *Shakespearian* texts. A more robust if more old-fashioned way of making a similar point would be to say: why read an interesting but second-best and largely derivative revenge play such as Q1 *Hamlet* when you can read a first-rate and startlingly original revenge play such as (setting aside Q2/F *Hamlet*) *The Spanish Tragedy*? Perhaps the most convincing answer to this hypothetical question is that a short quarto can productively be read as a counterpoint to its longer companion. Its strength lies in its limitation: namely, the severity of its release from authorial control. Its particular interest lies in how an initially Shakespearian text can become otherly from Shakespeare. That interest therefore depends, paradoxically but entirely, on a concept of authorship in the first instance. A short quarto tells us what others did with the play Shakespeare first wrote, and, perhaps literally, what others found memorable in Shakespeare.

The New Bibliographers' theory that actors memorially reconstructed some plays has been fundamental to the description of 'bad' quarto texts. In recent decades some elements of the theory have been called in question or discredited. In particular, it is no longer acceptable to assume that these books were printed surreptitiously because the manuscripts were illegally obtained.[54] Over and above these advances in scholarship, there has been a strong desire for the theory to go away. It seems reluctant to do so. Two major full-length studies have addressed the question anew, and although both adopted approaches that were in their distinctive ways militantly sceptical towards the theory, both ended up affirming that memorial transmission was at least part of the explanation for at least some of these texts. Kathleen Irace thought her computer-assisted statistical investigation would overturn the theory of memorial reconstruction by actors,[55] but in the event she affirmed the presence of memorial transmission in all of the six 'short' texts she examined. Irace found that certain roles were, as Greg and others had suggested, more fully accordant with the fuller text than others. She showed too that to a lesser extent the text was more accordant when the same actors would have been on stage but were not speaking. This pattern of varying correspondence according to whether the actor was off-stage, on-stage but silent, or speaking is more clearly demonstrated in some texts than others. When it can be demonstrated, it is hard to ignore and even harder to explain away except as evidence of variable competence in the actor's ability to transmit the text by memory. Laurie Maguire adopted very different assumptions and techniques, and her findings differ considerably from those of Irace. For Maguire, a major flaw in the textual criticism of these plays as developed by the New Bibliography lay in its dependence on subjective comparison between the two substantive texts. There are indeed innumerable variants that have been put forward as evidence of memorial reconstruction that can be explained in other ways. Rather than conduct the same enquiry in a more disciplined way, as Irace attempted, Maguire rejected the comparative approach entirely, and based her study on the intrinsic characteristics of the suspected text itself 'as if no parallel text existed'.[56] The task of identifying intrinsic and distinctive features of memorial transmission, though Maguire handles it with considerable care, presents unavoidable difficulties of its own. Is it methodologically better to evaluate a text according to an abstract conception of how it should be, rather than according to a comparison with how elsewhere it actually was? Part of Maguire's explanation for her approach is that it puts the two-text Shakespeare plays on the same basis as other non-Shakespeare plays where there is only one text to consider. The point is reasonable, but, however plausibly it is justified, the effect of excluding comparison between variant texts is to seal off a rich quarry of potentially significant evidence. It is not surprising that Maguire identifies relatively few texts as memorial reconstructions. Though *Merry Wives* is 'probably' a memorial reconstruction, even the notorious First Quarto of *Hamlet* remains a doubtful case ('Possibly MR, but if so, a very good one'), and texts such as Q1 *Henry V* and *Romeo and Juliet* escape the taint entirely.[57] Though since her work appeared two other critics have come to similar conclusions about *Romeo and Juliet*, which is the most carefully transmitted text in the group,[58] Maguire's negative results need interpreting as 'not proven' rather than 'not memorial reconstruction'. Her positive findings deserve treating with considerable respect.

Where Maguire complains that as a theory memorial reconstruction is too capacious, a possible riposte is that for some texts a capacious theory seems to be needed, and that few are available. No-one to date has advanced coherent explanations of all the 'bad' quartos that do away with memorial transmission entirely. The positive advance of recent years has been to show that these texts have other interesting claims on our attention. It has been useful to put memorial reconstruction to one side.

Revision theory and the recent attempt to rehabilitate the 'bad' quartos can be seen as two points on a textual-critical continuum. Quarto *King Lear* used to be regarded as a superior example of a memorially contaminated text, but that view is not often heard today.[59] Opposing it is the impressive authority of Peter Blayney's work on the Quarto printer Nicholas Okes, which is an important example of how printing-house studies can make a decisive contribution to the study of Shakespeare's text.[60] The revision theory would be vulnerable without Blayney's conclusion that the Quarto is for a number of reasons an unusually poor piece of printing.

Once the compositors' propensity to err is taken into account, no substantial barrier remains to viewing the copy for Q1 as an authorial draft. If Quarto *King Lear* can effectively be reclassified, then why not Greg's other 'doubtful' quarto, *Richard III*, why not the 'bad' quartos themselves? Such was the direction of Urkowitz's enthusiastic enquiries.

If one keeps in mind the polemical critiques that have been advanced by Werstine, the categorical instability of Quarto *King Lear* might expose fallacies in the project of critical editing itself. Yet it would hugely exaggerate both the historical starting point and the current position to claim that previous certainty had given way to universal scepticism. Coherent editing based on information and reasonable inference about the text is still more than possible. Editions continue to be needed and, if this is an age of 'Editing after the End of Editing',[61] they continue to be produced with vigour in a wide range of series. Whilst in their generalizable features the Arden 3, Cambridge, and Oxford series are sometimes uncomfortably similar to each other, each series offers its editors the possibility of making a distinctive and original contribution. The Cambridge series is supplemented with the beginnings of a sub-group of editions based on secondary quarto texts. Alongside the mainstream imprints there is space for quarto and Folio facsimiles, for the Shakespearean Originals series reprinting the earliest text of each play more or less letter for letter, for economical but respectably edited series such as the New Penguin, New Folger, and Signet, and for school editions such as the Cambridge School Shakespeare. *King Lear* is currently available as the conflated text, as separate *History* and *Tragedy* within the Oxford Complete Works, as a Folio-based text (Arden 3), as separate editions representing Quarto and Folio (Cambridge), as Michael Warren's 1989 innovative and anti-editorial portfolio of separate facsimiles of Q1, Q2, and F and parallel facsimile texts, as René Weis's 1993 parallel-text edition, as a modified reprint of the Quarto in the Shakespearean Originals, and, within the 1997 Norton Shakespeare, as three texts comprising the *History*, the *Tragedy*, and the traditional conflation. Stanley Wells's forthcoming Oxford World's Classics edition will be based on the Quarto only.

For the most part, even the more prestigious Shakespeare editions have lost any aspiration to set themselves out as monumental and definitive.[62] They admit that there are many possible outcomes to the editorial process, and they recognize their own contingency. In some recent editions, typographical devices such as special brackets, alternative type-faces and indented text draw attention to the problematic nature of the materials from which editors work.[63] More generally, the discussions of text are no longer esoteric and sealed off from other segments of the edition; they aim to be more accessible and to stress the significance of textual matters to the play. These changes go alongside a more positive response to the history of the play in performance and a closer approach to current critical thinking. All such innovations add to the value and relevance of editions; but they perhaps cannot respond fully to what has been called the crisis in editing without ceasing to exist. Paradoxically, one or two scholars whose work destabilizes critical editing are themselves editors, and Werstine is one of them. Another is Stephen Orgel, who has himself wryly drawn attention to the paradox: 'I am the first to admit that my own practice in my Oxford *Tempest* and *Winter's Tale* hasn't done much to take into account my own arguments in "What is a Text?" and "The Authentic Shakespeare" '.[64] Orgel nonetheless contributes fine examples of the editorial craft. There is no discernible attempt here to decompose the discourse from within.[65]

To some extent the crisis in editing is a crisis of confidence in the print medium and a realization that things can be done differently. Though most commentators agree that the book will be around for the foreseeable future, the specific advantages of electronic editing are fully evident. The utility of the book is that by imposing choices it presents a finite object that can be managed in its entirety. Print favours the single text, and presses strongly the question of what matters most. The utility of electronic text is that it opens new possibilities both for research and for acts of reading by making available material that the print editor reluctantly or gladly excludes. Sheer volume figures prominently here, and it enables a qualitative change in the nature of the edition. The hard decisions typified in a choice of copy text or a choice between variant readings can be bypassed with inclusive solutions at every level. As J. Yellowless Douglas dramatically expresses it, 'They are all laid out before us: the genuine postmodern text rejecting the objective paradigm of reality as the great "either/or" and embracing, instead, the "and/and/and." '.[66] Given the condition "and/and/and", the concept of a standard edited text is disfavoured, and the need for it is no longer immediately self-evident. The corollary of choice is that electronic *reading* is necessarily selective. Jim Rosenberg notes that 'the typical hypertext link may be described as a disjunctive link: if lexia X has links A, B, C, D, the user may choose A or B or C or D (or to go nowhere, of course!)'.[67] The path of reading becomes an arbitrary line drawn without intrinsic regard for beginning, middle, and end, passing to and fro on an effectively unfillable space. Like going on holiday, there is perhaps always a melancholy of departure from X on account of all the brochure destinations that are thereby excluded.

Such reflections apart, it is clear that electronic editions can add a valuable dimensionality to reading. The other texts (however determined) are always available, and the Arden CD-ROM, by providing hyperlinked source texts, glossary, dictionary of bawdy, and grammar, as well as the standard Arden commentary, suggests that in the future we may be able to consult plural, specializing, and purpose-designed commentaries.[68] More radical is the notion of a database edition that provides no more than the materials for readers to construct their own texts.[69] It is easy to become entranced by the abstract *possibilities* of electronic text (and sound and moving image), to the extent that the practical issues of editing seem about to vanish entirely. They will not. New editorial issues emerge, and they do not simply displace the old ones.[70] For instance, for most purposes a search engine is most usefully applied to an edited modernized text. Current CD-ROMs and electronic databases accessed through the Worldwide Web usually present such a text, and this will probably continue to be the case. Some of the currently available electronic texts are based on out-of-copyright editions that were designed for print publication many years ago. This practice is seen strikingly in the widely consulted and widely copied MIT Complete Works, whose text is itself copied from a CMC ReSearch CD-ROM and internet text prepared by Grady Ward; this in turn claims to be based on an untraced '1911' Stratford Town edition edited by Arthur Bullen.[71] Such editorial practices are clearly in the longer term unsatisfactory. Electronic editions, like print editions, need to be prepared with full cognizance of the current state of textual and bibliographical study. They should also be designed from the ground up with the electronic medium in mind. Peter Shillingsburg's prescient book-title *Scholarly Editing in the Computer Age* addresses a field of study that is still emergent. But one should not overlook that the computer age still requires printed books. Here editorial practice needs not merely to be distracted by the 'New Textualism', but enabled to produce editions fit for our times.

REFERENCES

1. Michael Warren, 'Quarto and Folio *King Lear* and the Interpretation of Albany and Edgar', in *Shakespeare, Pattern of Excelling Nature*, ed. David Bevington and Jay L. Halio, Newark: University of Delaware Press, and London: Associated University Presses, 1978, 95–107: 105.
2. Taylor, Gary and Warren, Michael (eds.) (1983), *The Division of the Kingdoms: Shakespeare's Two Versions of 'King Lear'*, Oxford: Clarendon.
3. William Shakespeare, *The Complete Works*, gen. ed. Stanley Wells and Gary Taylor, also ed. by John Jowett and William Montgomery, Oxford: Clarendon, 1986; textual documentation in Wells and Taylor, with John Jowett and William Montgomery, *William Shakespeare: A Textual Companion*, Oxford: Clarendon, 1987.
4. Important here have been revisionary accounts of the history of editing, notably Margreta de Grazia's Foucauldian *Shakespeare Verbatim: The Reproduction of Authenticity and the 1790 Apparatus*, Oxford: Clarendon, 1991, on Malone and the First Folio; and Laurie E. Maguire, *Shakespearean Suspect Texts: The 'Bad' Quartos and Their Contexts*, Cambridge: Cambridge University Press, 1996, on Greg and the New Bibliography. For a recuperative account of eighteenth-century editing, see Marcus Walsh, *Shakespeare, Milton, and Eighteenth-Century Literary Editing: The Beginnings of Interpretative Scholarship*, Cambridge: Cambridge University Press, 1997.
5. Kastan, David Scott (1996), 'The Mechanics of Culture: Editing Shakespeare Today', *Shakespeare Studies* 24, 30–37.
6. Irace, Kathleen O. (1994), *Reforming the 'Bad' Quartos: Performance and Provenance of Six Shakespearean First Editions*, Newark: University of Delaware Press, London and Toronto: Associated University Presses.

7. Greg, W.W. (1955), *The Shakespeare First Folio: Its Bibliography and Tex-tual History*, Oxford: Clarendon, 103. What Greg describes as 'perhaps a rash venture', his attempt to classify play manuscripts, does not result in a system of categories but an attempt to isolate the clearer examples of one particular kind of manuscript, prompt-books, from others that are of mixed, doubtful, or different characteristics: Greg, *Dramatic Documents from the Elizabethan Playhouses*, 2 vols. Oxford: Clarendon, 1931, 1, 191. For a recent critique of Greg's *Dramatic Documents*, see Paul Werstine, 'Plays in Manuscript', in *New History of Early English Drama*, ed. John D. Cox and David Scott Kastan, New York: Columbia University Press, 1997, 481–97.

8. Greg, W.W. (1974), 'Introduction: Ronald Brunlees McKerrow 1872–1940', in *Ronald Brunlees McKerrow: A Selection of His Essays*, John Phillip Immroth, ed., Metuchen, N.J.: Scarecrow Press, 1–23, 15.

9. For a defence of New Bibliographical procedures, see G. Thomas Tanselle, *Textual Criticism Since Greg: A Chronicle 1950–1985*, Charlottesville: University Press of Virginia, 1987.

10. For a full discussion of authorship attribution, see Gary Taylor, 'The Canon and Chronology of Shakespeare's Plays', in *Textual Companion*, 69–144. I mention here for convenience some post-1986 studies: Eliot Slater, *The Problem of 'The Reign of King Edward III': A Statistical Approach*, Cambridge: Cambridge University Press, 1988; Donald W. Foster, *Elegy by W.S.: A Study in Attribution*, Newark: University of Delaware Press; London and Toronto: Associated University Presses, 1989; M.W.A. Smith, 'The Author-ship of *The Raigne of King Edward the Third*', *Literary and Linguistic Computing* 6 (1991), 166–74; M.W.A. Smith, '*Edmund Ironside*', *Notes and Queries* 238 (1993), 202–5; Jonathan Hope, *The Authorship of Shake-speare's Plays: A Socio-Linguistic Study*, Cambridge: Cambridge University Press, 1994; Gary Taylor, 'Shakespeare and Others: The Authorship of *Henry the Sixth, Part One*', *Medieval and Renaissance Drama in England* 7, ed. Leeds Barroll, Madison, Teaneck: Fairleigh Dickinson University Press; London and Toronto: Associated University Presses, 1995, 145–205; Brian Boyd, 'Common Words in *Titus Andronicus*: The Presence of Peele', *Notes and Queries* 240 (1995), 300–307; MacD.P. Jackson, 'Stage Directions and Speech Headings in Act 1 of *Titus Andronicus* Q (1594): Shakespeare or Peele?', *Studies in Bibliography* 49 (1996), 134–48; Ward E.Y. Elliott and Robert J. Valenza, 'Glass Slippers and Seven-League Boots: C-Prompted Doubts About Ascribing *A Funeral Elegy* and *A Lover's Complaint* to Shakespeare', *Shake-speare Quarterly*, 48, (1997), 177–207.

11. de Grazia, Margreta and Stallybrass, Peter (1993), 'The Materiality of the Shakespeare Text', *Shakespeare Quarterly*, 44, 255–83, 257.

12. De Grazia and Stallybrass themselves go on to discuss the unit of the word, but with reference to modernization.

13. For a maximal statement of Shakespeare as reviser, see Grace Ioppolo, *Revising Shakespeare*, Cambridge, Mass., and London: Harvard University Press, 1991.

14. Blayney, Peter W.M. (1982), *The Texts of 'King Lear' and Their Origins*, vol. 1, *Nicholas Okes and the First Quarto*, Cambridge: Cambridge University Press, 1982.

15. *Textual Companion*, 510.

16. Meyer, Ann R. (1994), 'Shakespeare's Art and the Texts of *King Lear*', *Studies in Bibliography*, 47, 128–46.

17. Halio, Jay L. (ed.) (1994), *The First Quarto of 'King Lear'*, The New Cambridge Shakespeare, The Early Quartos, Cambridge: Cambridge Univer-sity Press, 1994, text at 3.4.86, discussed 16–17.

18. Honigmann, E.A.J. (1996), *The Texts of 'Othello' and Shakespearian Revision*, London and New York: Routledge, 1996.
19. Murphy, Andrew (ed.) (1995), *The Tragedy of Othello, The Moore of Venice*, Shakespearean Originals: First Editions, Hemel Hempstead: Prentice Hall International, 1995.
20. Honigmann, 144–5.
21. Meyer, Ann R. (1995), 'Shakespeare's Art'; Richard Knowles, 'Revision Awry in Folio *Lear* 3.1', *Shakespeare Quarterly*, 46, 32–46; Robert Clare, '"Who is it that can tell me who I am?": The Theory of Authorial Revision between Quarto and Folio Texts of *King Lear*', *The Library*, VI, 17 (1995), 34–59; Paul Hammond, 'James I's Homosexuality and the Revision of the Folio Text of King Lear', *Notes and Queries*, 242, (1997), 62–4.
22. Foakes, R.A. (1996), 'French Leave, or Lear and the King of France', in *Shakespeare Survey* 49, 217–223. See also his Arden 3 edn. (Walton-on-Thames: Thomas Nelson, 1997).
23. Goldberg, Jonathan (1986), 'Textual Properties', *Shakespeare Quarterly* 37, 213–17, 214 and 217. See also Marion Trousdale, 'A Trip Through the Divided Kingdoms', *Shakespeare Quarterly*, 37 (1986), 218–23. For a response to postmodernist approaches to editing, see Ian Small, ' "Why edit anything at all?": Textual Editing and Postmodernism: A Review Essay', *English Literature in Transition*, 38, (1995), 195–203.
24. Graham Holderness, in his Shakespearean Originals edition of *King Lear*, (Hemel Hempstead: Prentice Hall, 1995), 27 and 9.
25. de Grazia, Margreta (1988), 'The Essential Shakespeare and the Material Book', *Textual Practice*, 2, 69–85; de Grazia and Peter Stallybrass, 'Materiality'; Graham Holderness, Bryan Loughrey, and Andrew Murphy, '"What's the Matter?": Shakespeare and Textual Theory', *Textual Practice*, 9, (1995), 93–119.
26. Donald Reiman, ' "Versioning": The Presentation of Multiple Texts', in *Romantic Texts and Contexts*, Columbia: University of Columbia Press, 1987, 167–80; Hans Zeller, 'A New Approach to the Critical Constitution of Literary Texts', *Studies in Bibliography*, 28, (1975), 231–64 ('In the most extreme case a version is constituted by a single variant', 236; Zeller is referring specifically to *authorial* variants); Jack Stillinger, *Coleridge and Textual Instability: The Multiple Versions of the Major Poems*, (New York and Oxford: Oxford University Press, 1994), 118–40 ('A *version* of a work is a physically embodied text of the work', 132).
27. Compare Peter Shillingsburg: 'A version has no substantial existence, but it is represented more or less well or completely by a single text', (*Scholarly Editing in the Computer Age: Theory and Practice*, Athens: University of Georgia Press, 1984; 3rd edn., 1996, 44).
28. The point is made succinctly from a Marxist perspective by Gabriel Egan in 'Myths and Enabling Fictions of 'Origin' in the Editing of Shakespeare', *New Theatre Quarterly*, 49, (February 1997), 41–7.
29. Holderness, Graham., Loughrey, Bryan and Murphy, Andrew (1995), '"What's the Matter?": Shakespeare and Textual Theory', *Textual Practice*, 9, 93–119.
30. See William B. Long, 'Stage-Directions: A Misinterpreted Factor in Determining Textual Provenance', TEXT 2 (1985), 121–37; Long, ' "A bed / for woodstock' ", in *Medieval and Renaissance Drama in England* 2 (1985), 91–118; Paul Werstine, ' "Foul Papers" and "Prompt-Books": Printer's Copy for Shakespeare's *Comedy of Errors*', *Studies in Bibliography*, 41, (1988), 232–46; Werstine, 'McKerrow's "Suggestion" and Twentieth-Century Shakespeare Textual Criticism', *Renaissance Drama*, n.s. 19 (1988), 149–73;

Werstine, 'Narratives about Printed Shakespeare Texts: "Foul Papers" and "Bad" Quartos', *Shakespeare Quarterly* 41 (1990), 65–86; Long, 'Perspective on Provenance: The Context of Varying Speech-heads', in *Shakespeare's Speech-Headings*, ed. George Walton Williams, Newark: University of Delaware Press; London: Associated University Presses, 1997, 21–44. The fullest statement of the position is Werstine's 'Narratives', which draws most significantly on Long for the position on foul papers, Urkowitz (see n. 23) for the position on bad quartos, and Goldberg, 'Textual Properties', for the theoretical stance.

31. Tanselle, G. Thomas (1989), *A Rationale of Textual Criticism*, Philadelphia: University of Philadelphia Press, 1989, 78.

32. Greg, W.W. (1950–51), 'The Rationale of Copy-Text', *Studies in Bibliography* 3, 19–36.

33. For the principle, see Joseph Moxon, *Mechanick Exercises on the Whole Art of Printing (1683–4)*, ed. Herbert Davis and Harry Carter, London: Oxford University Press, 1962, 192, where Moxon says it is '*a task and duty incumbent on the* Compositor . . . *to discern and amend the bad* Spelling *and* Pointing *of his Copy, if it be in English*'. The practice is clearly in evidence where printers can be seen setting from known copy, whether manuscript or print.

34. Stanley Wells (1979), *Modernizing Shakespeare's Spelling*, with Gary Taylor, *Three Studies in the Text of 'Henry V'*, Oxford: Clarendon; Wells, 'Re-Editing Shakespeare for the Modern Reader: Based on Lectures Given at the Folger Shakespeare Library, Washington, D.C.', Oxford: Clarendon, 1984.

35. Randall McLeod, 'Spellbound', in *Play-Texts in Old Spelling*, ed. G.B. Shand and Raymond Shady, New York: AMS, 1984, 81–96; 'The Psychopathology of Everyday Art', *The Elizabethan Theatre*, 9, (1981), 100–168.

36. Random Cloud [Randall McLeod], '"The very names of the Persons": Editing and the Invention of Dramatick Character,' in *Staging the Renaissance: Reinterpretations of Elizabethan and Jacobean Drama*, ed. David Scott Kastan and Peter Stallybrass, London and New York: Routledge, 1991, 88–96; expanded as Randall McLeod, 'What's the Bastard's Name?', in *Shakespeare's Speech-Headings: Speaking the Speech in Shakespeare's Plays*, ed. George Walton Williams, Newark: University of Delaware Press, and London: Associated University Presses, 1997, 133–209.

37. Mowat, Barbara A. (1996), 'The Problem of Shakespeare's Text(s)', *Shakespeare Jahrbuch* 132, 26–43; Annabel Patterson, ed., *The Most Excellent Historie of The Merchant of Venice*, Shakespearean Originals: First Editions, Hemel Hempstead: Prentice Hall, 1995, 21–2.

38. McLeod, 'Bastards', 140.

39. Bristol, Michael D. (1990), *Shakespeare's America, America's Shakespeare*, London and New York: Routledge, 103.

40. In his defence of modernization, Stanley Wells cites Philip Gaskell, an opponent of modernization, who concedes that 'Plays are different from the works of literature that we have been considering so far because they are completed and primarily communicated not as books to be read but as performances in the theatre' (Wells, *Re-Editing*, 12–13, citing Gaskell, *From Writer to Reader*, [Oxford: Clarendon, 1978], 9).

41. Greg, W.W. (1942), *The Editorial Problem in Shakespeare: A Survey of the Foundations of the Text*, Oxford: Clarendon, 3rd edn, 1954, x.

42. For instance, 'Shakespeare: Man of the Theatre' is the title of Chapter 2 in Stanley Wells, *Shakespeare: A Dramatic Life*, London: Sinclair-Stevenson, 1994.

43. *Textual Companion*, p. 15 and p. 63, n. 34; Jerome J. McGann, *A Critique*

of Modern Textual Criticism, Chicago and London: University of Chicago Press, 1983, 54.

44. Taylor (*Textual Companion*, p. 64, n. 53) cites James Thorpe, 'The Aesthetics of Textual Criticism', *PMLA*, 80, (1965), 465–82: the 'integrity of the work of art' derives from 'those intentions which are the author's, *together with those others of which he approves or in which he acquiesces*'. See also T.H. Howard-Hill, 'Modern Textual Theories and the Editing of Plays', *The Library*, VI, 11 (1989), 89–115.

45. De Grazia and Stallybrass; Mowat, 'The Problem'. Mowat is one of the few commentators to have paid serious attention to the second point.

46. Bentley, G.E. (1971), *The Profession of Dramatist in Shakespeare's Time, 1590–1642*, Princeton: Princeton University Press, 1971.

47. Masten, Jeffrey (1997), *Textual Intercourse: Collaboration, Authorship, and Sexualities in Renaissance Drama*, Cambridge Studies in Renaissance Literature and Culture, vol. 14. Cambridge: Cambridge University Press.

48. Taylor, Gary (1989), *Reinventing Shakespeare: A Cultural History from the Restoration to the Present*, London: Vintage, 376–7.

49. John Jowett, '*Richard III* and the Perplexities of Editing', forthcoming in *TEXT*, 11, (1998).

50. Dillon, Janette (1994), 'Is there a Performance in this Text?', *Shakespeare Quarterly*, 45, 74–86.

51. Dillon is criticizing the transhistorical appeal to theatrical performability that partly replaces the authorial orientation in the Shakespearean Originals series.

52. In particular Steven Urkowitz, ' "Well-sayd olde Mole": Burying Three *Hamlets* in Modern Editions', in *Shakespeare Study Today*, ed. Georgianna Ziegler, New York: AMS, 1986, 37–70; Urkowitz, 'Reconsidering the Relationship of Quarto and Folio Texts of *Richard III*', *ELR* 16 (1986), 442–66; Urkowitz, ' "If I Mistake Those Foundations Which I Build Upon": Peter Alexander's Textual Analysis of *Henry VI Parts 2 and 3*', *ELR* 18 (1988), 230–56; Urkowitz, 'Good News About "Bad" Quartos', in *'Bad' Shakespeare: Revaluations of the Shakespeare Canon*, ed. Maurice Charney, London and Toronto: Associated University Presses, 1988, 189–206; Urkowitz, 'Five Women Eleven Ways: Changing Images of Shakespearean Characters in the Earliest Texts', in *Images of Shakespeare*, ed. Werner Habicht, D.J. Palmer, and Roger Pringle, Newark: University of Delaware Press, and London and Toronto: Associated University Presses, 1988, 292–304; Urkowitz, 'Back to Basics: Thinking about the *Hamlet* First Quarto', in *The 'Hamlet' First Published (Q1, 1603): Origins, Forms, Intertextualities*, ed. Thomas Clayton, Newark: University of Delaware Press, and London and Toronto: Associated University Presses, 1992, 257–91; Leah Marcus, *Unediting the Renaissance: Shakespeare, Marlowe, Milton*, London and New York: Routledge, 1996.

53. See for example *Textual Companion* (see note 3), 27 and 398.

54. An important scholarly revaluation of the topic is Peter W.M. Blayney, 'The Publication of Playbooks', in *A New History of Early English Drama*, ed. John D. Cox and David Scott Kastan, New York: Columbia University Press, 1997, 383–422.

55. Irace, *Reforming* (see note 6), 165.

56. Maguire, *Suspect Texts*, 155.

57. Maguire, *Suspect Texts*, 286, 256, 258, 302.

58. Jay L. Halio, 'Handy-Dandy: Q1/Q2 *Romeo and Juliet*', in *Shakespeare's 'Romeo and Juliet': Texts, Contexts, and Interpretations*, ed. Halio, Newark: University of Delaware Press, and London: Associated University Presses,

1995, 123–50; David Farley-Hills, 'The "Bad" Quarto of *Romeo and Juliet*', *Shakespeare Survey* 49 (1996), 27–44.

59. For an exception see Sidney Thomas, 'The Integrity of *King Lear*', *Modern Language Review* 90 (1995), 572–84. The texts of Christopher Marlowe's *Doctor Faustus* have undergone more spectacular reclassification, with the 'A' text similarly shifting from alleged 'bad' quarto to 'good' quarto. For detailed analysis and reference to other studies, see Eric Rasmussen, *A Textual Companion to 'Doctor Faustus'*, Manchester and New York: Manchester University Press, 1993.

60. Blayney, *Nicholas Okes*.

61. The title of Paul Werstine's article in *Shakespeare Studies* 24, ed. Leeds Barroll, Madison, Teaneck: Fairleigh Dickinson University Press; London: Associated University Presses, 1996, 47–54.

62. This comment is especially true of the approach adopted by the editors themselves. The term 'definitive' makes, however, an unexpected come-back in the publicity material for the Arden edition, which on the launch of new Arden 3 series in 1995 elevated itself from 'the standard scholarly edition' to 'the definitive edition' in equivalent statements on the rear cover of the paperbacks.

63. See, for example, the bracketing systems in texts in the New Folger series edited by Barbara A. Mowat and Paul Werstine (New York: Pocket Books); the use of braces and an alternative type-face in Jonathan Bate's Arden 3 edn. of *Titus Andronicus*, (London and New York: Routledge, 1995); the provision of superscript 'Q' and 'F' markers around passages unique to Q and F in R.A. Foakes's Arden 3 *King Lear*, Walton-on-Thames: Thomas Nelson and Sons, 1997; and the indentation within the text of passages printed in the Oxford Shakespeare as Additional Passages after the text in plays such as *Hamlet* in *The Norton Shakespeare: Based on the Oxford Edition*, gen. ed. Stephen Greenblatt, also ed. by Walter Cohen, Jean E. Howard, and Katherine Eisaman Maus, New York and London: W.W. Norton, 1997.

64. Orgel, Stephen (1996), 'What Is an Editor?', in *Shakespeare Studies*, 24, 23–29: 25.

65. Compare *Roland Barthes by Roland Barthes*, trans. Richard Howard, New York: Hill and Wang, 1977; originally published as *Roland Barthes par Roland Barthes*, Éditions du Seuil, 1975, 63.

66. Douglas, J. Yellowlees (1991), 'Understanding the Act of Reading: the WOE Beginner's Guide to Dissection', *Writing on the Edge*, **2**, (2).

67. Jim Rosenberg, 'Navigating Nowhere / Hypertext Infrawhere', online at <*http://www.well.com/user/jer/NNHI.html*>, accessed 8 January 1998.

68. The Arden CD-ROM, Walton-on-Thames: Thomas Nelson, 1997.

69. As described, for example, by Orgel.

70. For practical discussion of the design of an electronic Shakespeare edition based on a modernized text, see Michael Best, 'From Book to Screen: A Window on Renaissance Electronic Texts', *Early Modern Literary Studies* 1:2 (August 1995), online at <*http://unixg.ubc.ca:7001/0/e-sources/emls/01-2/bestbook.html#13*>; and the preliminary prospectus of the Internet Shakespeare Editions project, online at <*http://castle.uvic.ca/shakespeare/index.html*>; both accessed 8 January 1998.

71. The MIT Shakespeare is online at *http://the-tech.mit.edu/Shakespeare/*; accessed 23 January 1998. I am grateful to Hardy M. Cook for information about its origins. For comment on the variation between Grady's internet text and Bullen's 1904–7 edition, see also Ian Lancashire, 'The Public Domain Shakespeare', paper given at Modern Language Association conference,

New York, 29 December 1992; available in the archive files of the SHAKSPER electronic conference (enquiries to the editor, Hardy M. Cook, at *editor@WS.BOWIESTATE.EDU*). Another example of electronic resources based on variably satisfactory print material is the Arden CD-ROM, where the texts and editorial material are from the printed Arden 2 Shakespeare; some of the editions go back to the 1950s. Compare the emerging Shakespeare Internet Editions project, which aims 'to make scholarly, fully annotated texts of Shakespeare's plays available in a form native to the medium of the Internet'.

5   The Old and the New Materialising of Shakespeare

Richard Levin

The term 'materialism/materialist' has been very prominent in Shakespeare criticism for almost 15 years. It appears in the titles of four anthologies (Dollimore and Sinfield 1985, 1994, Wayne 1991, Crewe 1992, Kamps 1995),[1] and in the names chosen by two major critical schools, 'cultural materialism' and 'materialist feminism', and it is invoked regularly by many critics to define and validate their own work and often to invalidate the work of their non-materialist predecessors. As a result the term has taken on a number of different meanings, some of which are only tenuously connected to what we usually think of as physical materiality, although this problem is seldom addressed or even noticed since in current critical discourse 'materialism' does all the testing and is not itself tested.[2] I would like to rectify this situation by subjecting the uses of the term to an interrogation or, as we now say, by putting them in question. While most of my evidence will be drawn from interpretations of Shakespeare, my arguments should also apply to other fields that have experienced similar kinds of 'materialising'.

Any interrogation of the uses of this term by what I will call the old materialist critics of Shakespeare must begin with the recognition that it derives from the Marxist tradition (in fact it often serves as a synonym for Marxism), and that in this tradition it has to carry a very heavy ethical and political burden within a Manichean binary, since 'materialism' is supposed to be not only right but also good (progressive or revolutionary), while its opposite, usually called 'idealism', is not only wrong but evil (reactionary).[3] The connection is crucial and helps to explain the semantic plight of 'materialism' in this body of criticism, since the ethical-political imperative is so much more powerful than any need for a logically consistent definition of the term, which must undergo adjustments (now known as slippages) in its relation to physical materiality in order to serve this imperative, as we will see.

Until quite recently, almost all critics who claimed to be materialists defined their position in terms of the Marxist doctrine that activity in the material economic 'base' is the cause of all other activity, which is relegated to the noneconomic 'superstructure'.[4] This ought to present a problem because many superstructural pursuits like hawking and dancing are just as material as working on a farm or in a dark, satanic mill; but that is not 'material', for the materialism of this doctrine is highly selective and that selectivity is determined, as I said, by politics – here by the need to place the cause of all social ills (and hence their cure) in the economic system. Moreover, since the economic base is the cause of all activities in the superstructure, it is seen as prior to, more important than, and in a sense more real than, these activities (which is analogous to the Freudian 'unconscious' that operates like the Marxist base as the real cause of events in the 'conscious' superstructure). Anyone who fails to acknowledge this, who accepts these activities at their face value, is committing a gross 'idealization' or 'mystification' or 'misrecognition' of social reality.

One definition of the old materialist criticism of Shakespeare, then, is that it tries to prove that the apparently noneconomic concerns of his characters, such as their personal relations, are really determined by the economic base of their society. In Jonathan Dollimore's reading of King Lear, the play 'discloses' that 'human values' like 'kindness' are 'informed' by, 'dependent' on, and 'operate in the service' of, the 'material realities' of 'power and property' that are 'prior to' them (1984, 197–8, 202, 285), which ignores the 'immaterial' fact that only the unsympathetic characters (Goneril, Regan, Edmund) exemplify this concept of human values, while the sympathetic ones (Cordelia, Edgar, Kent) go right on being kind to Lear and Gloucester after these two men lose all their power and property. And Kathleen McLuskie also claims that family feelings in this play must be understood in terms of 'property and power', since these are the 'material conditions which lie behind' them, and which determine the 'real socio-sexual relations in King Lear' (1985, 100, 105–6). She differs from Dollimore in arguing that this underlying material reality is obscured rather than disclosed by the play, but she assumes the same 'base-ic' sense of 'materialism'.

Another sense of the term in the old materialist critics comes from the Marxist doctrine that the crucial feature of the economic base is the relation of the different classes to the means of production and to each other. Thus 'materialism' in this sense means the focus upon class, and especially class conflict, as the real cause of all other aspects of society. The problem is that class itself is not material; it is an abstraction derived from a selection of material facts and so is no more material than other abstractions, derived from other facts, that we use to categorize human beings, such as sex and age. Indeed it is less material than these two, for by examining people's bodies or even skeletons we can tell their sex and age but not their class. That kind of materiality, however, is immaterial to the materialists, who insist that class is always more basic and real than these other categories.

This gives us a second definition of the old materialist criticism of Shakespeare: it is an approach that tries to prove that his plays, whatever they appear to be about, are really about class conflict. There is a clear example in Kiernan Ryan's essay on *King Lear*, which locates the real 'causes' of the tragedy in 'the injustices of a stratified society' that is 'class-divided' (1995, 102–4). In fact all the main characters belong to the same class,[5] but he always already knows that class-division must be the cause of their tragedies. Peter Stallybrass claims that, even though the issues of *Othello* seem to involve the first two terms of the race–gender–class triad, they actually center on the third, because Othello's love for Desdemona is 'class aspiration ... displaced onto the enchanted ground of romance', and 'the construction of Othello as "black"' is 'the displaced condition' of this aspiration, and the class tensions of the play are 'displaced' onto Iago (1986, 134–5, 140). In a similar move, Dollimore states that the explicit sexual anxieties of the rulers in *Measure for Measure* are a 'displacement' of 'much deeper fears ... corresponding to more fundamental social problems' of class conflict (1985, 80). The concept of 'displacement' comes from the Freudians and serves the same purpose: since it always proceeds 'from below upwards' – from the Freudian unconscious or Marxist base to their effects in the conscious mind or superstructure, it can be deployed to prove that the apparent subject of the play is only a 'displacement' of another subject that the critic considers more important. Thus a Marxist would never find that class anxiety is a displacement of sexual anxiety, just as a Freudian would never find that fear of castration is a displacement of fear of a head injury.[6] It also proves that the subject that the Marxist critic focuses on is, in Dollimore's words, 'much deeper' and 'more fundamental' than the apparent subject that earlier critics took at face value.[7] And it shows us again the highly selective nature of the materialism of these materialists, since the apparent subject that they explain away as a displacement is usually no less material than the economic issues it is supposed to be displacing.

The Marxist base-superstructure paradigm mandates, not only that the superstructural concerns of the characters in a literary work must be treated as effects of something in the base of *their* society, but also that the work itself must be treated as part of the superstructure of *its* society, and so becomes the effect of some external social cause. Thus we have a third definition of the old materialist critics of Shakespeare: they try to prove that his plays are reflections of, or reactions to, events in his world, which they call 'historicizing' the plays. Not just any events will do, however, for here too their materialism is very selective. One might think, for example, that *Hamlet* could be 'historicized' by relating it to the death of Shakespeare's father, but even though that is certainly a material event, it is not 'material' to the materialists since it does not involve the economic base or its class structure. When Arnold Kettle says that it is 'essential to see Hamlet's problem historically', this means we must see it in terms of the materialist question he poses: 'what adequate actions could a young man take who, in the year 1600, could no longer look at society from the point of view of the ruling class?' (1964, 155). A more common tactic is to relate the plays to what these critics view as the most important basal event of this period, the transition from a feudal to a capitalist economy, so that their task is to determine whether each play is 'progressive' (welcoming this change) or 'reactionary' (opposing it). They can disagree on the answer – A.A. Smirnov argues that *King Lear* is forward-looking because Lear comes 'to sense the monstrous injustice of the feudal–aristocratic system', and the 'progressive characters', Cordelia and Edgar, represent 'the new era' and 'hope for a better future' (1936, 69–71), while Paul Delany finds that the play reveals Shakespeare's 'nostalgia' for 'feudal-heroic values' and his inability 'to reconcile himself with the emerging bourgeois forces' (1995, 36) – but they agree that it is the correct question to ask.

Since Marxists also know that the economic base of every society (except a socialist one) is torn by class conflicts and irreconcilable contradictions, their base-superstructure paradigm also mandates that these conflicts and contradictions must underlie every other aspect of that society, no matter how unified or harmonious it may seem to be. This then gives us another sense of materialism, grounded in another opposition between appearance and reality. It is explicit in Dollimore's attack on 'the belief in, or desire for, [a] profound unity . . . in the individual psyche [or] the social body, . . . a unity beyond the actual strife and disunity of existence' (1990, 422). Note that unity is just a 'belief' or 'desire', while disunity is an 'actual' fact of 'existence'. One could object that the unifying forces in individuals and societies are just as real as the disunifying forces, and that they must be more powerful than those forces in all viable individuals and societies, which otherwise would not be viable; but that is not 'material' to these critics because their selective materialism dictates that only disunity has a material reality and unity is only an appearance. This, too, follows from their political purpose, as Malcolm Evans acknowledges when he advocates 'a materialism for which contradiction in the social formation and the subject takes priority as the dynamic of historical change' (1986, 254).

A fourth definition of the old materialist criticism of Shakespeare, therefore, is that it tries to prove that there is a basic disunity in his plays and in his society wherein they are 'historicized'. A major industry has grown up around the campaign to demolish the absurdly harmonious Renaissance England presented in Tillyard's *The Elizabethan World Picture* and Lovejoy's *The Great Chain of Being*, and to replace it with an equally absurd picture of anarchy. Catherine Belsey calls on us to 'reverse' the 'enterprise of constructing (inventing) a lost organic world' of 'uncontested order' in the Renaissance by joining an enterprise that 'uncovers a world of violence, disorder and fragmentation' (1992, 44).[8] The order is invented; the disorder is uncovered. There is a similar campaign to uncover the real disunity in Shakespeare's plays and literary works in general, and to reject their apparent unity as a fiction that is usually blamed on 'humanist' critics, who serve the same function here as Tillyard and Lovejoy in the revisionist history. We are told by Jean Howard that literary texts 'seem' to be unified 'only when their heterogeneity is suppressed by [humanist] criticism' (1992, 32); and by Malcolm Evans that the 'fictional unity' of literary works must be 'torn apart' to reveal the 'disorder' that 'actually shapes the work' (1986, 254); and by Catherine Belsey that we need a materialist criticism that 'distance[s] itself from the imaginary coherence of the text' and recognizes 'the play of contradictions which in reality constitutes the literary text' (1980, 128); and by Pierre Macherey and Etienne Balibar that we must reject 'the illusory representation of the unity of a literary text', which is a 'mythical unity', since 'in itself, the text is . . . disparate' and 'contradictory' (1981, 49, 58).[9] We should note again that unity is always stated in terms that deny its existence – 'seem', 'fictional', 'imaginary', 'illusory', 'mythical' – while the disunity 'actually shapes' and 'in reality constitutes' the text 'in itself' because it is supposed to be more material than unity.

My fifth and final definition of the old materialist critics proceeds directly from the political imperative that, I argued, determines their uses of this term. Their approach is materialist because its purpose is to 'bring down capitalism' (Sinfield 1985, 154) and promote some form of socialism (very different from any materially existing form), which is implicit in the codewords 'activist', 'committed', 'emancipatory' and 'transformative' that they apply to it and that function like 'materialist' as synonyms for Marxist. But this purpose is not materialist in any ordinary sense of the word – surely no more materialist than promoting a materially existing capitalism, which they accuse nonmaterialist critics of doing. The same must be said of the tactics used in their readings of Shakespeare to achieve this purpose. One is to find that the play is advocating socialism, in defiance of the chronology of historical materialism: Kettle says that *King Lear* rejects both feudal and bourgeois values and ends in a promise of 'future harmony' in a classless society, so its meaning 'cannot be confined within the limits of seventeenth-century social thinking' (1964, 170–1), and Ryan insists that this play 'leaves us no choice but to identify the problem as . . . the injustices of a stratified society, and to seek the implied solution' in socialism (1995, 103–4). A more common tactic is to assert that some aspect (always a bad one) of Shakespeare's world or the world of his play is basically the same in our world, often by translating it into an abstract problem (like class-division) that floats free of history and the many material differences between our society and his.[10] That does not 'matter' so long as their equation of the two worlds enables them to derive from the play a Marxist lesson for today.

* * *

These five definitions do not cover all the old materialist criticism of Shakespeare, but I think they summarize its most important features and so can be used for a comparison with the new materialist criticism that recently emerged. Obviously there is no sharp chronological or logical division between the two: the old materialism is still being produced, though no longer at the cutting edge, and some precursors of the new materialism go back as far as 1980, which now seems like ancient history. One is the multiple-text school of bibliography, which maintains that the different early texts of plays like *King Lear* are not imperfect versions of a single Shakespearean original but separate and equal authorial constructs.[11] A more general influence is post-structuralist Theory, which put in question (i.e., put *out* of the question) many of the 'post-Englightenment' concepts assumed in conventional criticism. Some of this Theory was adopted by the cultural materialists, who can in this sense be viewed as a bridge from the old to the new materialism (even though many of them do not like what they see at the other end). It affected the way they 'historicized' Shakespeare (my third definition), since they did not refer to 'progressive' elements in the play but found instead that it contains 'subversive' elements undermining the concepts rejected by poststructuralism – that it 'refuses' any 'essentialist mystification' and exposes 'the radically contingent nature' of 'individual identity' (Dollimore 1984, 202, 229), or that it 'disrupt[s] sexual difference itself' and 'the notion of identity itself' (Belsey 1985b, 180, 187), and so on. Such elements cannot be called 'progressive' since they do not lead to anything in the succeeding bourgeois era, which did not refuse or disrupt the concepts of essentialism, sexual difference, or individual identity.[12] In fact many cultural materialists and other recent critics insisted that the concepts were imposed during this later period (i.e., 'post-Enlightenment'), which empowered them to discover in Shakespeare an anachronistic 'subversion' of these concepts that confirmed their own post-structuralist creed. This new way of 'historicizing' his plays does not seem very historical or materialist, but it provides another link to the new materialists who share that creed.

My purpose, however, is not to trace the genealogy of the new materialism but to examine its current state as a body of doctrines and the ways in which these doctrines invoke the idea of materiality. I will therefore focus on a well-known article by Margreta de Grazia and Peter Stallybrass, 'The materiality of the Shakespearean text' (1993), which, fortunately for my purpose, collects the doctrines in a kind of manifesto of the movement. The first thing to note is the new meaning of 'material' signalled by the title, which refers, not to the economic base or class conflict or any other aspect of the social system, but literally to a concrete, physical reality we can see and touch. There is a parallel change in the meaning of 'text'. Cultural materialists, along with many other critics influenced by post-structuralism, preferred to speak of Shakespeare's 'texts' rather than his 'works', in a gesture toward 'demystifying' the latter term, yet they still treated them, like the prepoststructuralists, as language or 'discourse' – that is, as sequences of sentences conveying ideas that are not material. But this article promises in its title and introduction to treat 'the Shakespearean text,' again literally, as a material object – as pieces of paper covered with black marks that were bound together in a quarto or folio and that should be 'looked *at*, not seen *through*' (p. 257). It is a promise, we will see, that is not and cannot be kept.

The first section of the article sets out to prove that Shakespeare's works/texts are unstable, unsettled, unfixed, uncertain, fluid, mutable, variable, diverse, disuniform, and nonidentical with themselves. The principal exhibit is the claim of the multiple-text critics, mentioned earlier, that the quarto and folio texts of *Lear* are not imperfect versions of one authoritative original but two separate plays that editors have illegitimately conflated. De Grazia and Stallybrass tell us that because of this claim 'Shakespeare studies will never be the same' (255), although the debate about it is far from settled.[13] I will not enter that debate, however, since I am only concerned with the role of materialism in the case that is presented by the multiple-text critics and applauded by this article. It must be a highly selective materialism since their evidence does not include differences between the quarto and folio in the location of ink smudges or broken letters, or even in the spellings of words. It is limited to passages that appear in one text and not the other, and that is because they do not 'look *at*' those material marks on the page but ignore some of them as irrelevant and 'see *through*' the rest to the immaterial ideas they convey, which, I noted, is what we mean by treating the text as discourse or, in the vernacular, by reading it,[14] just as the old materialists and most other critics did. Since we are going to encounter many more instances of this kind of slippage in the materialism avowed by the article, I will for convenience refer to it as matbending.

The materialism of the multiple-text critics endorsed by this article is also very selective in another sense. In their arguments they deal exclusively with the material differences between Quarto *Lear* and Folio *Lear* and never mention the much greater material differences between either of these texts and the text of another play. And the reason for this selectivity must be that they assume that *King Lear* constitutes some kind of entity, even if embodied in different versions, which is wholly distinct from any other play. The multiple-text argument cannot even be stated without this assumption, as we see when the article asks, 'how many variants between texts of *a given play* warrant the reproduction of *the play* in multiple forms?' (260, my emphasis), which makes sense only if the term 'play' refers to a single entity. We say of people who use circular reasoning that they assume what they think they are proving, but here is a case of people assuming what they think they are disproving. Since we will find many more examples of this kind of logic in the article, I am going to refer to it hereafter as asdisping.

The authors also present other arguments for textual instability that are even more problematic. One is based on the fact that in this period the same work/text can be referred to by different titles and the same title can refer to different works/texts. But this turns out to be another case of asdisping, since here again the argument cannot be stated without treating each text as self-identical: 'Titles for *a given play* vary', 'Thus *the play* published' under one title 'appears in Henslowe's diary' under two other titles (258–9, still my emphasis). It is assumed to be the same stable 'play', no matter how many titles it has. Moreover, in listing Henslowe's titles for 'the play' in question (it is *Sir Thomas Wyatt*), they do not include any titles he used for, say, *Tamburlaine*, because they assume that these are two distinct entities. This applies as well to the converse argument: their claim that 'one title could comprehend different texts' (an example is Shakespeare's and Wilkins's *Pericles*) only makes sense if the texts actually are different from each other and self-identical. It is also noteworthy that they do not include Quarto *Lear* and Folio *Lear* as an example here, which suggests that they do not actually regard them as 'different texts' comprehended by 'one title'.

In their second section they perform the same kind of operation on Shakespeare's words that they performed on his works – claiming that they are really (i.e., materially) unstable, unfixed, unsettled, indeterminate, plastic and mutable, and engage in 'linguistic errancy', 'verbal vagrancy', 'semantic slipping and sliding', 'convergence' and 'intermingling', and that this reality is once again concealed by the editors, only now their modernizing of the original spelling rather than their conflating of the original texts is to blame. The main argument boils down to the observation that before orthography was standardized, the same word could be spelled in different ways and the same spelling could be used for different words. But this implicates them in matbending. They must abandon their avowed materialism because a word is not a material object; as I already indicated, it is an immaterial idea that may be embodied in material writing or speech that we 'see *through*' or 'hear *through*' to reach the idea,[15] and this is what they are doing when they tell us about the instability of words, which cannot refer to material letters on the page. The argument also implicates them in asdisping, since their statement that 'the word *one* itself multiplies promiscuously in the sixteenth and seventeenth centuries, appearing as "an", "ain", "yane", "oon"', etc. (262)' assumes what it is supposed to be disproving – the existence of a single, discrete, stable, immaterial entity ('the word') that all these material spellings are spellings of, and that therefore does not multiply at all. Moreover, they do not include any spellings in their list (such as 'two') that they assume are embodiments of a different single, discrete, stable word.

Their other argument is based on the concept of a 'semantic field' that supposedly existed in the language's 'preregulative' phase when the 'boundaries that separate' words 'had not yet been drawn' (266), and that enabled the words to engage in the actions I listed. They try to prove this by drawing connections between 'air', 'heir' and 'hair' in some passages in *Macbeth*; but here again they are guilty of both matbending and asdisping. Their semantic field is not material, and while they often seem to be attributing the activity (slipping, sliding, etc.) that creates these connections to the early modern words themselves, it can only occur in the mind of a reader or hearer – indeed their demonstration involves some elaborate interpretations that come dangerously close to what we used to call a 'close reading'. This demonstration, moreover, assumes that the words really are separate: a statement like '*Hair* and *heir* also combine' (265) necessarily defines them as distinct entities that *can* combine, and this applies as well to the converging and intermingling that the authors ascribe to them.[16] In the immortal phrase of the father of countertransference, it takes two to intermingle. No 'semantic field' can do it to itself, no matter how errant or vagrant it may feel.

The third section tries to prove that Shakespeare's characters, like his works and words, are really unstable and that this instability is concealed, again, by modern editors because they insert lists of dramatis personae and regularize the variable speech prefixes. The argument based on the dramatis personae lists contends that, since they were not in the early play-texts, readers were 'without a program and therefore not programmed to encounter a group of unified characters, they instead had to negotiate an array of positionalities relating to rank, family, gender, age' (267). But surely most people who read these texts had been to the theatre where they saw that characters were presented in the unified material bodies of actors, and so would be 'programmed' to encounter unified characters in the texts as well. Without such an expectation they could not comprehend the play they were reading since 'positionalities' cannot speak or act. Even the authors themselves, in their account of the air–heir–hair 'semantic field' in *Macbeth*, treat Macbeth, Banquo, and Macduff as unified, stable characters and not as 'positionalities'.

The argument that uses variable speech prefixes to destabilize the characters is an example of asdisping because, like their arguments attempting to disprove stability by citing the variable titles of a play and the variable spellings of a word, it cannot even be stated without assuming that the variants point to a stable entity: 'the "Lady Capulet" of modern editions is fractured into "*Ca. W.,*" "*Capu. Wi.,*" "*La.,*" "*M.,*" "*Mo.,*" "*Old La.,*" "*Wi.,*" and "*Wife.*" In the stage directions there is a further proliferation of her names' (268). Clearly they believe that all the designations in their list, along with their pronoun 'her', refer to an unfractured, stable Lady Capulet. And they do not include '*Jul.*' or '*Rom.*' in their list because they believe these prefixes belong to entirely different unified characters.

At the end of this section they shift the meaning of 'character' so that it refers not to Shakespeare's dramatic characters but to the characters of those characters, and they maintain, not that character in this sense is unstable in Shakespeare's texts, but that it did not exist in his culture and was 'imagined' by later critics. They do not present an argument but simply quote Jonathan Goldberg's claim that in the Renaissance 'there is no notion of human character save as a locus of inscription' (1988, 316). They tell us 'he has done nothing less than overthrow almost three centuries of "character study"' (273) – a bit of hype comparable to 'Shakespeare studies will never be the same' – but he does not offer any real evidence and ignores a mass of evidence proving that early modern subjects believed that both living and fictional persons had characters. Since I have assembled some of this evidence elsewhere,[17] I will not discuss his claim here except to note that it is a good example of the new mode of 'historicizing' Shakespeare I mentioned earlier that reads back into his texts an anachronistic poststructuralist 'subversion' of allegedly 'post-Englightenment' concepts like personal identity.

About half of this section is devoted to another post-structuralist anachronism – the assertion that in the Renaissance 'the latter-day incontrovertible male/female binary . . . was not yet in place' (272).[18] While the connection of this assertion to the stability of Shakespeare's characters is not clear, the arguments supporting it are worth examining because they show the new materialism at its most immaterial. We might expect that card-carrying materialists would find their evidence in the material practices of the society – in the presence of women judges and bishops, for instance, and in sex-blind inheritance laws and same-sex marriages.[19] They do not cite any such evidence because there is none; instead they base their case on arguments that are matbendingly removed from this material reality, and that often involve asdisping. They point to Shakespearean crossdressing and ask, 'If the binaries were that clear cut, would the transvestism of a Ganymede or Cesario be imaginable?' (270). The answer is that the transvestism is imaginable only *because* of the clear-cut male/female binary since there must be a boundary to 'trans'; without the binary, transvestism would not exist and Rosalind's donning a doublet would be no more significant than her donning a new farthingale.[20] They also argue that the 'controvertibility of gender' is proved by 'a theater that assigned female roles to males' (270), but this proves just the opposite since the incontrovertible binary prohibited women from appearing on stage; without it there would have been women actors to play female (and male) roles. Another argument finds evidence in the 'widespread fascination' with 'the hermaphrodite' (270); but that assumes the basic importance of the gender binary, without which a hermaphrodite would be no more fascinating than someone born with an extra toe.

Their other arguments take them even further from materialism. They invoke 'the Galenic one-sex model' of anatomy, which they assert, relying on Thomas Laqueur (1990), 'obtained in the Renaissance' (270, 272). Laqueur is wrong, for this was not the dominant model then, as Janet Adelman (1997) has shown;[21] but even if it were, we have no reason to think that this theory (or any other) affected the material practices that enacted the gender binary. There is the same kind of double error in their appeal to William Lily's Latin *Grammar* (1567, sig. A6r), which 'classifies nouns into seven genders, including male, female, neuter (neither male nor female), doubtful gender (either male or female), and epicene (both male and female)' (272). They are asdisping again: the last three classes assume a prior male/female binary, without which 'neither', 'either' and 'both' are meaningless.[22] But even if their evidence were valid, it would still be irrelevant since grammatical and human gender cannot be equated and the material operation of the gender binary does not depend on grammar – if it did, our unisex third person plural pronoun would prove that 'the latter-day incontrovertible male/female binary' is not 'in place' even in this 'latter day'. All the material evidence we have shows that this binary was very much 'in place' in the Renaissance; post-structuralist Theory has now put it in question, but that is not retroactive.[23]

Their fourth section starts out trying to destabilize the author of the Shakespearean text. They argue that attributions of plays in this period are problematic because of collaboration[24] and the role of the dramatic company and stationer in determining what appears on the quarto title pages, which is supposed to prove 'the relative insignificance of the author' (274). But they ignore all the obvious evidence, much of it collected by Barbara Mowat, (1996) that proves the opposite – that people in the Renaissance attached a great deal of significance to authors and even celebrated them. One major piece of evidence is the First Folio itself, which owes its very existence to the belief in the constitutive role of a stable authorial Shakespeare.

They then return to the multiple-text criticism they praised in the first section, but now they condemn it because it retained 'the category of author' by positing Shakespearean manuscript revisions to account for the multiple texts, so that its 'emphasis on materiality was betrayed' by 'a higher devotion to the authorial holograph' that has a 'purely imaginary and idealized status' (276–7).[25] This marks a crucial shift from destabilizing 'the category of author' to eliminating it entirely (along with the manuscript it depends on), and it promises a definition of the new meaning of 'materialism', which they invoke in opposition to 'idealized' – this being, as I noted earlier, how the old materialism defined itself. But it is not easy to understand what conception of materialism is betrayed by positing an authorial manuscript behind the text, for this is the kind of inference – or 'imagining' – from a seen material effect to an unseen material cause that we all rely on. If in the morning I notice material puddles on my lawn, I infer that there was some material rain the night before, and I am sure they would do the same – indeed they could not function without making hundreds of such inferences every day. Those authorial manuscripts require more inferences, but they are all of this kind. From inspecting the material quarto we infer that it is the result of a material compositor setting material type. The new materialists also infer this but refuse to go any further; yet it is obvious that the compositor must have followed some copy when he set the type, and that in a first edition this must have been a manuscript.[26] It only requires one more inference of this kind to conclude that the manuscript was an authorial holograph or was descended from it, which is confirmed by extant non-Shakespearean dramatic manuscripts, some in the dramatist's handwriting, that prove the material existence of these 'purely imaginary and idealized' documents.[27] And in this article the authors infer that there was an authorial document behind each critical text they cite, for otherwise they could not use such locutions as 'Taylor argues' and 'Goldberg notes' that retain the banished 'category of author'. By the end of the section, therefore, we still cannot tell what concept of 'materialism' is being invoked to prohibit any inferences from the material Shakespearean text to a material Shakespearean manuscript.

The fifth and final section provides some answers to this problem, but they create new problems of their own. The authors begin by arguing that studies of Shakespeare's texts should 'reject depth [or 'interior significance'] as the object of analysis' since it is produced by the 'illusion' that 'Shakespeare's "meaning"' (their scare quotes) 'can be seen through the text', and focus instead on the 'exterior surface' by 'conceptualizing the text' in 'the materials of the physical book itself: in *paper*', which leads them to trace the transformations of these materials from cloth to paper and to conclude that 'the Shakespearean text' is to be viewed as 'a provisional state in the circulation of matter' (280). This is a clear definition of the new materialism and it defines a feasible project. The trouble is that it would, to adapt their praise of Goldberg, do 'nothing less than overthrow' in one move (formerly stroke) all their previous remarks about the work, word, character and author, since these concepts are derived not from the paper but from what is printed on it, which is immaterial (in both senses) to this project, and so their entire article up to this point would be guilty of matbending.[28]

They then shift their 'object of analysis' from the paper to the activities of the printshop and assert that we should be studying 'these material practices' instead of 'a transcendent "text" imagined as the product of the author's mind' (282). This too is a feasible project and one that, unlike the study of paper, is compatible with at least some of their earlier commentary, but it creates another problem since those 'material practices' are discerned not by 'looking *at*' the printed page but by 'seeing *through*' it, so if the idea that Shakespeare 'can be seen through the text' is an 'illusion' (280), why does this not also apply to the practices? The fact is that we infer them from the text by the same effect-to-cause logic that produced our knowledge that it rained and that compositors copied a manuscript. But this logic also enables us to proceed from Shakespeare's text to his mind and meaning (no scare quotes), which involves the same kind of causal inferences (though more complex) from words to intended meaning that we make whenever we receive a verbal communication – in fact without them communication would be impossible. Even the authors do not hesitate to make them when dealing with a modern critical text, as we just saw in their references to what Taylor and Goldberg said and meant, which they do not consider 'imagined'. It would seem then that our search for a satisfactory definition of the new materialist approach to the Shakespearean text has led to this unsatisfactory formulation: it privileges some inferences from the text that its practitioners approve of and call 'materialist', and condemns other inferences that they disapprove of and call 'imagined', 'idealized' and 'illusory'.

* * *

Our interrogation of this approach must move on, therefore, to ask how it determines which inferences are in the approved materialist category, and here it will be helpful to draw some comparisons to the old materialism, which we saw was also highly selective in bestowing its materialist imprimatur. The most obvious criterion used by the new materialists is found in their search for textual instability, which resembles the old materialists' search for textual disunity, described in my fourth definition. Both approaches regard this instability/disunity as fundamental to their analysis, and they both try to establish its privileged status by a distinction between reality and appearance, based on what I called the Manichean binary of good materialism *v* bad idealism: textual instability or disunity is supposed to be real because it is material, while textual stability or unity is supposed to be an immaterial or idealized 'illusion'. They both blame this illusion on the enemy – for the old materialists it was the humanist critics with their concept of organic unity, and for the new ones it is the editors with their conflated texts, regularized spellings, etc.[29] They both also assume that one of their main tasks is to defeat this enemy by demystifying or de-idealizing the illusion in order to prove the material reality of the disunity or instability that they prize. Since we found that this 'real' disunity/instability is really no more real or material than the 'apparent' unity/stability, the belief of both old and new materialists in it, and in the materialist-idealist binary that justifies it, gives us one explanation of the selectivity of their materialism.

There are, however, two important differences between the old materialist disunity and the new materialist instability. The old materialists, we saw, treated the text as discourse and so sought – and found – disunity in its discursive meaning, usually in the form of ideological contradictions. But the new materialists (claim to) reject any attempt to 'see *through*' the physical text to its discursive meaning and so seek – and find – within that text itself an instability in 'the four categories basic to the dominant post-Enlightenment treatment of Shakespeare': the 'single *work*', 'discrete *word*', 'unified *character*' and 'autonomous *author*' (257). The other major difference is the result of the old materialists' concern (in my third definition) with relating the text, as part of the superstructure, to the material base of its society, which leads them to argue that the contradictions they find in it 'reflect the historical contradictions of early modern culture', as Holderness, Loughrey and Murphy explain in defining their 'materialist' approach to Shakespeare (1997, 85).[30] There is no equivalent to this in the new materialists, who show little interest in the contradictions of early modern culture or the Marxist base-superstructure paradigm. The closest they come to it is in their efforts to connect some textual instabilities to the practices of the printers, publishers and theatrical companies, and to the ideas (or rather nonideas) of the time, as we noted in their claims (which I have been calling 'poststructuralist anachronisms') that the imagined stability depends on 'post-Enlightenment' concepts that did not exist in early modern culture.

The new materialists' special interest in the production of the physical text gives us another explanation of their selective materialism, which is similar to the old materialists' special interest (in my first definition) in activities within the economic base, since they both regard this kind of work as more material and therefore more important than other things that people do. Moreover, they both regard their valorization of this work as part of the campaign against their idealist foes, who attach less importance to it than to the author's work. Thus Michael Bristol objected to the 'binary opposition' that 'separates the life of the mind from the sphere of manual labor' and privileges the mind (1990, 106). De Grazia and Stallybrass endorse his objection (277) but instead of responding with a post-structuralist deconstruction of the binary they reverse it to privilege manual labor, as is evident in their 'thick' descriptions of the 'vatmen, couchers, and layers' who made paper and of the printers who 'used urine to soak the leather casing' of their inkballs (280, 282) and in their dismissal of the author, without even a thin description of his physical activity, as 'an impoverished, ghostly thing' compared to them (283). Of course, his labor required ink and paper that were just as material as the substances they handled, and their labor, since we must also infer it by effect-to-cause logic, is just as ghostly as his, but that does not 'matter' because the selective concept of materialism being applied here is limited to the working class. But there is, again, a major difference between old and new materialists in this principle of selectivity: the old ones were interested in working-class labor because of its relation to the economic system and class struggle, while the new ones view it as something interesting in itself. Their vatmen and printers are engaged, not in a conflict with the bosses over the extraction of surplus labor, but in a competition with the author (and his play) for our attention, in an impoverished and ghostly simulacrum of the Marxist class struggle.

This last point leads to what I think is the most important difference between the two materialisms since it underlies the others. As I explained in my fifth definition, the old materialists were Marxists who saw materialism as a weapon to 'bring down capitalism', and this purpose determined their selective applications of the term that locate it in the economic base, and class conflict, and the relation of the text to its society, and the disunity or contradictions within it, since they want to connect these locations to the problems of our own 'late capitalism' and to the need to 'transform' it. The new materialists have no discernible political purpose and I am not suggesting that they should have one,[31] but in the absence of any other goal we cannot tell what determines their selective location of materialism in instability and manual labor. They say these things are more interesting, which is indisputable if they only mean more interesting to *them*, but they also want them to be more interesting to *us* – to become 'the objects not only of our labors but also of our desires', as their final sentence puts it. The only reason given is that they are more material (i.e., real) than the imaginary and idealized objects of our mistaken labors and desires. But this materialist principle of selectivity, we saw, is itself based on a very selective principle of what is material, and so we are left running around in hermeneutic circles.

As the final step in our interrogation of the new materialism, we should ask what its consequences would be for the study and teaching of Shakespeare, but this will require us to distinguish between a 'strong' and 'weak' version of the authors' project. If we adopted the 'strong' version, then their initial assertion that 'Shakespeare studies will never be the same' would become an understatement because these studies would no longer exist. He and his canon would be abolished along with the 'post-Enlightenment' 'category of author', and the misguided pursuit that we call 'Shakespeare studies' would be replaced by studies of early modern papermaking and printing and other 'material practices'. Of course we might choose *King Lear* to exemplify these practices, but that would be wholly arbitrary since it is no more useful for this purpose than Swinhoe's *The Unhappy Fair Irene*.[32]

The authors, however, also have a 'weak' or fall-back version of their project: apparently it is acceptable to study a Shakespeare play if we strip it of all editorial contamination, as in Michael Warren's facsimile reproduction of the three texts of *King Lear*.[33] In one of their more amusing passages, they quote with approval (258) his complaint that in modern editions the play is 'processed for easy consumption' (1989, vii), which will surprise anyone who has taught the play in a modern edition to undergraduates (let alone high-school students), who certainly do not find it easy. If we are only allowed to teach it by confronting students with all three texts, and presenting these texts in facsimiles with the original spelling and even the printers' errors left intact, the task becomes so difficult that it could only be attempted in a graduate seminar. But even on this level it is hard to see what we could do. We could not apply a 'humanist' approach to the play by discussing the author's meaning or his characters or their characters, which have all been prohibited, nor could we discuss its artistic value because de Grazia tells us, in her reply to Pechter, that the play 'predat[es] the very emergence of the *literary*' (1997, 71).[34] We are also prevented from applying the old materialism or any other political or historical approach, since these too require inferences about discursive meaning. Nor could we examine the relation of the three texts to each other, lest our students be tempted to speculate about a process of revision, which is a betrayal of materialism (276) and of poststructuralism, which 'has taught us to suspect … a metaphysics of origin' (256). We could not even talk about the material of the facsimile since its paper is a post-modern product and so is its lettering, which bears no traces of early modern urine. Apparently we are restricted to 'looking *at*' the facsimile pages and savoring them as our closest approach to 'the materiality of the Shakespearean text'.

REFERENCES

1. See also the titles of Charnes, 1994; de Grazia, 1988; de Grazia and Stallybrass, 1993; Goldberg, 1990; Grady 1991, and Holderness, Loughrey and Murphy, 1995. The Australian and New Zealand Shakespeare Association announced that its conference in July 1998 will be on 'Material Shakespeare'.
2. The most important exceptions known to me are Jackson, 1994; Holderness, Loughrey and Murphy, 1995; and Pechter, 1997; whose critiques of the uses of materialism come from three very different directions.
3. Dollimore observed that 'As a term of abuse idealism is second only to fascism' (1983, 115). The term can be used to attack Marxists who have strayed – Aers (1991, 23–4) finds that Barker, 1984; Dollimore, 1984; Belsey, 1985a; and Eagleton, 1986 are guilty of 'gross idealism', and Goldberg, 1986, (75) criticizes Dollimore, 1984 for 'the idealism that haunts his materialism'.
4. Some of the more recent critics, influenced by Althusser and others, say they have loosened up the causal nexus by granting the superstructure a kind of quasi-autonomy, but they still find that 'in the last analysis' or 'ultimately' the basic cause is always in the base.
5. Edmund has a different legal status than the other main characters but bastards are not a separate economic class in the Marxist sense – his source of income (from the labor of others) and life style are the same as theirs.
6. A number of nonmaterialist critics claim that the blinding of Gloucester and the beheading of Macbeth are really displaced castrations.
7. A Freudian would assume the opposite – that the apparent sexual subject of *Measure for Measure* evokes 'much deeper fears' than the 'social problems'. Ryan also claims that his reading of *Lear* will 'delve deeper' than earlier ones (1995, 101), and Heinemann that the 'causes of disaster' that she discovers in this play 'lie deeper' than those previously proposed (1991, 78).
8. See also Hawkes, 1995, 13, 65. Moisan notes that this view of a strifetorn Renaissance now 'run[s] the risk of acquiring the aura of unimpeachable orthodoxy previously accorded the Great Chain of Being' (1994, 482).
9. For a fuller discussion of this point, see Levin 1996, 139–42.
10. See Charnes, 1992, 11–2; Eagleton, 1986, 104; Greene, 1981, 39–40;

Heinemann, 1991, 78; Holderness, 1991, 177; Ryan, 1995, 98, 102; Sinfield, 1992, 106; and Wynne-Daviesm 1991, 129.

11. The school won recognition with Urkowitz 1980 and Taylor and Warren 1983. There is a useful list of multiple-text studies of *King Lear*, *Hamlet*, *Othello*, *Troilus and Cressida*, and *Henry V* in de Grazia and Stallybrass, 1993, nn. 6–8.

12. This is one of Goldberg's objections (1986, 75) to Dollimore, 1984.

13. They add that its 'significance ... cannot be overestimated'; Holderness, Loughrey and Murphy say, in turn, that the 'importance' of the de Grazia-Stallybrass article 'cannot be underestimated' (1995, 100), which I hope is a Marxist slip.

14. This point is made in Pechter, 1997, 58.

15. Our word 'word' can refer to an immaterial idea or its material embodiment, but the idea determines whether what we see or hear is a word or a meaningless sequence of letters or sounds. And we can think of words without seeing or hearing them; in fact we always do this before we write or speak, even when we protest that we spoke 'without thinking'.

16. If early modern people did not separate the three ideas conveyed by these words they would miss the connections, and in their material lives they might try to breathe hair or comb their hair or bequeath their estate to the air.

17. See Levin, 1990, 438–44, 466–9, and also Aers, 1991. Goldberg's main 'evidence' (my scare quotes) for this claim comes from Renaissance writing manuals, which he dragoons into service by some fancy slipping and sliding between different meanings of 'hand' and 'character'.

18. Although they do not mention it, their assertion would do 'nothing less than overthrow' two decades of feminist studies of early modern patriarchy, which assume that the binary was firmly 'in place' then.

19. If early modern marriages were not determined by this binary, we would expect about 25 per cent of them to be between two women, 25 per cent between two men, and only 50 per cent between a woman and a man. And if it did not determine the laws of inheritance, why was Edward VI crowned before his two older sisters?

20. How would they account for transvestism in real life and drama during later periods when the gender binary is supposed to be 'in place'?

21. Other critics, as she points out, also accept this model uncritically, including Crewe, 1995, 120; Greenblatt, 1988, 79–80; Orgel, 1989, 13–4; and Sinfield, 1992, 134.

22. This is also true of the two remaining classes, 'Commune of two' (male and female) and 'Commune of three' (male, female and neuter).

23. They also endorse, as a kind of corollary, the recent claim that 'neither heterosexuality nor homosexuality existed as categories in early modern Europe' (272), but this binary goes back to the Bible (Leviticus, 18:22, 20:13) and is assumed in the early modern sodomy laws.

24. They cite Bentley (1971, 204–5) on frequency of collaboration in the plays of this period and complain that the implications of this 'have hardly begun to register in Shakespeare studies' (275). But very few of Shakespeare's plays or the other Renaissance plays that we value most are collaborations. I suspect this is not a coincidence.

25. In her 1988 essay de Grazia calls this manuscript a 'figment of the ... imagination', an 'immaterial abstraction', an 'imagined rarefication', 'hypothetically flimsy', 'metaphysically mystified', 'unscientific or unbibliographic', 'idealist', 'incarnational', 'ghostly' and a 'spectre' (71, 82).

26. The only alternatives I can think of are that he made up the play himself as

he went along or else picked the type from his case at random and so produced the play accidentally. Would they say that these explanations are *not* 'imaginary and idealized'?

27.   I will not even mention Heminge and Condell's description, in their epistle in the First Folio, of the Shakespearean holographs ('his papers') that they 'receiued from him', which were certainly not imaginary.

28.   They also do 'nothing less than overthrow' their entire article in another way when they acknowledge later that, since 'there is no "original"', then 'there is no intrinsic reason *not* to have a modernized' edition of Shakespeare (282), presumably with conflated texts, regularized spellings and speech prefixes, and all the other editorial interventions they have been arguing against. Bristol points this out (1990, 117).

29.   Even the language is similar: compare their claim that modern editors 'smooth away' or 'efface' textual instabilities (256, 266, 279, 282) with the claims in Belsey (1980, 109) and Dollimore (1984, 60, 67) that humanist critics are guilty of 'smoothing out contradiction' or 'smoothing over contradictions' or 'effacing' them.

30.   In an earlier article, however, they endorse the new materialists' command 'to look *at* rather than *through*' texts (1995, 117), although they qualify this in their reply to Pechter (1997, 84).

31.   It troubles some old materialists: Howard complains that they 'fetishize materiality' and neglect historical materialism (1997), and Holderness, Loughrey and Murphy that their 'worthy' materialism is 'uneasily linked to' (i.e., contaminated by) their poststructuralism (1995, 115).

32.   I chose this play for two reasons: it is the worst one I ever encountered, and it should augment my cultural capital since few people have heard of it.

33.   They suggest that readers 'assemble any number and combination' of the facsimile pages (283, 258). In their separate replies to Pechter, they both retreat to this 'weak' version (with no mention of reassembling pages) and insist it was what they really meant all along (1997, 71, 72, 73, 74, 78); but that it not what they said at the end of their article. In these replies they both appeal to their intended meaning ('we did not ... mean to suggest', 'we certainly were not trying to replace', etc.) to show that Pechter misrepresented them, although in their article, as we saw, they placed authorial 'meaning' in scare quotes and argued that it was an 'illusion' and that an appeal to it was a betrayal of materialism (280, 276).

34.   She does not explain what Sidney thought he was defending in his *Defence of Poetry* or what Meres thought he was discoursing about in his 'Comparative discourse of our English poets' in *Palladis Tamia*.

BIBLIOGRAPHY

Adelman, Janet (1997), 'Making defect perfection: Shakespeare and the one-sex model' in Comensoli, Viviana, and Anne Russell (eds), *Enacting Gender on the English Renaissance Stage*, Urbana: University of Illinois Press.

Aers, David (1991), 'Reflections on current histories of the subject', *Literature and History*, 2 (2), Autumn.

Barker, Francis (1984), *The Tremulous Private Body: Essays on Subjection*, London: Methuen.

Belsey, Catherine (1980), *Critical Practice*, London: Methuen.

———— (1985a), *The Subject of Tragedy: Identity and Difference in Renaissance Drama*, London: Methuen.

———— (1985b), 'Disrupting sexual difference: meaning and gender in the comedies' in Drakakis, John (ed.), *Alternative Shakespeares*, London: Methuen.

———— (1992), 'Literature, History, Politics' in Wilson and Dutton.

Bentley, Gerald Eades (1971), *The Profession of Dramatist in Shakespeare's Time, 1590–1642*, Princeton: Princeton University Press.

Bristol, Michael D. (1990), *Shakespeare's America, America's Shakespeare*, London: Routledge.

Charnes, Linda (1992), 'What's love got to do with it? Reading the liberal humanist romance in Shakespeare's *Antony and Cleopatra*', *Textual Practice*, 6 (1), Spring.

———— (1994), *Notorious Identity: Materializing the Subject in Shakespeare*, Cambridge: Harvard University Press.

Crewe, Jonathan (ed.) (1992), *Reconfiguring the Renaissance: Essays in Critical Materialism*, Lewisburg: Bucknell University Press.

———— (1995), 'In the field of dreams: transvestism in *Twelfth Night* and *The Crying Game*', *Representations*, 50, Spring.

De Grazia, Margreta (1988), 'The essential Shakespeare and the material book', *Textual Practice*, 2 (1), Spring.

De Grazia, Margreta, and Peter Stallybrass (1993), 'The materiality of the Shakespearean text', *Shakespeare Quarterly*, 44 (3), Fall.

———— (1997), 'Love among the ruins: response to Pechter', *Textual Practice*, 11 (1), Spring.

Delany, Paul (1995), '*King Lear* and the Decline of Feudalism' in Kamps.

Dollimore, Jonathan (1983), 'Politics teaching history', *LTP: Journal of Literature Teaching Politics*, 2.

———— (1984), *Radical Tragedy: Religion, Ideology and Power in the Drama of Shakespeare and His Contemporaries*, Brighton: Harvester (2nd edn 1989).

———— (1985), 'Transgression and Surveillance in *Measure for Measure*' in Dollimore and Sinfield.

———— (1990), 'Critical Developments: Cultural Materialism, Feminism and Gender Critique, and New Historicism' in Wells, Stanley (ed.), *Shakespeare: A Bibliographical Guide*, 2nd edn, Oxford: Clarendon.

Dollimore, Jonathan, and Alan Sinfield (eds) (1985), *Political Shakespeare: New Essays in Cultural Materialism*, Manchester: Manchester University Press (2nd edn 1994).

Eagleton, Terry (1986), *William Shakespeare*, Oxford: Basil Blackwell.

Evans, Malcolm (1986), *Signifying Nothing: Truth's True Contents in Shakespeare's Text*, Brighton: Harvester.

Goldberg, Jonathan (1986), Untitled review, *Modern Philology*, 84 (1), August.

———— (1988), 'Hamlet's Hand', *Shakespeare Quarterly*, **39** (3), Fall.

———— (1990), *Writing Matter: From the Hands of the English Renaissance*, Stanford: Stanford University Press.

Grady, Hugh (1991), *The Modernist Shakespeare: Critical Texts in a Material World*, Oxford: Oxford University Press.

Greenblatt, Stephen (1988), *Shakespearean Negotiations: The Circulation of Social Energy in Renaissance England*, Berkeley: University of California Press.

Greene, Gayle (1981), 'Feminist and Marxist criticism: an argument for alliances', *Women's Studies*, **9** (1).

Hawkes, Terence (1995), *William Shakespeare: 'King Lear'*, Plymouth: Northcote.

Heinemann, Margot (1991), '"Demystifying the mystery of state": *King Lear* and the world upside down', *Shakespeare Survey*, **44**.

Holderness, Graham (1991), 'Production, Reproduction, Performance: Marxism, History, Theatre' in Barker, Francis, et al. (eds), *Uses of History: Marxism, Postmodernism and the Renaissance*, Manchester: Manchester University Press.

Holderness, Graham, Bryan Loughrey and Andrew Murphy (1995), '"What's the matter?" Shakespeare and textual theory', *Textual Practice*, **9** (1), Spring.

———— (1997), 'Busy doing nothing: a response to Edward Pechter', *Textual Practice*, **11** (1), Spring.

Howard, Jean E. (1992), 'The New Historicism in Renaissance Studies' in Wilson and Dutton.

———— (1997), 'Necessary irritations', unpublished paper presented at the meeting of the Shakespeare Association of America, Washington, DC.

Jackson, Leonard (1994), *The Dematerialisation of Karl Marx: Literature and Marxist Theory*, London: Longman.

Kamps, Ivo (ed.) (1995), *Materialist Shakespeare: A History*, London: Verso.

Kettle, Arnold (1964), 'From *Hamlet* to *Lear*' in Kettle, Arnold (ed.), *Shakespeare in a Changing World*, London: Lawrence and Wishart.

Laqueur, Thomas (1990), *Making Sex: Body and Gender from the Greeks to Freud*, Cambridge: Harvard University Press.

Levin, Richard (1990), 'Unthinkable thoughts in the new historicizing of English Renaissance drama', *New Literary History*, **21** (3), Spring.

———— (1996), 'The Cultural Materialist Attack on Artistic Unity and the Problem of Ideological Criticism' in Harris, Wendell V. (ed.), *Beyond Poststructuralism: The Speculations of Theory and the Experience of Reading*, University Park: Pennsylvania State University Press.

Lovejoy, Arthur O. (1936), *The Great Chain of Being: A Study of the History of an Idea*, Cambridge: Harvard University Press.

Macherey, Pierre, and Etienne Balibar (1981), "Literature as an ideological form: some Marxist propositions', trans. James Kavanagh, *Praxis*, **5**.

McLuskie, Kathleen (1985), 'The Patriarchal Bard: Feminist Criticsm and Shakespeare: *King Lear* and *Measure for Measure*' in Dollimore and Sinfield.

Moisan, Thomas (1994), Untitled review, *Shakespeare Quarterly*, 45 (4), Winter.

Mowat, Barbara A. (1996), 'Constructing the Author' in Parker, R.B., and S.P. Zitner (eds), *Elizabethan Theater: Essays in Honor of S. Schoenbaum*, Newark: University of Delaware Press.

Orgel, Stephen (1989), 'Nobody's perfect: or why did the English stage take boys for women?' *South Atlantic Quarterly*, 88 (1), Winter.

Pechter, Edward (1997), 'Making love to our employment; or, the immateriality of arguments about the materiality of the Shakespearean text', *Textual Practice*, 11 (1), Spring.

Ryan, Kiernan (1995), *Shakespeare*, 2nd edn, London: Prentice Hall.

Sinfield, Alan (1985), 'Give an Account of Shakespeare and Education' in Dollimore and Sinfield.

——— (1992), *Faultlines: Cultural Materialism and the Politics of Dissident Reading*, Berkeley: University of California Press.

Smirnov, A.A. (1936), *Shakespeare: A Marxist Interpretation*, trans. Sonia Volochova, New York: Critics' Group.

Stallybrass, Peter (1986), 'Patriarchal Territories: The Body Enclosed' in Ferguson, Margaret, Maureen Quilligan and Nancy Vickers (eds), *Rewriting the Renaissance: The Discourses of Sexual Difference in Early Modern Europe*, Chicago: University of Chicago Press.

Taylor, Gary, and Michael Warren (eds) (1983), *The Division of the Kingdoms: Shakespeare's Two Versions of 'King Lear'*, Oxford: Clarendon.

Tillyard, E.M.W. (1943), *The Elizabethan World Picture*, London: Chatto and Windus.

Urkowitz, Steven (1980), *Shakespeare's Revision of 'King Lear'*, Princeton: Princeton University Press.

Warren, Michael (ed.) (1989), *The Complete 'King Lear' 1608–1623*, Berkeley: University of California Press.

Wayne, Valerie (ed.) (1991), *The Matter of Difference: Materialist Feminist Criticism of Shakespeare*, Ithaca: Cornell University Press.

Wilson, Richard, and Richard Dutton (eds) (1992), *New Historicism and Renaissance Drama*, London: Longman.

Wynne-Davies, Marion (1991), '"The Swallowing Womb": Consumed and Consuming Women in *Titus Andronicus*' in Wayne.

6 Shakespeare in Performance

John Russell Brown

A student of Shakespeare at the end of the twentieth century will not suffer from lack of possibilities. Any scholar has always realized that the more we know the more we become aware of what we do not know and wish to discover. The present situation is different: having studied a play or plays from one point of view and method of criticism or scholarship, we find that both viewpoint and method are unsatisfactory. Continually, more techniques have to be learnt and new vistas of published work attract our attention. We have to choose from among many directions for the next stage of our study.

The study of 'Shakespeare in performance' is, perhaps, the clearest and most worrying example of this. Three lines of work used to be distinguishable. A play's 'Stage History' would give an account of major productions down the centuries and draw attention to their achievements and differences with a focus, for the early centuries, on star actors and, from the end of the nineteenth century onwards, on directors and designers. George C.D. Odell's wide-spanning *Shakespeare – from Betterton to Irving* in two volumes (1920, reprinted 1963)[1] formed the basis from which many other histories traced the course of change, usually dealing with one play at a time. It was symptomatic of the isolated nature of this work, that the Stage Histories included in volumes of the 'new' Cambridge Shakespeare in the years after World War II were usually by another hand than the edition itself. Nevertheless, they set a model for other stage histories of book-length scope.

A different line of work produced detailed studies of individual productions. Michael Mullin's *'Macbeth' Onstage* (1976)[2] reproduced promptbook, director's notes, interviews, and criticism in as wide a gamut as practicable for Glen Byam Shaw's production of 1955 with Laurence Olivier in the title-role. Arthur Colby Sprague's *Shakespeare and the Actors* (1948)[3] cast a much wider net, collecting traditional and highly original items of stage-business from numerous productions from the earliest recorded to those of its own day. Marvin Rosenberg's compendious volumes on the major tragedies, notably his *Masks of 'King Lear'*(1972),[4] further varied this effort of documentation by collecting descriptions of how leading actors dealt with the texts, especially at crucial points where their 'interpretations' could create notably different 'characters.'

A third group of scholars examined the texts of the plays microscopically to discover what the dialogue and stage-directions (in so far as they were thought to be either authorial or theatrical) could yield by way of information or, at least, hints about Elizabethan theatre practice and the playing of individual scenes and incidents; in numerous articles, Rudolph Stamm, George F. Reynolds in his study of staging at the Red Bull Theatre (1940), and Bernard Beckerman, in *Shakespeare at the Globe* (1962),[5] were pioneers in this.

All these three modes of research are still being pursued energetically today. Jonathan Bate and Russell Jackson's *Shakespeare: an Illustrated Stage History* (1996)[6] is by numerous and variously knowledgeable authors and amply illustrated. Two new series, *Shakespeare in Performance*[7] and *Text and Performance*,[8] offer stage histories of individual plays and also deal in considerable detail with particular productions. Alan Dessen's *Recovering Shakespeare's Theatrical Vocabulary* (1995)[9] adds meticulous comparison to analysis of details of many dramatic texts in an effort to break the codes used by theatre practitioners in the lost manuscripts which lay behind the early printed texts. In *Shakespeare, Theory, and Performance* (1996),[10] edited by James C. Bulman, a number of specialists discuss a wide range of these lines of study as they are being followed in the 1990s.

Yet the study of Shakespeare in Performance is now moving in directions scarcely dreamt of in the 1980s and not represented adequately in any of the books mentioned above. Most obviously, the rise of 'Performance Studies' in Theatre departments in universities across Europe and in North America, and in some English departments too, has produced new and less impressionistic ways of studying any play in performance. Performance Studies are not primarily concerned with how texts are 'interpreted' (which hitherto has been the chief topic in Shakespearean stage histories and performance studies) but with asking what is the nature of the performances throughout a play and of the progressive experience of an audience: what happens in actors and audiences and, crucially, what happens between them. Role-playing, simultaneity, co-existence, transgression, performative function, foregrounding, improvisation, ritual, ceremony, sign, signifier, presence, transformation: these are some of the terms now being redefined and made available for describing what happens in a theatre and in theatre-like events elsewhere. Richard Schechner's *Performance Theory*[11] (1988) blazed trails for numerous other general and particular books bringing these terms into wider usage. Linked to Performance Studies are Communication Studies and Reception Theory, dealing with word-acts, body language, stereotypes, rituals, and interpersonal communication of all kinds. Key books are Erving Goffman's *The Presentation of Self in Everyday Life* (1959)[12] and *Interaction Ritual* (1967).[13] All these forms of study, Shakespeareans are begining to realise, have much to say about the nature of Shakespeare's plays in performance. Marvin Carlson's *Performance: a Critical Introduction* (1996),[14] provides a careful introduction to this field of study.

Despite their large claims for attention, Performance Studies are not the only current extension to earlier work on Shakespeare on the stage. Theatre History, including the histories of acting, directing, design, and production or administration, together with the history of theatre criticism, are all being brought to bear on the study of what happens when a Shakespeare play is performed at a particular place and time or, more daringly, at no particular place or in the theatre of his own time. No longer can theatre records be read as if they were straightforward evidence: they have to be interpreted or reconstructed as very inadequate evidence of what the players were doing or how the audience was reacting. Many of the early stage histories read naïvely today, as if their writers thought that theatre had always used very much the same sort of system of presentation or as if a descriptive detail plucked from one person's account of a production was an accurate accounting of stage practice and represented the value of any moment in the progressive experience of the play in a theatre. An early and admirable example of the integration of theatre history and the study of one actor's performances and productions was Alan Hughes, *Henry Irving, Shakespearean* (1981).[15]

With recognition of the importance of Theatre History came a new resolve to relate Shakespeare's text to what can be learned about theatre practice. For a study of early performance, some sense of the physical, psychological, technical, and administrative engagement that all theatre shares is a necessary preparation for evaluating the evidence: it will also supply language to deal with the issues raised. Peter Thomson's *Shakespeare's Theatre* (1983)[16] and *Shakespeare's Professional Career* (1992)[17] show the advantages of this practical knowledge in reappraisal of evidence about the earliest performances and in renewed study of the texts. It is still more necessary for understanding the complicated production processes and equally complicated stage effects of theatre in the present technologically advanced age. A series of anthologies, called *Players of Shakespeare*,[18] has usefully collected actors' accounts of the processes of rehearsal and performance in British theatre today. But, beyond the actors' work on the text, a student of Shakespeare in Performance must also study a production's visual effects. Dennis Kennedy's *Looking at Shakespeare: a Visual History of Twentieth-Century Performance* (1993)[19] has almost single-handedly opened up this new field of study.

Acting and visual display are only part of a theatre performance; it involves an engagement between audience and actors in a particular place and a crucial element in this is the form of the building in which a performance is given. In studying this, scholarship has been aided by contemporary theatre practice which has, in a growing number of instances, returned to an open stage and the encouragement of audience participation. The new Globe Theatre in London has brought these experiments to public attention as well as concentrating on staging Shakespeare. Increasingly scholars will be more able to place an imagined performance of a text in a physical context in many ways similar to that for which the plays were written. Iain Mackintosh's *Architecture, Actor and Audience* (1993)[20] is the most useful guide available into this territory.

One effect of viewing performances in different forms of theatre is to direct attention to how much work has yet to be done on the effect of audiences on performance: the new Globe can provide something like the original structure of a theatre, but cannot begin to deliver its audience. Several studies have been concerned with the demographics of Shakespearean audiences, Andrew Gurr's *Playgoing in Shakespeare's London* (1987)[21] the most balanced and usable among them. But this enquiry proved only the beginning of a huge new subject for research: how did these people respond, together and individually, and how did that response alter the players' performances and the effect of the play on their minds? Much of present research uses verbal evidence about attitudes and does not tackle audience activity, as may be exemplified by Jean E. Howard's *The Stage and Social Struggle in Early Modern England* (1994).[22] The more practical aspects of this subject are still waiting exploration with the help of Performance Studies.

Intercultural studies are also proving useful. Instead of concentrating on so-called famous or successful productions in English-speaking theatres, the study of Shakespeare in Performance has recently been aided by comparisons from across the oceans. The 1991 Congress of the International Shakespeare Association proved a strong influence by bringing hundreds of Shakespeare scholars from the West (as they would have said) to visit Tokyo where they found themselves in company with fellow scholars from South Korea and other Asian countries besides Japan. They saw performances in the ancient traditions of Noh and Kabuki and modern productions using spectacle, music, and performance styles unfamiliar at home. Numerous scholarly initiatives followed of which the Congress papers proved to be only the beginning. Dennis Kennedy's anthology of studies by various hands, *Foreign Shakespeare* (1993),[23] is almost entirely confined to European examples, but it has proved to be the leader in a new line of studies that together will offer a global view. A number of anthologies already at press bring together scholars familiar with widely different theatrical traditions who together seek to remove contemporary and European preconceptions that have little to do with the theatre for which Shakespeare's plays were written and to open up further possibilities in production and criticism.

Moving still further from the conditions of what is usually referred to as Shakespeare's theatre (although the variety and unusual nature of many cultural circumstances of that time are increasingly seen to make that way of reference seem very inapposite) are the many scholars who have special-ized in studying Shakespeare in performance in the cinema or on television. The subject has its own present-day interest in raising questions about the means of adaptation and film-making, but here, too, scholars have found a new awareness of the actions and interactions which are inherent in the lines of dialogue as present in the printed texts. One of its advantages is that the evidence can readily be consulted many times and presented on any occasion in the classroom. The interest of this new branch of the study of Shakespeare in Performance as well as the dangers of equating a lens medium with theatre can be sampled in *Shakespeare and the Moving Image* (1994),[24] an anthology edited by Anthony Davies and Stanley Wells.

* * *

Textual and editorial studies have recently outgrown that surge of new activity after World War II which was prompted by the 'New Bibliogra-phy' and new editions now follow each other at frequent intervals using rather different editorial rules and preferences. Some of this was the prod-uct of new technology but more has been a direct result of taking on new channels of work. E. A. J. Honigmann's *The Stability of Shakespeare's Text* (1965)[25] upset accepted notions and a simple-minded pursuit of a 'definitive' text by making a comparative study of other poets who, unlike Shakespeare, have left clear evidence of how they composed and worked through various versions and, in the light of that, returning to re-consider variants in the early editions of Shakespeare. This was analogous to the new comparative study of Shakespeare in performance around the world and slowly other editors began to listen and change their expectations.

Other innovative editorial work followed a realisation that punctua-tion, stage directions, and presentation of verse and prose on the printed page could not be left to rule-of-thumb grammatical correctness and modern publishers' style-books. Editors who took on the stage histories of their plays and studied actual rehearsals and performances could not be content to accept old procedures on the nod. Some were to make intrusive addi-tions to stage directions in their texts, but almost all became more wary in these matters and their annotations began to include discussion of acting possibilities and of stage business and movements as part of an explication of the text and also to explain editorial decisions about choice between readings from different texts or in crucial matters of punctuation where, for example, a question mark instead of a full stop could change what the play is in performance as radically as a change of word or words.

A recent initiative has set out to use the new, more practical study of Shakespeare in Performance to annotate texts in single-volume editions, the *Applause Shakespeare Library* (1997 and in progress).[26] With the dialogue printed on the verso of each opening, the facing recto gives both the usual glosses and a more extensive commentary on the play in performance written by theatre director or actor. The aim is to enable a reader to 'see' the play as he or she reads the text and also to realise some of the more crucial decisions that are involved when actors make the words part of a complete, on-stage performance.

* * *

Critics, as distinguished from scholars, have long recognized the many channels their work can follow. From the earliest years of the twentieth century, they would switch around among numerous accepted ways of approaching a text: studies of genres, sources, structure, language, imagery, versification; discussions of the play's background or, as would be said today, its context, intellectual, philosophical, theological, political, cultural, social, biographical, geographical, theatrical; examination of its action, characters, argument or theme, spectacle, dialogue, music; and an understanding of all this according to psychological, historical, contemporary, or personal definitions. The criticism of Shakespeare's plays has long been a complex maze in which an explorer might well not know which way to turn.

Yet in recent years a general increase in specialization and an acceptance of the plurality of thought have together opened up Shakespeare's plays to new and intense speculation. Anthologies of self-proclaimed 'new' criticism will be found in all bookshops and libraries. *Alternative Shakespeares* (1985),[27] edited by John Drakakis, was followed by *Alternative Shakespeares 2* (1996).[28] The series of anthologies of criticism known as Casebooks, published by Macmillan over several decades and some of them issued in updated versions in the early nineteen-nineties, are in the process of being entirely replaced by collections of still newer new work on each of the principal plays. Now almost any kind of new or specialist knowledge can be brought on screen to give a different entrance to a text. Only a few deades ago, 'Feminist' or 'Gay and Lesbian Studies' were unknown or not recognized as such; now they are established sections in publishers' lists and scholarly conferences. A great deal of energetic study is fostered by bringing such issues of every-day living to bear on the criticism of the plays. This has always been part of the critical impulse, but seldom seen or presented as such. More remains to be done: one might have expected that the annual meeting of the Shakespeare Association of America in Washington, DC, in April 1997 to have scheduled a seminar on business management, promotion and hospitality where the practical expertise so much in evidence there might have been brought to bear on the records of seventeenth-century theatre companies and textual references to such matters. More surpisingly still, in the multi-racial society of modern North America, was the absence of an interest in this unique social and political phenomenon in the choice of seminar topics and the total absence of persons of color among speakers and almost total absence among attending members.

While much remains to be done among the multiple approach routes of contemporary criticism, the product of the last decades of the twentieth century is impressive for its variety and idiosyncrasy. This is a parallel development to the recognition that the study of Shakespeare in Performance cannot be practised without some entry into the many-faceted nature of performance, but here the very nature of understanding, the infinite possibilities of cognition, is a prime factor in opening up study to many different clusters of approaches each with its own appropriate methods and expertise. Terence Hawkes put this wittily in *Meaning by Shakespeare* (1992):[29]

> The point of Shakespeare and his plays lies in their capacity to serve as instruments by which we make cultural meaning for ourselves. . . . They don't in themsleves, 'mean'. It is we who mean, by them ' (147)

No predilection or intellectual concern need be unsatisfied, readers were told and then roused to enjoy and indulge this freedom and be as industrious as he was himself in nailing down every new meaning he came across. To put this provocatively, he made Lear's 'Give me the map there' (I.i.36) the key to an understanding of the entire play, turning its locks with scholarly explication about what used to be thought (or at least written) about maps and a discourse on the changing frontiers on maps in the critic's own times.

Seemingly, any arcane piece of knowledge can be shown to be relevant to some part of a Shakespeare text and then used to prize the play open and show what is inside, as if for the first time. Choice of key is as personal or accidental as that made between numerous television channels on any evening. We should not be surprised when Stephen Greenblatt starts an essay about *King Lear* with a long quotation from the *American Baptist Magazine* of 1831,[30] or Catherine Belsey[31] finds the web-footed, cross-dressed Venetian croupier heroine of a 1988 novel by Jeanette Winterson useful in explicating The *Merchant of Venice*, or Jonathan Dollimore[32] appropriates what Foucault has said about sexuality in the nineteenth and twentieth centuries to an understanding of *Measure for Measure*. So, too, the theories of literature which have supported much of this huge increase in explication have their place in providing means for critical enquiry; sometimes it is recommended that a study of theory should accompany or take priority over all study.

In *Shakespearean Negotiations* (1988),[33] Greenblatt acknowledged that 'there is something slightly absurd' in using a tract about colonial schemes to explicate a comic scene in *Henry IV*, but he argued that Shakespeare's theatre was not 'isolated by its wooden walls' from such ideas or from the wielding of power that they represent (45–6). According to this view, criticism setting off from maps or from pamphlets about parental authority, vagabonds, colonists, morality, and a million other topics is justified by the formulation of these ideas somehow, somewhere, and for some reason, as much as by any direct reference to them in playtexts or any possibility that Shakespeare might have read them at some time. As Stephen Greenblatt has said, the ultimate justification is that these ideas might have circulated among various audiences in the various theatres in which the plays were performed. The critical study of Shakespeare's texts in its most bookish and literary forms comes back to the question of audiences which, as we have seen, is one of the major new issues in the study of Shakespeare in Performance.

*   *   *

In a new multi-channelled world, contact needs to be maintained between workers in different lines of approach. This applies not only to such obviously cross-channelled subjects as audience behaviour. It will seem very strange to a scholar versed in Performance Studies or in older-fashioned stage histories to find critics quoting words taken from the dialogue of a play without regard to why and how they are said, or to whom and to what effect, and then applying them to some interpretation without regard to what is happening on stage at the time and to what the play does to its audience. Equally strange to critics will be a study of Shakespeare in Performance which generalises easily about audiences and considers theatrical enactment without a strict attention to time and place and the ideas and behaviour then in evidence or which pays little attention to the declared intentions of theatre patrons and their political masters. Textual students will be puzzled by critics or performance specialists who quote the words of a play without remembering that they represent only one version of the work, in some cases known to be either early or late in the play's composition, or who do not realise that punctuation or verse-lining may have very little authority.

Perhaps the chief challenge facing all students of Shakespeare at the end of the twentieth century is that study is becoming more particular in reference and specialized in method at the very time that it is being opened up to wide-ranging exploration. Some means must be found for maintaining contact outside any particular project that is absorbing a student's attention. In this situation the *Shakespearean International Yearbook* is a welcome initiative, especially if its editors can devise effective cross-referencing.

REFERENCES

1. O'Dell, D. (1920), (reprinted 1963), *Shakespeare – from Betterton to Irving*, 2 vols.
2. Mullin, Michael (1976), *Macbeth Onstage*, Columbia and London: University of Missouri Press, New York: Scribner's sons, New York: Dover Publications.

3. Sprague, Arthur Colby (1948), Cambridge, MA: Harvard University Press.
4. Rosenberg, Marvin (1972), *Masks of 'King Lear'*, Berkeley, Los Angeles, London: University of California Press.
5. Stamm, Rudolf, Reynolds, George F. and Beckerman, Bernard (1962), *Shakespeare at the Globe*, New York: Macmillan.
6. Bate, Jonathan and Jackson, Russell (1996), *Shakespeare: an Illustrated Stage History*, Oxford: Oxford University Press.
7. *Shakespeare in Performance*, 1998, Manchester: Manchester University Press.
8. *Text and Performance*, 1998, London: Macmillan.
9. Dessen, Alan (1995), *Recovering Shakespeare's Theatrical Vocabulary*, Cambridge: Cambridge University Press.
10. Bulman, James, C. (ed.) (1996), *Shakespeare, Theory and Performance*, London: Routledge.
11. Schechner, Richard (1988), *Performance Theory*.
12. Goffman, Erving (1959), *The Presentation of Self in Everyday Life*, New York: Doubleday.
13. Goffman, Erving (1967), *Interaction Ritual*, New York: Anchor Books.
14. Carlson, Marvin (1996), *Performance: a Critical Introduction*, New York: Routledge.
15. Hughes, Alan (1981), *Henry Irving, Shakespearean*, Cambridge: Cambridge University Press.
16. Thomson, Peter (1983), *Shakespeare's Theatre*, London and New York: Routledge.
17. Thomson, Peter (1992), *Shakespeare's Professional Career*, Cambridge: Cambridge University Press.
18. Brockbank, Philip *et al.* (ed.) (1985), *Players of Shakespeare*, Cambridge: Cambridge University Press.
19. Kennedy, Dennis (1993), *Looking at Shakespeare: a Visual History of Twentieth-Century Performance*, Cambridge: Cambridge University Press.
20. Mackintosh, Iain (1993), *Architecture, Actor and Audience*, New York: Routledge.
21. Gurr, Andrew (1987), *Playgoing in Shakespeare's London*, Cambridge: Cambridge University Press.
22. Howard, Jean, E. (1994), *The Stage and Struggle in Early Modern England*, London and New York: Routledge.
23. Kennedy, Dennis (ed.) (1993), *Foreign Shakespeare*, Cambridge: Cambridge University Press.
24. Davies, Anthony and Wells, Stanley (ed.) (1994), *Shakespeare and the Moving Image*, Cambridge: Cambridge University Press.
25. Honigmann, E.A.J. (1965), *The Stability of Shakespeare's Text*, London: Edward Arnold.
26. Brown, John R. (ed.) (1997), *Applause Shakespeare Library*, New York: Applause Books.
27. Drakakis, John (ed.) (1985), *Alternative Shakespeares*, London and New York: Methuen.
28. Hawkes, Terence (ed.) (1996), *Alternative Shakespeare 2*, London and New York: Routledge.
29. Hawkes, Terence (1992), *Meaning By Shakespeare*.
30. Greenblatt, Stephen (1990), 'The Cultivation of Anxiety: King Lear and His Heirs' reprinted in *Learning to Curse: essays in early modern culture*, New York and London, pp. 80–98.
31. Belsey, Catherine in 'Love in Venice', *Shakespeare Survey 44*, Cambridge: Cambridge University Press.

32. Dollimore, Jonathan, 'Transgression and Surveillance in *Measure for Measure*' in *Alternative Shakespeares* (op. cit., n. 27), pp. 72–87.
33. Greenblatt, Stephen (1988), *Shakespearean Negotiations*, Oxford: Oxford University Press.

PART 2

The Globe, Old and New

7   Staging the Globe

Ros King

The dominant theories as to the form of Shakespeare's theatre are now solidly embodied – in timber, lime and hair on London's South Bank. This is the problem, of course. While the current Globe's board of directors have given an assurance that they would find the funds to dismantle the timber frame and re-build it, should firm evidence be found that these design solutions are wrong, Sam Wanamaker's theatre does seem to have a permanence and solidity which some people find unsettling. Those most closely involved with the reconstruction however, are the first to admit that what has been built is merely 'a' Globe, not 'the' Globe. They are all acutely aware that at every step, faced with conflicting and ambiguous evidence – or more usually, lack of any real evidence – decisions have had to be made on the basis of best guess and compromise. They themselves have no confidence at all that they have got it right, merely that it is as right as possible given the present state of knowledge (Mulryne and Shewring, 1997)

The most frustrating part of the situation at present is that the tantalising archaeological remains of the first and second Globes discovered in 1989, remain unexcavated under Anchor Terrace and the approach road to Southwark Bridge. A radar survey carried out by the Museum of London Archaeology Service, through the metre-thick eighteenth century concrete basement of Anchor Terrace in those parts of the building which were easily accessed and not over rat-infested, in the Autumn of 1996, showed some 71 parabolic shapes indicating solid objects in the clay below the concrete. But without a much more systematic radar survey over the full estimated area of the site, ideally combined with the opportunity to test dig in some areas, it is impossible to say whether these hits describe a significant pattern.

We still tend to talk about 'the' Elizabethan theatre, but if there is anything that the chance archaeological discoveries of the last ten years have told us, it is that there were probably as many theatre designs as there were theatres. Indeed, there were two distinct designs at the Rose, the circular 1587 construction and the 1592 rebuilding which stretched the circle into a horse-shoe with the result that the original squashed hexagonal stage became slightly deeper and more thrust. Neither of these Roses bears much resemblance to what, through the De Witt drawing of the Swan and therefore the Globe film set for Laurence Olivier's *Henry V*, is firmly entrenched in the popular imagination as 'Shakespeare's theatre'. Unfortunately our need to know, now bears a heavy cost tag, for the Anchor Terrace redevelopers would have to be compensated for any delay due to late archaeological work. In any case, English Heritage has a firm (if controversial) policy of allowing only rescue archaeology on scheduled monuments, arguing that sites become endangered by bacterial attack once they are disturbed. It is clear that only solid archaeological evidence from the original Globe site will finally settle the questions as to whether the theatre was one hundred feet in diameter (as reconstructed) or smaller; whether its stage was rectilinear (as now) like the Swan drawing, or tapered like both Rose stages; and where exactly the controversial stage pillars were positioned. No amount of archaeology however will provide us with much evidence for anything else above ground level. For that, we have to draw analogies from other extant buildings of the period. For insight into the way in which the theatre was originally used, we are being thrown back both on the internal evidence of the manuscript and early printed playtexts of the period and, at the other end of the normally accepted scale of evidence, on our contemporary experiences as audiences and performers. This too is a problem. The current research interest in the use of the building is historical, but carrying out that research necessarily flies in the face of normal historicist methodology since it uses living people, actors and audiences, as both tools and subjects. Use of the building can thus be seen either as an experiment in, or a metaphor for, historic practice – that is in so far as it is not seen as historical tourism, or indeed just tourism.[1]

The very existence of the Globe looks like an attempt to deny one of the basic tenets of current literary theory: that there is irreducible difference between different societies and historical periods. It certainly requires a transcendence of the dichotomising polarities within the Shakespeare industry: between theatre and academia; text and performance; theory and practice; authenticity and modern interpretation. Whether the Globe can positively aid a transformation in critical thinking about Shakespeare remains to be seen, but there are many who would prefer to have done with it now and see it sold to Madame Tussaud's. The building is thus the site of an extraordinarily broad struggle between the conflicting demands of tourism, education, the business of running a theatre, and the ideologies of different types of scholarship. No-one should underestimate the difficulty of keeping the whole thing in balance.

Some of these problems – like the accusation of 'theme-park Shakespeare' – were anticipated. Some are surprising. Some are simply bizarre results of pragmatism. An example of the last is the discrepancy between the artistic policy of pegging standing tickets to £5 until at least the millennium so as to foster a sense of people's theatre, while being forced by lack of capital to contract out the catering, with the result that someone who could only afford to spend £5 on a ticket, could not afford to buy a coffee. The fact that one can even contemplate including such a point in an academic article on Shakespeare's theatre and staging highlights the challenge to our perceptions and practices that the Globe embodies. This sum was deemed to be the modern equivalent of the penny charged for yard admission in Elizabethan London. Accordingly, there have been several occasions in the last two years – such as for first preview performances – when yard admission has been reduced to the single penny (albeit 1p rather than 1d). Is this authenticity or PR; charming or kitsch? This article is therefore, unashamedly and necessarily at this point, a personal response to recent academic research on staging at the Globe and to three summers of workshops and productions during the workshop, prologue and opening seasons 1995–7. It is coloured by my research interests in bibliography and historical staging; by my experience as a director and as an adviser to theatre companies committed to reaching new audiences for Shakespeare; by being an audience member at the Globe on multiple occasions; and being dramaturg for the Globe prologue season production of *Damon and Pythias*. It is part of an on-going project to theoretise what we mean by 'authenticity' in Shakespearean performance, and by bringing the various normally discrete areas of architecture, text, actor technique and audience response together in one discourse, attempts to set out the conflicts and problems in both practice and academic methodology which are highlighted by the Globe's existence.

Whatever one thinks about it, the Globe is of enormous cultural importance and has constituted news with a level of staying power unheard-of in an arts story. It is the only classic theatre in Britain that is making money rather than losing it, and its influence on the popular perception of Shakespeare will be enormous. Both last year's prologue and this year's opening seasons were sell-out successes with a recent MORI poll commissioned by the Globe, finding, perhaps surprisingly, that 45 per cent of audiences had come from the London area with only 17 per cent overseas visitors.

Few people would presume to challenge the research into joints and mortises made by the theatre's latter day Peter Street, the craftsman historian, Peter McCurdey. Neither would they know, without being told, that the evident visual authenticity of the internal joinery depends on the fact that an initial plan to save time and money by turning balusters by machine had been rejected in favour of bodging each one individually on a pole lathe. The casual observer's sense of the rightness of the interior woodwork is unwittingly dependent on the infinite infinitesimal variations which resulted. The painting of the stage, tiring house façade and the musicians' gallery similarly used historically researched pigment and paint in a design inspired by both figurative and *trompe-l'oeil* marble paint effects in buildings and pictures of the period. However, the over-familiarity of the De Witt drawing – but not the Latin travelogue that accompanies it – plus the ubiquitousness of black-and-white Victorian and stock-broker tudor meant that here the casual observer has a clear (if misled) impression of what an Elizabethan building should look like and once initial amazement at all the colour and detail wears off, reaction to the very high level of decoration has sometimes been wary if not hostile.

At the time of writing (November 1997), one of the decisions still to be taken in time for next year is the extent to which the rest of the house should now be decorated. There is an historical argument for rendering the entire outside of the building – even making it look like rusticated stone-work – and thus perhaps from a distance giving the appearance of the round rather than polygonal building that appears in some of the early panoramic views of London. McCurdey however, is worried about the rot that can attack timber unseen when it is covered up in this way. There is also an aesthetic argument for painting all the remaining bare interior surfaces, although not necessarily all to the same level of detail as that on the *frons scenae*. Resistance to this comes both from people clinging to a sense of presumed Elizabethan wood and plaster simplicity, and from those arguing that the stage should be the focus of the building. This objection is at odds with the building's circularity and its same light conditions, which together mean that the audience are as much players in the action as those on the stage.

The commentary accompanying the De Witt drawing[2] is not concerned with English ethnic architecture but only with those aspects of London architecture and visual culture which most nearly approximate to that which can be found on the continent. In De Witt's eyes, the London amphitheatres are splendid precisely in so far as they look like Roman ones, with painted marble effects so well executed as to fool the 'nosiest' people (*nasutissimos*). A century's tradition of bold but essentially undecorated stage sets however, has contributed to an anxiety felt by some modern actors and directors, that an audience may not be able to see their work against such a busy background, and there have been attempts both this season and last to cover the decoration with plain cloth.

In contrast to this, Jenny Tiramani, the designer responsible for much of the decorative research, warns us to stop regarding the stage as if it were a set, but to start thinking of it instead as a 'framework'[3] for the action. She suggests that it even looks wrong when actors touch the pillars or the tiring house during the action and thinks they should rely on stage hands to open and close the entrance doors. Two plays written for the Rose theatre in 1599, *Englishmen for my Money* by William Haughton and *Two Angry Women of Abingdon* by Henry Porter indicate that other Elizabethan writers were aware of the tension between real actor, representative set and stage framework on these stages. Haughton's play demands an upper playing level, and a winch capable of hoisting an actor in a basket to the 'window' of a 'bedroom' while the stage itself variously represents the inside of a house, the street outside it and the exchange. But he also plays hilariously with false localisation in which, under cover of 'pitch darkness', the clown leads a foreign merchant a merry dance telling him as the actor staggers about bumping into the stage posts, that one of these is the 'may-pole on Ivy Bridge going to Westminster' and the other, just three lines later, the may-pole 'at the farthest end of Shoreditch' on the other side of the town (ll. 1654, ff.). In *Two Angry Women*, a similar night-time collision causes the character Dick Coomes to exclaim, 'A plague on this post! I would the carpenter had been hanged that set it up for me' (l. 2250), a sentiment that Globe actors and directors have been echoing for the last three years. It is therefore perhaps the case that the actors and writers in the Elizabethan theatres were only too aware of the limitations of their theatre buildings – as indeed actors always are – and that the dramatists exploited these difficulties to theatrical effect. Haughton's and Porter's jokes are self-reflexively about the theatre building, and depend on the premise that the characters cannot see what they are bumping into and are deluded into believing it to be something else. The scenario thus builds on the artifice rather than breaking with it: as far as the audience is concerned, the post is still the stage post and emphatically not the may-pole on Ivy Bridge. The clown meanwhile occupies the showman's position between the delusion and the reality. Therefore it is not perhaps so much the touching of the building that matters, as the semiotics of the touch. An actor playing in the stage balcony will inevitably touch the balustrade – if only because in the current design, it is necessary to lean out in order to be fully visible. But the balustrade here exists in the same realm as the actor performing – he needs it to be safe while standing on what we will accept as a metaphor for a real-life high-up space, be it city walls, monument or bedroom window.[4]

The opening of the building coincides with increasing interest amongst academics in considering Shakespeare as a writer for the theatre, but the current critical methodology belongs to literary criticism and cultural studies, and is not entirely equipped to deal with performance. Ironically, those who are most conscious of this as a problem for theatre studies in general, are performance artists who are least likely to be concerned with research into a body of work which they tend to avoid as logocentric and canonical. A collection of essays (Bulman (ed), 1996), marking the 20th anniversary of the publication of J.L. Styan's *The Shakespeare Revolution*, argues that Styan was deceived in claiming a common purpose and approach to Shakespeare amongst theatre professionals and academics. Two contributors suggest that this perception arose simply from the accident that so many British directors of the sixties and early seventies had been educated at Cambridge by F.R. Leavis (93, 163). Literary critical practices have changed radically since then. There is a far wider interest in problems associated with the transmission of the text, as well as a political commitment to retrieving marginalised voices. Yet there is no coherent theory for the analysis of texts connected with performance, and critics even within a single literary school (e.g. New Historicism) therefore cannot agree as to whether any given play of the early modern period is an example of political subversion or of political containment. The situation is no more uniform in the theatre. While actors tend towards a personal aesthetic of practical criticism combined with that of Stanislavskian method, directors usually claim the right to refashion the play – although radical design does not necessarily equate with radical reappraisal of the text. This conflict of approach has seen the rise of a number of actor-led companies over the last ten years, and an increasing number of actors taking to directing – although the result is perhaps most frequently a demonstration of a contradiction in terms. All this marks a real conflict of interest which is hindering the development of effective academic and journalistic criticism of Shakespeare and performance.

Apart from the Globe's design team, only theatre historians are currently much interested in the way in which the physical nature of the sixteenth and seventeenth century theatre building itself may have influenced the choices made by writers and performers for that theatre. However the historians' desire to establish what 'must' happen, as determined mostly by documentary or textual evidence, raising as it does both the spectre of an original writer and the presence of prescriptive academicism, pleases none of the other groups.[5] Theatre historians, used to what Michael Bristol calls the 'particularist' school of scholarship, (Bristol, 1996, 29–35) may have to get used to the messier human pragmatics of practical day to day invention. There will be no written documentary evidence for many of the solutions that are found.

In the months leading up to the start of the Globe's 1996 prologue season, Professor Andrew Gurr both hoped and regularly urged: 'the building will tell us what to do'. This sentiment, while very different from the appeals to the 'ghost of Shakespeare' made at the same time by some of the actors involved with the project, is not in itself unlike the sensitivity to the spirit of place invoked by contemporary theatre artists involved in devising site-specific work. It also bears comparison with the phrase 'genius of the place' used by eighteenth century landscape designers. In all cases the speakers are searching for a sense of authentic human engagement with a particular environment, and are appealing to human sensibility. This search is inevitably coloured by the individual's agenda as well as by training and experience, and by the exercise of something that the eighteenth century would have described by that now-maligned term 'taste'. Denis Salter records a similar hope made in connection with the construction of the first ever purpose-built Elizabethan-type theatre reconstruction:

> When, in the early 1950's, that looming patriarch of British theatre, Tyrone Guthrie, insisted on building a neo-Elizabethan open platform stage in, of all places, Stratford, Ontario, many people felt persuaded that a singularly 'Cana-

dian' style of performance would eventually emerge from what was billed as a daring New World experiment in classical actor training. (Salter, 120)

There is a good deal of sociological evidence to suggest that buildings do influence behaviour, but while actors tend to regard themselves as creatures of instinct, they also bring with them personal preferences for specific learned, professional techniques which are not accessible to instinctive change. Salter goes on to argue that Guthrie's was a reactionary indeed colonial ideal 'designed to ensure that an essentialising "Canadian-ness" ... could *never* be expressed at Stratford' and that, in its mixture of the modern, (particularly the use of realistic sets) and the 'historical' the theatre is culturally dislocated. This is an argument about authenticity in performance which has also been mirrored in critical responses to the Globe this season. Is it possible for actors, and indeed audiences, in such a strange, familiar yet alien, a-historically historical space to be themselves? How is one supposed to act, either as actor or as audience in such a theatre?

While stressing that 'firm conclusions, neat distinctions and confident truth claims do not emerge from the extant evidence', Alan Dessen (1996, 62) argues that a dramatist 'could assume a theatrical vocabulary shared by both players who knew their craft and playgoers ... [and] fall back upon some formula' to indicate the level of scenery or props needed to suggest specific places like courts, shops or gardens (50). He draws attention to the precise form of words in stage directions distinguishing between 'discovered', 'set forth' and the formulations: 'as if'; 'as in'; and 'as to'; arguing that Elizabethan writers and actors wanting to suggest, say, a shop 'had various options: (1) to draw a curtain so as to discover figures in a shop (and set up an initial tableau); (2) to have figures set forth "the shop" by means of furniture, costume, and properties (... the carrying onto the stage of a stall and merchandise ...); or (3) to have figures enter working or with the tools of their trade', the 'as if' option (59–60). As he points out, the level at which the scene change is effected has an effect on the pace of the performance. Practitioners working within the twentieth century tradition for bare-stage Shakespearean production are well-aware of such choices, but Dessen's article suggests that the precise wording of the stage direction may contain a code for performance. Whether this code is to be considered as authorially directive or simply a record of a particular performance will depend on one's view both of the bibliographical provenance of the text, and of the level of supremacy of the writing author in the collaborative business of play production. Dessen, deploring a current tendency to fall back on the catch-all strategy of textual 'indeterminacy' is urging us to make the effort to understand what might be meant.

This painstaking documentary approach to historical theatre practice cannot in itself answer the urgent needs of modern actors faced with playing the Globe space. Stanley Wells, some time ago asked, the fundamental question of principle as to the degree to which actors attempting reconstructions of early performances should feel free to elaborate on the evidence supplied by the early texts. The scholarly nature of the enterprise would appear to dictate an austere rejection of stage business for which there is no evidence, yet it is difficult to believe that the Elizabethans would have been similarly austere (Wells, 1991).

In other words, if it *can* be done using the technology available to Elizabethans, there cannot be any good reason to say that it *should not* be done, despite a complete lack of documentary evidence that it *was* done. This is the principle behind some of the empirical work being done with students in university drama departments with suggestions as to the multiple uses for a set of stage hangings (Carnegie, 1996) and principles for the use of the stage doors (Fitzpatrick, 1995). The problem here is that, given sufficient conviction and skill on the part of the performers and a readiness to accept a convention on the part of the audience, virtually anything *can* be made to work – at least for a limited period.

Discussion about the use of the doors has arisen partly because we do not absolutely know whether the Globe had two doors or three and partly from a chance remark made by Bernard Beckerman in refutation of a suggestion by George Reynolds that players maintained 'a continuing identification of one place with one entrance'. Beckerman concludes:

> As good evidence ... can be offered for a theory that actors almost always obeyed the convention of entering at one door and leaving at the other, regardless of location. ... I offer this suggestion not as a theory but as a warning against such reconstructed staging as Reynolds proposes' (Beckerman 1962, 72–3)

In fact, Reynolds' suggestion is appropriate for *some* plays. The court records of expenditure for Christmas 1564–5 show a sum paid for 'canvas to cover divers townes and howses' for use in a performance of 'Edwardes tragedy'. The play is not named, but both the date and the painted subjects fit *Damon and Pythias*. In production, we found that this play ran smoothly with one door suggesting the town and the other the court. But *Damon* is very straightforward in its disposition of characters within scenes and both entrances and exits tend to be marked by statements as to whence characters have come and where they are going. Shakespeare's plays are both much less localised and more complex in their use of mid-scene entrances and exits. This complexity, coupled with a realisation that companies maintained a turnover in performance of six plays a week with no more than two weeks between receiving a new play and its first performance, has led academics to suppose that some system must have been in use to help actors remember which door to use and prevent them colliding into one another. This is a suggestion that has not been well-received by actors, unsurprisingly. Two weeks, though short in modern terms is longer than the weekly repertory system in which older members of the profession were trained; actors are used to being physically aware of themselves and others on stage; while the combination of physical movement with a line of text, in my experience, is a fairly foolproof way of imprinting the memory. The supposition that they need anything else, is insulting. The 'revolving door' principle of staging however is now being seriously entertained and is firmly connected with Beckerman's name – which should be a lesson to us all not to make suggestions we do not believe in. During the workshop season, Tim Fitzpatrick with some students, partly in order to argue for a two door rather than a three door Globe, demonstrated a combination of the Reynolds and Beckerman theories with one door representing locations 'further in' and the other locations 'further out'. This system represents geography, but it is also relative from scene to scene, so that for example, an exit to the market place could be by one door (further out) in a scene located in a house in the town, but by another door (further in) in a scene located in the country outside the town. Although the students made it work, it did not strike me as an easy rule to remember, or particularly helpful to audiences visually.

I suggest instead that Shakespeare's plays with their high incidence of unlocalised scene settings, requirements for extensive doubling, and entrances and exits within the scene, may be using the doors dramaturgically, as a technique for telling a complex story to the audience. This approach relates the envisioning of the dramatist as story-teller, to the reception of the audience, and is easy for an actor to operate. It also raises the possibility that only a proportion of those scenes which require characters to meet each other at the beginning of the scene actually commence with a specific stage direction to enter at different doors (see *Macbeth* 1.3.0). It is predicated on two principles. Firstly that a character has to have a reason to bring him on stage over and above the fact that the author has given him lines to say, i.e. the character needs to be going somewhere – although this might be a mental journey as much as or more than a physical one. Secondly that entrances and exits need to give visual dramaturgical clues to the audience, not only on the geography of the scene, but more importantly, on the characters' interactions with each other. A character must therefore always exit by a different door from the one by which he entered, unless his exit is specifically stated to be back in the geographical direction of his entrance in that scene. But in order for us, the audience, firstly to maintain a mental image of what that character is doing while he is absent from the stage, secondly to understand both literally and metaphorically where he is coming from at his next entrance, and perhaps even distinguish between that character and another character doubled by the same actor, he should re-enter from the door at which that character previously exited. This gives rise to a simple rule: exit from a scene by the door opposite to your entrance door unless otherwise directed by the dialogue, and re-enter in your next scene as that character by that character's previous exit door. Following this directive, exits and entrances in the plays that I have so far examined, (*Twelfth Night, Macbeth*) are found to follow a logical arrangement: within any given scene, characters coming from the same place use the same entrance doors – because this is the way the action has been envisioned. Such a scheme may not necessarily apply to texts which preserve pre-performance versions of the play. It will be seen that only in those instances where a meeting by several doors requires actors to break the 're-enter by character's previous exit door' rule (as at *Twelfth Night* , 2.2.) is the stage direction 'enter by several doors' or 'enter character A by one door and character B by another' actually required. The operation of this rule in *Twelfth Night* reveals numerous instances in which multiple-character entrances which might have been assumed to be by the same door become much more dynamic onstage meetings, conveying significant dramaturgical information.

The process of designing the decorative scheme for the stage and *frons scenae* at the Globe reconstruction has had an entirely unexpected effect on thinking about the conceptual extent of the playing space. A decision to incorporate the ceiling of the musicians' gallery and Lords' rooms in the tiring house, into the scheme for the heavens, in order to unite the gallery and its playing space visually with the stage, had the added advantage of rendering the total playing area almost a square within the circle of the theatre, thus better conforming to Renaissance principles of design. It also drew attention to the immediate backstage area behind the *frons* at stage level. Half-way through the season, it was decided to paint the stage floor, continuing the colour backstage correspondingly with the gallery above. The total playing space conceptually, now includes those areas hidden to the audience but which might be thought of as containing any characters speaking 'within'. This has interesting implications for both directors and editors. The passage in which Horatio and Marcellus are looking for Hamlet (*Hamlet*, 1.5.113–20) for example, might become a mini off-stage scene. Neither Q1 nor Q2 contains any direction 'within' prior to these characters' entrance in this scene, but F contains that word for their shared line 'My lord, my lord' immediately prior to their entrance which is marked a line later than in Q2. *Pace* Oxford's *Textual Companion* the entrance is marked indeterminately in Q1, in the margin. The dialogue that follows between people who still cannot see each other, seems so difficult to bring off without unwanted risibility when fully visible to the audience, that it is often cut. F reads as follows:

> [*Hamlet* contd.] It is; Adue, Adue, Remember me: I have sworn't.
> *Horatio and Marcellus within.* My Lord, my Lord.
>
> *Enter Horatio and Marcellus*
>
> | Marcellus. | Lord Hamlet |
> | Horatio. | Heaven secure him. |
> | Marcellus. | So be it.   (NB. not in Q1; ascribed to Hamlet in Q2) |
> | Horatio. | Illo, ho, ho, my lord. |
> | Hamlet. | Illo, ho, ho, boy; come bird, come. |
> | Marcellus. | How is't my Noble Lord? |
> | Horatio. | What newes, my Lord? |

F's ascription of 'So be it' to Marcellus is not absolutely wrong in itself, but compared with Q2's ascription to Hamlet, it is syntactically odd, less interesting and therefore probably a printing error. The version in Q2 gives us, linguistically, two parallel scenes, with Hamlet still finishing his vow to 'remember' his father, but it does not direct the staging except to call conventionally for an entrance for Marcellus and Horatio immediately before they speak. F's 'within' (and arguably Q1's indeterminate entrance) demand some use of the offstage space. If F's marking of the entrance is regarded as the introduction of an error through collation with Q2 – and it has long been suggested that this process is operating in *Hamlet* (Walton, 1971, 175–193) – then the entire exchange can be seen as making drama-turgical use of the off-stage space, the actual entrance being delayed as long as the actors need it to be, probably down to, 'How is't, my noble lord?'.

Hitherto, the editing of Shakespearean texts has been a bibliographical process, coloured (often unacknowledgedly) by literary taste and theatrical tradition. It is now beginning to be recognised that theatrical considera-tions need to be more consciously incorporated into the editing process (Foakes, 1997). To directors this understandably looks like an encroach-ment on their domain by people insufficiently skilled in the practical business of theatre, although it must be stressed that most directors, ac-tors, students and indeed literary critics are unaware of the extent to which their interpretations have always been skewed by the reprinting of traditional but not necessarily original stage-directions. Neither Iago's ac-quisition of the handkerchief by 'snatching it' from Emilia (3.3.319, first printed by Rowe) nor his wounding of Cassio in the leg (5.1.26, first printed by Theobald), are the only, let alone the best, possible performance choices, yet they remain, albeit in square brackets, in the latest Arden edition, and the latter at least occurred in the 1997 production at the Royal National Theatre in London.

The notion of textual instability has led to renewed interest in the eight-eenth and nineteenth century acting versions of Shakespeare (Ripley, 1996; Osbourne, 1996). These co-existed with the literary (usually Folio based editions) to which modern editions are heir. In my view however it is a mistake to regard these *re-written* texts, interpretations of the original – changed, eked out, 'improved' to fit very culturally-specific moral impera-tives – as if they are equivalent to the performance versions played by the company of which Shakespeare himself was a member. Unlike the earlier texts, the language of these plays allows only a very narrow range of possible meanings and they therefore remain irredeemably implacable to interpretation on anything but their own terms. The problem is that these versions of Shakespeare, pandering to specific social, political or moral attitudes, spawned theatrical and critical traditions and preconceptions which have tended to outlast the restoration of original textual readings. It is not enough just to declare that all readings are necessarily situated in their own time and place. We need to re-examine every part of our current readings and question whether we are not in fact still unwittingly abiding by readings which emanate from other historical, but not Shakespearean, times and places – traditional Shakespeare, maybe, but not authentic either to ourselves now, or to the 'originals' – whatever we take those to be.

Traditional, establishment Shakespeare, is something cultured out of eighteenth and nineteenth century textual accretions but it is too often equated with 'authentic' or even 'original' Shakespeare. It is time to separate these terms. Original Shakespeare is, to us now, unknowable. It would depend on replicating not just the text and the conditions of a particular performance, but the particular mix of mind-sets in the audience that witnessed that performance and their individual responses to it. Authentic Shakespeare by contrast is something which would be critically cognisant of currently best guesses at the text and of original performance practice, and would continually be developing a performance style capable of mediating that to contemporary audiences. Far from being pickled in aspic, as traditional Shakespeare is, it would necessarily change with new research, and developing audience/performer experience, just as, in the last twenty years, the authentic movement in music has developed and changed out of all recognition, broadening knowledge, understanding and experience in the process, and bringing insight and new clarity even to over-familiar works in the classical and romantic repertoires.

Whether or not the descriptions of rowdiness to be found in antitheatrical tracts (of all periods) accurately describes the authentic behaviour of sixteenth century audiences, the modern public certainly believes that this is how 'they' behaved. This season's Globe audience members regularly exchanged such information amongst themselves and, encouraged by newspaper reports, came prepared to play that part, albeit mostly in a very restrained way. Very few people actually threw things, and while comparatively large numbers fainted (for some as yet unexplained reason) no-one in the audience was assaulted. In comparison with the genuinely authentic rowdy behaviours displayed at football matches it was rather poorly acted. Additionally, the regeneration of the South Bank which the Globe rightly sees as being in part at least due to its presence, and which is without doubt a desirable thing in principle, means that the ambient area is rapidly ceasing to be a place of danger, and now for the first time since the Medieval period, reflects, rather than contrasts with, the wealth of financial London facing it across the river. It has become domesticated, indeed pretty (as well as pretty pretentious).

Bryan Reynolds has argued that 'transversal power radiates from the [Elizabethan] public theatre, such that everyone exposed to this theatrical nexus's efflorescing reach, including its most fervent enemies, was infected with transversal thought' (Reynolds, 1997, 143–167). If Reynolds is right, and 'Instead of reflecting or affirming a "sensibly" ordered society, this transversal theatre served as a transmitter for the novel idea that the world

is negotiable, performative, manipulable' (154), then an authentic historical performance of plays of that period needs to be capable of raising
similar fundamental questions of real psychological, social and political
importance to a modern audience. This is where, to my mind, the 1997
Globe production of *Henry V* went so badly wrong. A directorial decision
to find and concentrate on a 'mythic' element in the story, combined with
a readiness to accept and indeed encourage rabidly anti-French play-acting
in the audience as if it were both genuine and morally unproblematic,
meant that all subtlety – all sense of the play as 'negotiable' – was lost.
Sure, the audiences enjoyed themselves, but they will have come away
reinforced in the (erroneous) belief that the play is simply a piece of
pageantry glorifying England at war with her nearest neighbour. The
American actors playing the French, initially personally distressed by the
response they were arousing, and seemingly unaware that they were themselves encouraging this with significant looks and pregnant pauses, actually
described their characters as 'villains' on the TV documentary that was
made to mark the opening of the theatre (Channel 4, 1997). This treatment of the French was only matched by the simultaneous sentimentalising
and de-legitimising of Bates and his fellows, and (with the notable exception of Toby Cockerell's graceful Katherine) by the pantomime-dame
presentation of the female characters by male actors. By focusing on
Henry's personal agony of responsibility under the yoke of mythic kingship, the production failed to give due weight to the play's dissenting
voices. There was no real moral or intellectual contest on the stage; nothing to challenge received notions about the meaning of the play; and
therefore no possibility of anything but cod-Elizabethan acting from the
audience. As an audience member – on three occasions – opposed to
gratuitous racial abuse I was deeply angered by feeling that I was being
allowed only one option: to join in the booing. Anything else was outside
the contract that had been set up from the stage and therefore, bizarrely,
would actually be offensive behaviour. In the end I remained silent, hating
myself for not objecting more actively, simultaneously aware that if my
stony face was spotted from the stage it would do nothing for actor/
academic relations and resenting being put in such an impossible position.
So much for authenticity.

A similar reaction is recorded by Athenaide Dallett in an analysis of
audience behaviour at an avowedly revolutionary theatre event staged on
a university campus during a period of actual political protest in 1968.
Here the actors were expecting to elicit revolutionary behaviour from the
audience, by inviting them to decide on the outcome of the play, although
only within certain carefully-controlled parameters. The result was, it is
claimed, manifestly less revolutionary than that with which the audience
were themselves engaged on the campus. A member of the audience is
quoted as observing that silence was the only effective protest to the
production, as verbal objection would have been playing the actors' rather

inadequate game. Dallett contrasts this incident with the riots that attended the first production of Synge's *Playboy of the Western World* , in which the audiences took violently hostile exception to what they perceived to be the message of the play, and concludes that when a performance is disrupted by the spectators whether by unwanted silence or unwanted riot, 'it is usually the case that the rioters deem their uprising a justified response to some sort of abrogation of the theatrical contract by the performance' (Dallett, 1996, 323–4).

This observation should make us question the motivation behind the standard anti-theatrical (and here we can now read anti-film and anti-TV) argument that theatre incites lawlessness. A politically engaged response in accord with the content of the play – such as attended Middleton's parable on the Spanish marriage, *A Game at Chess* in 1624 or Ion Caramitrou's production of *Hamlet* in Bucharest immediately prior to the fall of the Ceauscescu regime – might be expected to be more likely to produce a passionate desire to *see* the show, not to disrupt it. Much more work therefore needs to be done on the nature of the contract between audience and performer, and again, because evidence for any one period is so scanty it will be necessary to draw analogies from differing times and places. Jane Moody thus uses Stephen Greenblatt's famous essay 'Invisible Bullets' as a springboard to argue for potentially revolutionary voices in nineteenth century nautical melodramas but her conclusions can usefully be reapplied back to the renaissance:

> Greenblatt seems to interpret theatrical spectatorship wholly in terms of unconscious process. This language of apprehension – manifestation, engagement, prohibition – characterises audiences as an unindividuated group in silent and complicit absorption of spectacle. Greenblatt's definition of theatricality would seem to be incompatible with the acknowledgement of spectators as capable, active human agents' (Moody, 1996, 64).

Greenblatt of course is not alone in regarding audience behaviour in this way. The general consensus is that audiences are passive spectators simply because they do not normally alter the actual outcome of the story although it is universally accepted that their response might feed back to the actors, altering the quality of the performance. A modern audience allowed to play-up as undifferentiated groundlings at the new Globe, without reference to their own individual beliefs, highlights the dangers of pastiche historicity. The plays presented in the opening season covered four genres, two, if not three, original playhouses and also enjoyed performances at court.[6] Each of those playing spaces would have had different audience profiles (Gurr, 1987, 151–3), with perhaps different styles of performance (Sutcliffe, 1996, 128), and different standards of audience behaviour. No matter what the attempts to recreate historic costumes and performance conditions on the stage, the only place for an audience to be, emotionally and intellectually, is in the present, in direct and honest interaction with the story that is being presented to them.

Performers in the *Henry V* company at the Globe did not want to be on the receiving end of baguettes lobbed from the pit as they were on one occasion, but none of the actors felt that it was their job to attempt to control the audience overtly from within the persona of their character – as for example a stand-up comic would do, and as the *Damon and Pythias* company had been encouraged to do. Without the control that comes from dimming the lights, it seemed difficult even to begin the show. At the post-season review John Orrell suggested using a blast of trumpet, but this might be coming at the problem from the wrong side – replacing the clue of the lights rather than re-discovering what actors had done before lights. *Henry V* used pre-performance off-stage drumming with wooden staves, which was then brought onto stage and stopped with a hand-signal from Rylance – this had also been conceived as an aural time capsule, transporting the audience back to another world. *Damon and Pythias* had taken its clue from one of the opening lines 'Silence in all ears bent, I plainly do espy' so that Anna Niland as Prologue came on stage and waited, eye-balling the audience until they were attentive. Indeed, throughout this production, we found that it was unabashed eye-contact that made the difference, enabling Pythias (Patricia Kerrigan) to prevent audience reaction from getting out of hand, and Stephano (Julie Markey) to whip it up so that they incited her to beat up the villain Carisophus.

Henry Irving's dimming of the auditorium lights marked the culmination of the two hundred and fifty year process of retreat into a three-dimensional illusionist set. It left actors free to concentrate on the verisimilitude of the emotional experience of the character, and militated against the meta-theatricality of direct character/audience interaction that is written-in to Shakespearean and pre-Shakespearean texts. While few actors today would want to restrict themselves to a fourth wall theatrical experience – at least for Shakespeare – the largest part of their training and their rehearsal practice, *including* that for Shakespeare, is actually predicated on such a presupposition. Of this the single largest part, is voice training as promulgated by the work of Cicely Berry, Patsy Rodenburg and Kristen Linklater – although ironically the single most frequently repeated journalistic criticism of Shakespeare productions is probably that the actors concerned could not speak the language intelligibly. Richard Knowles, suggests 'that the influence of Berry on the RSC has been significantly more direct than that of Brook, or arguably of any other single figure, though as a voice coach (gendered female) she has been less celebrated' (Knowles, 1996, 95). He goes on to question the mystical nature in which these three authors write of 'freeing the natural voice' a concept which goes beyond the purely physical skills required for breath control and voice production to encompass the much vaguer concepts of personal freedom, personal growth and 'organic' wholeness, with Berry urging the actor to remain 'free to our basic primitive response to [the language] – primitive in the sense of being less consciously organised, and less culturally based' (Berry, *The Actor and His Text,* cited Knowles, 97). As Knowles points out, even the apparently neutral skills of breathing 'properly' are actually culturally determined – as can be attested by the different timbres of the spoken and particularly the singing voice in different cultures around the world and even within different styles of western classical music. The idea that actors should be 'primitively' aware of Shakespeare's language may be one reason why the critics despair of modern Shakespearean verse-speaking.

A similar strongly critical line on the professed anti-intellectual, emotionally therapeutic stance of voice work is taken by Sarah Werner, but from a specifically feminist angle:

> For the feminist actor, this emphasis on psychological healing and the prioritisation of therapy over political action limits her ability to call attention to the politics in the text ... Language that is organic and natural is not language that challenges societal structures. (Werner, 1996, 250).

Werner's approach, premised on the belief that Shakespeare's plays present an unredeemed misogynist message, is as ideological as that of the three voice specialists she castigates and is at odds with the transactional approach favoured by Reynolds (13 above). However her observation that the tendency of the actor to 'explain characters' actions and emotion in terms they are familiar with' (252) was certainly the motivation behind actor/director Jack Shepherd's direction of *Two Gentlemen of Verona* for the prologue season in 1996. Much of the rehearsal time was spent in improvising new scenes tangentially to the play's story (e.g. Silvia visiting her shrink) with the result that the cast simply ran a mile from the difficult philosophical and culturally specific concepts enclosed in lines like 'All that was mine in Silvia I give thee' (5.4.83). Blocking was similarly determined on the basis of what people would do in the situations that had been imposed on the text (e.g. sitting in a café for the opening scene), and ignored both the structures of the language, and the sight-line problems of the stage. These are considerable, but only if scenes are blocked as if the stage were a proscenium arch looking to the front. It was to me the greatest disappointment of the 1997 season that the seating price structure quite unhistorically reinforced that orientation and that none of the directors took the challenge of playing to the sides, or exploring ways in which staging might be inspired by an awareness of patterns and rhythms in the language.

However the use of single-sex casts in both 1996 and 1997, all male for *Henry V* and all female for Richard Edwards' *Damon and Pythias* written for the boys of the Chapel Royal, provided some useful evidence. Toby Cockerell's Katherine was indeed a piece of *trompe l'oeil* capable of deceiving the nosiest spectators and should finally have nailed the often-repeated, suggestion, unsupported except by reference to those ubiquitous and biased anti-theatrical propagandists, that boys wearing dresses provided a sexual frisson, *as boys,* for male audience members. Cockerell himself was both no longer a boy in the accepted age limits of the term, and also, ironically, much more convincing as Katherine than he was in his doubled role as Boy. His performance corroborated two less theatrically hostile English Renaissance eye-witness responses to boy actor perform- ances. One is the report of Queen Elizabeth warmly congratulating and rewarding the boy playing Emilia in Edwards' lost play *Palamon and Arcite* during her 1566 visit to Oxford – this despite the fact that the part was interpreted by members of the audience as urging her to marry. The other, is Henry Jackson's famous letter of 1610, describing a moving performance of the death of Desdemona in which the boy actor is repeat- edly referred to as 'she', and which Anthony Dawson adduces as evidence that it 'puts into question the reading of the victimised, subjected Desdemona that some recent critics have seen as central to the cultural work the play is said to have performed' (Dawson 1996, 35).

I had wanted to use an all-female cast for *Damon and Pythias*, as a multiple exercise in defining authenticity. Firstly, it would extend the range of parts available to female actors – as necessary to the authenticity of our present age and society as the extension of classic roles to non-white actors; secondly it would explore a dislocation between actor and character that might be analogous to the playing of adult male roles by boys – the only way in which it would now be possible to do this in a professional context. The production was generally enthusiastically received by an audience of 900 people and was very well reviewed.[7] Two other cross-gendered produc- tions in the UK during these two years, Fiona Shaw's performance as Richard II in Deborah Warner's production (1996) and Kathryn Hunter's perform- ance of King Lear (1997), both generated a great deal of media interest. These four productions together raise theoretical questions about the nature of cross-gendered casting generally: is the purpose of such practice to play the opposite gender, or to play the specific role? Are we trying to deceive, or is the tangential light which can be cast on a role when the actor's own gender is visibly at odds with that of the character, useful or disturbing? Toby Cockerell's performance demonstrated that sixteenth century English theatrical practice was capable of presenting convincing femininity as a piece of deception. Edwards' writing for *Damon and Pythias* in contrast presents an entire parallel universe, self-reflexively aware of the play's in- tended performance by schoolboys. It incorporates their daily activity reading the classics, and plays on their relative sizes, both to each other and to adult males – it has no female characters. It was this dislocation that we were trying to capture with a cast of women, not trying to pass as men, but simply wearing male clothes. Fiona Shaw's own gender similarly shone through her presentation of Richard as male, but for different reasons and to different effect. In Deborah Warner's subsequent estimation, it was suc- cessful because, far from dislocating actor and character, it highlighted perceived feminine aspects of the role. Shaw's effect on cast and audiences was not what Warner had anticipated:

> I wanted everybody who came across Richard to have a great big problem when they met this person who must be male through virtue of being a king, yet who looked like a woman and was effeminate. I was very much looking forward to that being a problem that everybody would have to work with. In fact the company completely accepted that this was Richard II and I have to say now in the light of that, that this is Shakespeare's play. Whoever plays the role, everybody will readily accept them as Richard. So having thrown in a very rich colour, it was somehow diluted within the drama. (Cousin and Warner, 233).

This raises questions as to what constitutes 'Shakespeare's play', not to mention a monarch and a 'woman'. But if casting has been done on the basis of the best *person* for the character, could not that character be presented in the same sex as the actor, so as to ensure that the casting is seen as casting and not as cross-gendering? Since Elizabeth I reputedly described herself as Richard II, I would like to see what Shaw would make of the part if it were simply re-presented as female, rather than cross-gendered as 'effeminate'.

One of the other reasons for the sense of dislocation in *Damon and Pythias*, in addition to its use of boys, is its genre. The play is the first tragi-comedy to be written in English. At one point, Patricia Kerrigan singing Pythias' extremely emotional lament, which during the dress-rehearsal had brought tears to the eyes of the few individuals scattered about the auditorium, had difficulty in holding back the mirth of a two-thirds capacity house. It was a genuine spectator-sport tussle and she won, but it was a difficult few minutes. Had the production mis-fired in its choice of music? Or is there something in the mixture of comedy and high-tragedy that we need to explore and exploit in our productions of renaissance tragedies? While in the privacy of an empty (or darkened) auditorium we did (and might) have gone with the fiction of virtuous self-sacrifice that this play recounts, in full light, surrounded by nine hundred other people who might not behave so selflessly for a friend, the audience perhaps found it unworldly and slightly ludicrous. Therefore, because they knew they should not be laughing at such a display of serious virtue, it was shocking – which provoked more laughter – an uneasy tension which was only resolved by the play's own comedic conclusion.

So, where are we now? In a state of flux certainly, and perhaps on the cusp of exciting change. The representation of Shakespeare's theatre that has been staged in Sam Wanamaker's Globe is probably not accurate but it is authentic to its materials and its builders and is as close as we are currently likely to get to the concept 'Elizabethan theatre'. Since as we now know, the original buildings were all variations on a theme rather than identical structures it does not in fact invalidate the experiment if this one is different too. The salient feature of the design which marks it off from all other twentieth-century British theatres, is that it supports an audience on multiple levels relatively close to and on all sides of the stage who share the same light as the performers. Perhaps most importantly, part at least of that audience is on its feet. An audience which is lit knows that it is itself on show, while a standing audience has a completely different level of energy and involvement from one that is seated because its members are making a considerable physical investment. The building is influencing audience behaviour, and it would be interesting to see what would happen if standing room were to be allowed in the galleries where people (all seated) currently feel and behave much more detached than those in the yard. However the performances which until now have appeared on the stage itself have been far from authentic either to the texts or to the experience and needs of late twentieth century humankind, and this in turn has encouraged inauthentic play-acting in the audience. Playing the Globe demands greater strength, vigour, pace, flexibility and guts than anything we have seen on the stage so far. I do not think we go to such a theatre simply to witness displays of emotion within the actor. Instead we need actors with the confidence to play the whole space three-dimensionally and thereby to play us, the audience, as individuals: to face us and confront us; to know that they can draw us in by *turning away* to confront some other part of the house; to push and to pull so that it is *our* emotions which are made to turn on the knife-edge between mirth and tragedy, and *our* intellects that engage in the dialectic of the drama. The experiment on Bankside demands new approaches to actor training, to textual editing and to criticism. It will make us aware of the ghosts of sixteenth-century staging practices in the writing of the plays of the period which would otherwise remain invisible. What we do with these insights and the ways in which we incorporate or transcend them in modern performance, both at the Globe and elsewhere, will remain a subject for discourse.

REFERENCES

1. See Shackley, 'When is the past? Authenticity and the Commoditization of Heritage', *Tourism Management*, 15, (5) 1994.
2. 'A Note on the Swan Theatre Drawing', *Shakespeare Survey*, 1, 1948, 23–4.
3. 'Framing Shakespeare', Directors' Guild of Great Britain conference, 30 June, 1997.
4. Consideration of the stage as a metaphor for a real place rather than an imitation of reality allows us to entertain ideas about practices which would otherwise seem completely alien. The Original Shakespeare Company (dir. Patrick Tucker) uses a fully visible on-stage prompter whose presence quickly gets forgotten by the audience. This is little different from classical Japanese conventions about invisible stage attendants and reflects a practice recorded in 1602 in Cornwall by Richard Carew, see Butterworth, Philip (1992), 'Book-carriers: Medieval and Tudor Staging Conventions', *Theatre Notebook*, Vol. XLVI, No. 1.
5. Alan Dessen's '"Taint not thy Mind": Problems and Pitfalls in Staging Plays at the New Globe', in *New Issues in the Reconstruction of Shakespeare's Theatre*, ed. Franklin J. Hildy, (New York: Peter Lang) 1990, unfortunately expresses his advice to the players in the form of ten commandments.

6. *Henry V, The Winter's Tale, The Maid's Tragedy,* at the Globe, the latter two probably also written with the Blackfriars in mind, *Chaste Maid in Cheapside* at the Swan. WT, *H5* and *MT* are known to have played at court.
7. The *Guardian*, 11.9.96, the *Scotsman* 13.9.96.

BIBLIOGRAPHY

Beckerman, Bernard (1962) *Shakespeare at the Globe 1599–1609,* New York; London: Collier; Macmillan.

Bristol, Michael D. (1996) 'How Good Does Evidence Have to Be?' in Pechter (1996).

Bulman, James C. (ed) 1996), *Shakespeare, Theory and Performance,* London; New York: Routledge.

Carnegie, David (1966), 'Stabbed Through the Arras: The Dramaturgy of Elizabethan Stage Hangings', in Kerr, Heather; Eaden, Robin; Mitton, Madge (eds), *Shakespeare: World Views,* Newark; London: University of Delaware Press; Associated University Press.

Cousin, G. and Warner, D. (1996), 'Exploring space at Play, The Making of the Theatrical Event, An Interview with Deborah Warner', *New Theatre Quarterly,* Vol. 12, No. 47, 229–236.

Dallett, Athenaide (1996), 'Protest in the Playhouse: Two Twentieth Century Audience Roits', *New Theatre Quarterly,* **12,** (48), November.

Dawson, Anthony B. (1996), 'Performance and Participation: Desdemona, Foucault, and the Actor's Body', in Bulman (1996).

Dessen, Alan C. (1996) 'Recovering Elizabethan Staging: A Reconsideration of the Evidence' in Pechter (1996)

Fitzpatrick, Tim (1995) 'Shakespeare's Exploitation of a Two-Door Stage: Macbeth' *Theatre Research International,* **20,** (3) 207–230.

Foakes, R.A. (1997), 'On Finishing a Commentary on King Lear', in *Shakespearean Continuities: Essays in Honour of E.A.J.Honigmann,* John Patchelor, Tom Cain, Claire Lamont (eds), London; New York: Macmillan; St Martin's Press.

Gurr, Andrew, (1987) *Playgoing in Shakespeare's London,* Cambridge: Cambridge University Press.

Hamilton, Derek (1995) *Shakespeare's Use of Doors on the Elizabethan Stage,* Dissertation, University of New Brunswick.

Haughton, William (1616), *Englishmen for my Money,* ed. W.W. Greg (1912), Malone Society Reprints, Oxford: Oxford University Press.

Knowles, Richard Paul (1996), 'Shakespeare, Voice, and Ideology: Interrogating the Natural Voice' in Bulman (1996).

Moody, Jane (1996), 'Silence of New Historicism: A Mutinous Echo from 1830', *Nineteenth Century Theatre,* **24,** (2), Winter.

Mulryne, Ronnie; Shewring, Margaret (eds) (1997), *Shakespeare's Globe Rebuilt,* Cambridge: Cambridge University Press.

Osbourne, Laurie E. (1996), 'Rethinking the Performance Editions: Theatrical and Textual Productions of Shakespeare', in Bulman (1996).

Pechter, Edward (ed.) (1996), *Textual and Theatrical Shakespeare: Questions of Evidence,* Iowa City: University of Iowa Press.

Porter, Henry (1599), *Two Angry Women of Abingdon,* ed. W.W. Greg (1912), Malone Society Reprints, Oxford: Oxford University Press.

Reynolds, Bryan (1997), 'The Devil's House, "or worse": Transversal Power and Antitheatrical Discourse in Early Modern England', *Theatre Journal,* 49, (2) May.

Ripley, John (1996), 'Coriolanus as Tory Propaganda', in Pechter (1996).

Salter, Denis (1996), 'Acting Shakespeare in Postcolonial Space' in Bulman (1996).

Sutcliffe, Christopher (1996), 'Kempe and Armin: The Management of Change', *Theatre Notebook,* 50, (3).

Walton, J.K. (1971) *The Quarto Copy for the First Folio of Shakespeare,* Dublin: Dublin University Press.

Wells, Stanley (1991), 'Staging Shakespeare's Ghosts', in Biggs, Murray *et al* (eds), *The Arts of Performance in Elizabethan and Early Stuart Drama: Essays for G.K.Hunter,* Edinburgh: Edinburgh University Press.

Werner, Sarah (1996), 'Performing Shakespeare: Voice Training and the Feminist Actor', *New Theatre Quarterly,* XII, (47) August.

8   The Still-Elusive Globe: Archaeological remains and scholarly speculations

John G. Demaray

Of the three principal places where Shakespeare's dramas were staged in the late-sixteenth and early-seventeenth centuries – the Globe and other open-air public theatres; the Inns-of-Court chambers and private indoor playhouses, most notably Blackfriars; and the royal chambers and Masquing House at Whitehall – research and interpretation in recent years has focused with keenest intensity upon the Globe. 'Shakespeare's theatre' retains a hallowed fascination in its own right; and the publication of each new speculation on its possible design stirs extended technical debates, some shedding helpful light on issues of performance criticism.

Court staging at Whitehall, and its influence on Shakespeare's imagination, has by contrast been swept somewhat into the background in recent years given the excitement and debate generated by the hurried, partial Southwark excavations in 1989 and 1991 of the foundations of the Rose theatre just off Maiden Lane, and of small segments of what are probably Globe foundations off nearby Park Lane. A deluge of popular and scholarly commentary on 'Shakespeare's theatre' has been generated too by the highly publicized opening in June, 1997, in Southwark, not far from the excavations of the two theatres, of a full-scale reconstruction of the Globe. As is well known, the original theatre, first erected in 1599, was destroyed by fire in June 1613, rebuilt on the original foundations and reopened in 1614, and then torn down in 1644.

Have the excavation findings, and the design problems posed in trying to recreate a modern copy of the early theatre, actually added anything authoritative to knowledge about the original Globe? The answer has to be a tentative yes. But to place the excavation results and design considerations in perspective, it is helpful to note how conflicted are both past and recent speculations about structural details of the Globe. Like the ghost of Hamlet's father, the theatre remains rather mysterious because early documentation is lacking on its exact dimensions and features, documentation of a kind abundantly available for court theatrical spaces such as the Whitehall Masquing House and Grand Chamber.

Until the excavation reports were published beginning in 1989, past design commentary has always rested heavily on the confusing primary evidence of early drawings and etchings which hardly inspire scholarly confidence about the theatre's form. Two *Civitas Londeni* maps by John Norden published in 1600 (one revised from his 1593 *Speculum Britanneae* map, with the Globe added) reveal the theatre, open to the sky at its core, as having exterior walls respectively circular and then hexagonal. In the hexagonal-sided rendering, the Globe has a tower. Yet the theatre is seen with octagonal walls sloping inward in a panoramic depiction of London by Claes Jan Visscher published in Amsterdam in 1616. On the other hand, the eye-witness drawings of Bohemian artist Wenceslaus Hollar, reconstituted and etched in Antwerp in 1647, reveal a 'Long View' of London with the second Globe, mis-labelled in the etching as a 'Beere bayting' arena, appearing as a circular structure oriented to the north. This second Globe is ringed with a single line of windows, abutted by two seeming stairwells respectively on its eastern and western façade, and surmounted to the south by a dome-like turret rising above a stage roof.[1]

Precise data on the dimensions of an early public playhouse surfaced in 1790 when Edward Malone published a contract, which mentioned the Globe in passing, for the building of Henslowe's Fortune Theatre, a square structure having an over-all width of 80-foot, a 55-foot-wide square inner courtyard, and a 43-foot-wide stage. Finally, a drawing by Johannes de Witt discovered in 1888 shows a public playhouse interior, apparently that of the Swan erected in 1595, with a large rectangular or possibly square stage. At the rear of this performing space are two doors at stage level and a gallery with a railing on a second level. From the stage rise two circular pilasters supporting a roof which overhangs both stage and rear gallery.

Of the most reliable primary sources for insights into Globe design – Hollar's relatively detailed eye-witness drawings and etching, the Fortune theatre contract, and the de Witt interior drawing – only the Hollar illustrations actually have the Globe as their subject, and this is the second Globe erected in 1614. Although these materials together with circumstantial evidence leave most basic design questions unanswered or moot, a previous generation of scholars used them, along with stage directions and textual materials, hypothetically to re-create, with much speculative and imaginative elaboration, accounts and drawings of a complete and fully-furnished first Globe playhouse. This Globe of 1599 was regularly presented, sometimes with the aid of photographs of miniature three-dimensional models built by the authors or their students, as a polygon with six or eight external sides, a generally circular interior, a two-level stage with rear chambers closed by a curtain on each level, and with a roof or 'heaven' projecting over the stage and supported by two small, square pilasters. This general hypothetical theatre-type emerges in works such as John Cranford Adams's *The Globe Playhouse: Its Design and Equipment*; C. Walter Hodges's *The Globe Restored*; Irwin Smith's *Shakespeare's Globe Playhouse* which made frequent use of Adam's projections; and Leslie Hotson's *Shakespeare's Wooden O*.[2]

A provocative and encompassing general design theory, one resting on occultist materials but in accord with Renaissance notions of cosmic correspondence and hierarchy, was advanced in the 1960s by Frances A. Yates in *Theatre of the World*.[3] But it was a theory that did little convincingly to establish concrete components of the Globe's structure. The Globe should be considered a microcosm, Yates argued, built to correspond to the wider universe, the macrocosm, with a necessarily square stage signifying humanity, a stage roof on its painted underside signifying the heavens, an earthen pit signifying the world, and the pit's circular interior form signifying cosmic patterns manifest in the perfect circles of the nested spheres. Her specific comments on the construction of the rear stage, however, came from occultist materials well removed from any actual documents about the Globe itself.

In recent books published before excavation results were announced, C. Walter Hodges and John Orrell attempted to uncover a range of specific features of the second Globe through minute analysis of Hollar's pencil sketches made from the tower of St Saviour, now Southwark Cathedral. Convinced of the general accuracy of Hollar's illustrations, Hodges in *Shakespeare's Second Globe: The Missing Monument*, derived from partly imaginative and at times doubtful speculations a quite splendid playhouse 92 feet in diameter with a lofty stage roof supported, not by pilasters rising from the stage, but by buttresses arching outward from the side galleries.[4] These buttresses were imagined by Hodges to be like those employed to hold up the roofs of Elizabethan great halls (44–51). According to this hypothetical plan, the estimated 43 by 27½- foot stage was thus open and clear of obstructing supports. The 'heavens' were in turn uplifted to the painted undersides of a very high gabled stage roof, one with a turret dome containing 'lantern' windows admitting a well of light upon the performing space below (61–72). Hodges also reasoned that, although the Globe might look circular from a distance and was so drawn by Hollar, the exterior probably had an estimated sixteen sides. He pointed out, in an argument that has gained wide acceptance, that Elizabethan carpenters, including Peter Street who was in charge of constructing the second Globe, were unskilled in erecting circular timber-framed buildings and instead would have put up a many-sided polygon of intersecting straight timbers.

In an extremely meticulous study of the same Hollar illustrations, one produced in 1983 but subsequently important in the evaluation of the Globe excavations of 1989 and 1991, John Orrell, in *The Quest for Shakespeare's Globe* went beyond Hodges in maintaining that Hollar had traced his drawings, with the second Globe immediately in view, using a topographical 'glass' that insured considerable dimensional accuracy. Orrell, working with John Horsley, made intricate trigonometrical projections calculating distances and sizes on the basis of facts known about the dimensions of other drawn buildings.[5] He properly took exception to a number of Hodge's interpretive diagrams – especially Hodge's projections of inferred interior features developed from Hollar's illustrations – on the grounds that the theatre is incorrectly 'viewed through a plane of intersection at right angles to the line of sight', when in fact ... the lines of sight intersect the plane at angles ranging from 77.5 (little zero) (right) to 72.5 (little zero) (left). (122). Orrell thus calculated the Globe to be about 102 feet across with an undetermined number of sides – and allowing for 2 per cent error – concluded that 100 feet seemed the correct diameter. The stage was now conjectured to be 49.6 feet wide, with a yard of some 70 feet across, with a main building height of 33 feet (120). This second Globe, Orrell further speculated, was built on the foundations of the first and would have had similar dimensions.

With the Globe and Rose excavations underway and the neighbouring 'third' Globe theatre just beginning construction, Andrew Gurr in 1989 outlined in *Rebuilding Shakespeare's Globe* 'third' Globe design decisions made up to that point, with Orrell contributing, among other essays, a chapter on the design of a future, indoor Inigo Jones theatre to be erected next to the new Globe.[6] The committee – guided by Gurr and Orrell and including Hodges, Glynne Wickham, architect Theo Crosby, and many others – deserves high marks for struggling to produce a reasonable replica of the original Globe on the assumption that the experienced Kings Men company to which Shakespeare belonged had created a practical outdoor theatre that 'worked' in the past and that, despite modern audience expectation of comforts, could still 'work' today. But with so many gaps in knowledge, the design was inevitably a hybrid. The 'third' Globe, built as an attempted replica of the original theatre of 1599–1613, was given the general 'Swan Theatre' stage pilasters, back wall, and stage gallery; a 43-foot-wide stage as in the Fortune contract, but a stage placed to the south as suggested by Hollar's exterior illustrations of the 'second' Globe; a 5-foot stage height like that in the Red Lyon playhouse; a stage roof with a single gable reflecting the assumed first design rather than the 'second' Globe's double-gabled stage roof with dome-like turret drawn by Hollar; and the large size – about 100 feet in diameter – that it is believed once held an estimated. crammed-in Elizabethan audience of some 3,000 but would now hold some 1,500 contemporary persons of larger physical stature.[7] In drawing up plans and in the initial construction in 1989, the 'third' Globe was then designed with 24 exterior sides, the same number as that of the 'Swan' as derived from an analysis of de Witt's interior drawing. Using photographs of a model of the new Globe, and of a spotlight representing the sun, a unique illustrated explanation is included of the fall of moving sunlight and shadow in the outdoor theatre during play-production hours in the afternoon.

Late in 1989 construction halted on the new Globe because of unexpected Rose excavation findings, hoped-for but as yet uncovered Globe excavation discoveries, and resulting design disputes; and also because of serious funding difficulties. In reviewing excavation activities, it must be admitted that the archaeological campaign in congested Southwark proved to be exasperating, subject as it was to day-to-day decisions by the British courts. Unlike famed turn-of-the-century British archaeological 'digs' in distant lands involving huge teams of workers labouring over many years, the Southwark 'dig' was 'worked' by a few experts over a matter of weeks with the largest local 'teams' composed, not of archaeologists, but of opposed lawyers and politicians. Imry Merchant, owner of the Rose site, and Anchor Terrace flat owners, who controlled the Globe site, attempted alternately to halt or limit the 'digs, facing off in the courts against the Museum of London excavators and their supporters from the English Heritage organization and various theatrical groups. The 'digs' ran into a legal and political morass and had to be abandoned.

The Rose theatre 'dig' just off Maiden Lane first went forward for about a month from January to mid-February 1989. Then after being shut down on 19 February, was resumed again for a few days early in May only to be closed on 15 May. Excavations began once more for a brief period in 1991 before being permanently ended. Still, there was sufficient time to uncover about three-fifths of the Rose Theatre foundations.[8]

The results were illuminating. The first phase of the Rose construction in 1587 was found to survive in foundations and mortar showing a building facing south approximately 72 feet in diameter, with a stage to the north with 16 feet 5 inch depth, and a pit of mortar sloping toward the stage which possibly did not have a roof in the first construction phase. Uncovering the front line and the oblique east wing of the stage foundations, the excavators found a stage 26 feet 10 inches in front, and about 36 feet 9 inches in the rear. During the second phase of the Rose's construction in 1592, the theatre, the excavators discovered, was expanded to about 79 feet in diameter with the enlarged stage area now marked by seeming post foundations for a covering roof. The stage depth was increased accordingly to 18 feet 4 inches, and the pit floor was now constructed of ash, compacted earth, cinders, pea grit, and hazelnut shells. It appeared to excavators that the building had about 12 sides plus a backstage wall area, or 14 sides if a possible angle in the backstage wall is counted as two sides.[9]

By contrast, the Globe dig of 1989, east of the present Anchor Terrace Apartments on the corner of Southwark Bridge Road and Park Lane, proved intellectually tantalizing if in many respects inconclusive. The excavators uncovered small portions – not over about seven meters long in any one place – of what appeared to be the remains of the inner and outer gallery-wall foundations of a polygonal building, one possibly constructed in two different phases. Protruding from the eastern side of the outer wall foundation, excavators found parts of a brick structure surviving in two L-shapes, each one not over two meters in length, with the shorter lengths of each L-shape touching the main outer wall. This brick structure has been interpreted as a foundation segment for a possible stairwell or lobby, a protuberance of the kind showing in the Hollar drawings and etching.

At the northern end of the dig, there was discovered the seeming remains of the outer main foundation wall consisting simply of chalk rubble 'apparently set around timber stakes.' To the south of this rubble, excavators exposed a short line of red bricks set within chalk flecked mortar, materials considered possibly a segment of the main foundations of the second Globe rebuilt after the 1613 fire.[10]

In the hope of finding more conclusive remains, the excavators in 1991 gained legal permission to dig four small trenches within the basement of Anchor Terrace where it was assumed a major portion of the theatre would have been situated – one trench each at either end of the basement, and two adjacent to one another at the centre. But only the central trenches revealed features of interest: occasional charcoal mortar and brick flecks which might have been part of a pier base. Legalities prevented digging below the bottom level of the Anchor Terrace foundations. A Surface Radar Survey of the entire area recorded further 'interesting features' but no clear pattern of past construction.

In an evaluation of the Globe excavation, Simon Blatherwick and Andrew Gurr concluded – assuming the L-shaped abutments to be a possible stairwell foundation seemingly oblique to the main part of the Globe – that the theatre was possibly 80 feet or more in diameter in its first phase, and perhaps 100 feet in diameter after reconstruction. They considered the foundation remains uncovered, however, too fragmented and slight to allow for a conclusive determination of the number of the building's sides. John Orrell, in an appendix containing 'additional comments' that rely in part upon the visual evidence of Hollar's 'Long View' of London, now maintained that the supposed stairwell remains are at right angles to the main foundations and as such do in fact define the form of a building, in both its first and second phases, of some 20 sides with approximately a 100-foot diameter. These last calculations were adopted with only a minor adjustment as part of the design plan, as will be seen, when construction on the new Globe started up again.

At present, the legal, political, and financial situation is such that the excavations themselves have come to what appears to be a permanent end. The Rose excavations will survive in a basement, uplifted on special pillars, of the Rose Court flats off Maiden Lane. The bulk of the Globe excavations, next to the Anchor Terrace flats on Southwark Road, are to be covered over and used as a car park.[11]

Given the state of the evidence on the form of the Globe, disagreements persist. Tim Fitzpatrick in a recent issue of the *Shakespeare Bulletin*, offers an original analysis of the angles of the excavated foundation, and of the angled eastern abutment, in relation to the disputed positioning of alternately penciled and etched lines in Hollar's illustrations. Noting the 80-foot diameter of the square Fortune Theatre as listed in Henslowe's contract, Fitzpatrick puts together a new if problematical argument for the original Globe's having 16, not 20 sides, and being 80 feet across – a possible diameter tentatively proposed by Gurr for the first Globe.[12]

Perplexing design issues of this kind, together with summaries of the New Globe construction project instigated and pressed forward by the late Sam Wanamaker, fill the pages of recent books: namely, Barry Day's informal and highly readable *This Wooden 'O': Shakespeare's Globe Reborn*; and the scholarly collection of essays in *Shakespeare's Globe Rebuilt*, edited by J.D. Mulryne and Margaret Shewring, with Andrew Gurr as advisory editor.[13] Another account of present opinions on the Globe appears in Andrew Gurr, Ronnie Mulryne, and Margaret Shewring, *The Design of Shakespeare's Globe*.[14] To give some idea of the difficulties confronted in making architectural decisions, Barry Day, a Director of the International Shakespeare Globe Centre, recounts the varied views of a committee trying finally to decide the number of the new Globe's exterior sides taking into account excavation results and other evidence:

> There was no shortage of suggestions. 18–sided and 94 ft. . . .18 sided and 90 ft. . . . 21 sided and 100 ft. Even 32 ft.-sided! Support for 24 sides dwindled rapidly. In the end it came down to a vote between 20 sides and 99 ft. (Orrell's revised recommendation after discussion with Peter McCurdy) and 18 sides and 90 ft. Orrell was supported by fourteen of the twenty votes and all participants agreed to accept the conclusion in the light of probability but by no means certainty. The new Globe would now be built to those dimensions [*sic*].[15]

In considering both archaeological discoveries and scholarly knowledge, it should be observed that the excavations, so exciting in their large possibilities, were somewhat disappointing in their ultimate results. Most significant is the fact that there is now after several centuries actual physical archaeological evidence that a building with perhaps from 16 to 20 angled foundation sides, consistent with what is known or inferred of the Globe, stood on the Globe site; and that it was a building with an L-shaped protruding foundation on the eastern side apparently for a stairwell or entrance lobby. In accord with the Hollar drawings and etchings, the stage would then probably have been on the south side, aligned at its back to the midsummer solstice, as were giant, uplifted, 'marker' boulders on the southern reaches of circular Stonehenge. At the Globe in the late afternoon hours of the British winter, deep shadows would have engulfed players, thus providing saturnine lighting for fifth-act scenes of suffering and death. Members of the audience surprisingly faced the light, with top-gallery audience members apparently warmed by the sun's rays in the winter early afternoons. The building appears to have been up to 100 feet in diameter, a size expansive enough to accommodate large Elizabethan audiences. Moreover, the excavated Rose with its 12 to 14 sides, sloping pit, and its stage – a structure tapered outward at the sides from front to rear, located in the north instead of the south, and possibly without a roof when first constructed in 1587 – provides new evidence of sharp differences in public theatre design, differences manifest too in the contract for a Fortune theatre that is square.

While a range of circumstantial evidence and a great variety of conflicting scholarly opinions on the Globe abound, basic scholarly and archaeological findings make clear how little about the theatre, particularly the first Globe, is actually known. It would have been especially helpful to historical performance criticism, for example, had the first or even the second Globe's stage-area – in its exact dimensions, form, and features – been uncovered by recent excavations, but such has not been the case. So much has been written over the past thirty years on such sandy evidential foundations, with so many fully appointed but largely imaginative Globe 'models' illustrated in textbooks and scholarly monographs, that generations of readers have grown up with false security in their acquaintance with the assumed 'real' accoutrements of a theatre that has in considerable measure been a hypothetical creation of wishful scholarly conjecture. The actual wooden, fire-prone, public playhouse of 1599 – standing beyond city limits near brothels, a bear baiting arena, and a cock-fighting pit, and constructed from the timbers of an earlier shattered theatre – was in its time considered unworthy of preservation in formal architectural plans. By contrast, the designs of court theatres and stages created by architect Inigo Jones survive in a copious body of drawings.[16] As John Orrell has rightly suggested, the specific plans for the Globe in its day-to-day construction most likely existed only in the mind of its major carpenter-builder, Peter Street.[17]

Reasoned future hypothetical designs for the Globe by modern commentators will always be welcome. But consideration should be given to presenting at least some authoritative scholarly illustrated reconstructions in just a few lightly-sketched, suggestive outlines without imaginatively 'filled-in' concrete details. The outlines could be accompanied by the usual reproductions of the differing but well-known early etchings, drawings, and documents associated with Globe scholarship. Such a suggestive combination of illustrations, used with primary texts, might further stimulate performance and dramatic criticism centred on early public-theatre staging. And because so much more is known about the specifics of royal and revels staging than public Globe staging, stage-design and historical performance criticism can beneficially stress, with the meticulousness in argumentation displayed in recent disputes about the Globe, further new speculations about the mounting of Shakespeare's plays on court and aristocratic stages as part of revels activities.

REFERENCES

1. See the collection of early illustrations of the Globe collected in 'The Bankside Theatres: Early Engravings', *Shakespeare Survey*, 1 (1948): 27–28 and 30. See also the small, unreliable, circular outline of the Globe by Jodocus Hondius, who did not work from on-site viewings, in the inset panorama of London dated 1610 in John Speed's atlas *The Theatre of the Empire of Great Britain* (1611–12). A 'circular' Globe is visible as well in one of two small, rough alternative sketches by Inigo Jones for William Davenant's masque *Britannia Triumphans* (1638). The sketches are reproduced in Irwin Smith's (New York, 1956), plates 14–15.

2. See John Cranford Adams (1942), *The Globe Playhouse: Its Design and Equipment*, (Cambridge, Mass.); C. Walter Hodges (1954), *The Globe Restored*, (New York); and Irwin Smith (1959), *Shakespeare's Globe Playhouse*, which cites many of Adam's calculations and diagrams; and Leslie Hotson, *Shakespeare's Wooden O*, (London).

3. Frances A.Yates (1969), *Theatre of the World*, (London). See also the occultist materials related to theatrical tradition in Yates's (1966), *The Art of Memory*, London.

4. C. Walter Hodges (1973), *Shakespeare's Second Globe: The Missing Monument*, London, Toronto, Melbourne.

5. John Orrell (1983), *The Quest for Shakespeare's Globe* (Cambridge, London, New York). See also Orrell's (1990), 'Beyond the Rose: design problems for the Globe reconstruction', *New issues in the reconstruction of Shakespeare's theatre: proceedings of the conference held at the University of Georgia, February, 16–18, 1990*, ed. F. J. Hildy New York, 95–118.

6. Andrew Gurr, with John Orrell (1989), *Rebuilding Shakespeare's Globe*, New York, 53–123.

7. See the discussion of the variety and size of the Globe audience in Andrew Gurr (1980), *Playgoing in Shakespeare's London*, Cambridge and New York.

8. See the chronology of the Rose excavation campaign in Christine Eccles (1990), *The Rose Theatre*, New York, xi–xiii.

9. Eccles, ibid., 95–146.

10. See S. McCudden (1989), *Report on the evaluation at Anchor Terrace Car Park, Park Street, SE1*, Museum of London (Department of Greater London Archaeology), and his 'The discovery of the Globe Theatre, London', *Archaeologist*, 6 (1990): 143–4.

11. Simon Blatherwick and Andrew Gurr, with John Orrell (1992), 'Evaluating the archaeological evidence from the 1989 and 1992 digs at the site of the Globe', *Antiquity* 66, (251) , 315–33, June. Orrell's 'additional comments' appear 329–33. See also Gurr's 'Entrances and Hierarchy in the Globe Auditorium', *Shakespeare Bulletin: A Journal of Performance Criticism and Scholarship*, 14, (4) 11–13, Fall.

12. Tom Fitzpatrick (1996), 'The Fortune Contract and Hollar's Original Drawing of Southwark: Some Indications of a Smaller First Globe', *Shakespeare Bulletin: A Journal of Performance Criticism and Scholarship*, 14, (4) 5–10, Fall.

13. See Barry Day (1996), *This Wooden 'O': Shakespeare's Globe Reborn*, London; and J.D. Mulryne, and Shewring, ed. (1997), *Shakespeare's Globe Rebuilt*, Cambridge. Disagreements about design decisions for the New Globe are recorded in Franklin J. Hildy (1992), 'A Minority Report on the Decisions of the Pentagram Conference', *Shakespeare Bulletin*, 10 (4) 9–12, Fall; and in Paul Nelsen (1992), 'Reinventing Shakespeare's Globe? A Report on Design Choices for the ISGC Globe', *Shakespeare Bulletin*, 10 (4) Fall, 5–8.

14. Andrew Gurr, Ronnie Mulryne, and Margaret Shewring (1993) *The Design of Shakespeare's Globe*, London.
15. *This Wooden 'O'*, (see n. 13), 221–22.
16. See the extant designs of royal theatres in John Orrell (1985), *The Theatres of Inigo Jones and John Webb*, London, New York, New Rochelle. Individual chapters focus on designs for Christ Church, Oxford; the Cockpit in Drury Lane; Somerset House; the Cockpit-in-Court; and the Whitehall Masquing House and the Great Hall.
17. See the account of Orrell's opinions on how Street worked in *This Wooden 'O'* (see n. 13), 93–94.

PART 3

Shakespeare and Renaissance Ideas

9   The Reign of James VI: A survey of recent writings

Johann P. Sommerville

In recent years, many literary scholars have adopted a historical, or at least historicist, approach to the texts of Shakespeare and his contemporaries. The political nature of much literature has won wide recognition, and political as well as social and cultural history have come to seem increasingly important for literary criticism. Understandably, though, people working in literature have limited time to examine historical sources, either primary or secondary. So they often rely on the works of just a few recent and authoritative historians. The trouble is that the historians are sometimes not quite as recent, authoritative or reliable as the literary critic supposes. Commonly, writers on English Renaissance literature draw on works which specialists in early modern British history consider a bit dated. Sometimes the literary scholar accepts as established views that are vigorously contested. Often, current discussion amongst historians goes unnoticed by people working on literature. The paragraphs below survey recent historical scholarship on the Jacobean age. Obviously, a short essay will omit much; and a great deal of fine scholarship has been passed over in silence. In particular, it says almost nothing about works on literary history or biography, since the reader is doubtless already familiar with them. But the pages that follow do discuss some of the main debates that have exercised historians since the mid-1980s, and they do list books and articles through which students can easily develop a comprehensive bibliography of James and his age. An excellent bibliographical tool for British history in general is worth mentioning here: The Royal Historical Society's *Annual Bibliography of British and Irish History*[1] – a very full listing of relevant material published each year since 1975.

There is no really definitive biography of James. The standard academic biography is D. H. Willson's *James VI and I*,[2] but it is now badly dated. Willson strongly disliked James and made his feelings apparent. Lately, historians are much less harsh on the king than they used to be. He was formerly regarded as lazy, conceited, corrupt and incompetent, but nowadays he is often seen as an able and effective ruler. Two accounts that present the modern, rehabilitated monarch are Maurice Lee, *Great Britain's Solomon: James VI and I in his Three Kingdoms*[3] and Christopher Durston's pamphlet *James I*.[4] Jenny Wormald is working on a full-scale biography. At a much more popular level, the most recent biography is Bryan Bevan, *King James VI of Scotland & I of England*.[5] An older book with virtually the same title is by Antonia Fraser.[6] Both are readable but to be used with caution. The King's own political writings are available in two twentieth-century editions: *The Political Works of James I*,[7] and King James VI and I, *Political Writings*.[8] Each contains material which the other omits. One reason why James has come to seem a more able king than he once did is that the charges of corruption and extravagance no longer look as convincing as they used to. As the first king of a new dynasty, James had to spend heavily to secure support. An important contribution in this area is Linda Levy Peck, *Court Patronage and Corruption in Early Stuart England*.[9] Two books by fine historians introduce a wider period but also cover James's reign: Derek Hirst, *Authority and Conflict: England 1603–1658*,[10] and Mark Kishlansky, *A Monarchy Transformed: Britain 1603–1714*,[11] (paperback Penguin Books, 1997).

Scholarship on the history of Jacobean England has centred for some years on debate between so-called 'revisionists' and their critics. The key revisionist idea is that the English Civil Wars of the 1640s did not have long-term origins. Earlier scholars argued that the reign of James I witnessed mounting conflict between the king and his parliaments, and that the conflict continued after James's death in 1625, eventually culminating in civil war in 1642. Some of them – J. H. Hexter is an example – saw the conflict as a struggle over the constitution, between a king eager to extend his powers and a House of Commons bent on preventing him from doing so. Others – for instance Christopher Hill and Lawrence Stone – rooted political strife in social and economic tensions. In his best-selling *The Causes of the English Revolution 1529–1642*,[12] Lawrence Stone located the causes of the Civil War in structures and events stretching as far back as Henry VIII's Reformation and the Dissolution of the Monasteries which followed it. Revisionists, by contrast, find little trace of the Civil War's origins before 1625 or even 1637. The most prominent of the revisionists is Conrad Russell (the fifth Earl Russell, and son of Bertrand), whose works include *The Causes of the English Civil War*,[13] which remarkably does not mention either Stone or Hill – an indication of just how far the revisionists have moved from earlier scholars. Russell's *Causes of the English Civil War* is an excellent statement of the revisionist case. It develops and refines ideas which he expressed earlier in a number of books and articles including his very influential 'Parliamentary History in Perspective',[14] and his detailed account of the parliamentary politics of the 1620s, *Parliaments and English Politics 1621–1629*.[15] A lengthy companion volume to *The Causes of the English Civil War* is Russell's *The Fall of the British Monarchies 1637–1642.*[16]

Russell and other revisionists (including Kevin Sharpe, John Morrill, and Glenn Burgess) argue that James I's reign was a peaceful period. They claim that life in Jacobean England was marked by social and political consensus, not marred by conflict. Parliament, they say, was not struggling with the crown for sovereignty, but was declining in importance in the opening decades of the seventeenth century. Within Parliament, the House of Lords was much more powerful than the Commons, and many members of the Lower House were clients of nobles. Often, what looks like conflict between crown and Commons is really a political struggle between noble factions, of which one mobilizes support in the House of Commons while the other relies on royal favour. Of course, the revisionists admit, there were occasional political disagreements, but they resulted from factional conflict and from clashes of personality rather than from serious social strains or from deep-rooted disagreements on matters of constitutional or religious principle.

At times, the revisionists argue so forcefully in favour of their thesis about consensus, that the Civil War becomes something of an embarrassment to them. How could such a prolonged and destructive war spring so suddenly from such peaceful and harmonious origins? Russell has some answers. Though he claims that religious consensus reigned in Jacobean times, he argues that divisions on theology became important after about 1625, when the rise of Arminianism destroyed the harmony of the English Church. He sees the dispute between the Arminians and Calvinists under Charles I as one cause of the Civil War, but he also stresses the problem of multiple kingdoms: James I and Charles I ruled in England, Scotland and Ireland, but each of these kingdoms had its own separate administrative machinery, and there were no institutions of government to coordinate policy for all three. Russell stresses the importance of developments in Scotland and Ireland for explaining what happened in England. His work has stimulated the interest of English historians in Irish and Scottish history, and in adopting a British perspective on English politics.

Russell's views on Jacobean England receive some confirmation from the work of two fine historians of the Church and religion – Patrick Collinson and Nicholas Tyacke. In his *The Religion of Protestants: The Church in English Society, 1559–1625,*[17] Collinson claimed that the Church under James was broadly united. There were, he admitted, differences of emphasis amongst leading churchmen on inessential points, but they commonly endorsed a single set of views on key theological questions, and most adopted a basically Calvinist outlook on the fundamental issues of grace, salvation, and predestination. Collinson drew on important earlier works by Tyacke. In 1987 Tyacke published his long-awaited book, *Anti-Calvinists: the Rise of English Arminianism c.1590–1640.*[18] He argued that most of the leaders of the Jacobean Church were Calvinists, but that some theologians (including Lancelot Andrewes) took a different line, rejecting Calvinist ideas on predestination. Critics of Calvinism came to be called Arminians, after the Dutch theologian Arminius – though Arminius was just one of the thinkers who influenced the English writers, and English anti-Calvinism predates the Dutchman's impact. Under James I, Tyacke argues, anti-Calvinists were relatively insignificant, but things altered rapidly in the 1620s and especially when Charles I and Laud took over Church and State. Tyacke's interpretation emphasizes that the really revolutionary religious changes of the early-seventeenth century occurred from the mid-1620s onwards, and were introduced by the Arminians – who enforced new ceremonies, and used censorship to muzzle Calvinists. Earlier, Christopher Hill and others had emphasized the revolutionary nature not of Arminianism but of *puritanism*, and they argued that the puritan movement had been gathering strength long before 1625. Tyacke does not deny that there were puritans, nor that they played a part in the events of the early-seventeenth century (see especially his 'The "Rise of Puritanism" and the Legalising of Dissent, 1571–1719', in O.P. Grell, J.I. Israel, and N. Tyacke, (eds), *From Persecution to Toleration: The Glorious Revolution and Religion in England*.[19] But he stresses that what really shook the peace of the Jacobean Church was the rise of Arminianism. Conrad Russell, Tyacke's colleague in London, claimed that the rise of Arminianism was not just a highly important episode in England's religious history, but a leading cause of the Civil War.

Tyacke's thesis has been challenged by a number of scholars, including Peter White, Julian Davies, and Kevin Sharpe. In his *Predestination, Policy and Polemic: Conflict and Consensus in the English Church from the Reformation to the Civil War*,[20] White argues that the strife between Calvinists and Arminians was much less important than Tyacke claims. According to White, the English Church from Elizabeth's reign onwards pursued a *via media* between theological extremes. He sees Whitgift's Lambeth Articles of 1595 not as a statement of Calvinism (the view of Tyacke and others) but as an attempt to steer a middle course between Calvinists and anti-Calvinists. Again, James I sent a delegation to the Synod of Dort, which condemned Arminianism in 1619, and this is commonly seen as clear evidence that the official doctrinal position of the Jacobean Church was Calvinist. But White insists that the British delegates at Dort were moderates rather than Calvinists. What Tyacke describes as the Arminian revolution of the 1620s and 30s, appears in White's account as the triumph of traditional Anglican views, which were suspicious of religious extremes and of overly precise definitions of subtle points of doctrine.

In *The Caroline Captivity of the Church: Charles I and the Remoulding of Anglicanism*,[21] Julian Davies, like White, rejects Tyacke's thesis about the rise of Arminianism. He admits that things went wrong with the Church after 1625, but he attributes what happened to Charles I's policies on ceremonies and not to anti-Calvinism. Tyacke rooted the ceremonial changes of the 1630s – especially the railing in of altars (as communion tables were now renamed) at the east end of churches – in the sacramentalism of Arminian churchmen such as Laud. Davies argues that it was Charles I himself and not Laud who was responsible for the altar policy, linking the king's attitude towards ceremonies with his high opinions on royal power. The new ceremonies, says Davies, resulted from Charles I's ideas on sacramental kingship, not from Arminianism.

A third book which challenges Tyacke's thesis is Kevin Sharpe's *The Personal Rule of Charles I*.[22] This stout volume, which extends to almost 1,000 pages, is one of the most extreme statements of revisionism, on both religious and secular issues. Russell claims that people divided on religion from the mid-1620s but agreed on political and constitutional matters. John Morrill – another leading revisionist – has similarly stressed the religious causes of the wars, which he calls 'England's Wars of Religion' (a number of his writings on this theme are collected in his *The Nature of the English Revolution*).[23] Sharpe, on the other hand, maintains that harmony reigned in both Church and State until long after Charles I came to the throne. It was only with the onset of the Scottish troubles in 1637, he says, that the king began to encounter really serious problems. On Sharpe's account, the idea that the English Civil War had deep roots in social or religious conflict was an invention of Whig and Marxist historians, without foundation in the evidence. In reality, he says, the war resulted from strains which arose only after Charles I attempted to foist a new Prayer Book on the Scots.

The ideas of White, Davies, Sharpe and their allies have been attacked by a number of scholars, sometimes implicitly, on other occasions more overtly. Definitely in the category of explicit assault is Tyacke's response to them – 'Anglican Attitudes: Some Recent Writings on English Religious History, from the Reformation to the Civil War'.[24] Tyacke reasserts his earlier thesis, claiming that his critics have misinterpreted the evidence, or simply ignored it. In particular, he charges them with persistent failure to distinguish between sublapsarian and supralapsarian predestination, a key distinction in contemporary debates. Though English anti-Calvinism is often equated with Arminianism, Tyacke's article stresses its roots in earlier Lutheran ideas, and especially in the thinking of the sixteenth-century theologian Niels Hemmingsen – who exercised considerable influence on English divines and on Arminius himself. As we saw, Russell's revisionism drew on Tyacke's ideas, arguing that the Civil War resulted from the rise of Arminianism rather than from political or constitutional disputes. Tyacke himself sees things rather differently, suggesting that the war had political as well as religious causes, and that the government of the early Stuart kings displayed absolutist tendencies. It is, however, the work of Sharpe rather than Russell which arouses his severest strictures. Sharpe, he notes, 'wishes to elevate short-termism to an unprecedented height' (165–6), and he comments that time will tell how far his 'massive book' 'comes to look like some great beached leviathan, stranded by the receding tides of revisionism' (162).

Tyacke notes that 'stress on the role of Arminianism has had the unfortunate consequence of distracting attention from puritanism' (166) and he has himself tried to correct this in his recent work. The *doyen* of historians of puritanism is Patrick Collinson, whose many writings include a fine recent collections of essays – *Elizabethan Essays*.[25] While Collinson portrayed the Jacobean Church as broadly united, some younger scholars have modified the picture, though still contrasting James with Charles. The work of Peter Lake is particularly important, combining vast reading in early modern religious writings with subtlety of argument. In *Anglicans and Puritans? Presbyterianism and English Conformist Thought from Whitgift to Hooker*,[26] Lake examines Elizabethan debates on a wide range of religious issues, arguing that Richard Hooker pioneered a distinctive style of divinity which exercised a profound effect on later Arminianism: 'All the ideological ingredients which were to give English Arminianism its distinctive flavour were present in English protestant thought by the 1590s' (245). Like the later Arminians, Hooker combined a sacrament-centered piety with anti-Calvinism, and in James's reign the same was true of Andrewes and others. But while James ruled, the disagreements between Calvinists and their opponents were not allowed to destroy the unity of the Church. Charles, on the other hand, pursued far less conciliatory policies. An excellent overview of the policies of the two kings is Kenneth Fincham and Peter Lake's 'The Ecclesiastical Policies of James I and Charles I', in Kenneth Fincham, (ed), *The Early Stuart Church, 1603–1642*;[27] the material on James I is a revised and shortened version of the same authors' 'The Ecclesiastical Policy of James I', in *Journal of British Studies*.[28] Other important essays in Fincham's *Early Stuart Church* include John Fielding's study of the diocese of Peterborough,[29] and Anthony Milton on English attitudes towards the Church of Rome.[30] More recently, Milton has published a much fuller treatment of the same subject: *Catholic and Reformed. The Roman and Protestant Churches in English Protestant Thought, 1600–1640*.[31] This is a very thorough and well-researched book, running to nearly 600 pages.

While revisionists disagree about the religious changes of the early-seventeenth century, they all take the view that the Civil War did not originate in conflict over constitutional principle. Before 1640 or so, their argument goes, virtually everyone adopted a single outlook on constitutional questions. This notion of political and constitutional consensus features in many revisionist writings, including Kevin Sharpe's *Politics and Ideas in Early Stuart England*,[32] but easily the most accomplished statement of the case is in Glenn Burgess's *The Politics of the Ancient Constitution. An Introduction to English political Thought, 1603–1642*,[33] and the same author's *Absolute Monarchy and the Stuart Constitution*.[34]

Also worth mentioning is Paul Christianson's 'Royal and Parliamentary voices on the Ancient Constitution, c. 1604–1621', in a fine collection of essays edited by Linda Levy Peck, *The Mental World of the Jacobean Court*,[35] and Christianson's more recent *Discourse on History, Law and Governance in the Public Career of John Selden, 1610–1635*.[36] Both Burgess and Christianson argue that pretty well everyone in early-seventeenth century England endorsed the theory of the ancient constitution, and that there were very few absolutists there. One difference between the two concerns King James himself: for Christianson, the King was an absolutist in his earlier days, but became converted to constitutionalism some time before giving a famous speech to Parliament in 1610; for Burgess, on the other hand, James was a constitutionalist much earlier, and his *True Law of Free Monarchies* (published in 1598) was not an absolutist work, though it is commonly seen as such.

The revisionist notion that consensus prevailed on matters of political principle has been attacked by a number of writers, including Derek Hirst in 'Revisionism Revised: the place of principle', in *Past and Present*,[37] and at greater length in J. P. Sommerville, *Politics and Ideology in England 1603–1640*[38] – a book which argues that there were sharp divisions on matters of political principle in the early seventeenth century, and that they contributed to political strife which culminated in civil war. It claims that there were absolutists, including James I, and that their ideas and policies aroused the fear and suspicion of people who believed that kings hold only limited power, and that they are obliged to abide by ancient customary laws or by contractual obligations imposed upon their ancestors when monarchs were first instituted. The arguments of Burgess and Christianson take issue with these ideas, as does Conrad Russell in 'Divine Rights in the Early Seventeenth Century', in John Morrill, Paul Slack, and Daniel Wolfe, (eds), *Public Duty and Private Conscience in Seventeenth-Century England: Essays Presented to G. E. Aylmer*.[39] The debate revolves around two crucial connected questions: how widespread was absolutist thinking, and was the theory of the ancient constitution dominant? Two recent contributions on these topics are Johann Sommerville, 'English and European Political Ideas in the Early Seventeenth Century: Revisionism and the Case of Absolutism', in *Journal of British Studies*,[40] and the same writer's 'The Ancient Constitution Reassessed: the Common Law, the Court and the Languages of Politics in Early Modern England', in Malcolm Smuts, ed., *The Stuart Court and Europe. Essays in Politics and Political Culture*.[41] The first of these essays claims that revisionists have misconstrued the nature of absolutism, and that what they say to show that there were few or no English absolutists can readily be extended to prove that no absolutists existed anywhere – since quite a number of English authors said the same things as Continental thinkers who are normally seen as absolutists. The second essay questions the thesis that virtually everyone subscribed to the theory of the ancient constitution espoused by Sir Edward Coke and other common lawyers. Admittedly, some lawyers stressed the sacrosanct nature of England's ancient customs and argued that they themselves were the only fit interpreters of them – since they alone possessed the 'artificial reason' which was needed to grasp the law's true meaning. But it is doubtful that these ideas were anything like universal. Not everyone liked lawyers.

A dozen years ago, revisionism was rapidly becoming the new orthodoxy. Now it is embattled. This is largely the result of work by so-called 'post-revisionists', who accept some of the detailed findings of revisionists but reject their main claim – that England was a happy and harmonious land until just before civil war broke out. Leading post-revisionist writings include Ann Hughes' excellent local study of *Politics, Society and Civil War in Warwickshire, 1620–1660*,[42] and a very valuable study of both national and local politics just after the death of James I – Richard Cust's *The Forced Loan and English Politics 1626–1628*. Both Cust and Hughes find substantial evidence of serious strains in English society in the 1620s. They have also joined forces to edit a fine collection of post-revisionist essays, *Conflict in Early Stuart England*,[44] which provides a forceful critique of revisionism from many angles. Ann Hughes' *The Causes of the English Civil War*[45] is a readable and well-argued overview of a central topic. Another outstanding example of post-revisionism is Thomas Cogswell's *The Blessed Revolution: English Politics and the Coming of War, 1621–1624*,[46] an excellent, detailed account of foreign policy and domestic politics in James's last years. Cogswell is also the author of an important essay on the links between literature and politics: 'Underground verse and the transformation of early Stuart political culture', in *Political Culture and Cultural Politics: Essays presented to David Underdown*, (ed), Susan D. Amussen and Mark A. Kishlansky, 277–99.[47] Also on the cultural aspects of politics, though not particularly concerned with the debate over revisionism, is Kevin Sharpe and Peter Lake, eds., *Culture and Politics in early Stuart England*.[48] Post-revisionists like Cogswell, and pre-revisionists such as Jack Hexter are both represented in J. H. Hexter, ed., *Parliament and Liberty from the Reign of Elizabeth to the English Civil War*.[49]

Revisionists attacked Marxist efforts to root the origins of the Civil War in social conflict. Crude attempts to portray early-seventeenth century England as a society divided on class lines between a rising bourgeoisie and a feudal aristocracy have fallen out of fashion, but a more subtle account of social and cultural differences, and their political ramifications, features in the work of many critics of revisionism, including David Underdown. In *Revel, Riot and Rebellion. Popular Politics and Culture in England 1603–1660*,[50] he linked side-taking in the war with local variations in geography, farming, popular culture, and religion. Underdown explored similar themes in *Fire from Heaven. Life in an English Town in the Seventeenth Century*,[51] a detailed and entertaining account of Dorchester especially in the first four decades of the century. A more recent statement of his views is in *A Freeborn People. Politics and the Nation in Seventeenth-Century England*.[52]

Much writing on social history and on popular culture deals with periods much longer than James's reign. One noteworthy item is Ronald Hutton's *The Rise and Fall of Merry England. The Ritual Year 1400–1700*,[53] which is about traditional rituals and attempts to reform them; it discusses such things as maypoles, church ales, Boy Bishops, and Lords of Misrule. The Protestant calendar is the subject of David Cressy's *Bonfires and Bells. National Memory and the Protestant Calendar in Tudor and Stuart England*,[54] which talks about the political uses of the calendar – for example, in thanksgiving for the defeat of the Armada, and the discovery of the Gunpowder Plot. An interesting recent collection of essays on various aspects of social history is Paul Griffiths, Adam Fox and Steve Hindle, eds., *The Experience of Authority in Early Modern England*.[55] A very good, full discussion of an important social group is Felicity Heal and Clive Holmes' *The Gentry in England and Wales 1500–1700*.[56]

Witches continue to attract scholarly interest. Two notable recent works are James Sharpe's fine, judicious and informed survey *Instruments of Darkness. Witchcraft in Early Modern England*,[57] and Stuart Clark's massive *Thinking with Demons: the Idea of Witchcraft in Early Modern Europe*.[58] Clark's book runs to over 800 pages and discusses all aspects of modern scholarship on European as well as English witchcraft. Its very full bibliography provides an excellent research tool for anyone interested in witches. Far more has lately been published on women, gender, and the family than can possibly be mentioned here. Some highlights are Susan Dwyer Amussen, *An Ordered Society: Gender and Class in early Modern England*[59] which combines a local study with more general observations; Amy Louise Erickson, *Women and Property in Early Modern England*,[60] which provides an excellent and well-researched account of the law and practice of property-owning by women, showing that they in fact had much more control of property than legal theory would suggest; and M. R. Sommerville, *Sex and Subjection: Attitudes to Women in Early Modern Society*,[61] which is a fine analysis of the views of sixteenth and seventeenth-century theorists, and draws on a wealth of primary materials.

Another topic that has interested many scholars lately is national identity. The resurgence of nationalism in Europe and elsewhere, and political events in Ireland and Scotland, have lent topicality to early modern ideas of nationhood, and to the history of relations between different parts of the British Isles. Debate over Russell's ideas on multiple kingdoms have added an extra twist. The reign of James VI and I is, of course, particularly relevant to the subject of Anglo-Scots relations, since James united the crowns of the two countries, and tried to introduce a still more 'perfect union'. Roger A. Mason has edited an excellent collection of essays on *Scots and Britons: Scottish Political Thought and the Union of 1603*.[62]

Still more recent, and on a wider range of topics, is Brendan Bradshaw and John Morrill, ed., *The British Problem, c. 1534–1707. State Formation in the Atlantic Archipelago*,[63] which contains a number of important essays by eminent historians. They demonstrate that British questions are topical, but that there is no agreement on what the British problem is. Unless that is the problem.

It seems fairly clear that current interest in national identity has at least as much to do with recent developments as with what happened in the past. Maybe modern writings on this subject tell us more about ourselves than about James I and his contemporaries. Perhaps the same goes for work on other currently debated ideas, including revisionism itself. Partly, of course, revisionism can be explained in terms of the defects of earlier scholarship and the perpetual academic search for innovation. Some historians had undoubtedly over-emphasized the inevitability of the Civil War, and over-stressed the bitterness of social divisions. But it looks unlikely that the pre-revisionists (who were dominant before 1976), and the post-revisionists (who have been increasingly prominent since 1986) have all entirely misconstrued the evidence. So why did it become fashionable to downplay past divisions on social and political matters in the mid-1970s? In England, the 1970s were a decade of economic decline, rising prices, strikes, social conflict, and political instability – as power swung from left to right and back again. Arguably, people who stressed that division and conflict were aberrations and not part of the country's heritage had the best interests of the nation at heart. Arguably, too, what they said bore only a limited resemblance to what happened in Jacobean England.

REFERENCES

1. Royal Historical Society (1976), *Annual Bibliography of British and Irish History*, Brighton: Harvester Press.
2. Willson, D.H. (1956), *James VI and I*, London: Jonathan Cape.
3. Lee, Maurice (1990), *Great Britain's Solomon: James VI and I in his Three Kingdoms*, Urbana and Chicago: University of Illinois Press.
4. Durston, Christopher (1993), *James I*, London and New York: Routledge, Lancaster Pamphlets.
5. Bevan, Bryan (1996), *King James VI of Scotland & I of England*, London: The Rubicon Press.
6. Fraser, Antonia (1974), *King James VI of Scotland, I of England*, London: Weidenfeld and Nicolson.
7. James I (1918), *The Political Works of James I*, ed., Charles Howard McIlwain, Cambridge, Mass.: Harvard University Press.
8. James VI and I (1994), *Political Writings*, (ed.) Johann P. Sommerville. Cambridge Texts in the History of Political Thought, Cambridge: Cambridge University Press.
9. Peck, Linda Levy (1990), *Court Patronage and Corruption in Early Stuart England*, London: Unwin Hyman.

10. Hirst, Derek (1986), *Authority and Conflict: England 1603–1658*, Cambridge, Mass.: Harvard University Press.
11. Kishlansky, Mark (1997), *A Monarchy Transformed: Britain 1603–1714*, London: Allen Lane (paperback, Penguin Books).
12. Stone, Lawrence, (1972), *The Causes of the English Revolution 1529–1642*, London: Routledge and Kegan Paul.
13. Russell, Conrad (1990), *The Causes of the English Civil War*, Oxford: Clarendon Press.
14. Russell, Conrad (1976), 'Parliamentary History in Perspective', in *History*, 61, 1–27.
15. Russell, Conrad (1979), *Parliaments and English Politics 1621–1629*, Oxford: Clarendon Press.
16. Russell, Conrad (1991), *The Fall of the British Monarchies 1637–1642*, Oxford: Clarendon Press.
17. Collinson, Patrick (1982), *The Religion of Protestants: The Church in English Society, 1559–1625*, Oxford: Clarendon Press.
18. Tyacke, Nicholas (1987), *Anti-Calvinists: the Rise of English Arminianism c. 1590–1640*, Oxford: Oxford University Press.
19. Tyacke, Nicholas (1990), 'The "Rise of Puritanism" and the Legalising of Dissent, 1571–1719', in O.P. Grell, J.I. Israel, and N. Tyacke, (eds), *From Persecution to Toleration: The Glorious Revolution and Religion in England*, Oxford: Clarendon Press, 17–28.
20. White, Peter (1992), *Predestination, Policy and Polemic: Conflict and Consensus in the English Church from the Reformation to the Civil War*, Cambridge: Cambridge University Press.
21. Davies, Julian (1992), *The Caroline Captivity of the Church: Charles I and the Remoulding of Anglicanism*, Oxford: Clarendon Press.
22. Sharpe, Kevin (1992), *The Personal Rule of Charles I*, New Haven: Yale University Press.
23. Morrill, John (1993), *The Nature of the English Revolution*, Longman: London and New York.
24. Tyacke, Nicholas (1996), 'Anglican Attitudes: Some Recent Writings on English Religious History, from the Reformation to the Civil War', *Journal of British Studies*, 35, 139–67.
25. Collinson, Patrick (1994), *Elizabethan Essays*, London: Hambledon Press.
26. Lake, Peter (1988), *Anglicans and Puritans? Presbyterianism and English Conformist Thought from Whitgift to Hooker*, London: Unwin Hyman 1988.
27. Fincham, Kenneth, and Lake, Peter (1993), 'The Ecclesiastical Policies of James I and Charles I', Kenneth Fincham, (ed), *The Early Stuart Church, 1603–1642*, London: Macmillan, 23–49.
28. Fincham, Kenneth and Lake, Peter (1985), 'The Ecclesiastical Policy of James I', *Journal of British Studies*, 24, 169–207.
29. Fielding, John (1993), 'Arminianism in the Localities: Peterborough Diocese 1603–1642', Kenneth Fincham, (ed), *The Early Stuart Church, 1603–1642*, London: Macmillan, 93–113.
30. Milton, Anthony (1993), 'The Church of England, Rome and the True Church: The Demise of a Jacobean Consensus', in Kenneth Fincham, (ed), *The Early Stuart Church, 1603–1642*, London: Macmillan, 187–210.
31. Milton, Anthony (1995), *Catholic and Reformed. The Roman and Protestant Churches in English Protestant Thought, 1600–1640*, Cambridge: Cambridge University Press.
32. Sharpe, Kevin (1989), *Politics and Ideas in Early Stuart England*, London: Pinter.

33. Burgess, Glenn (1993), *The Politics of the Ancient Constitution. An Introduction to English Political Thought, 1603–1642*, University Park, Pennsylvania: Pennsylvania State University Press.
34. Burgess, Glenn (1996), *Absolute Monarchy and the Stuart Constitution*, New Haven: Yale University Press.
35. Christianson, Paul (1991), 'Royal and Parliamentary voices on the Ancient Constitution, c. 1604–1621', in Linda Levy Peck, (ed) *The Mental World of the Jacobean Court*, Cambridge: Cambridge University Press, 71–95.
36. Christianson, Paul (1996), *Discourse on History, Law and Governance in the Public Career of John Selden, 1610–1635*, Toronto: University of Toronto Press.
37. Hirst, Derek (1981), 'Revisionism Revised: the place of principle', in *Past and Present*, 92.
38. Sommerville, Johnann P. (1986), *Politics and Ideology in England 1603–1640*, London: Longman.
39. Russell, Conrad (1993), 'Divine Rights in the Early Seventeenth Century', in John Morrill, Paul Slack, and Daniel Wolfe, (eds), *Public Duty and Private Conscience in Seventeenth-Century England: Essays Presented to G.E. Aylmer* (Oxford), 101–20.
40. Sommerville, Johann P. (1996), 'English and European Political Ideas in the Early Seventeenth Century: Revisionism and the Case of Absolutism', *Journal of British Studies* 35, 168–94.
41. Sommerville, Johann P. (1996), 'The Ancient Constitution Reassessed: the Common Law, the Court and the Languages of Politics in Early Modern England', in Malcolm Smuts, (ed), *The Stuart Court and Europe. Essays in Politics and Political Culture*, Cambridge: Cambridge Univesity Press, 39–64.
42. Hughes, Ann (1987), *Politics, Society and Civil War in Warwickshire, 1620–1660*, Cambridge: Cambridge University Press.
43. Cust, Richard (1987), *The Forced Loan and English Politics 1626–1628*, Oxford: Oxford University Press.
44. Cust, Richard, and Hughes, Ann (1989), eds., *Conflict in Early Stuart England*, London: Longman.
45. Hughes, Ann (1991), *The Causes of the English Civil War*.
46. Cogswell, Thomas (1989), *The Blessed Revolution: English Politics and the Coming of War, 1621–1624*, Cambridge: Cambridge University Press.
47. Cogswell, Thomas, 'Underground verse and the transformation of early Stuart political culture', in Susan D. Amussen and Mark A. Kishlansky, (eds)., *Political Culture and Cultural Politics: Essays presented to David Underdown*, Manchester: Manchester University Press, 1995, 277–99.
48. Sharpe, Kevin, Lake, Peter (1994), eds., *Culture and Politics in early Stuart England*, London: Macmillan.
49. Hexter, J.H., ed. (1992), *Parliament and Liberty from the Reign of Elizabeth to the English Civil War*, Stanford: Stanford University Press.
50. Underdown, David (1985), *Revel, Riot and Rebellion. Popular Politics and Culture in England 1603–1660*, Oxford: Oxford University Press.
51. Underdown, David (1992), *Fire from Heaven, Life in an English Town in the Seventeenth Century*, New Haven: Yale University Press.
52. Underdown, David (1996), *A Freeborn People. Politics and the Nation in Seventeenth-Century England*, Oxford: Clarendon Press.
53. Hutton, Ronald (1994), *The Rise and Fall of Merry England. The Ritual Year 1400–1700*, Oxford: Oxford University Press.
54. Cressy, David (1989), *Bonfires and Bells. National Memory and the protestant Calendar in Tudor and Stuart England*, Berkeley: University of California Press.

55. Griffiths, Paul, Fox, Adam, and Hindle, Steve, eds (1996), *The Experience of Authority in Early Modern England*, London: Macmillan.

56. Heal, Felicity, and Holmes, Clive (1994), *The Gentry in England and Wales 1500–1700*, London: Macmillan.

57. Sharpe, James (1996), *Instruments of Darkness. Witchcraft in Early Modern England*, London: Hamish Hamilton, paperback edition Philadelphia: University of Pennsylvania Press, 1997.

58. Clark, Stuart (1997), *Thinking with Demons: the Idea of Witchcraft in Early Modern Europe*, Oxford: Clarendon Press.

59. Amussen, Susan Dwyer (1988), *An Ordered Society: Gender and Class in early Modern England*, Oxford: Basil Blackwell.

60. Erickson, Amy Louise (1993), *Women and Property in Early Modern England*, London: Routledge.

61. Sommerville, Margaret R. (1995), *Sex and Subjection: Attitudes to Women in Early Modern Society*, London: Edward Arnold.

62. Mason, Roger A., ed. (1994), *Scots and Britons: Scottish Political Thought and the Union of 1603*, Cambridge: Cambridge University Press.

63. Bradshaw, Brendan, and Morrill, John, eds (1996), *The British Problem, c. 1534–1707. State Formation in the Atlantic Archipelago*, London: Macmillan.

10   Studies on Shakespeare's Language: An overview

Norman Blake

In this chapter I shall deal with the basic features of language, such as grammar and lexis, and not with the more applied areas of language study such as rhetoric and style, which are handled elsewhere. It may be difficult to keep the two areas completely separate, as some scholars have used language studies as a means of focusing on style and rhetoric. As it happens, rhetoric and style are very popular areas of investigation at present for they represent aspects of language which literary specialists feel competent to deal with, because they do not necessarily involve any familiarity with modern approaches to language. There exist relatively few linguists trained in historical language work who have turned their attention to Shakespeare. I start by considering the principal aspects of Shakespeare's language which can be dealt with under broad headings such as *grammar* and *dictionaries,* and then review more general works which cover several aspects of Shakespeare's language or which are more introductory or applied in nature.

GRAMMARS

Few grammars of Shakespeare's language have been written, and a new grammar remains one of the main desiderata in Shakespearean studies. The two grammars most frequently cited (though both are out of print) are those by Abbott and Franz.[1] Abbott's *A Shakespearean Grammar* has as its subtitle 'An Attempt to illustrate some of the Differences between Elizabethan and Modern English for the Use of Schools'. This sub-title is significant, because the aim of this grammar is modest. The book is based on traditional grammar and works through adjectives, adverbs, articles, conjunctions, prepositions, pronouns, and verbs, before going on to what it calls irregularities, compound words, prefixes and suffixes. It has a long section on prosody, together with a shorter section on similes and metaphors. As a grammar it is not complete. It has, for example, no sections on nouns or word order. Indeed, it makes no attempt at completeness, for Abbott was mainly concerned to highlight differences between Elizabethan and Modern English. His attitude is one that looked back from a period of grammatical regulation and standardization (the nineteenth century) to one where any possible variation to the rules of language, as he understood them, was permissible.

His introduction opens with this sentence:

> ELIZABETHAN English, on a superficial view, appears to present this great point of difference from the English of modern times, that in the former any irregularities whatever, whether in the formation of words or in the combination of words into sentences, are allowable. (5)[2]

He then gives examples of these irregularities. His book has helped to foster two attitudes among modern readers and editors. The first is that almost anything is possible in Shakespeare's English and that, therefore, one should only comment on the most extreme form of irregularity in an edition or discussion. No attempt is made to provide a description of Shakespeare's language on its own terms since the focus is always on what is different. The second is that the language is studied through modern editions; Abbott used the Globe Shakespeare. Modern editions have modern spelling and punctuation. Inevitably the edition one uses influences the aspects of language one might comment upon, because the modern spelling and punctuation throw up 'irregularities' much more starkly since they can less easily be accommodated in a modern form of the language. Because Abbott wrote in English and most editors and critics of Shakespeare are Anglophone with only a limited or no knowledge of German, his grammar has remained the most influential, as its inclusion on a CD-ROM attests.

This is regrettable since the grammar by Franz is altogether a more scholarly piece of work and he points out some of the shortcomings of Abbott's work (iv). But even Franz, somewhat modestly, disclaims the attempt to write a comprehensive grammar of Shakespeare's English; he will only gather together the characteristic features of Shakespeare's English.[3] He does set his grammar within a historical context and he quotes extensively from other writers both before and after Shakespeare. But he too sees Shakespeare's English in contrast with the spoken English of better-class English speakers of his day.[4] He used the editions by W.A. Wright (London 1891–93) for his study, but he made use of the quarto facsimiles by W. Griggs and the First Folio when he felt it necessary. The grammar contains sections on morphology and syntax, each of which tackles the various parts of speech in detail as necessary. It was supplemented by a second volume on spelling, phonology and word-formation.[5] Compared with Abbott, Franz is a professional scholar whose work is both detailed and well documented. He was familiar with the scholarship of his time and his books remain major contributions to a study of Shakespeare's language, though it is unfortunate that they are rarely exploited. In addition to being revised and reprinted, a shortened version of the grammar appeared as *Die Grundzüge der Sprache Shakespeares* in 1902.[6]

Two modern books, one English and one German, have the basic features of grammars, but they are much shorter than the works by Abbott and Franz.[7] They are also somewhat more modern in that they give attention to such features as semantics, rhetoric, dialect and register. Brook included few examples because he refers readers to Abbot and Franz for further discussion and exemplification of many points. He does, however, quote from the First Folio and key the quotations to the Globe edition. But as his book contains only 200 pages, there is little room for extensive discussion of grammatical points, many of which are stated baldly and with few or no examples. He relies heavily on the earlier grammars. Scheler's book is even shorter and is divided almost equally between syntax and lexis, with a short introduction on spelling and phonology. He used the first edition of the Norton facsimile of the First Folio and keys the lines to the lineation in the Alexander edition. He also characterises the language of the time as showing a lack of regulation and of functional coherence in syntactic forms.[8] Neither book appears to have made much impact on editors or other scholars; for they are referred to infrequently.

DICTIONARIES AND GLOSSARIES

Although there are bilingual dictionaries of Shakespeare, this section refers only to those in English.[9] Naturally editors from the time of Thomas Hanmer have usually included a glossary of difficult words in their editions of the plays.[10] The most complete dictionary is that by Schmidt, first published in 1874–75 and revised for a third edition by Sarrazin in 1902.[11] As Schmidt explains in his preface, the purpose of the book was different from that of glossaries hitherto which had only explained those words which had become obsolete or unintelligible to modern readers. His dictionary would 'contain his whole vocabulary and subject the sense and use of every word of it to a careful examination' (v). The dictionary uses the modern spellings of the Cambridge edition, but it does not include etymologies. The original intention to include every quotation which illustrated every sense of every word was abandoned and not even full references were given in every case. But the dictionary does include what Schmidt considered the different meanings of each single word, though he scrupulously avoided those difficulties which sprang from grammar or sentence structure. An indication of its comprehensiveness is that *go* occupies almost three full sides and is exemplified in sixteen senses with numerous quotations and references. The book contains a series of four appendices with 1) grammatical observations; 2) provincialisms; 3) words and sentences taken from foreign languages; and 4) list of the words forming the latter part in compositions [i.e. the second, bound element in compounds], though these appendices seem to be very rarely consulted.

The main glossary used today is that by C.T. Onions, though it is quite slight when put next to Schmidt's dictionary.[12] This glossary concentrates in supplying 'definitions and illustrations of words or senses of words now obsolete or surviving only in provincial or archaic use' (iii). It is typical of the glossary type with modernised spelling, no etymologies, and brief definitions with one or two illustrative quotations of the senses provided. It has five senses of *go* together with a list of phrasal verbs with *go*. The entry occupies less than half of a column on a double-column page. Because it is handy and available, it is often the work consulted first by many readers.

A full dictionary of Shakespeare will be difficult to compile until a dictionary of Early Modern English is available. Naturally any scholar of Shakespeare will rely heavily on the *Oxford English Dictionary* which is now available in its second CD-ROM edition.[13] This contains the etymologies and the uses by other contemporary writers which are needed for a proper understanding of Shakespeare's lexis. As modern editors sometimes emend forms out of their texts, this dictionary enables the scholar to check whether their emendations are acceptable. There are also glossaries of specialised vocabularies of this time. The earliest devoted to words from Shakespeare and his contemporaries was compiled by Robert Nares in 1822; a later one by Skeat and Mayhew was devoted to Tudor and Stuart words.[14] Such collections contain a restricted list of words with a few meanings, and they are often collected on the basis that they are unknown in modern times.

The most significant recent development is the Shakespeare Dictionary Database Project based at the University of Münster and directed by Professors Spevack and Neuhaus. The first fruit of this project is *A Shakespeare Thesaurus*[15] which tries to group Shakespeare's lexis into categories based on their superordinate and subordinate status. The book suffers the shortcomings of a thesaurus, though it is a brave attempt to categorise Shakespeare's vocabulary. The project will issue a volume on Shakespeare's morphemes and a CD-ROM which will contain his complete vocabulary, the thesaurus and details of his word-formation and morphemes together with G.B. Evans's Riverside edition (the base text) and facsimiles of the First Folio and quartos.[16] A trial CD-ROM is already available and the main CD-ROM has been promised for a little while now. Other CD-ROMs with various texts on them are also available and these should transform the study of Shakespeare's lexis and morphology depending on the flexibility of the programs included as part of the package.

Another spin-off of the Münster Database has been the various concordances complied by Professor Spevack.[17] This has not entirely superseded the older concordance by Bartlett, which is still found in many libraries and has been frequently reprinted.[18] The new concordance by Spevack is fuller and is arranged in several different ways: complete works, tragedies, comedies and histories, and individual plays. This concordance is now the basic tool for the study of Shakespeare's vocabulary, though it is being replaced by the CD-ROMs.

Specialised studies on individual aspects of Shakespeare's lexis have appeared in glossaries, though they are often incomplete and may be compiled by those who are not lexicographers by training. Most need to be used with caution and should be supplemented by the *Oxford English Dictionary* and Spevack's concordance. The most common subject for such dictionaries is Shakespeare's bawdy or sexual language.[19] Though many aspects of his vocabulary still need detailed study, those glossaries dealing with restricted aspects of his vocabulary are often more complete and reliable than those which treat his sexual language, for that can be a somewhat problematic area. For example, the work of Mats Rydén on flower names in Shakespeare and W.B. Whall on his sea terms are fairly comprehensive.[20]

A book which falls within the scope of dictionaries is the index of Shakespeare's proverbs collected by Dent.[21] This attempts to upgrade the Shakespearean entries in Tilley's list of sixteenth and seventeenth century proverbs, though there is little general discussion as such.

PUNCTUATION AND ORTHOGRAPHY

Grammars of Shakespeare's language often contain brief sections on orthography and punctuation, though such studies are not common if only because most modern editions of Shakespeare are presented in a modernised spelling and punctuation. It is not a subject which occupies more than a few lines in most modern editions. Some specialised studies have appeared. The fullest and most systematic account of Shakespeare's punctuation is that by Simpson, though his book is slight and is not based on a complete survey.[22] The best modern account of punctuation is to be found in various contributions by Vivian Salmon, who has studied not only Shakespeare's own works but also those by other writers of his time and grammars written contemporaneously.[23] These works do not form a comprehensive account of Shakespeare's punctuation, but she has highlighted for editors and literary scholars many of the points which need to be taken into account especially when editing the plays. Unfortunately, the books in which these contributions are published are not widely used or perhaps available, and so her work has not been as influential as it deserves to be.

Among other works, which are mainly designed to call attention to some of the dramatic implications of the original punctuation but which do not provide a comprehensive account of the punctuation, the most recent is a book by Graham-White.[24] This attempts to show developments in punctuation and its use in playscripts, but it is somewhat superficial. However, it and other works do emphasise the significance and value of the original punctuation, since so many modern literary scholars entertain a very prejudiced view of the Quarto and Folio punctuation. It still remains a common view among editors of his plays that the punctuation of quartos and folios is so bad that it can be ignored. Works such as that by Graham-White and others go some way to showing this to be an untenable position to adopt.

Less work has been done on Shakespearean orthography, once more because of the modernisation of his texts today. Two areas have received most attention. The first is aspects of non-standard and colloquial language, especially in the work of A.C. Partridge.[25] This, as its title indicates, deals particularly with clipped forms and contractions in the plays, though it also has a useful section on the orthography found in *Sir Thomas More*. A second book by Partridge, despite its title, deals principally with spelling and punctuation in the non-dramatic works.[26] The second is prompted by discussion of the principles of modernising Shakespeare's language which necessarily involves commenting upon the orthography found in the Quarto and Folio versions.[27] There have been a number of articles which have followed up the work done by Wells on modernisation, and it may be said that the debate still continues about the principles involved.[28] However, a full study of Shakespeare's orthography is still lacking, though to some extent there is naturally an overlap between writings on orthography and his phonology.

In some respects the most significant contribution to a study of punctuation and orthography in Shakespeare's works has been made by Charlton Hinman in his study of the First Folio.[29] Through his work it was possible to trace the various stints by the different compositors and thus to study what system each one preferred and how each compositor may have been influenced by the copytext which he was using. In this way it was theoretically possible to gain some insight into what the spelling and punctuation system of the copytext was and to assume that certain features in spelling and punctuation are attributable to Shakespeare himself. This has in its turn allowed comparison of the systems found in manuscript fragments like *Sir Thomas More* to determine whether the spelling is similar to what one can deduce about the copytext's system and thus to attribute the handwriting and composition to Shakespeare himself.[30] Even so, most of this work has appeared in shorter pieces and has not led to a comprehensive account of Shakespeare's orthography.

Perhaps the most fundamental treatment of punctuation and spelling which has surfaced recently has been the rejection by some scholars of Greg's distinction in editing between substantives and accidentals. It is this distinction which has provided the justification for editions in modern spelling and punctuation. As one scholar has indicated 'we should not work as if meaning is confined to lexical codes'.[31] A number of scholars, working often from a bibliographical position, have complained about the loss of material which takes place when a text from this period is modernised; their view is that this division into substantives and accidentals is both divisive and wrong.[32] However, these significant methodological advances appear to have had little impact so far on editors of Shakespeare.

PHONOLOGY

Phonology is a feature of Shakespeare's language which is rarely raised in modern editions except in so far as they suggest that certain words have the same sound either in rhyme or, more especially, in puns. Yet it is this feature of Shakespeare's language which has received extensive study in the post-war years. The problem for those who study Shakespeare's phonology is that by the time the Quartos and First Folio were printed the writing system had achieved a fair degree of standardisation, even though there was some variation in the stints by the different compositors. This means that it is difficult to see through the spelling system used in the plays to determine precisely how it might represent Shakespeare's pronunciation. This has led to a dispute about the nature of the available evidence both in printed versions of his texts and in material available in grammars written at the time. There have been two views on this matter.

The first finds particular expression in the work of Henry Wyld and Helge Kökeritz.[33] In their view the work of the grammarians on pronunciation at this time was bedevilled by an attempt to systematise and regularise what they thought was appropriate for English rather than to recount what was actually happening to the development of sounds. Inevitably grammarians tend to be conservative and committed to as much regularity as possible. Hence these scholars claim that the grammars are often out of date and usually idealisations of what was happening to the language. They claim that a much better understanding of what was happening at the time can be seen through rhymes, puns and, especially, unusual spellings found in the writings of less well-educated people. The attempts by such people to write as they speak while also trying to match what they considered the more acceptable spellings of their day reveal what was actually taking place in the language. While Wyld has relatively little to say about Shakespeare, Kökeritz devotes a whole book to Shakespeare's sound system and an analysis of his rhymes and puns.

The second and opposed approach is found in the work of Eric Dobson and Fausto Cercignani.[34] These scholars think that the spellings of less well-educated speakers are difficult to interpret, because one cannot tell what vowel may be meant from any given spelling, though it may be easier to do so with consonants. Such speakers are not necessarily accurate in the way they represent their own sounds. Furthermore, it is necessary to make sure that one has an accurate transcript of what they wrote, for many ghost spellings through faulty editing have entered the literature. Without some system, it is difficult to interpret what sounds are represented by rhymes or puns; one may deduce that certain words rhyme together, but that does not reveal what precise sound is represented by the rhyme. The grammarians may be guided by the wish to construct a system and they may sometimes be a little idealistic in what sounds they prefer, but there were competent phoneticians among them and some of them also tried to describe the way that the sounds are made. With judicious interpretation, it is possible from what they write to gain a much clearer idea of the development in sounds at this time. Naturally, this representation is clearest for what was happening within the metropolitan area of London, and it need not follow that Shakespeare's own pronunciation had been fully assimilated into that of London, within which a great deal of variation existed then as it does today.

Cercignani's book represents the most comprehensive account of Shakespeare's pronunciation available, and as part of that account he has to deal extensively with the spellings found in the quartos and the folio. It is unlikely that this book will be superseded in the near future. The material presented is somewhat dense and one must be careful not simply to pick out some statement without seeing it within the context in which Cercignani places it. Although some of the information needs to be treated with caution and the book itself is somewhat difficult to work through, it can readily be used as a work of reference. If one uses it in this way, one must make sure to understand all the implications of what is being proposed, because there are frequent variations in the sounds found in individual words.

SYNTAX

Syntax overlaps with grammar and what has been written in the section on grammar will not be repeated here. It is important to stress that no modern accounts of Shakespeare's syntax have been forthcoming, although considerable information about the syntax of Shakespeare's time can be discovered from Visser's *An Historical Syntax of the English Language*.[35] Syntax is a difficult aspect of language to order in a simple and coherent way, and some find it difficult to find their way through this book. Otherwise, modern scholars have been satisfied simply to shed light on Shakespeare's syntax by discussing individual features, especially in relation to character. As such these books come very close to being studies in style rather than syntax.

One of the earliest of these studies was that by Dolores Burton.[36] This book is partly programmatic in seeking to show that style study could be applied successfully to Shakespeare and outlining how it might be done. The computer was to be used to collect and sample the data. She looked at various features such as interrogatives and imperatives, hypotaxis and occurrence of adjectives. The book contains a large number of tables with statistical information and outlines of the procedures adopted. A more recent book which exploits syntactic structures is that by John Houston.[37] He does not provide a complete analysis of any play. He takes various features of word order within a sentence, clause or group and studies what stylistic implications different word orders might have. He also sees the development of syntax chronologically since he accepts that there is development in Shakespeare's use of syntactic structures from the early plays through to the final ones. A nominal style is, for example, characteristic of early plays such as *Romeo and Juliet,* whereas a much more compressed and asyndetic style is more common in later plays like *Coriolanus.* There are no statistics in this book and the data are somewhat impressionistic, for a large number of features and plays are covered. The general effect is to illuminate style rather than to elucidate syntax.

Work which is more linguistic in its orientation is found in the writings of Teresa Fanego.[38] This studies infinitive complements in detail and shows that their occurrence depends on the type of discourse employed (they are more common in verse than prose) and on the date of composition of the individual plays (for infinitive complements are more common in later than in earlier plays). One might, therefore, regard them as part of the growing complexity of Shakespeare's language as he matured. The conclusions of this book are complemented by a study published in *Studia Neophilologica* on finite complement clauses.[39] The appearance of her book in Spain highlights a growing trend in this type of work. Several syntactic studies on specialised points of Shakespeare's language have been published in non-English-speaking countries by local university presses. Such works may be difficult to get hold of, and they have therefore had less impact on Shakespearean studies than they deserve. This is particularly true, of course, of works published in countries of the former Eastern Block and in Japan.[40] Such works often contain valuable material of a detailed linguistic nature, but their rarity in English-speaking countries means that they have had little impact on Shakespearean studies.

GENERAL STUDIES

In this section I include books which cannot so readily be placed in any of the preceding ones. The books I shall deal with here do not attempt to provide a systematic investigation of Shakespeare's language, for they deal with Shakespeare as part of a wider investigation or they restrict their comments to introducing Shakespeare's language or showing how information about his language can help to enrich a reading of Shakespeare. Apart from general histories of the language, there are books devoted to the development of the English language in the early modern period. The two most significant are by Barber and Görlach.[41] Both go through the various features of language which have been dealt with above, but because their limit is larger they do not have the space to comment extensively on Shakespeare. They do, however, provide an informed understanding of the language of his time.

A.C. Partridge's book on the language of Renaissance poetry is more lexical and stylistic, though it does have a section devoted to Shakespeare.[42] A similar approach is adopted by Ronberg in his book, though his approach is rather more linguistically oriented than that by Partridge, although he too seeks to show how the language is used in Renaissance literature.[43] A book by Ian Michael on the teaching of English contains many valuable insights, since he isolates many of the attitudes towards grammar found at this time as exemplified in the extant grammars and educational works.[44] He provides the background to the kind of education Shakespeare might have received and the attitudes he could have assimilated. Jane Donawerth seeks to provide an account of philosophical attitudes to language at this time and how they can be traced in Shakespeare's plays.[45] The two parts of the book are not always mutually illuminating.

Of more specialised Shakespearean relevance are general books which introduce Shakespeare's language. That by Blake highlights various aspects of language and seeks to show how they can help in an understanding of Shakespeare's meaning.[46] This book is presented with a more modern linguistic methodology, though it should be comprehensible to anyone with a basic traditional grammar. It considers such things as varieties, vocabulary, the verbal group, the nominal group, other word classes, and word order in turn. In a short book he cannot give many examples or produce a systematic account. Hussey's book concentrates more on Shakespeare in his time.[47] He concentrates on vocabulary and syntax, and his study tends towards stylistic appreciation.

An impotant general book is that by Hilda Hulme who uses local records from Warwickshire and surrounding counties to elucidate the meaning of some of Shakespeare's usages, especially lexical ones.[48] She shows how he might have been influenced by his own dialect in his choice of vocabulary. W.F. Bolton has written a book on the language of Shakespeare's history plays.[49] Using a computer database, he studies a single play against a single linguistic feature: sounds in *Richard III*, vocabulary in *King John*, pragmatics in *Henry VIII* and so on. Inevitably the coverage is superficial and the discussion of specific theoretical concepts is slight. The book is not as helpful as it might have been.

Two important collections of essays repay close attention. The first by Salmon and Burgess is divided into the following sections, aspects of colloquial Elizabethan English, studies in vocabulary, Shakespeare and Elizabethan grammar, studies in rhetoric and metre, punctuation and the linguistic context of Shakespearean drama.[50] There are many important articles in this volume which repay careful study, but which have not necessarily provoked much further enquiry into the area of linguistics covered. The other book is that by Blake, which includes a selection of the essays written by him over the last ten years.[51] These often introduce more general comments on Shakespeare's language or highlight how new approaches associated with modern linguistics could be applied to Shakespeare.

One of the areas covered in both volumes is Shakespeare and nonstandard language. It is difficult to know where to fit this feature in, since it is something which overlaps with many areas in linguistic studies. The main concerns have been firstly to isolate what sounds may have been implied by the non-standard features Shakespeare uses, the problem of what is meant by colloquial and how colloquiality may be detected in Shakespeare's works, and the question of what spellings to use in any modernisation and how far those spellings should be imposed on the text. Non-standard language passes over easily into questions of register. For example, how far is swearing nonstandard and how far is it a matter of discourse style and register. These concerns are raised to some extent in the book by Shirley on swearing.[52]

A number of books are more concerned with style and literary matters than with language. This is particularly true of some earlier books which may have *language* in their titles, such as B. Ifor Evans, *The Language of Shakespeare's Plays* (3rd edition, 1964). But it applies also to some more modern books, quite apart from those which are specifically devoted to rhetoric. Among them may be mentioned *Shakespeare Meaning & Metaphor,* and *Shakespeare's Poetic Styles.*[53] The former attempts to apply critical theories of metaphor to Shakespearean usage and the latter analyses Shakespeare's use of high and low styles.

MODERN LINGUISTIC APPROACHES

The development of modern linguistic theories about and approaches to language was relatively slow in having any impact on the study of Shakespeare's language. But increasingly these have tended to inform new studies. Three areas in particular may be said to have been significant: sociolinguistics, discourse analysis and pragmatics. It is, however, true to suggest that some older studies could be said to fall within what today would be regarded as these approaches even though their authors might not have been familiar with linguistics as such. Inevitably some style studies overlap with discourse analysis and pragmatics, and sociolinguistics today may not be too far away from register in older studies. Some scholars simply study a feature in Shakespeare's plays which they find interesting, such as his forms of address, without necessarily approaching it with a methodology which could be said to be informed by any linguistic theory. It is only recently that these approaches have tended to produce book-length studies, for it is more characteristic that a scholar seizes on a particular feature and examines it in one or two plays.

Approaches which might be termed sociolinguistic have concentrated especially on Shakespeare's use of the second person of the personal pronoun, for it is often assumed that there is a significant difference between his characters' use of the *thou/thee* and *ye/you* forms. The latter are neutral, whereas the former may imply intimacy, anger or contempt. Studies of this feature in one or more plays are common enough and examples are found in the Salmon and Burgess reader.[54] But it needs to be remembered that we cannot be certain that the forms which survive are those which Shakespeare himself introduced, for studies of the differences between quartos and First Folio have shown that there is variation between the usage of these forms which is probably the work of the compositor rather than of the author. The variation in vocabulary is also frequently related to social and stylistic factors in modern studies. The use of malapropism and colloquialisms are often referred to social status and etiquette. However, a complete study has yet to be made of his usage of these features.

A book which relies on sociolinguistic and sociohistorical linguistic evidence is that by Jonathan Hope.[55] This book uses three linguistic features, the auxiliary *do,* relative markers such as *who, which* and *that,* and the personal pronouns *thou* and *you,* to determine the authorship of various plays which have at one time or another been attributed in whole or in part to Shakespeare. This means trying to resolve which parts of plays are Shakespeare's in his collaborative ventures with Fletcher and then Middleton, and which plays in the apocrypha may be entirely or partly his. The methodology employed is tracing the chosen linguistic features in the historical development of the language and comparing their use in the known plays by Shakespeare with those by other authors. Although the aim of the book is a study of authorship, it inevitably produces a lot of data of Shakespeare's use of the named linguistic features. How far the principal aim, the resolution of the debate about authorship, may be achieved, the book provides valuable insights into the use of language by Shakespeare and others at his time. It is certainly a book whose methodology could be extended to other plays and other authors.

Discourse analysis and pragmatics in Shakespearean studies were given some impetus by Keir Elam, who introduced the topic for many Shakespearean scholars, although he was building on suggestions made by other scholars for its general application to literature, especially drama.[56] Elam emphasises some of the problems in studying Shakespeare's language:

> Studies, especially book-length studies, of Shakespeare's language run two main risks. The first is the risk of tautology, or, what amounts to the same thing, of getting lost in a virtually limitless terrain. In the textual form in which we have received it, Shakespearean drama is *all* language. . . . The second risk is the opposite one, namely of too severe a delimitation of the critical and dramatic territory. Whatever its descriptive value, criticism that abstracts from

the plays a given linguistic function or level – Shakespeare's syntax, Shakespeare's imagery, Shakespeare's lexicon, etc. – will not normally be able to integrate its findings into an overall account of linguistic structure. (2–3).

He uses the speech-act framework proposed by the philosopher J.L. Austin and developed by others to highlight discourse structures in the comedies and to provide some means of understanding the language games found in them. At this point his book tries to marry the speech-act approach to critical appreciation of how language is used in these plays. The result is to diverge from a straightforward linguistic approach and to discuss the plays in more general terms, especially in the application of rhetoric, though using language as the centre around which his discussion can be built.

A more thorough linguistic study along similar lines is that by Kay Wikberg who analyses questions and answers in Shakespeare.[57] This study relies on a somewhat older methodology, though it pays some attention to transformational grammar and its overall approach has much in common with modern approaches to discourse. The author studies questions and replies in all Shakespeare's plays, though some are given special emphasis. The question-answer patterns in Shakespeare are much the same as those in modern English, but their analysis can yield interesting results for style and understanding how various scenes operate. But the major results of this study are data-oriented and the actual analysis is much less significant for the appreciation of the plays than for an understanding of the nature of questions and answers more generally.

Discourse in Shakespeare was given some attention in a book on discourse analysis, which is not likely to be the usual reading of most Shakespearean scholars.[58] In this book Coulthard applied the analysis of conversation which had been developed in classroom practice to literature and he used *Othello* as one of his examples of how discourse analysis could help to elucidate meaning and significance in a text. In his analysis Coulthard is able to propose how Othello so easily falls prey to Iago's suggestions through the discourse pattern of the play. 'Iago rouses Othello's suspicion by a sequence of unanswered questions, not simply because they are unanswered but because they are avoided clumsily and in fact deliberately so, in order to suggest to Othello that Iago is deliberately concealing something.' (185).

Coulthard's lead has been followed by other scholars such as Blake who have broadened his field of enquiry. A number of approaches have been tried, one of the most prominent being that of discourse markers. Considerable attention has been devoted to discourse markers in modern English and the way in which they can frame talk, and this has then been given a historical dimension by such scholars as Laurel Brinton and Deborah Schiffrin.[59] Several essays by Blake, found in the collection of essays noted above (fn.51), have built on these foundations. He has studied how editors have paid insufficient attention to the nature of *why* and *what* as discourse markers, because they can function both as markers and as interrogative adverbs. The tone of a passage can be significantly altered depending on how one interprets one of these words. In another essay he analyses the opening of *Hamlet* as it is found in quarto and First Folio to show how a review of their discourse strategies can tell us something about the play and its setting.

Much work on discourse in Shakespeare has been done outside Britain and the United States. An example of this work is the collection of essays by Shigenobu Fuami.[60] Some of these essays are devoted to a consideration of the use of *well* in various plays. He discusses which verbs it is used with and how in some plays like *Henry V* its association with some verbal phrases indicates an intention which is fulfilled later in the play. Other essays are devoted to the marking of emphasis, and in this area he pays particular attention to the language of women and to certain lower class characters. He analyses the means of creating emphasis and how these means are deployed by different characters.

Pragmatic approaches overlap with discourse analysis and again much of this work has been done by scholars outside the English-speaking world. Some of these works are introductory and others more specialised. A more introductory work is that by Juhani Rudanko.[61] His book explores the application of distinct linguistic approaches in each of his five major chapters: questions and requests as found in adjacency pairs, establishment of dominance in a conversation, interactional discourse among two characters, the use of speech-act theory, and politeness theory. Each chapter looks at what has been proposed as a theoretical background to the concept and then applies it to a different play or section of a play to test what has been written so far and how it might be extended to Shakespeare. The book's purpose is 'to give some indication of the range of linguistic methods that are available or that can be made available' (191) in investigating Shakespearean drama. The theories exploited are those which were developed in the first instance to explain or elucidate natural conversation in the modern period and not for the study of literature. Rudanko seeks to show how these techniques can readily be adapted for the study of texts, especially dramatic ones.

His last chapter builds upon the work of Brown and Gilman on politeness theory.[62] They review politeness theory and how in the form of evaluating the power, distance and ranked extremity of each speech act it can reveal so much about the development of the plays and the interaction of their characters. They conclude 'Dramatic texts offer good possibilities for the study of politeness theory. They offer wide social and characterological scope, and because the speech is not elicited from informants but was invented by authors for purposes of their own, dramatic texts can surprise analysts, as Shakespeare has surprised us, into discoveries they had not envisioned' (208).

A slightly more specialised approach is taken by Marta Gabinska in her work.[63] She tries to analyse the functioning of language at two different levels, the fictive world and the world of text and its reader, through studying the openings of certain plays and some crucial scenes in others. Particular attention is paid to misunderstanding and lack of communication between characters. This book shows how it is possible to combine a linguistic approach with a more theoretical critical approach, and takes the application of linguistic theories in a slightly different direction.

CONCLUSION

This has been a cursory survey of where we stand today in language studies in Shakespeare. A review may be found in an article by Partridge and further bibliographies are available in many of the books cited in the footnotes.[64]

It may be said that the study of Shakespeare's language is in a state of transition. There are only a few major works devoted to a study of his language, and recently such thorough studies have usually been directed towards his phonology and orthography.[65] Increasingly attempts are made to apply modern linguistic approaches to Shakespeare, but most studies so far are exploratory rather than definitive. No one play has yet been subjected to a thorough-going analysis of its language. A new grammar remains an important desideratum, and the publication of the much-delayed CD-ROM of Shakespeare's vocabulary may give a boost to studies of his lexis and word-formation. Too much of what editors and literary critics have to say about Shakespeare's language is based on rather out-of-date approaches, but the absence of a comprehensive account of his language using modern approaches makes it difficult for non-linguists to adapt what they have to say about Shakespeare's language to an appropriate direction. The bifurcation of literary and linguistic studies has not been a blessing for the study of Shakespeare's language, but there are signs that this gap is now closing.

REFERENCES

1. Abbott, E.A. (1869), *A Shakespearean Grammar*, London: Macmillan, often revised and re-issued, and Franz, W. (1898–1900), *Shakespeare-Grammatik* (Halle: Niemeyer), frequently revised and re-issued. The grammar by Abbott is to be included on the CD-ROM on Shakespeare with the Arden texts.
2. I quote from the reprint of the third edition.
3. 'nur eine übersichtliche Zusammenfassung der charakteristischen Züge des Sh.schen Englisch' (iii).
4. 'die gesprochene Sprache der Gebildeten von heute' (iii).
5. Winter, Carl (1905), *Orthographie, Lautgebung und Wortbildung in den Werken Shakespeares mit Ausspracheproben*, Heidelberg.
6. It was published in Berlin by Emil Felber.
7. Brook, G.L. (1976), *The Language of Shakespeare*. The Language Library, London: Deutsch) and Scheler, Manfred (1982), *Shakespeares Englisch, Eine*

sprachwissenschaftliche Einführung. Grundlagen der Anglistik und Amerikanistik 12, Berlin: Schmidt.

8.   'ein häufig Mangel an Regelgebundenheit und funktionaler Eindeutigkeit der synt. Ausdrucksmittel' (85).

9.   See, for example, Leon Kellner (1922), *Shakespeare-Wörterbuch.* Englische Bibliothek 1, Leipzig: Tauchnitz. Although fairly inclusive, this dictionary is rather restricted in its definitions and references.

10.   A list of these may be found in Arthur G. Kennedy (1927), *A Bibliography of Writings on the English Language from the Beginning of Printing to the End of 1922*, Cambridge Mass.: Harvard University Press, rptd New York: Hafner, 1961, p. 250 ff.

11.   Schmidt, A. *Shakespeare Lexicon. A Complete Dictionary of all the English Words, Phrases and Constructions in the Works of the Poet.* 2 vols. (Berlin: Reimer, London: Williams and Norgate, 1874–75), and *Shakespeare-lexicon*, rev. by Gregor Sarrazin. 2 vols. 3rd edn. (Berlin: Reimer, New York: Stechert, 1902).

12.   Onions, C.T. (1911), *A Shakespeare Glossary*; 3rd edn enlarged and revised throughout by Robert D. Eagleson (Oxford: Clarendon, 1986).

13.   J.H. Murray, *A New English Dictionary on Historical Principles* (Oxford Clarendon, 1884–1928), reissued as the *Oxford English Dictionary* 13 vols (Oxford: Clarendon, 1930), 2nd supplement ed Burchfield, R.W. 13 vols (Oxford: Clarendon, 1972–86). Available in CD-ROM 2nd edn (Oxford, 1992).

14.   Nares, Robert (1822), *A Glossary; or Collection of Words, Phrases etc., which have been thought to require Illustration, in the Works of English Authors and particularly Shakespeare and his Contemporaries*, London: Triphook; W.W. Skeat (1914), *A Glossary of Tudor and Stuart Words especially from the Dramatists* edited with additions by A.L. Mayhew Oxford: Clarendon; rptd Hildesheim: Olms, 1968.

15.   Spevack, Marvin (1993), *A Shakespeare Thesaurus*, Hildesheim: Olms.

16.   Neuhaus, H. Joachim (c.1997), *Shakespeare's Word-Formations* (Hildesheim: Olms) and his *Shakespeare Database CD-ROM*, Hildesheim: Olms, c.1997.

17.   Spevack, Martvin (1968–75), *A Complete and Systematic Concordance to the Works of Shakespeare.* 9 vols, Hildesheim: Olms.

18.   Bartlett, John (1894), *A New and Complete Concordance or Verbal Index to Words, Phrases and Passages in the Dramatic Works of Shakespeare with Supplementary Concordance to the Poems*, London and New York: Macmillan; last rptd 1979.

19.   The best known is Eric Partridge (1947), *Shakespeare's Bawdy*, London: Routledge & Kegan Paul; rev.edn 1975. See also Frankie Rubinstein, *A Dictionary of Shakespeare's Sexual Puns and their Significance*, London: Macmillan, 1984, 2nd edn 1988; Gordon Williams, *A Dictionary of Sexual Language and Imagery in Shakespearean and Stuart Literature.* 3 vols, London: Athlone, 1994; and his *A Glossary of Shakespeare's Sexual Language*, London: Athlone, 1997.

20.   Rydén, Mats (1978), *Shakespearean Plant Names: Identifications and Interpretations*, Stockholm: Almqvist & Wiksell, and W.B. Whall (1910), *Shakespeare's Sea Terms*, Bristol: Arrowsmith, London: Simpkin, Marshall, rev. edn 1911.

21.   Dent, R.W. (1981), *Shakespeare's Proverbial Language: An Index*, Berkeley CA: University of California Press.

22.   Simpson, Percy (1911), *Shakespearian Punctuation*, Oxford: Clarendon.

23.   Salmon, Vivian 'The spelling and punctuation of Shakespeare's time,' in *William Shakespeare, The Complete Works Original-Spelling Edition*, ed.

Stanley Wells and Gary Taylor, Oxford: Clarendon, 1986, xlii–lvi; *The Study of Language in Seventeenth-Century England* (1988), Amsterdam: Benjamins, and 'English punctuation theory 1500–1800', *Anglia* 106 (1988): 285–314.

24. Graham-White, Anthony (1995), *Punctuation and its Dramatic Value in Shakespearean Drama*, Newark: University of Delaware Press, London: Associated University Presses.

25. Partridge, A.C. (1968), *Orthography in Shakespeare and Elizabethan Drama: A Study of Colloquial Contractions, Elision, Prosody and Punctuation*, Lincoln: University of Nebraska Press, and 'Shakespeare's orthography in *Venus and Adonis* and some early quartos,' *Shakespeare Survey* 7 (1954): 35–47.

26. *A Substantive Grammar of Shakespeare's Nondramatic Texts* (1976), Charlottesville: University Press of Virginia. Partridge sees this book as a useful aid to preparing old-spelling editions.

27. Stanley Wells and Gary Taylor (1979), *Modernizing Shakespeare's Spelling, with Three Studies in the Text of 'Henry V'*. Oxford: Clarendon.

28. See, for example, N.F. Blake (1990), 'Modernizing language and editing Shakespeare,' *Poetica* (Tokyo) 34: 101–23 [rptd in his *Essays on Shakespeare's Language 1st series* (Misterton: Language Press, 1996), 63–105.]

29. Charlton Hinman (1973), *The Printing and Proof-reading of the First Folio of Shakespeare*. 2 vols, Oxford: Clarendon, and see the introduction to *The Norton Facsimile: The First Folio of Shakespeare*, 2nd edn prepared by Peter W.M. Blayney, New York and London: Norton, 1996.

30. An introduction to some of the problems surrounding *Sir Thomas More* is found in Partridge (1964) 43–66

31. Lennard, John (1995), 'Punctuation: And – "Pragmatics"', in *Historical Pragmatics: Pragmatic Developments in the History of English*, ed. Andreas H. Jucker, Amsterdam: Benjamins, 87.

32. See Lennard fn.31 65–98 and his *But I Digress: the Exploitation of Parentheses in English Printed Verse* (Oxford: Clarendon, 1991) and references there.

33. Wyld, H.C. (1936), *A History of Modern Colloquial English*. Oxford: Clarendon, 3rd edn, and H. Kökeritz (1953), *Shakespeare's Pronunciation*, New Haven: Yale University Press, 1953.

34. Dobson, E.J. (1968), *English Pronunciation 1500–1700*, Oxford: Clarendon, 2nd edn, and Fausto Cercignani (1981), *Shakespeare's Works and Elizabethan Pronunciation*, Oxford: Clarendon.

35. Visser, F.Th. (1963–73), *An Historical Syntax of the English Language*, Leiden: Brill, 3 vols.

36. Burton, Dolores (1973), *Shakespeare's Grammatical Style. A Computer-Assisted Analysis of 'Richard II' and 'Antony and Cleopatra'*, Austin and London: University of Texas Press.

37. Houston, John Porter (1988), *Shakespearean Sentences: A Study in Style and Syntax*, Baton Rouge and London: Louisiana State University Press.

38. See especially her *Infinitive Complements in Shakespeare's English*, Santiago de Compostela: University of Santiago.

39. 'Finite complement clauses in Shakespeare's English,' 62 (1990): 3–21 and 129–49.

40. As examples one may quote P. Katietek (1972), *Modal Verbs in Shakespeare's English*, Poznan: Universytet im Adama Mickiewicza and Shigenobu Fuami (1997), *Essays on Shakespeare's Language: Language, Discourse and Text*, Kyoto: Apollon-sha.

41. Görlach, M. (1991), *An Introduction to Early Modern English*, Cambridge: Cambridge University Press, and C.Barber (1976), *Early Modern English*. The Language Library, London: Deutsch.

42. Partridge, A.C. (1971), *The Language of Renaissance Poetry*, London: Deutsch.

43. Ronberg, Gert (1992), *A Way with Words: The Language of English Renaissance Literature*, London: Arnold.

44. Michael, Ian (1978), *The Teaching of English From the Sixteenth Century to 1870*, Cambridge: Cambridge University Press.

45. Donawerth, Jane (1984), *Shakespeare and the Sixteenth-Century Study of Language*, Urbana and Chicago: University of Illinois Press.

46. Blake, N.F. (1983), *Shakespeare's Language: An Introduction*, Basingstoke: Macmillan, [reissued as *The Language of Shakespeare* in 1989].

47. Hussey, S. (1982), *The Literary Language of Shakespeare*, London: Longman; 2nd edn 1992.

48. Hulme, Hilda (1962), *Explorations in Shakespeare's Language: Some Problems of Word Meaning in the Dramatic Text*, London: Longman, 2nd edn 1977.

49. Bolton, W.F. (1992), *Shakespeare's English: Language in the History Plays*, Oxford:Blackwell.

50. Salmon, V. and Burgess, E. (1987), *Reader in the Language of Shakespearean Drama*, Amsterdam: Benjamins.

51. Blake, N.F. (1996), *Essays on Shakespeare's Language 1st Series*, Misterton: Language Press.

52. Shirley, Frances A. (1979), *Swearing and Perjury in Shakespeare's Plays*, London: Allen & Unwin.

53. Thompson, Ann & John O. (1987), *Shakespeare Meaning & Metaphor*, Brighton: Harvester, and John Baxter (1980), *Shakespeare's Poetic Style: Verse into Drama*, London: Routledge & Kegan Paul.

54. An early study is Geraldine Byrne, *Shakespeare's Use of the Pronoun of Address, its Significance in Characterisation and Motivation* (New York, 1936).

55. *The Authorship of Shakespeare's Plays: A Socio-linguistic Study* (Cambridge: Cambridge University Press,1994).

56. Elam, Keir (1984), *Shakespeare's Universe of Discourse: Language-Games in the Comedies*, Cambridge: Cambridge University Press.

57. Wilkberg, Kay (1975), *Yes-No Questions and Answers in Shakespeare's Play: A Study in Text Linguistics*. Acta Academiae Aboensis Ser. A Humaniora 51.1, Abo: Abo Akademi.

58. Coulthard, Malcolm (1985), *An Introduction to Discourse Analysis*. London: Longman, 2nd edn, [1st edn 1977]), 179–92.

59. Brinton, Laurel J. (1990), 'The development of discourse markers in English', in Jacek Fisiak, *Historical Linguistics*, Amsterdam: Benjamins, 31–53, and Schiffrin, Deborah (1987), *Discourse Markers*, Cambridge: Cambridge University Press.

60. Fuami, Shigenobu (1997), *Essays on Shakespeare's Language: Language, Discourse and Text*, Kyoto: Apollo-sha.

61. Rudanko, Juhani (1993), *Pragmatic Approaches to Shakespeare: Essays on Othello, Coriolanus and Timon of Athens*, Lanham, London and New York: University Press of America.

62. Brown, Roger and Gilman, Albert (1989), 'Politeness theory and Shakespeare's four major tragedies,' *Language in Society*, 18: 159–212.

63. Gabinska, Marta (1987), *The Functioning of Language in Shakespeare's Plays: A Pragma-Dramatic Approach*, Krakov: Jagellonian University.

64. Partridge, A.C. (1979), 'Shakespeare's English: a bibliographical survey', *Poetica* (Tokyo) 11: 46–79.

65. See further, N.F. Blake, 'Shakespeare's language: past achievements and

future directions', in *Proceedings of the XIXth International Conference of Aedean*, edited by Javier Pérez Guerra et al., Vigo: Universidade de Vigo, 1996, 21–35.

11   Shakespeare and Religion

Donna B. Hamilton

The topic of Shakespeare and religion causes stir. There remains resistance to readings that represent Shakespeare as holding specific positions on religion or politics, and there is the state of the evidence as to Shakespeare's religious convictions: according to Patrick Collinson, while the evidence for saying that Shakespeare's father was a Catholic is 'very nearly conclusive,' about William Shakespeare, 'we cannot say'.[1] Nevertheless, current work on early modern religion, literature, and politics – taken for granted to be crucial to studies of Sidney, Spenser, Marlowe, Dekker, Daniel, Jonson, and Donne, as well as to history of the book, early modern women's writing, and metropolitan and provincial culture – is increasingly understood to be relevant to Shakespeare. This essay reviews trends in current historical and literary studies that affect how work proceeds on the subject of Shakespeare and religion. As opportunities to access this topic increase, opportunities to avoid the subject dwindle.

No contribution to the issue of Shakespeare and religion has been more important than the validation of the relevance of religion to the study of Tudor and Stuart drama. Central has been the overturning of the long-held assumption that, under Elizabeth, and following the injunctions against printing religious materials instituted by Mary, theological topics and religious controversies were not represented on stage. Paul W. White has shown that the 1559 proclamation 'Prohibiting Unlicensed Interludes and Plays, Especially on Religion or Policy' was not enforced, and that representation of religion on stage was vigorously continued through the 1570s as a tool for the more effective protestantisation of England. Summarizing recent research, White has concluded that the notion that there were no religious plays after Dr. Faustus is 'insupportable'; rather there was a 'continuing theatrical representation of Protestant orthodoxy, occultist practice, and libertine humanist reaction to religion throughout the early modern era'. Richard Dutton has argued that the 1589 order which established a licensing commission appointed by the Archbishop of Canterbury and the Lord Mayor of London to guard against matters of divinity in plays did not remain in effect, and in general, that the Master of the

Revels, whose role included negotiating the politics of patrons, fostered the liberty of the theatre as much as its repression.[2]

An earlier assumption, that poets who wrote to please patrons reified official government positions is thus replaced by a notion of a less tightly controlled theatre, and even of a nobility which, itself characterized by political and religious differences, ensured not uniformity but a theatrical and literary diversity. Although their emphases differ, both Janet Clare and Cyndia Susan Clegg have described censorship practices as contingent on changing social and political situations, a point Clegg has made in a different way in an essay on press censorship and *Richard II*, 'There exists . . . a surprisingly small number of texts written and printed in England that the government deemed transgressive, and these locate Elizabethan press censorship quite precisely in the politics of personality, patronage, and national interest'.[3] These treatments of censorship – influenced by Annabel Patterson's descriptions of self-censorship and by David Norbrook's view that poets 'developed elaborate strategies to try to preserve a degree of independence for their writing'[4] – have reshaped assumptions about what topics were represented in drama and poetry, despite the fact that censorship was primarily driven by concerns over managing religious reform.

Even as a significant realignment has taken place in theatre history in relation to religion, so has there been a realignment across early modern literary studies in relation to Shakespeare. Prior to the 1980s, few books treated Shakespeare alongside his contemporaries. A representative example of such exclusive practices is Elizabeth Story Donno's edition of *Elizabethan Minor Epics*, which did not include the text of *Venus and Adonis*. Two decades later, the books that offered models for different practices were books that would stimulate change across Renaissance studies, many of which also treated religious matter. Other scholars have described the intellectual event represented in Stephen Greenblatt's *Renaissance Self-Fashioning*; for Shakespeare studies, a major contribution was Greenblatt's merely having included Shakespeare in a book that also discussed More, Tyndale, Wyatt, Spenser, and Marlowe; Jonathan Dollimore and Alan Sinfield belonged to the same destabilizing camp. But Shakespeare lined up alongside his contemporaries is still a Shakespeare confined to a parallel column rather than set down on a road intersecting with and trespassing the territories of others. An important move was Helgerson's analysis of the institutions by means of which England fashioned a national identity, a thematized organizational structure that placed Shakespeare both within and in relationship to the larger building blocks – law, church, theatre, epic, cartography – of English culture. Now essays on Shakespeare and religion appear in collections of essays on other early modern writers.[5]

In her sustained project on religion, Debora Shuger has addressed the problem of a literary history of the Renaissance that omits religion. Defining her work in the context of cultural materialism and New Historicism,

Shuger has commented that 'the almost total neglect of society's religious aspects in favour of political ones – a reaction against the theological bias of earlier Renaissance criticism – has produced in recent literary scholarship a curiously distorted picture of the period'. Emphasizing the importance to intellectual history of the role of religion, Shuger has declared, 'Religion during this period supplies the primary language of analysis. It is the cultural matrix for explorations of virtually every topic: kingship, selfhood, rationality, language, marriage, ethics,and so forth. Such subjects are . . . articulated in it; they are considered *in relation to* God and the human soul. That is what it means to say that the English Renaissance was a religious culture, not simply a culture whose members generally were religious'.[6] Like revisionist historians who have resituated their work within the assumption that consensus was a more fundamentally driving force in politics than conflict and opposition, Shuger has situated her approach to intellectual history as a description of the dominant culture, and thus of Protestant writing. That Shakespeare has almost always been seen as a writer whose work is rich in religious reference and yet difficult to theorize or pin down theologically makes Shuger's work important to Shakespeare studies. The impact of her contribution will be felt on Shakespeare studies by scholars who supplement it with the recent historiography of the English reformation.

A statement by Patrick Collinson locates one agenda of the new history of Protestantism: 'A long-running dispute about Spenser, whether he should be classified as a Protesant or a Puritan, is sterile, since it rests on a distinction which cannot in fact be made . . . Puritanism was neither alien to Protestantism nor even distinct from it but was its logical extension, equivalent to its full internalization'.[7] That statement suggests how Collinson's narrative of Protestantism has shifted away from the emphasis that prevailed in *The Elizabethan Puritan Movement* (1967), where it was the divisions among Protestants – those satisfied with the Elizabethan Settlement and those looking for further reform – that interested him. In his later work, Collinson has aligned more closely with the political revisionists (among them, Conrad Russell and G. R. Elton) who, departing from a Whig historiography, have defined English politics as characterized not by conflict but by consensus. In her survey of current historiography, Margo Todd summarizes, 'As [Collinson] argued in *The Religion of Protestants* (1982), most protestants, puritans and bishops alike, were bound together by a common theology and evangelical commitment and determined to work together within the national Church to bring about reform at the popular level, to impose a new, disciplined, protestant culture centered on the Word of God'.[8]

Historians who participate in, while taking exception to, revisionist versions of Protestant consensus include Peter Lake and Peter White. Concentrating on the group he calls 'moderate puritans', Lake has insisted on the divisions caused both by the theologies of predestination which divided people between the elect and the reprobate, and by theologies (especially Arminianism) which rejected predestinarianism. Lake's studies of the rhetoric of Protestant conservatives and of anti-Catholic rhetoric delineate the discourses by means of which consensus was constructed. Also emphasizing the differences that existed within the English church, Peter White shows the extent to which theological positions associated with one group or one period can be found across a wider spectrum of individuals and years;[9] his discussion is an antidote to labelling in general, and to the facile characterizations of puritanism that continue to be practiced by literary scholars.

The new historiographies of consensus as well as of differences arm us against assuming that a religious allegiance was necessarily the same as or determined social and political allegiances. As Gordon McMullan has noted, both the Beaumonts and the Treshams were known 'for persistent recusancy . . . yet their political and social connections' were 'preeminently Protestant, even militant Protestant, in credential'.[10] And, in an important though later example, David L. Smith has described Edward Sackville, fourth Earl of Dorset, as a 'slippery customer for those modern historians who wish to see unbridgeable confessional gulfs' in early Stuart England: 'A detailed study of him reveals ambiguities of position that confused his contemporaries and confound modern categorization'.[11] The revisionist historiographers' attention to a consensus politics, White's attention to diffuse categories of differences, together with observances like these by McMullan and Smith, make Shakespeare's seemingly elusive religious positioning less a barrier to thinking about religion in his plays and poems.

Recent historiography also pursues intersections of religion, law, and politics, often by way of the languages that these intersections produced and through which they occurred. Working with the languages of common law, civil law, and theology during the later Elizabethan and Stuart periods, Glenn Burgess has studied how audience and context governed which language might be used on certain occasions for a particular topic, such as the relationship between king and law, or the obedience of subjects.[12] As a constitutive part of many fields of knowledge and relationships, the language of theology could serve as a consensus-building language for a variety of situations. By the same token, the languages of law and politics were central to ecclesiastical matters. Elizabethan ecclesiastical policy – under the eager careerism of the arch-conformist Archbishop Whitgift and canon lawyer Richard Cosin, and despite the opposition of common lawyers James Morice and Robert Beale – supported a growing monarchical absolutism. Like the practitioners of censorship, these engineers of absolutism relied on the developing institutions and language of the protestant church to forge their futures. One avenue was through expansion of *ex officio* prosecutions in the ecclesiastical courts during the 1590s. Affecting Protestant and Catholic dissidents, such prosecutions included the watershed case of Robert Cawdrey, as well as the trials of

Thomas Tresham and Thomas Cartwright. Writes John Guy, 'when Bancroft succeeded Whitgift, the conformist drive for hierarchy and order was further intensified'.[13] Because such policies affected a broad spectrum of people, the elite as well as the middling sort, literary texts, including drama, can be expected to register these issues.[14]

Notions of a Protestantism that is both more consensus-driven and diverse, as well as the tool of absolutists, carry a range of implications in the context of what has been the forceful reintroduction of Catholicism to the scene of early modern studies. The work of four scholars has been especially at issue as theses regarding the rate and means by which the protestantisation of England occurred and by which Catholicism had been eliminated or experienced revival have undergone revision: A. G. Dickens had described a Protestant reformation that was both rapid and from below, a 'swift advance at the popular level . . . driven by strong ideological strain toward an improved religion'. G. R. Elton had argued that the reformation was rapid, from above, and virtually in place by 1553. On the catholic side, John C. H. Aveling had understood that English medieval catholicism had died out between 1534 and 1570, and thereafter a combination of spontaneous revival in England and missionary effort in England by the seminaries abroad developed a new catholic body. John Bossy had argued that after 1570 a defunct catholic community was recreated by the seminary priests and Jesuits.[15] The common denominators in these theses were Protestant strength and Catholic absence.

The new Catholic historiography, led by Christopher Haigh, J. J. Scarisbrick, and Eamon Duffy, has constructed sixteenth-century English religious culture as characterized by a strong catholic presence over a wider geographical area for a longer period of time, and has argued for a general populace that was more reluctant, conservative, and resistant in the face of reform than had earlier been held. According to Haigh, the new evidence 'is likely to shift the consensus of historical generalization towards a recognition that the early phases of the Reformation were indecisive, and that major Protestant advance took place mainly in the Elizabethan period. Only in the latter part of the sixteenth century, when a Protestant regime remodelled commissions of the peace and diocesan administrations to give power to supporters of reform, when the redistribution of clerical patronage weakened conservative interests and when the universities produced a supply of committed preachers of the new religion, did Protestantism have a real and widespread impact'.[16]

The implications of a continuing, as opposed to obliterated, later sixteenth-century catholicism include the variety of subject positions that Catholics assumed, including the phenomena of church papism (outward conformity to protestantism), of recusancy (the refusal to obey the church attendance laws), and of conversion back and forth between Protestantism and Catholicism, all of which further deconstruct the notion of an impermeable, essentialized protestant presence. Haigh's contribution has included his view that 'separated English Catholicism, with its important churchpapist penumbra, was not a new post-Reformation creation of missionaries from the Continent; it was a continuation of traditional English Catholicism shaped by the circumstances of the Reformation in England' (207), and was hurt more than helped by the returning Jesuits who, rather than cultivating the established but poorer Catholic communities in the north, located in southwestern gentry houses.[17]

Focusing on church papists from the 1580s to the second decade of the seventeenth century, Alexandra Walsham has argued that church papism was the non-recusant catholic choice that provided safety from fines, loss of property, and imprisonment; it 'was not a posture of apathy, but one of moral dilemma – a scrupulous as well as pragmatic answer to the problem of proscription'. And she has linked the practices of Catholics and those of dissenting protestants in concluding that church papism illustrates the degree to which 'Elizabethan and Jacobean Catholicism appears a religious culture of dissent marked in practice by a decisive degree of cooperation and compromise ... Just as the godly [within puritanism] were able to engage in additional and alternative pious practices while remaining within the embrace of the ecclesiastical establishment, so too could the church of England cosily accommodate the equally eccentric religiosity of church papists. In some respects, Tudor and early Stuart Catholicism might also be better characterised as semi-separating'. Working along related lines, Michael Questier has turned away from political and ecclesiastical categories and focused on the belief system itself, on the concern with salvation and with moving the will. Arguing that these categories exist largely outside the polemical debates along which historians usually organize discussion of ecclesiastical matters, he has shown how much shifting about occurred, as individuals changed their minds about their belief systems across and within the traditional protestant and catholic divides and back again.[18] The dominant culture was protestant, but that the old faith was no longer within the thinking and knowledge of those living in later Elizabethan and early Stuart England is not a viable working assumption. A rethinking of many aspects of literary, including dramatic, culture has begun and will continue within these historiographical modifications.

Although we have yet to see the impact of this revised religious history on Shakespeare studies, in general Shakespeare criticism has become unusually responsive to research on an issue or tradition in relationship to which Shakespeare has previously been constructed. A key contribution, then, is Annabel Patterson's having extricated Holinshed from having previously been almost only read within the context of Shakespeare's plays. Her analysis of *The Chronicles of England, Scotland, and Ireland* as a history pieced together by a collection of authors invested in a range of political, economic, religious, and legal issues authenticates an identity for the *Chronicles* separate from the use any reader might subsequently make of them. As she notes, Elizabethan policy on Catholic issues 'define the period from 1570 through 1584', and also highlight the censorship issues for the 1587 edition of the *Chronicle*. Especially relevant to Shakespeare is her analysis of the shifting valency of the Oldcastle story of Lollardry and rebellion as it was retold by Bale, Hall, Foxe, and Holinshed; attention to these historians' self-consciousness about the rewriting of the Oldcastle story emphasizes the religious and ideological importance of the Oldcastle/ Falstaff material that Shakespeare reworked.[19] Patterson's invitation to reread Holinshed implicitly invites further interrogation of the sources of other Shakespeare plays.

If religion has caught on slowly in Shakespeare studies, new work on religion and Shakespeare's contemporaries is already abundant. To Blair Worden, Sidney's *Arcadia* is deeply constituted of the protestant-catholic religious politics surrounding Elizabeth's marriage negotiations with Anjou. Leah Marcus has initiated new discussion of Marlowe with her argument of the shift in protestant religious positioning in the two texts of *Dr. Faustus*. John King's studies of Tudor iconography and of Spenser as a reformation poet have become standard works, cited by historians and literary scholars. Literary representations of the Irish and of Ireland have dominated work on Spenser, especially as it is related to the interest in the development of British national identity; analysing the range of protestant positioning for this project is as important as the catholic–protestant conflict. Objecting to notions of Dekker as an unprincipled writer 'willing to write on the Protestant or the Catholic side', Julia Gasper has described Dekker as a militant protestant and 'political Puritan.' Suggesting 'the probable alliance in opposition to persecution between Donne's family and the houses of Percy and Stanley, especially through the missionary work of Donne's Jesuit uncle, Jasper Heywood, from 1581 to 1585,' Dennis Flynn has studied Donne's connection to Henry Percy, ninth Earl of Northumberland, and Donne's service 'through the late 1580s, with Henry Stanley, fourth Earl of Derby'.[20]

Studies of what women wrote, whether they conformed, whom they married, and to whom they gave patronage have become resources of major significance for understanding a range of religious and social practices.[21] Forthcoming editions of John Foxe, under the direction of David Loades, and of Samuel Daniel, edited by John Pitcher, will affect how we define Shakespeare's milieu, as will new studies of Francis Bacon, by Lisa Jardine and Alan Stewart, and of the earl of Essex, by Paul Hammer, of Edward Alleyn, by Susan Cerasano, and of the earl of Oxford, by Alan Nelson. The Oxford edition of *The Complete Works of Thomas Middleton*, general editor Gary Taylor, will increase access to Middleton's protestant persona. Studies of dramatic contexts not previously given extensive treatment include Scott McMillin and Sally-Beth MacLean's *The Queen's Men and Their Plays: 1583–1603*.

Forthcoming books that focus on religious culture include Alison Shell on catholics and 'controversial imagination', Richard McCoy on the 'sacred', and Fran Dolan on legal and literary representation of the Catholic menace during crises in Protestant-Catholic relations, from 1605–1680. Arthur Marotti's extensive work on Catholic and anti-Catholic discourses in England, 1580–1680, has begun to appear.[22]

A marked change in work on Shakespeare is the ease with finding in Shakespeare representations of both Protestant and Catholic traditions and perspectives, a movement consistent with revisionist historiography, where both Protestant and Catholic paradigms have seen significant change. To Greenblatt, *King Lear* can be read from both Protestant and Catholic points of view. Gary Wills has demonstrated *Macbeth*'s equivocating reliance on the language of the Gunpowder Plot, including traditions associated with the execution of Edmund Campion and other Jesuits. Huston Diehl has read the plays of Kyd, Marlowe, Middleton, and Shakespeare as rehearsals and explorations of the period's anxieties, confusions, and struggles over the changing nature of religious assumptions regarding the concepts that formed the bedrock of beliefs – the eucharist, images and spectacles, death and memory, and conscience. Religions other than Christianity are also receiving more attention; scholars who suggest that representations of Turks, Moors, and Jews in Shakespeare's plays indicate that his subject is Turks, Moors, and Jews need also to be aware of how such terms function in the religious discourses of Catholics and Protestants.[23]

A Protestant-leaning approach is that of Robert N. Watson who argues by way of *Othello* for a construction of Shakespeare as a Protestant polemicist; despite the reversibility of such a reading, Watson shows the availability of such a polemic for an audience inclined to find it there. Similarly, a Catholic-leaning study will be available from Alison Findlay, who considers how knowledge of conventual lifestyle might have affected the way Shakespeare's female spectators viewed the trade-off between Isabella's retreat to a nunnery and oppressive 'fatherly' religious doctrine; similarly, she reads *Richard II* in the context of the struggles for power among Elizabeth I, Mary Queen of Scots, and Arabella Stuart, with comparisons of Mary's religious poetry and Richard II's attitudes to kingship, subjectivity and God.[24]

Both literary scholars and historians have become adept at studying conscience, antipopery, atheism, puritanism, and martyrdom as intellectual and rhetorical constructs, but as Michael Questier has emphasized, empirical investigation supplements those approaches for instances in which we want to know 'in practice' what people were doing. A different focus on the Protestant program, then, is Curtis Breight's shifting attention from Queen Elizabeth to William Cecil, Lord Burghley, and setting himself against New Historicist views of the court as dependent on the ceremony and spectacle of a virgin queen.[25]

Sensitive to the impact of assumptions on interpretation, Collinson has addressed the matter of what we might say about Queen Elizabeth's and Shakespeare's private religious beliefs. For Elizabeth, Collinson has delineated a religious conservatism. During the reign of Mary Tudor, Elizabeth 'conformed outwardly to her sister's religion and regularly heard mass'; later, she did not ask that her catholic suitors 'abandon the practice of their own religion'. While she agreed to the eradication of stone altars, she continued 'use of the old catholic oaths', retained the cross in her own chapel, held a 'deep prejudice against clerical marriage', and 'nursed a negative prejudice against the preaching ministry'.[26] On Shakespeare's religious situation, Collinson has begun with Stratford, where he has deemed it 'probable that most members of this community were church papists' during the early decades of Elizabeth's reign, and 'not until the mid-1580s are there any signs of a watershed in the religious culture of Stratford or evidence of any local influence that could have brought about ... a conversion'. With the coming of the vicar Richard Barton, 'in 1585, Stratford at last embarked on the first steps of ... transformation ... In 1587 and 1588 Cartwright himself preached at Stratford, accompanied by Throckmorton, the town marking these notable visits by gifts of wine and sugar'.[27]

Collinson agrees 'with De Groot that some explanation of John Shakespeare's withdrawal from public life must be found other than in business failure and the reason is likely to have been religious. Shakespeare's father was most probably an unreconstructed Catholic of the old sort who was a potential and perhaps an actual "convert" of the missionary priests who had penetrated to the vicinity of Stratford by 1580.' Probably around 1583, 'John Shakespeare concealed in the roof of his house in Henley Street the copy of St Charles Borromeo's "Last Will of the Soul" to which he had apparently set his name, article by article ... making it the personal confession of "John Shakespeare, an unworthy member of the Holy Catholik religion"' 'There is no conclusive evidence of John Shakespeare's Catholicism', says Collinson, 'but this is very nearly conclusive'. As for William Shakepeare and Catholicism, Collinson speculates that 'he may well have leaned in that direction', although his echoes from the Bible in his early plays are from the Bishops' Bible, in later plays from the Geneva.[28] I understand Collinson to be saying that, in his view, Shakespeare was closer in heritage to Catholicism than many people have assumed, but if he leaned that way he also leaned toward Protestantism. As is true for many of Shakespeare's contemporaries, the languages of accommodation and consensus are often among the best resources we have to explain certain aspects of what we see in the life and writing of a major public figure.

Of current scholars who argue that Shakespeare was Catholic – Peter Milward, E.A.J. Honigmann, Gary Taylor, Eric Sams, and Richard Wilson – and that the Catholicism is apparent in the plays,[29] Milward, Honigmann, Taylor, and Wilson are similar, except that Wilson appropriates the Catholicism for a distinctly dissident Shakespeare. These arguments have two points of anchorage, the Borromeo testament of John Shakespeare and the assumption that the William Shakeshafte, known to have been a schoolmaster in the home of the Hoghtons, a wealthy Catholic family of Lancashire, was William Shakespeare. Important to this narrative are the connections between the Hoghtons and John Cottam, Shakespeare's schoolmaster in Stratford, and the fact that John's brother Thomas was tried with Edmund Campion, and executed in 1582, the year following Campion's execution.

Campion's story has existed in narrative form since his execution; a strategic advantage to associating the Shakespeare material with Campion is that this move gives narrative shape to what may otherwise appear to be a set of disconnected facts and speculations. With the arrival of the Jesuits and increased persecution of Catholics, many Catholics converted or accepted outward conformity; others adopted recusancy. It is speculated that at this time, and partly for his protection, Shakespeare made his way into the patronage of Lord Strange by way of the Stanley family, also located in Lancashire.

Taylor has concluded that Shakespeare's Catholicism is the explanation for the difficulty there has always been in describing Shakespeare; his 'invisibility . . . is an *act*', that is, an 'action' aimed at 'self-erasure', his 'initiating act of subversion is an act of self-containment'.[30] This thesis has a credibility, however, beyond its own argument; in a national state that required official uniformity in religion and politics, the fashioning of a public self was a taken-for-granted aspect of religious and political practices, including those of Protestant and Catholic nonconformity. The value of accommodation impels the formation of positions.

Nevertheless, one aspect of late Elizabethan consensualism was that it took for granted its own political and religious diversity. Current emphasis among revisionist historians on consensus has led Peter Lake and others to decry inattention to forms of opposition. I would argue that, far from diluting our sense of a non-unitary culture, a political situation governed by consensus politics may more appropriately be described as a situation which normalized dissent. Opposition did not reside in an opposition party, but in the daily practice of striving toward social and political solution. This point is important for synthesizing advances in historiography with those in censorship practices, as well as in suggesting the relationship between differing views of Shakespeare. As a writer whose inclination toward and skill in accommodation was perhaps unsurpassed, Shakespeare nevertheless developed shrewd and pointed critiques of the institutions and practices of his time which were detrimental to the life of the subject. His interrogations of the implications of state power were closely bound to the religious and spiritual concerns of his contemporaries. He repeatedly represented a monarchy dependent on the will and power of the people.

Lest we be too glib about these important generalizations, let us recall James Shapiro's description of how mainstream historians ignored Sidney

Lee's research on sixteenth-century Jews: 'Lee's entry [in the *Dictionary of National Biography* on Lopez and the Jewish presence in Elizabethan England] had little impact on how traditional British historians dealt with early modern England's Jewish presence'.[31] Because mainstream historians, until the 1960s, argued that no Jew set foot in England between 1290 and 1656, editions of *Merchant of Venice* were also until that time repeating historical inaccuracies. Beginning in Shakespeare's own time and continuing until relatively recently, one task of the historians of England's past has been the construction of the Protestant English state. The Protestantisation of England in the sixteenth century occurred by way of changes made and enforced at all institutional levels, the churches, universities, censorship, printing trade, and court systems. The early goal of obliterating Catholicism was in part managed by enforcing Catholic silence in all of these arenas, a strategy closely linked to the creation of institutional and discursive worlds which then often succeeded in also representing Catholics as absent. Later historians wrote about what was in view.

Newly legitimated and in vogue, Catholic studies have opened up an area of research that is, to say the least, intriguing. It will take time to sort out what we think of Richard Wilson's having extended his argument about Shakespeare's Catholicism in an article on *The Tempest*, where he depends on the involvement of Robert Dudley in European Catholic politics for reading the play.[32] Richard Dutton's careful work on censorship practices foreruns his project of reading Shakespeare's history plays in the context of the constitutional politics related to the Duchy of Lancaster and in the context of *The Conference about the Next Succession* (1594), the central Catholic treatise on the succession issue.[33] Although many early modern scholars know *The Conference*, it is also certain that Marprelate, Perkins, and Hooker are far more familiar than Robert Parsons, Gregory Martin, or Thomas Stapleton. It is impossible to study whether or to what end the Catholic discourse made its way into early modern drama unless one can recognize its presence. And, as I suggested at the beginning of this essay, perhaps nowhere are the issues of intentionality and referentiality more difficult for us than when we identify religious discourse in the plays of Shakespeare.

Some examples from *Hamlet* may serve as illustration. Two key passages in *Hamlet* are the speeches where, at the end of Act 1, Hamlet tells his friends that he will adopt an 'antic disposition' to avoid the discovery of what he knows and what he is about, and where, just prior to seeing Ophelia in Act 3, Hamlet speaks the 'To be or not to be' soliloquy. I am not aware whether others have noted that these passages are similar to passages in Robert Parsons's *An Epistle of the Persecution of Catholics in Englande* (1582). Writing of the range of predicaments in which Catholics, previously of the dominant English religion, now found themselves, Parsons described how Catholics were forced to flee from their homes, hide in fields, and endure the humility of having their persons searched for hidden articles of their faith: 'Whether now have these exulcerate and rancorous conroversies towching matters of faith and religion thruste us?' (136). Describing how the catholic lived in constant fear of accidentally revealing his identity in a way that would place him in danger, Parsons illustrates: 'yf a woorde, yea a peece of a woorde slipp forth of a mans mouthe at unawares, or that he happen to geve but a wink with his eie, or a nod with his heade, whereby any suspition may arise, that he favoureth oure cause: there is then matter enogh, whereupon eyther to accuse hym, or to cast hym in prison' (140–41). Does Shakespeare parody that speech when he writes Hamlet's speech asking that his companions swear not to do anything that will give him away, or are these sentences too commonplace to allow any attribution? Later, describing the torments of persecution, Parsons asks how anyone can bear up under such duress: 'Now, what puissance and valew of mynd think yow might suffice? What noblenese of courage wer nedefull? what strong and steadfast constancie do yew judge requisite to make me hable to bear and endure those vexations . . . ? Those contumelies (I mean) and those despites? Those rebukes and dishonors? Those prisons, bolts, and shakles? Those deformities and disorder? . . . loothsome sights . . . stinking savours . . . putrifactions' (156). If the first example is not compelling, this second one surely pricks the interest in how the 'To be or not to be' passage came into being. That soliloquy also uses the language of 'enterprise' and 'resolution', which, from the perspective of catholic discourse names first their effort to return England to catholicism (the Enterprise of England), and second, the attitude needed to resist conformity. Hamlet speaks of 'enterprises of great pitch and moment' that 'lose the name of action'. Does Shakespeare write as a Protestant, dominating a Catholic discourse, or as a Catholic, reiterating the words of Parsons on the situation of the persecuted Catholic? Or as neither? The ambiguity in Shakespeare's recirculation of Parsons's language leaves the reader able to appropriate it for different readings, including an ironic one that would represent a Catholic failure. Whatever one concludes, the possibility that Shakespeare has used Parsons is the most important point. As early modern studies continue to pursue the history and discourses of religion, Shakespeare's place within that study will also have more consideration.

REFERENCES

1. Collinson, Patrick (1994), 'William Shakespeare's Religious Inheritance and Environment', *Elizabethan* essays, London: Hambledon Press, 251, 252, 219–52.
2. White, Paul W. (1993), *Theatre and reformation: Protestantism, patronage, and playing in Tudor England*, Cambridge: Cambridge University Press; White, Paul W. (1997), 'Theatre and Religious Culture', in John D. Cox and David Scott Kastan, (eds), *A New History of Early English* Drama, New York: Columbia University Press, 151, 133–51; Dutton, Richard (1991),

Mastering the Revels: The regulation and censorship of English renaissance drama, London: Macmillan, 77–78, 247–48. See also Margo Heinemann, (1980), *Putitanism and theatre: Thomas Middleton and opposition drama under the early Stuarts*, Cambridge: Cambridge University Press; Butler, Martin (1984), *Theatre and crisis, 1632–1642*, Cambridge: Cambridge University Press; and Hamilton, Donna B. (1992), *Shakespeare and the politics of Protestant England*, London: Harvester Wheatsheaf, 1–4; Diehl, Huston (1997), *Staging Reform, Reforming the Stage: Protestantism and Popular Theatre in Early Modern England*, Ithaca: Cornell University Press.

3. Clare, Janet (1990), *'Art made tongue-tied by authority': Elizabethan and Jacobean dramatic censorship*, Manchester: Manchester University Press, 211; Clegg, Cyndia Susan (1997), *Press Censorship in Elizabethan England*, Cambridge: Cambridge University Press; and Clegg, (1997), ' "By the choise and invitation of al the realme": *Richard II* and Elizabethan press censorship', *Shakespeare Quarterly*, 48 (436), 432–48.

4. Patterson, Annabel (1984), *Censorship and interpretation*: Madison: University of Wisconsin Press; and Norbrook, David (1984), *Poetry and politics in the English Renaissance*, London: Routledge & Kegan Paul, 6.

5. Donno, Elizabeth Story (1963), *Elizabethan Minor Epics* New York: Columbia University Press; Greenblatt, Stephen (1980), *Renaissance Self-Fashioning*, Chicago: University of Chicago Press; Sinfield, Alan (1983), *Literature in Protestant England, 1560–1660*, London: Croom Helm; Dollimore, Jonathan (1984), *Radical Tragedy: Religion, Ideology and Power in the Drama of Shakespeare and His Contemporaries*, Hemel Hemstead: Harvester Wheatsheaf; Helgerson, Richard (1992), *Forms of Nationhood: The Elizabethan writing of England*, Chicago: University of Chicago Press; Hamilton, Donna B. and Strier, Richard (eds), (1996), *Religion, Literature, and Politics in Post-Reformation England, 1540–1688*, Cambridge: Cambridge University Press; and McEachern, Claire and Shuger, Debora (eds), (1997), *Religion and Culture in Renaissance England*, Cambridge: Cambridge University Press.

6. Shuger, Debora K. (1990), *Habits of thought in the English Renaissance: Religion, politics, and the dominant culture*, California: University of California Press, 5, 6. See also Shuger, Debora K. (1994), *The Renaissance Bible: Scholarship, Subjectivity, and Sacrifice*, California: University of California Press; and Shuger, 'Subversive fathers and suffering subjects: Shakespeare and Christianity', in Hamilton and Strier, (eds), *Religion, Literature, and Politics in Post-Reformation England, 1540–1688*, 46–69.

7. Collinson, Patrick (1995), 'Protestant culture and the cultural revolution', in Margo Todd, (ed), *Reformation to revolution: Politics and religion in early modern England*, London: Routledge, 34–35. For primary materials, see Peter Milward (1977) (1978) two discursive bibliographies, *Religious Controversies of the Elizabethan Age: A survey of printed sources*, London: Scolar, and *Religious Controversies of the Jacobean Age: A survey of printed sources*, London: Scolar, 1978.

8. Todd, Margo (ed), (1967), headnote to Collinson, 'Protestant culture', in *Reformation to revolution*, 33. See Collinson, Patrick (1967), *The Elizabethan Puritan Movement*, Berkeley: University of California Press; Collinson, Patrick (1982), *The Religion of Protestants : The church in English society*, Oxford: Clarendon Press; Collinson, Patrick (1982), *The Birthpangs of Protestant England*, New York: St. Martin's; Russell, Conrad (1990), *The Causes of the English Civil War*, Oxford: Oxford University Press; Russell, Conrad (1990), *Unrevolutionary England, 1603–1642*, Oxford: Oxford University Press; and Elton, Geoffrey (1986), *The Parliament of England, 1559–1581*, Cambridge: Cambridge University Press.

9. See Lake, Peter (1982), *Moderate Puritans and the Elizabethan church*, Cambridge: Cambridge University Press; Lake, Peter (1988), *Anglicans and Puritans?: Presbyterianism and English conformist thought*, London: Unwin Hyman; Lake, Peter (1980), 'The significance of the identification of the Pope as Antichrist', *Journal of Ecclesiastical History* 31: 161–78; Lake, Peter (1987), 'Calvinism and the English church, 1570–1635', *Past and Present* 114: 32–76; and White, Peter (1992), *Predestination, Policy and Polemic*, Cambridge: Cambridge University Press.

10. McMullan, Gordon (1994), *The politics of unease in the plays of John Fletcher*, Amherst: University of Massachusetts Press, 71.

11. Smith, David L. (1196), 'Catholic, Anglican or puritan? Edward Sackville, fourth Earl of Dorset, and the ambiguities of religion in early Stuart England', in Hamilton and Strier, eds., *Religion, Literature, and Politics*, 115, 115–37.

12. Burgess, Glenn (1993), *The politics of the ancient constitution: An introduction to English political thought, 1603–1642*, University Park: Pennsylvania State University, 118, 115–38. See also Burgess, Glenn (1996), *Absolute monarchy and the Stuart constitution*, New Haven: Yale University Press; and Sommerville, J.P. (1986), *Politics and ideology in England, 1603–1640*, London: Longman.

13. Guy, John (1996), 'The establishment and the ecclesiastical polity', in John Guy, (ed), *The reign of Elizabeth I: Court and culture in the last decade*, Cambridge: Cambridge University Press, 148, 126–49. See also Hamilton, *Shakespeare and the politics of Protestant England*, 330–58.

14. Hamilton, Donna B. (1992), *Shakespeare and the politics of Protestant England*, London: Harvester Wheatsheaf; see also Hamilton, Donna B. (1990), *Virgil and The Tempest: The politics of imitation*, Columbus: Ohio State University Press; and Jordan, Constance (1998), *Shakespeare's Monarchies: Ruler and Subject in the Romances*, Ithaca: Cornell University Press.

15. Haigh, Christopher (1982), 'The recent historiography of the English reformation', in Todd, (ed), *Reformation to revolution*, 17, 15, 13–32; reprinted from *Historical Journal* 25: 995–1007. See Dickens, A.G. (1989), *The English Reformation* (2nd edition, London: B.T. Batsford, 1989); Elton, G.R. (1977), *Reform and Reformation: England 1509–1558*, London; Elton, G.R. (1972), *Policy and Police: The Enforcement of the Reformation in the Age of Thomas Cromwell*, Cambridge: Cambridge University Press; Aveling, John C.H. (1976), *The handle and the axe: The Catholic recusants in England from Reformation to emancipation*, London: Blond and Briggs; and Bossy, John (1976), *The English Catholic Community, 1570–1850*, New York: Oxford University Press.

16. Haigh, Christopher (1987), 'Recent historiography of the English Reformation', in Haigh, Christopher (ed), *Revising the Reformation*, Cambridge: Cambridge University Press; Haigh, Christopher (1993), *English Reformations: Religion, politics, and society under the Tudors*, Oxford: Clarendon Press; Scarisbrick, J.J. (1984), *The Reformation and the English people*, Oxford: Blackwell; and Duffy, Eamon (1992), *The stripping of the altars: Traditional religion in England c.1400–c.1580*, New Haven: Yale University Press.

17. Haigh, *Revising the Reformation*, 207, 200–1; Haigh, *English Reformations*, 264–66.

18. Walsham, Alexandra (1993), *Church papists*, Woodbridge: Boydell Press, 95, 94–95; Questier, Michael (1996), *Conversion, politics and religion in England, 1580–1625*, Cambridge: Cambridge University Press.

19. Patterson, Annabel (1994), *Reading Holinshed's Chronicles*, Chicago: University of Chicago Press, 128, 130–53.

20. Worden, Blair (1996), *The Sound of Virtue: Philip Sidney's 'Arcadia' and Elizabethan Politics*, New Haven: Yale University Press. Marcus, Leah (1989), 'Textual Indeterminacy in Marlowe's *Dr. Faustus'*, *Renaissance Drama*, 20: 1–29; on Marlowe, see also Grantley, Darryll and Roberts, Peter eds. (1996), *Christopher Marlowe and English Renaissance Culture*, Aldershot: Scolar Press; and Cheney, Patrick (1997), *Marlowe's Counterfeit Profession: Ovid, Spenser, Counter-Nationhood*, Toronto: University of Toronto Press. King, John (1989), *Tudor royal iconography: Literature and art in an age of religious crisis*, Princeton: Princeton University Press; and King, John (1990), *Spenser's Poetry and the Reformation Tradition*, Princeton: Princeton University Press. For Spenser and Ireland, see Hadfield, Andrew (1997), *Edmund Spenser's Irish experience: Wilde fruit and salvage soyl*, Cambridge: Cambridge University Press; for guidance to the work on Ireland, see Bradshaw, Brenden, Hadfield, Andrew and Maley, Willy (eds) (1993), *Representing Ireland: Literature and the origins of conflict, 1534–1660*, Cambridge: Cambridge University Press. Gasper, Julia (1990), *The Dragon and the Dove: The Plays of Thomas Dekker*, Oxford: Clarendon Press, 1, 4, 5, 9, 10; and Flynn, Dennis (1995), *John Donne and the Ancient Catholic Nobility*, Bloomington: Indiana University Press, 16.

21. For example, Rowlands, Marie (1985), 'Recusant Women 1560–1640', in Prior, Mary (ed), *Women in English Society 1500–1800*, London: Methuen, 149–66; Jordan, Constance (1990), *Renaissance Feminism: Literary Texts and Political Models*, Ithaca: Cornell University Press; Trill, Susan (1993), 'Religion and the construction of feminity', in Crawford, Patricia (ed.), *Women and Religion in England, 1500–1720*, New York: Routledge, 30–55; Woods, Suzanne (ed.) (1993), *The Poems of Aemilia Lanyer*, New York: Oxford University Press; Mueller, Janel (1994), 'Textualism, Contextualism, and the Writings of Elizabeth I', in *English Studies and History*, ed. David Robertson, Tampere English Studies, no. 4, Tampere, Finland: University of Tampere Press, 11–38; Lewalski, Barbara K. (1994), *Writing Women in Jacobean England*, Cambridge, Mass.: Harvard University Press; Walsham, *Church Papists*, 77–81; Wilcox, Helen (ed.((1996), *Women and Literature in Britain, 1500–1700*, Cambridge: Cambridge University Press; Hannay, Margaret (ed) (1985), *Silent but for the word: Tudor women as patrons, translators, and writers of religious works*, Kent, Ohio: Kent State University Press; Hannay, Margaret (1990), *Philip's Phoenix: Mary Sidney, Countess of Pembroke*, New York: Oxford University Press. See also Dove, Linda (1997), 'Women at Variance: Sonnet Sequences and Social Commentary in Early Modern England', University of Maryland diss., 1997; and Karen Nelson, 'Pastoral Literature and Religious Reform in England, 1575–1625', University of Maryland diss., 1998.

22. Bibliographic details available for new and forthcoming books include: Jardine, Lisa and Stewart, Alan (1998), *Hostage to Fortune: The Troubled Life of Francis Bacon*, London: Victor Gollancz (New York: Hill and Wang, 1999); McMillin, Scott and MacLean, Sally-Beth (1998), *The Queen's Men and their plays: 1583–1603*, Cambridge: Cambridge University Press; Richard McCoy, 'Love's martyrs: Shakespeare's "Phoenix and Turtle" and the sacrificial sonnets', in Claire McEachern and Debora Shuger, (eds) *Religion and Culture in Renaissance England*, 188–208; McCoy's new study will be *Alterations of state: Sacred kingship in the English reformation*; Fran Dolan's working title is *Whores of Babylon: Gender and Catholicism in Seventeenth-Century English Print Culture* ; Marotti, Arthur (1997), 'Southwell's Remains: Catholicism and anti-Catholicism in early modern England', (ed.) Cedric C.

Brown and Arthur F. Marotti, Basingstoke, Hampshire: Macmillan Publishers and New York: St. Martin's Press, 37–65.

23. Greenblatt, Stephen (1988), 'Shakespeare and the Exorcists', in *Shakespearean Negotiations*, Berkeley: University of California Press, 94–128; Wills, Gary (1995), *Witches and Jesuits: Shakespeare's 'Macbeth'*, New York: Oxford University Press; Diehl, Huston (1997), *Staging Reform, Reforming the Stage: Protestantism and Popular Theatre in Early Modern England*, Ithaca: Cornell University Press. See, for example, Shapiro, James (1996), *Shakespeare and the Jews*, New York: Columbia University Press; and Vitkus, Richard (1997), 'Turning Turk in *Othello*', *Shakespeare Quarterly*, 48: 145–76.

24. Watson, Robert N. (forthcoming) '*Othello* as Protestant propaganda', in McEachern and Shuger, (eds), *Religion and Culture in Renaissance England*, 234–57; Findlay, Alison (forthcoming) *A feminist perspective on Renaissance drama*, Oxford: Blackwell's.

25. Questier, (1997), 'Practical Antipapistry during the Reign of Elizabeth I', *Journal of British Studies* 36: 374, 371–96; Breight, Curtis C. (1996), *Surveillance, militarism, and drama in the Elizabethan era*, London: Macmillan.

26. Collinson, 'Windows in a Woman's Soul: Questions about the Religion of Queen Elizabeth I', in *Elizabethan Essays*, 104, 110, 111–13, 114.

27. Collinson, 'William Shakespeare's religious inheritance and environment', in *Elizabethan Essays*, 246, 247, 248, 219–52.

28. Collinson, 'William Shakespeare's religious inheritance', 250–52.

29. Milward, Peter (1973), *Shakespeare's Religious Background*, Bloomington: Indiana University Press; Honigmann, E.A.J. (1985), *Shakespeare: the 'lost years*, Manchester: Manchester University Press; Taylor, Gary (1985), 'The Fortunes of Oldcastle', *Shakespeare Survey* 38: 85–100; Taylor, Gary (1994), 'Forms of opposition: Shakespeare and Middleton', *English Literary Renaissance* 24: 283–314; Sams, Eric (1995), *The Real Shakespeare: Retrieving the early years, 1564–1594*, New Haven: Yale University Press; Richard Wilson, 'Shakespeare and the Jesuits', *Times Literary Supplement*, 4942, 19 December 1997; and Milward, 'Shakespeare and the Jesuits', *Times Literary Supplement*, 4944, 2 January 1998:15. See the review of Sams's book by Michael D. Bristol (1997), *Renaissance Quarterly* 50:607–09.

30. Taylor, 'Forms of opposition', 313–14.

31. Shapiro, *Shakespeare and the Jews*, 64.

32. Wilson, Richard (1997), 'Voyage to Tunis: New history and the old world of *The Tempest*', *ELH*, 64: 333–57.

33. Dutton, 'Shakespeare and Lancaster', *Shakespeare Quarterly* (forthcoming).

12   Magnanimity and the Image of Heroic Character in Shakespeare's Plays: A Reappraisal

John M. Steadman

Although Shakespeare rarely referred explicitly to his characters and their actions as 'heroic' or 'magnanimous', both of these concepts (along with the values traditionally associated with them: honour, nobility, fortitude, martial prowess) nevertheless occupied a central position in his dramatic works throughout his career, underlying the themes and plots of his history plays and tragedies alike. In the following pages I shall reconsider certain of the major trends in scholarship on this subject over the last few decades, focusing on twentieth-century controversies over the nature of Renaissance concepts of honour, on the degree of Aristotelian and/or Platonic influence on these concepts, and on recognizable affinities between epic and heroic poetry and the English history play. The last of these topics has not only engaged the attention of a variety of Shakespearean critics but also remains a potentially fruitful subject for further investigation.

After briefly distinguishing some of the diverse senses of the term *magnanimity* in early English usage and their bearing on the concept of the heroic, I shall re-examine Shakespeare's explicit evocations of these concepts as well as his references to the related ideas of greatness, nobility and honour. In the latter half of this study I shall essay a modestly comprehensive summary of some of the more influential books and articles on the subject.

I

Although the *locus classicus* of both magnanimity and heroic virtue is to be found in Aristotle's *Nicomachean Ethics*, the use of these terms in the Middle Ages and the Renaissance varied widely, comprehending a much broader range of connotations and associations than one would expect from their peripatetic context. Shakespeare himself rarely employed either of these terms, although he did indeed exploit much of their original content and meaning under other designations.

Aristotle had defined the *megalopsychos* ('great-souled' man) as 'one, who, rightly conscious of his own great merits, is indifferent to praise except from those whose approval is valuable, regards the chances of fortune with equanimity, and, while ready to confer benefits, will seldom condescend to accept them.' In accordance with this definition Sir Richard Barckley (1598) observed that Charles Martel 'shewed great magnanimitie in refusing principalities'.[1] In the following century John Milton would similarly adduce as a superlative example of magnanimity Christ's rejection of the kingdoms of the world.[2] Subsequently 'modified in accordance with Christian ideals, and blended with elements suggested by the L[atin] word' *animus* (which could be interpreted in the sense of 'courage'), magnanimity was frequently 'classed as a subdivision of "fortitude" ... ' Thus Thomas Hoccleve (c.1412) identified this virtue as 'strong herte or grete corage.' Similarly Alexander Barclay (1509) in *Shyp of Folys* associated 'strength and magnanimitie'; and Daus (1560) praised 'magnanimitie' (*animi fortitudo*) in 'great adversity'.[3]

In his discussion of the magnanimous man, Aristotle had specifically associated this virtue with the idea of greatness, whether in virtue or action or reward. Magnanimity 'seems even from its name (*megalopsychos*) ('great-souled' man) to be concerned with great things'. The *megalopsychos* 'thinks himself worthy of great things, being worthy of them'. Deserving and claiming 'great things, and above all the greatest things', he aims at honour, 'the prize appointed for the noblest deeds' and 'surely the greatest of external goods'. Moreover, he 'must be good in the highest degree', for 'greatness in every virtue would seem to be characteristic' of the magnanimous man. Magnanimity is thus ' a sort of crown of the virtues; for it makes them greater, and it is not found without them'.[4]

Reminiscent of Homeric allusions to the 'great-souled' heroes of the Trojan War, Aristotle's term patently signifies 'greatness of soul', but significantly its Latin equivalent *magnanimitas* might also denote 'greatness of mind' – a sense that recurs frequently in the vernacular poetry and prose of the Renaissance.

The issue of Shakespeare's knowledge (direct or indirect) of the *Nicomachean Ethics* has been raised by various twentieth-century scholars, among them Curtis Brown Watson and W.R. Elton. In *Shakespeare and the Concept of Honor* (Princeton, 1960, 71), Watson endorses Frederick Bryson's contention that Aristotle was 'the chief authority for the works of the Italian humanists on the code of honor and the duel' and that at least 'fifty works on honor and the duel go directly back to the *Nicomachean Ethics* for their basic definitions of honor' and its relationship to virtue. (Bryson's study, *The Point of Honor in Sixteenth-Century Italy: An Aspect*

of the Life of the Gentleman was first published at Chicago in 1935).)
Nevertheless Watson deliberately sidesteps the question as to whether
Shakespeare himself possessed first-hand knowledge of Aristotle's writings: 'If the code of honor and the duel springs so directly from the moral
notions of Aristotle, if this code is establishing the terms of honor for
every Renaissance aristocrat and every royal court of Europe, the question
whether Shakespeare himself read Aristotle is a matter of little significance'. Associating the ideas of magnanimity and honour, Watson maintains
that 'Shakespeare, like the humanist moralists, links courage with magnanimity, the master virtue' (340).

More recently, in his essay 'Aristotle's *Nicomachean Ethics* and Shakespeare's *Troilus and Cressida*', *Journal of the History of Ideas*, Vol. 58
(1997), 331–337, Elton has argued plausibly for the influence of this ethical
treatise on Shakespeare's drama. Pointing out significant parallels between
these two works, he observes that the *Nicomachean Ethics* was 'familiar to
Elizabethan higher education' and that it 'was reprinted in translations in
numerous editions, with commentaries, in the sixteenth century'. He also
notes that this work was 'mainly available in Latin (except for the 1547
abridged English version from the Italian and translations into this and
other non-English vernaculars'). In Elton's opinon, 'this circumstance would
have provided little impediment to . . . a Latin-familiar audience'.

Essential to Renaissance conceptions of magnanimity and to their representation in drama and heroic poetry were the closely related ideas of
honour and self-knowledge. Observing that magnanimity (*megalopsychia*)
'is concerned with honour on the grand scale' and that 'honours and
dishonours . . . are the objects with respect to which the proud [that is,
magnanimous] man is as he should be', Aristotle insists that the
megalopsychos must possess a true sense of his own worth. In sharp
contrast to the 'vain' man, 'who thinks himself worthy of great things,
being unworthy of them', and to the 'unduly humble', who 'thinks himself
worthy of less than he is really worthy of', the truly magnanimous man
'claims what is in accordance with his merits'. He recognizes his own
inherent virtues and the kind of rewards that they deservedly merit.

The motifs of self-knowledge and heroic identity underlie the tragedy of
Coriolanus[5] and that of Brutus. And in Shakespeare's Alexandrian drama
it is precisely the recurrence of these motifs that enhances the tragedy of
Antony, the 'great-souled' warrior who sins against his own heroic identity
yet regains it (though only in part) in defeat and death.

Although Aristotle insisted firmly on the superlative and comprehensive
virtue of the magnanimous man, he did not, in fact, identify magnanimity
with heroic virtue. Certain Renaissance writers, however, such as Tasso,
found little difference between these ideals; and many of his contemporaries
emphasized the magnanimous character of epic heroes. Aristotle himself,
moreover, had quoted Priam's eulogy of Hector (*Iliad*, Book 24, line 258f.)
as a basis for his definition of *virtus heroica*; 'superhuman virtue, a heroic

and divine virtue,' the virtue of the 'godlike man'.[6] Despite its comparative brevity, this definition received extensive elaboration among scholastic philosophers and among Renaissance moralists. It underlay Francesco Piccolomini's more extended discussion of heroic virtue in his *Universa Philosophia de Moribus* (Venice, 1583); and in Roman Catholic theology it provided the foundation for analysing the close relationships between heroic virtue and sanctity and its bearing on the veneration of the saints.[7] In this context it is not without significance that Spenser would devote the first book of his Protestant epic to the celebration of sanctitude or Holiness.

II

Closely associated with the idea of heroism and the heroic image both in England and on the Continent, references to magnanimity occurred frequently in Renaissance discussions of epic and drama. In his *Discorsi del poema eroica* Torquato Tasso maintained that the 'illustrious' element of the heroic poem was founded, *inter alia*, on 'the magnanimous resolution to die':

> Ma l'illustre de l'eroico è fondato sovra l'eccelsa virtú militare e sopra il magnanimo proponimento di morire, sovra la pietà, sovra la religione, e sovra l'azioni ne le quali risplendono queste virtú, che sono proprie de l'epopoeia, e non convengono tanto ne la tragedia.[8]

Similarly, in his *Discorso della virtù eroica e della carità*, (1582), Tasso argued that 'heroic virtue stands in the same relation to magnanimity, as glory to honour.' Whereas magnanimity aimed at honour as the only reward proportional to its merits, heroic virtue aimed at glory.[9]

Another influential Italian writer, Count Annibale Romei, explicitly associated magnanimity with Aristotle's conception of heroic virtue. According to *The Courtier's Academie*, 'The excess then of virtue, according to the Philosopher, is after this maner expressed: the which excesse is of such a nature, as it cannot passe into vice, but rather is properly that which maketh a man magnanimous, and it is called vertue heroicall, as that which participateth both of humanitie and divinitie' (Watson, 103). In Romei's view magnanimity was an essential 'adjunct of military profession . . . : for that warrior who hath not a loftie and magnanimous mind, shall never accomplish glorious enterprises' (Watson, 107). Romei's treatise was accessible to Shakespeare in John Keper's English translation, published in London in 1598.

Similarly, in *An Apologie for Poetrie* Sir Philip Sidney explicitly associated the heroic poem with the delineation of magnanimity:

> There rests the Heroicall . . . which draweth with it no lesse Champions then *Achilles, Cyrus, Aeneas, Turnus, Tideus* and *Rinaldo* . . . who maketh magnanimity and justice shine throughout all misty fearfulness and foggy desires . . . [10]

Again, in *Englands Heroicall Epistles* (1619) Michael Drayton virtually identified heroic virtue with magnanimity, specifically linking the 'heroical' with 'greatness of mind':[11]

> And though (Heroicall) be properly understood of Demi-gods, as of HERCULES and AENEAS, whose Parents were said to be, the one, Caelestiall, the other, Mortall; yet is it also transferred to them, who for the greatness of Mind come near to Gods. For to be borne of a Caelestiall Incubus, is nothing else, but to have a great and mightie Spirit, farre above the Earthly weakenesse of Men; in which sense OVID (whose Imitator I partly professe to be) doth also use Heroicall.

Later in the seventeenth century John Dryden would also stress the close relationship between magnanimity and heroic epic. In his *Dedication of the Aeneis* he included magnanimity among the 'characteristical' virtues that the epic poet bestows on his hero. According to *A Discourse Concerning the Original and Progess of Satire*, the virtues of 'a magistrate, or general, or a king' embrace 'active fortitude, coercive power, awful command, and the exercise of magnanimity, as well as justice.' As an heroic subject Dryden himself had considered the actions of 'Edward, the Black Prince, in subduing Spain, and restoring it to the lawful prince ... Don Pedro the Cruel' – an argument attractive 'for the greatness of the actions, and its answerable event; for the magnanimity of the English hero, opposed to the ingratitude of the person whom he restored ... ' In his criticism of Spenser's *Faerie Queene* Dryden further observed 'that magnanimity, which is the character of Prince Arthur, shines throughout the whole poem; and succours the rest [of the heroes], when they are in distress'.[12]

III

Shakespeare's occasional references to magnanimity usually exploit the widespread use of this term to denote valour and courage rather than the Aristotelian disregard of lesser honours. In some instances the concept of magnanimity is evoked in an equivocal or ironic context; in other cases a literal rather than an ironic sense is paramount. This is also true of Shakespeare's explicit references to the heroic.[13]

In *All's Well That Ends Well* (III, vi) Count Bertram tests the mettle of the boastful Parolles by professing to accept at face value his insincere proposal to retrieve a French drum lost to the enemy: 'Why, if you have a stomach, to't monsieur: if you think your mystery in strategem can bring this instrument of honour again into his native quarter, be magnanimous in the enterprise and go on; I wil grace the attempt for a worthy exploit'. (Riverside, 527).

In the same drama (II, i) it is again the braggart Parolles who evokes the heroic concept in bidding farewell to the French lords upon their departure for the Italian wars. 'Noble heroes! My sword and yours are kin'. (Riverside, 513).

In *Love's Labour's Lost* it is the braggart and fantastical Spaniard Don Adriano de Armado who evokes the *topoi* of magnanimity and heroic virtue in a condescending love-letter to the country wench Jaquenetta. 'More fairer than fair, . . . have commiseration on thy heroical vassal! The magnanimous and most illustrate King Cophetua set eye upon the pernicious and indubitate beggar Zenelophon . . . ' (Riverside, 191).

In *2 Henry IV* (III, ii), Falstaff makes sport of the woman's tailor Francis Feeble in filling up the muster-book for the wars, exploiting the resources of paradox and oxymoron: 'Well said, good woman's tailor! Well said, courageous Feeble! Thou wilt be as valiant as the wrathful dove or most magnanimous mouse'. (Riverside, 905).

In *Troilus and Cressida* allusions to magnanimity and heroism are placed in equivocal contexts. Though Hector maintains that the 'moral laws of nature and of nations speak aloud to have her [Helen] back return'd' (II, ii), he nevertheless yields to Paris and Troilus in resolving 'to keep Helen still, For 'tis a cause that hath no mean dependance / Upon our joint and several dignities.' Troilus in turn amplifies this theme: 'But, worthy Hector, / She is a theme of honour and renown, / A spur to valiant and magnanimous deeds . . . '(Riverside, 463). In a later scene (III, iii) the epithets 'magnanimous' and 'heroical' form an integral part of a deliberately inflated and hyperbolical style designed partly to discredit the pretensions of the boastful Ajax and partly as a significant element in the mock-heroic. Ajax is 'prophetically proud of a heroical cudgeling', and Achilles desires 'the valiant Ajax' to invite 'the most valorous Hector' to his tent and to procure safe conduct for his person from 'the magnanimous and most illustrious six-or-seven-time honoured Captain General of the Grecian army, Agamemnon . . . '

In other instances Shakespeare employs the term 'magnanimity' in the sense of valour or courage and without irony or equivocation. In *3 Henry VI* (V, iv) Prince Edward extols the power of Queen Margaret's martial eloquence but scarcely without hyperbole:

> Methinks a woman of this valiant spirit
> Should, if a coward heard her speak these words,
> Infuse his breast with magnanimity,
> And make him, naked, foil a man at arms.
> (Riverside, 701)

IV

In contrast to the occasional explicit references to magnanimity and heroism in Shakespeare's plays, the topic of honour (with its concomitant themes of suicide and on occasion, revenge) receives more frequent emphasis. The concept of magnanimity is, in fact, often subsumed under the category of honour.

In *Othello* (V, ii), the Moor's suicide is associated with greatness of mind (that is, magnanimity):

> This did I fear, but thought he had no weapon,
> For he was great of heart.

Hamlet debates (III, i) the alternatives of suicide and patient endurance of adversity:

> Whether 'tis nobler in the mind to suffer
> The slings and arrows of outrageous fortune,
> Or to take arms against a sea of troubles,
> And by opposing, end them.

On a later occasion he rephrases the issue of greatness in terms reminiscent of the Aristotelian definition of the magnanimous man.[14] Nevertheless he significantly qualifies the Aristotelian view in his comments on the imperatives of honour (IV, iv):

> Rightly to be great
> Is not to stir without great argument,
> But greatly to find quarrel in a straw
> When honour's at the stake.
> (Riverside, 1172)

The topos of suicide as an honourable death recurs subsequently in Horatio's abortive resolve to perish with Hamlet:

> I am more an antique Roman than a Dane.
> Here's yet some liquor left.
> (Riverside, 1185)

In several of the Roman plays suicide is associated with greatness of mind as a means of avoiding shame and of denying the victor the honour of conquest by triumphing over one's self. In *Julius Caesar* (V, i) Brutus initially blames Cato for committing suicide at Utica to prevent his being taken captive by Caesar. Immediately afterward, however, he professes his intent to seek death rather than be led in triumph through the streets of Rome:

> Think not, thou noble Roman,
> That ever Brutus will go bound to Rome;
> He bears too great a mind.
> (Riverside, 1129)

When Titinius slays himself with Cassius's sword (V, iii) he describes this action as 'a Roman's part'. (Riverside, 1131).

In V, iv, Lucilius assures Antony that

> no enemy
> Shall ever take alive the noble Brutus;
> The gods defend him from so great a shame;

> When you do find him, or alive or dead;
> He will be found like Brutus, like himself.
>
> (Riverside, 1131)

Believing Mardian's lying report of Cleopatra's death, Antony condemns himself for lacking

> The courage of a woman – less noble mind
> Than she which by her death our Caesar tells,
> 'I am conqueror of myself.'
>
> (Riverside, 1379)

In the following scene (IV, xv) both of the protagonists characterize Antony's self-slaughter as a victory over himself.

> *Ant.*   Peace!
> Not Caesar's valour hath o'erthrown Antony,
> But Antony's hath triumph'd on itself.
>
> *Cleo.*   So it should be, that none but Antony
> Should conquer Antony, but woe 'tis so!
>
> (Riverside, 1380)

In his last words before dying, Antony once again returns to the theme of self-conquest through self-inflicted death (V, xv):

> The miserable change now at my end
> Lament nor sorrow at; but please your thoughts
> In feeding them with those my former fortunes
> Wherein I liv'd, the greatest prince o' th' world,
> The noblest; and do now not basely die,
> Nor cowardly put off my helmet to
> My countrymen – a Roman by a Roman
> Valiantly vanquish'd.
>
> (Riverside, 1380–1381)

In contrast to Cleopatra's timorous pretence of suicide (a falsehood that leads paradoxically but directly to Antony's death), the reflections that precede her own death reveal not only her concern with her own honour and greatness but (more significantly) her resolution to emulate the nobility of her consort's example (IV, xv):

> Good sirs, take heart,
> We'll bury him; and then, what's brave, what's noble,
> Let's do't after the high Roman fashion,
> And make death proud to take us.
>
> (Riverside, p.1381)

In the concluding scenes of this tragedy Cleopatra recurs frequently to the motif of greatness, to the nobility of suicide and to conquest over the changes of Fortune.

Though Cleopatra primarily conceives her 'greatness' in terms of her queenly status and royal lineage (witness her disgust at the prospect of beholding 'Some squeaking Cleopatra boy my greatness / I' th' posture of a whore'), her final action brings her close to the greatness of mind that constitutes true magnanimity. The two motifs are ultimately fused as she dons her royal robe and crown for her posthumous meeting with her conquerors; and both are summed up afterwards by Charmian:

> It is well done, and fitting for a princess
> Descended of so many royal kings
> (Riverside, 1386)

and finally by Caesar.

Shakespeare's allusions to magnanimity and heroism – and to the closely related concept of honour – embrace the extremes of idealism and farce. They refer alternatively to true nobility and valour and to their spurious counterfeits. Recurring in a wide variety of contexts, these topoi transcend distinctions of literary genre: comedy, tragedy and heroic play. Even in the same drama they sometimes propose complementary or seemingly contradictory conceptions of heroic virtue. Such apparently incompatible ideas reinforce one another, and provide a clearer and more forceful image of true magnanimity through contrasting it with its opposites. The pretensions of the *alazon* – a Pistol or a Parolles or a Falstaff – serve as a foil for the merits of the genuine hero. In accordance with the well-established principles of Renaissance logic and rhetoric, they effectively define true virtue through juxtaposition with its contraries.

v

Early modern ideas of magnanimity of 'greatness of mind' comprehend a wide variety of senses over and above the Aristotelian definition. Significantly, thanks to these variants, in Renaissance literatures magnanimity often becomes practically indistinguishable from heroic virtue. Both of these concepts share many essential values in common: the ideals of courage and fortitude and nobility. The association with military prowess and the characteristic valour of the soldier. The superlative virtue of the hero and the magnanimous man and his awareness of his own merits and true worth. His concern with deserved honour – indeed with the highest honours – and his disdain of lesser rewards.

Much of the criticism devoted in recent decades to Shakespeare's representations of heroic character centers primarily on the Roman tragedies based on Plutarch (notably *Coriolanus* but also *Julius Caesar* and *Antony and Cleopatra*[15]) on the English history plays. In the scholarship on this subject one may recognize a number of recurrent themes and preoccupations in addition to the motif of valour and the idea of greatness: whether greatness in mind or in action, or in birth and estate. Among these concerns are, most notably, the relation between heroic epic and heroic tragedy; the affinities between Aristotle's *Nicomachean Ethics* (or the traditional moral philosophies influenced by this work) and Shakespeare's heroes; the interplay among diverse ideals of honour; the distinction or interaction between classical and Christian values.

Although Maurice B. McNamee's book *Honor and the Epic Hero: A Study of the Shifting Concept of Magnanimity in Philosophy and Epic Poetry* does not discuss dramatic poetry, it nevertheless provides a useful background for the representation of magnanimity and honour by Shakespeare and other Renaissance dramatists. As the epigraph for his study he appropriately quotes Falstaff's estimate of honour (*1 Henry IV*), remarking that 'in a play in which Hotspur embodies the madness of exaggerated pursuit of honor, Falstaff's view is not all jest' (vi). Hotspur's 'fervid protestations' on the subject and Falstaff's jesting are in fact 'echoes of very ancient and ever-recurring attitudes in life and in letters.' Subsequent studies by other scholars analyse Shakespeare's representations of magnanimity and honour in detail. In *Shakespeare's Magnanimity: Four Tragic Heroes, Their Friends and Families* (New York, 1978) Wilbur Sanders and Howard Jacobson re-examine the poet's images of the magnanimous man in *Hamlet*, *Macbeth*, *Antony and Cleopatra* and *Coriolanus*.

In *The Herculean Hero in Marlowe, Chapman, Shakespeare and Dryden* (New York and London, 1962) Eugene M. Waith similarly focuses on the heroic image in two of Shakespeare's Roman tragedies as well as in *Tamburlaine*, *Bussy D'Ambois*, *The Revenge of Bussy D'Ambois* and *Byron's Tragedy*. Linking the motifs of heroic valour and magnanimity (41, 52, 55, 92, 94, 108), he stresses Byron's 'great spirit' and Bussy's 'great spirit' and 'great heart'. In commenting on Antony's vengeful fury against Cleopatra (Act IV), whom he suspects of compounding with Caesar, Waith likens him to Seneca's 'Oetean Hercules': 'Each one feels that his death has been robbed of all honour. And each longs passionately for revenge and then death ... Rage is the characteristic response of the Herculean hero to an attack on his honour,' and both Antony and Hercules 'Want more than anything to recover some part of their lost honour in order to make themselves worthy of a hero's death' (118–119).

In his discussion of Coriolanus Waith again emphasizes many of the characteristic features of the 'great-souled man'. In his intemperate and scathing denunciation of the common people 'Caius Marcius ... reveals his reverence for valour, constancy and a great spirit, as well as his utter contempt for those who will never attain such virtues' (124). Upon defeating the Volscians at Corioles, he 'refuses any reward but the name of Coriolanus which he has earned' (125). Waith's subsequent but related study *Ideas of Greatness: Heroic Drama in England* (London, 1971) is centered primarily on the seventeenth century.

The motif of greatness and the principles of heroic characterization underlie Richard B. Ide's study *Possessed with Greatness: The Heroic Tragedies of Chapman and Shakespeare* (Chapel Hill, 1980). Noting that early in the Jacobean period Chapman and Shakespeare 'wrote five tragedies with a soldier as protagonist,' (*Othello, Bussy D'Ambois, The Conspiracy and Tragedy of Byron* and *Coriolanus*) Ide argues that in each of these dramas 'the soldier's attempt to realize a heroic conception of self brings him into fatal conflict with society' (xi). Of particular interest are the author's comments on the bearing of heroic epic on these heroic tragedies: 'Typically the dramatists evoke the style and subject matter of epic to convey the soldier's heroic idealism. The epic genre is thus used as a metaphor expressing a heroic conception of self that is at odds with "reality" as social consensus defines it' (xi).

In his discussion of *Coriolanus* (226) Ide observed that in *Paideia: The Ideals of Greek Culture*, tr. Gilbert Highet, Vol.1 (New York, 1939–44), 1–5, Werner W. Jaeger had linked 'Aristotle's concept of the "magnanimous" man to heroic *areté* . . .'

Shakespeare's heroic modes have engaged a number of other critics in addition to Richard Ide. In *The Heroic Image in Five Shakespearean Tragedies* (Princeton, New Jersey, 1965), Matthew N. Proser centres his attention on *Julius Caesar, Macbeth, Othello, Coriolanus* and *Antony and Cleopatra*. In his opinion (3) 'the tragedy in each of these plays partly ensues because of the discrepancy between the main character's self-conception and his full humanity as it is displayed in action . . . Although in each tragedy we find a major character who is confronted by a critical situation, the action the hero takes is as much determined by his conception of himself, his "heroic image," as by exterior circumstances.' David Riggs's study *Shakespeare's Heroical Histories: 'Henry VI' and Its Literary Tradition* (Cambridge, Massachusetts, 1971) re-examines the 'premises of heroical-historical drama' from 1587 to 1592 and the 'heroic example' from *Tamburlaine* to *Richard III*.

Subsequently in *The Heroic Idiom of Shakespearean Tragedy* (Newark, London and Toronto, 1985) James C. Bulman attempted a comprehensive survey of the dramatist's 'heroic mimesis', arguing (22) that 'the versimilitude of Shakespeare's heroes . . . depends on their relationship to heroic tradition.' Maintaining (51) that 'the idioms Shakespeare employed to delineate heroism in his early plays were too restrictive to allow him a personal signature,' Bulman emphasized the 'ironic heroism' of the dramatist's later plays: *Julius Caesar, Richard III, Richard II, 1 Henry IV, Hamlet*. Shakespeare's 'new heroes were characterized by their awareness of conventional expectations, and their tragedies arose from their failure to live up to them – from their inability to wear hand-me-down roles with any comfort or conviction' (51). Other chapters centre on *Troilus and Cressida, Timon of Athens, King Lear, Macbeth* and *Antony and Cleopatra*.

After an initial chapter on *Othello* Reuben A. Brower's *Hero & Saint: Shakespeare and the Greco-Roman Heroic Tradition* (New York and Oxford, 1971) re-examines the presentation of the heroic in Homer's Achilles, Virgil's Aeneas, and the poetry of Ovid and Seneca. Of Shakespeare's plays Brower singles out for detailed discussion *Titus Andronicus, Julius Caesar,*

Troilus and Cressida, Hamlet, Antony and Cleopatra, Coriolanus and *King Lear.*

Brower's primary emphasis falls not on the 'saint' (however one defines him) but on the 'hero' and (in particular) the martial hero. In the military honours bestowed on the dead bodies of Coriolanus, Brutus and Hamlet he finds a reflection of 'attitudes towards the life and death of a soldier-hero that had their origin in the epics of Greece and Rome' (29–30).

VI

The motif of honour in Shakespearean drama – so closely associated with the ideal of magnanimity – has attracted the attention of a large number of scholars. Despite criticism by later critics, Watson's study, along with those by Margaret Greaves and such revisionist critics as Paul N. Siegel and Norman Council, retains much of its original value. A salient feature of Watson's discussion of magnanimity and of other aspects of Renaissance ideas of honour is the emphasis that he places on the alleged conflict between Christian and pagan-humanist ethics and on Shakespeare's own ambivalence in regard to tensions between these value-systems. Stressing Shakespeare's affinities with 'the humanist moralists' (340), he insists that 'the pagan-humanist morality of the Renaissance was a unifed and integrated as the Thomistic ethics of the 13th century' and this unity was 'largely derived form the fact that the *Nicomachean Ethics* was as responsible for Renaissance moral formulations as it was, in a Christianized form, for the ethics of St. Thomas Aquinas' (420).

Watson's analysis of Renaissance concepts of honour – and in particular his emphasis on the antithesis between Christian and 'pagan-humanist' ethics – have been sharply criticized by other students of the period: Sears Jayne (1962), Siegel (1964), and Council (1973). In his review of Watson's book, Jayne objects that, in spite of numerous quotations, it fails to provide 'a definitive study of the Renaissance concept of honor.' Watson's primary materials are limited to works in English or in Tudor English translation, materials which have already been examined by others,' but even these English materials 'seem incomplete'. Moreover, 'like his primary materials', his 'secondary materials seem a little thin'; and, in spite of his 'thesis about "pagan-humanism" ' he makes only 'limited use of the copious literature on humanism' (358–359).[16]

Siegel, in turn, maintains that, although Watson has 'put us in a position to understand better an important aspect of Renaissance thought, he has confused the subject as much as he has clarified it.' In discussing Shakespeare he uses 'the plays to illustrate the various ideas on honor,' but 'does not explore any play thoroughly.' Moreover, he 'has confused two opposing Renaissance concepts of honour, what we might call the Christian humanist ideal of honor and the neo-chivalric cult of honor' (123–124).[17]

Instead of drawing a sharp distinction between Christian and humanist values, as Watson had done, Siegel tends to fuse the two in a single amalgam. In his view, 'the Christian humanist ideal of honor is expounded in the courtesy books and the works of moral philosophy,' and this ideal became 'an integral part of the new ideal of the courtier, in which the virtues of the humanistic scholar, learned in the classics and indebted to them, are united with those of the medieval knight, an ideal which governed the new Tudor aristocracy.' On the other hand, 'the neo-chivalric cult of honor is expounded in the duelling treatises' and 'stems primarily from the chivalric notion of personal military glory. Contrary to Watson, it is this feudal chivalric tradition rather than revived classicism which is in conflict with the Christian humanist ideal of honor' (124–125).

Siegel's study comprehends five Shakespearean dramas: Henry IV, Troilus and Cressida, All's Well That End's Well, Coriolanus and Timon of Athens. In these dramas, he maintains, 'Shakespeare does not draw similar portraits of the contemporary Italianate devotee of the neo-chivalric cult of honor. Instead, while presenting the destructiveness of the cult, he also, by associating it with military glory and the glamour of a bygone chivalry, makes a more complex use of it' (133).

Agreeing with Siegel that 'Watson's book introduces as much confusion as it does clarity into the study of Renaissance ideas of honour,' Norman Council likewise blames much of this confusion on the frame of reference and the methodology of Watson's study. His 'thesis, that most aspects of honour belong uniquely to the ethics of "pagan humanism" and so are incompatible with the ethics of Christianity, and his practice, using sections of the plays to illustrate the various categories of honour he has described, do confuse the matter. In his efforts to dichotomize, Watson fails to consider Christian uses of classical formulations of the idea which such theologians as Richard Hooker make, and he disregards those portions of secular arguments which claim a Christian origin for human honour.' Thus in his treatise Of Honour Robert Ashley 'easily accommodates the Aristotelian definition to a Christian context'. (32).[18]

Council's primary concern in this study falls on the plays themselves. After briefly discussing 'ideas of honour in Shakespeare's England,' he devotes the greater part of his book to analysis of six plays: 1 Henry IV, Julius Caesar, Troilus and Cressida, Hamlet, Othello and King Lear.

With a few exceptions, such as Greaves's study and Watson's book, twentieth-century analyses of Renaissance ideas of honour and/or its relation to English drama do not for the most part discuss magnanimity in detail. Nevertheless, inasmuch as a concern for honour traditionally remained a central preoccupation of the megalopsychos or magnanimous man, it is difficult to overestimate the importance of these studies as background for critical analysis or early modern conceptions of nobility and greatness of mind or soul.[19]

In order to place Shakespeare's adaptations of heroic motifs in clearer historical perspective and in their original intellectual and dramatic contexts we still need more comprehensive and detailed surveys and reassessments of the evolution and elaborations of ideals of the *megalopsychos* from antiquity and the Middle Ages to early modern times. (In several respects this should in all probability be our first priority.) Secondly, and more narrowly, such surveys should necessarily be complemented by close analysis and criticism of the variations on these ideas and heroic *topoi* among Shakespeare's near-contemporaries and his immediate successors. Studies such as these could potentially offer a firmer, more reliable basis for revaluing Shakespeare's own distinctive contributions to the heroic tradition and for reappraising with greater justice and accuracy the finer points of his dramatic art.

REFERENCES

1. See *The Oxford English Dictionary*, Second Edition, ed. J.A. Simpson and E.S.C. Weiner (Oxford: Clarendon Press, 1989; repr. 1991), *s.v. magnanimity; magnanimous*. The correlative adjective *magnanimous* has been defined as 'great in courage', 'nobly brave or valiant' and also as 'high-souled; nobly ambitious; lofty of purpose; noble in feeling or conduct.'
2. See John Milton, *Christian Doctrine*, tr. John Carey, ed. Maurice Kelley, in *Complete Prose Works of John Milton* (gen. ed., Don M. Wolfe), Vol. 6, New Haven and London: Yale University Press, 1973, 735–736.
3. *OED, s.v. magnanimity*
4. For Aristotle's discussion of magnanimity (*megalopsychia*), see *Ethica Nicomachea*, tr. W.D. Ross, in *The Works of Aristotle*, Vol.9 (Oxford: Clarendon Press, 1925), 1123ᵃ 34–1125ᵃ 16. Ross renders Aristotle's term as 'pride,' observing that this 'has not the etymological associations' of the Greek word, 'but seems in other respects the best translation'. Nevertheless in both scholastic and Renaissance humanist traditions the concepts of pride and magnanimity are usually as significantly diverse as vice and virtue.

    Professor W.R. Elton has kindly called my attention to the discussions of magnanimity by René Antonin Gauthier, Margaret Greaves, Giovanni Pontano, and Thomas Traherne. See Pontano, *De magnanimitate*, ed. Francesco Tateo (Firenze: Instituto nazionale di studi sul Rinascimento 1969); Traherne *Of Magnanimity and Charity*, ed. John Rothwell Slater, New York: The King's Crown Press 1942; Gauthier, *Magnanimité: l'idéal de la grandeur dans la philosophie païenne et dans la théologie chrétienne*, Paris, 1951; Greaves, *The Blazon of Honour: A Study in Renaissance Magnanimity* (New York: Barnes and Noble 1964).

    Traherne's discussion of magnanimity originally appeared in his *Christian Ethicks: or, Divine Morality*, London: printed for Jonathan Edwin 1675, 224–5. Equating magnanimity with 'Greatness of Soul,' Traherne maintains that this virtue 'includes invincible Patience, an immovable Grandeur, which is above the reach of Injuries, a contempt of all little and feeble Enjoyments, and a certain kind of Majesty that is conversant only with Great things; . . . a generous Confidence, and a great inclination to Heroical deeds . . . '

Greaves's survey of English representations of magnanimity and its variants ranges from the late Middle Ages through the seventeenth century and reconsiders the work of Chaucer and Malory, Sidney and Spenser, Shakespeare and Milton, and Dryden and Traherne. The section on Shakespeare (120–129) briefly re-examines variations of the heroic type ranging from admiration to mockery, especially in *3 Henry VI, Julius Caesar, Love's Labour's Lost, Troilus and Cressida*, as well as *Antony and Cleopatra* and *Coriolanus*. In her opinon Antony is 'the magnanimous man *manqué*,' Don Adriano de Armada a '"satirical antitype" of magnanimity', while Hector and Troilus are 'the only two men' in Shakespeare's Trojan drama 'who do not at their every appearance make a mockery of the heroic type, and even they are tarnished.'

5. Coriolanus's overbearing and insolent behaviour toward the Roman 'plebs' could appropriately be juxtaposed with Aristotle's description of the *megalopsychos*: 'It is a mark of the proud [that is, magnanimous] man also to ask for nothing or scarcely anything, but to give help readily, and to be dignified towards people who enjoy high position and good fortune, but unassuming towards those of the middle class; for it is a difficult and lofty thing to be superior to the former, but easy to be so to the latter, and a lofty bearing over the former is no mark of ill-breeding, but among humble people it is as vulgar as a display of strength against the weak.'

6. For Aristotle's discussion of heroic virtue, see *Ethica Nicomachea*, tr. W.D. Ross, 1145a 20. Significantly, like heroic virtue, the virtue of magnanimity involves a superlative, or 'extreme' degree of virtue. In the words of Aristotle, 'The proud man [the megalopsychos], then, is an extreme in respect of the greatness of his claims, but a mean in respect of the rightness of them.'
For discussion of the close relationship between magnanimity and heroic virtue in the Renaissance, see Merritt Y. Hughes, 'The Christ of *Paradise Regained* and the Renaissance Heroic Tradition', *Studies in Philology*, 35 (1938), 254–77.

7. For Piccolomini's discussion of heroic virtue and for the views of Agostino Nifo da Sessa, Fortunatus Scacchus, Lucas Castellinus and others on the relationship between heroic virtue and sanctity, see John M. Steadman, *Milton's Epic Characters, Image and Idol* (Chapel Hill: University of North Carolina Press, 1968), 31–33.

8. Tasso, Torquato (1935), *Prose*, Flora, Francesco (ed.) Milano and Roma: I Classici Rizzoli, 1935.

9. Guasti, Cesare ed. (1875), *Le prose diverse di Torquato Tasso*, Firenze: Successori Le Monnier in Firenze, 2, 193.

10. Smith, G. Gregory, ed. (1904), *Elizabethan Critical Essays*, Oxford, Oxford University Press, 179; reprinted 1937 London: Lowe and Brydone.

11. Hebel, J. William ed. (1932), *The Works of Michael Drayton*, Oxford, Shakespeare Head Press and B. Blackwell, 2, 130.

12. Ker, W.P., ed. (1926), *Essays of John Dryden*, Oxford: Clarendon Press, 2, (28), 31, 38, 159. See also Spenser's Letter to Raleigh, in Edmund Spenser, *The Faerie Queene*, ed. A.C. Hamilton (London and New York, 727) and *Nicomachean Ethics*, tr. Ross, 1122ª 18–1123ª 19. For discussion of representations of magnanimity in Spenser, see Maurice B. McNamee, S.J., (1960), *Honor and the Epic Hero: A Study of the Shifting Concept of Magnanimity in Philosophy and Epic Poetry*, New York: Holt, Rinehart and Winston, 137–159; Greaves, 75–93. For Milton's treatment of the concept of magnanimity, see McNamee, 160–178; and John M. Steadman, *Milton and the Renaissance Hero*, Oxford, Clarendon Press, 1967, 137–161, and *passim*; *Milton's Epic Characters, passim,* University of North Carolina Press; *Milton*

and the Paradoxes of Renaissance Heroism, Baton Rouge and London: Louisiana State University Press, 1987, 173–259; Greaves, 94–111.

13. All quotations from Shakespeare are based on *The Riverside Shakespeare*, ed. G. Blakemore Evans et al., Boston: Houghton Mifflin Co., 1974.

14. According to the *Nicomachean Ethics* the magnanimous man 'does not run into trifling dangers, nor is he fond of danger, because he honours few things; but he will face great dangers, and when he is in danger he is unsparing of his life, knowing that there are conditions in which life is not worth having.' It is characteristic of him ' not to aim at the things commonly held in honour, or the things in which others excel; to be sluggish and to hold back except where great honour or a great work is at stake, and to be a man of few deeds, but of great and notable ones.'

15. Standard works on these three plays include Derek Traversi's *Shakespeare: The Roman Plays*, Stanford, California: Stanford University Press, 1963); Maurice Charney's *Shakespeare's Roman Plays: The Function of Imagery in the Drama*, Cambridge, Massachusetts: Harvard University Press, 1961; and M.W. MacCallum's earlier study (1910) *Shakespeare's Roman Plays and their Background* (London: Macmillan, 1935).

16. For Jayne's review (1962) see *Shakespeare Quarterly*, 13, 357–359. See Curtis Brown Watson (1960), *Shakespeare and the Renaissance Concept of Honor* (Princeton: Princeton University Press).

17. Siegel, Paul N. (1968), *Shakespeare in His Time and Ours*, Notre Dame and London. Chapter Five ('Shakespeare and the New-Chivalric Cult of Honor') originally appeared in *The Centennial Review*, 8 (1964).

18. Council, Norman Briggs (1973), *When Honour's at the Stake: Ideas of Honour in Shakespeare's Plays*, New York: Barnes and Noble.

19. Among these studies, in addition to works already cited, the reader may profitably consult C.L. Barber, *The Idea of honour in The English Drama 1591–1700*, Göteborg: Elanders (1957); Fredson Thayer Bowers, 'Middleton's *Fair Quarrel* and the Duelling Code' *JEGP*, 36 (1937), 40–65; Frederick R. Bryson, *The Sixteenth-Century Italian Duel, A Study in Renaissance Social History*, Chicago: University of Chicago Press, 1938; Paul A. Jorgensen, *Shakespeare's Military World* (Berkeley and Los Angeles, 1956); V.G. Kiernan, *The Duel in European History: Honour and the Reign of Aristocracy*, Oxford: Oxford University Press (1988); Paul N. Siegel, *Shakespearean Tragedy and the Elizabethan Compromise*, New York: New York University Press, (1957); J.L. Simmons, '*Antony and Cleopatra* and *Coriolanus*, Shakespeare's Heroic Tragedies: A Jacobean Adjustment', *Shakespeare Survey*, 26, 95–101; and Harold S. Wilson, *On the Design of Shakespearean Tragedy*, Toronto and London: University of Toronto Press (1957). See also Mervyn James's discussion of this subject in *English Politics and the Concept of Honour 1485–1642* (1978). *Past and Present Supplement* 3. Of particular relevance are his discussions of the 'Bartolan tradition,' which 'emphasised the nature of honour as the reward of "virtue"' (3); of the role of the epic in conferring immortality on 'honourable deeds' (14); on Bacon's distinction between 'false' honour and 'the magnanimity of the man of wisdom' (88); and on the popularity of the former on the late Elizabethan and the Stuart stage (89). I am indebted to Professor W.R. Elton for this reference.

13   Shakespeare and the Law: An overview

R.J. Schoeck

GENERAL INTRODUCTION

'Every state or nation has a system of beliefs, of institutions, of laws, of customs, which must be seen as whole', the historian Arnaldo Momigliano has justly generalized.[1] To a considerable degree much in Shakespeare's plays can be seen not as a history of the laws and customs of Elizabethan England – of course Shakespeare was no mere historian – but rather as an ongoing effort to comprehend and criticise in dramatic terms the systems of law and the institution of kingship (which drew so richly and intricately from traditions of legal, and theological, thought, as E.H. Kantorowicz has detailed[2]), in which he lived. What makes Shakespeare's endeavour and achievement the more exciting is that he was keenly aware both of the larger traditions of the laws and of the transient nature of certain individual laws and customs as he wrote, and he was also aware of their interconnectedness: that the individual laws, customs, institutions and ceremonies were to be explained by other laws and customs and ceremonies. Thus, Shakespeare was something of a stucturalist and comparatist *avant la lettre*.[3] But he was not a theorist, nor even an historian: he was, as will bear repetition more than once, the writer of plays, a poet, a man of the theatre.

I propose in this chapter to discuss law and literature as a relatively recent field-concept, then to sketch very briefly structures of law in Shakespeare's dramaturgy (the role of equity, e.g.) followed by comments on certain studies of individual plays. A brief conclusion will follow, together with an appended note on the language of the law in Shakespeare. This essay is not to be taken as a bibliography of the subject Shakespeare and the Law; for necessarily much that has a different orbit and touches Shakespeare and the Law only tangentially – however fruitful that study might be in itself and for some other aspect of Shakespeare studies – had to be omitted.

One cannot approach so broad and complex a field[4] as is announced in the title of this essay without a number of preliminary caveats and several distinctions and delineations. For Shakespeare, it must be reiterated as a first principle of interpretation that we are dealing with plays, not treatises; that the primary end of each play is entertaining (although this does not preclude the handling of serious legal and other problems within the play); and that by virtue of the nature of dramatic structures no character in a Shakespeare play may be assumed to be representative of the author's own thoughts or convictions – that, indeed, some characters are capable of speaking errors (as with deliberate malapropisms spoken for theatrical effect) or making other misrepresentations that a contemporary audience, particularly one so sophisticated as an Inn of Court audience, would catch and appreciate.[5]

For The Law: in the Elizabethan world-picture that was real, provided we do insist, being too static, there were included not only positive law (statutory law, royal and papal decrees, maritime law, military law and laws of war, and still others), but also customary law, and above all else natural law and, through revelation in Scripture, even divine law. Of its nature, then, the Law was conceived as hierarchical, and there was a further distinction between the Old Law (roughly, the law of the Old Testament) and the New (roughly, the law of the New Testament). Few in Shakespeare's audience could have claimed expertise in fields outside the common law, and the common law was intricate enough in itself to baffle the layman (with further confusion or misunderstanding generated by the use of Law-French); but few would have denied the variability of the various kinds of law, however much they might have grumbled at or criticized inefficiency or corruption. The average theatregoer (if such existed, then or now) would have had personal experience in matters of marriage and wills, with a smattering of ignorance in contracts, and all would have had a layman's nodding acquaintance with such essentials as the marriage law of the church.[6] Yet the majority of Shakespeare's contemporaries, one has reason to think, would have accepted the notion that the various kinds of law were related and, indeed, in the largest reach of the Law, subsumed in a larger unity.[7]

Such generally used (though often argued) concepts as *ratio, ordo* and degree, and *lex divina, lex aeterna*, are central to our modern understanding of the late-medieval early-modern law; and in a work contemporaneous with Shakespeare's plays, Richard Hooker's *On the Laws of Ecclesiastical Polity*, we find those individual concepts handled with the meticulousness of a philosopher or theologian at the highest reach of his discipline, and then subsumed in a larger concept of law that charts the relations of man to God and to each other. Although Shakespeare wrote no treatise, unlike Richard Hooker, yet these and other concepts are imbedded in the dramatic action of many of his plays.[8]

Law and literature is a special field of study that has grown rapidly in the past quarter-century and now has its own literature;[9] a number of law schools in the United States now regularly offer courses in law and literature. When I offered such a course in the early 1960s it was a new thing, and I have repeated the offering, *mutatis mutandis*, a number of times, then narrowing the focus for a seminar on Shakespeare and the Law for the newly formed Folger Institute in Washington, DC, in 1974.[10]

In the past twenty years books and articles have appeared in growing numbers, generally dealing with Greek tragedy (especially the *Antigone*[11]), which often is dealt with comparatively in contexts that permit the inclusion of Shakespeare), with medieval sagas and other medieval literature,[12] and with Dante in particular,[13] as well as with Elizabethan and Jacobean drama,[14] and moving into nineteenth- and twentieth-century novels.[15] Radbruch briefly discussed the reasons for the fascinations of dramatists and novelists with trial scenes: primarily, and obviously, there is a ready-made conflict in such scenes. Any discussion of Shakespeare and the Law must be located at least in particular in this larger context of teaching and discussion. The appearance in 1973 of James Boyd White's *The Legal Imagination* in fact argued that the study of literature should be a part of legal education (thereby carrying into the curriculum and enjoinder of Judge Learned Hand that lawyers should be widely read in literature and philosophy from Plato to the modern day). At the same time it may well be argued that a complete view of the role of law in western society and culture should include at least an awareness of the thrust of law and legal thought into art; and in our own age there must be some consideration given to film and theatre as interpreters of the law and of various dramatic texts, from *Antigone* to *Merchant of Venice* and beyond.[16] There is as yet, however, no definitive treatment either of Law and Literature or of Shakespeare and the Law.

I shall not discuss at any length the argument that lawyers and students of the law constituted a major part of the audience for the performance of Shakespeare's plays for the Inns of Court; that must await another historian.[17] (For the approach of a legal historian to some of these question, see E.W. Ives, 'The Law and the Lawyers', *Shakespeare Survey*, 17 [1964] 72–86, which contains much that is valuable for further study and discussion.) Similarly, I shall not discuss the hypothesis that Shakespeare studied law, perhaps in Stratford. W. Nicholas Knight argues that Shakespeare was himself a lawyer, but such historical questions as the lack of extant records in the archives of the Inns of Court – even lawyers may be thwarted by the lack of evidence, to borrow from the inelegant phraseology of one academic committee – defeat that argument: Knight's case is at best a Scottish verdict of Not Proven.[18]

There is a rich harvest yet to be reaped in the study of the wills of the sixteenth century. In her review of E.A.J. Honigmann and Susan Brock, *Playhouse Wills, 1558–1642,* (Manchester: University Press, 1993), and Joyce Rogers, *The Second Best Bed,* (Westport, Connecticut: Greenwood Press, 1993), Laetitia Yeandle has compactly discussed the nature of the evidence and the conclusions which can be drawn from that evidence, in her review in *Shakespeare Quarterly*, 45 (1994) 373–4.

For a legalistic mind, thinking generally is anchored to specific cases (as in our generation so much discussion is tied to *Roe* v. *Wade*, e.g.), and the celebrated case of *Hales* v. *Petit* (1563), in which a suicide is judged a criminal, is related by Phillips to the question of Ophelia's doubtful death; and more careful identification is needed of cases that are figured in the action and language of the plays.

One of the themes that runs through a number of the plays – comedies and romances as well as tragedies – is incest. In Chapman's *Odyssey* the spotlight is turned on Oedipus:

> that beyond all law [Joycasta]
> Her own soone married, ignorant of kind . . .

All law is here a resonant phrase, and to be ignored of kind – that is, nature in general (*rerum natura*) and its laws – as in *Titus Andronicus* (at the first stage of Shakespeare's tragic development) – is to risk violating all natural law. (In a letter prefixed to More's *Utopia* in 1517 the celebrated French jurisprudent Guillaume Budé excoriated lawyers who ignored or were ignorant of the natural law.) Richard A. McCabe in *Incest, Drama and Nature's Law* (Cambridge: University Press, 1993) has studied the theme of incest in English Renaissance and Restoration drama. The figure of Richard III is seen as 'the ultimate expression of England's unnatural history, the ultimate despiser of the laws of kin' (157). Thus, 'The readiest way to make the wench amends/ Is to become her husband, and her father' (*Richard III*, I.i. 155–6). *Hamlet* plays with the consciousness, if not the conscience, of the prince; he muses upon a 'little more than kin, and less than kind' (I.ii. 65). Thus McCabe concludes (171):

> Pervaded by images of self-defeat, of engineers hoist with their own petard, of mistaken purposes fallen upon their inventors' heads, of poisons fatally returning (like incestuous offspring) to their point of origin, of mortal coil and spiritual recoil, *Hamlet* is the ultimate tragedy of family bondage, the quintessence of haunted dust.

In *King Lear*, McCabe reminds us, 'by emphasising the "bond" between parent and child, she [Cordelia] reminds Lear of the "natural" limits of filial affection, of the prohibitions as well as the privileges of kinship' in I.i. 96–8.

Incest is a terrifying spectre, Marilyn Williamson remarks in *The Patriarchy of Shakespeare's Comedies* (Detroit, 1986), 113; it is indirectly raised in *Pericles* and hinted at in *The Winter's Tale* and *Cymbeline* (113). Still larger and stronger elements of natural law are raised as well. John F. Danby argued in his much-cited essay on *King Lear* that there are two conflicting theories of nature in the play; but McCabe asserts that 'there are almost as many conceptions of the natural as there are characters to conceive it' (*Incest*, 175). Cf. John F. Danby, *Shakespeare's Doctrine of Nature: A Study of 'King Lear'* (London, 1949), which is not however a study of natural law so much as it is an exponent of 'Natural Philosophy.' A more wide-ranging and yet more probing study of natural law in More, Spenser, Sidney, Shakespeare and Milton is provided by R.S. White's study, *Natural Law in English Renaissance Literature* (Cambridge: University Press, 1996).

A cutting of the Gordian knot of much philosophical, legal and literary discussion is provided by R.S. White's useful conclusion to a discussion of the nature of fictions and the 'as-if' worlds that Shakespeare gave:

> ... Shakespeare wryly observes that the very tools of rhetoric and poetry are double-edged and ambiguous and that their truth value is at best relative, yoked to the moral vision of the literary work and its audience. The only way to resolve such ambiguities is by assuming some ethical dimension beyond man-made systems and positive laws, to a dimension said by Elizabethan theorists to be shared by all readers as by all humanity: to reason, conscience, and community 'needs': in short, to Natural Law. (White, *Natural Law*, 105–6)

In a text everywhere read in sixteenth-century England, More's *Utopia*, the natural law may be thought to be implicit; and in Budé's letter to Lupset (that appeared in the 1517 Paris edition and was frequently included in subsequent editions) lawyers who ignore or are ignorant of the natural law are excoriated.[19]

The importance of conscience in Elizabethan England has been discussed by a number of scholars, and in 1992 Donna B. Hamilton used Perkins' *A Case of Conscience* (1592) to argue that a central issue in *Measure for Measure* is its condemnation of 'laws which oppress subjects, and celebrates by contrast actions by rulers that "use the law to protect life and liberty" and so by implication to maintain the liberties of the subject which had been guaranteed, the common lawyers argued, by Magna Carta': *Shakespeare and the Politics of Protestant England* (Hemel Hempstead, 1992), 114–15 and 186.

The laws and customs of marriage amply figure in Shakespeare's plays, as they did significantly in Erasmus' *Colloquies*, which it is likely that Shakespeare used (as everyone else in the sixteenth century did). On *sponsalia de praesenti* and *de futura*, the distinction between which Erasmus minutely and with marvellous humour presented to sixteenth-century schoolboys – as in 'Courtship' and other colloquies on love and marriage[20] – see Margaret Loftus Ranald, who has studied marriage in several plays in her *Shakespeare Quarterly* articles, and now her *Shakespeare and His Social Context* (New York, 1987); and further Anne Barton on '"Wrying but a little": marriage, law and sexuality in the plays of Shakespeare', in *Essays, Mainly Shakespearean* (Cambridge: University Press, 1994), 3–30.

SOME INDIVIDUAL PLAYS

I have chosen for comment some plays in which legal elements are conspicuous – such as the trial scene in *A Merchant of Venice* and the mock trials in *King Lear*. It is not surprising that these are the plays that have evoked the greatest attention in discussions of Shakespeare and the Law, but it must not be thought that only in such plays is the law a conspicuous, or even a determinative element.

COMEDIES

A useful survey of criticism and scholarship in the first half of the century that dealt with the comedies is provided by J.R. Brown in 'The Interpretation of Shakespeare's Comedies: 1900–1953', in *Shakespeare Survey* viii (1955) 1–13, and in *Shakespeare and His Comedies* (1957). One of the more interesting of recent monographs that cut across a number of the comedies is that of Linda Anderson, *A Kind of Wild Justice: Revenge in Shakespeare's Comedies*, (Newark, Delaware: University of Delaware Press, 1987), which contends that revenge (a wild justice according to Bacon) is a central element in Shakespeare's handling of comic intrigue and, further, she looks to the connections of revenge in the legal systems represented in the plays.[21]

A Comedy of Errors

It can be argued, and it has been so argued by H. Brooks among others, that this play is concerned with serious issues of disorder and rebellion, in addition to the broad farce owed to its sources.[22] In *Shakespeare and His Comedies* J.R. Brown viewed the play as dealing with 'the follies and evils of possessiveness' in love, and, more to the concern of this essay, views *Comedy of Errors* as looking forward to *Merchant of Venice* in 'its contrasts of love, commerce, and justice'.

Merchant of Venice

If there be such a genre as problem comedy, then surely *Merchant of Venice* is one; but it is also a problem for critics and scholars more than for theatre-goers, who always have found the play great theatre, whatever the interpretation of Shylock. Together with the legalities of the play are woven themes from folk-tales (the savagery of the usurious creditor who demands his pound of flesh, as well as the motif of the choice of the right casket in order to win the lover's lady) and the urban myth of a wealthy Jew (inherited in part from the figure of Barabas in *The Jew of Malta*). Modern interpretations of Shylock and the play have moved back and forth on a spectrum ranging from the incarnation of the devil to a sentimental-ized daughter-wronged father-figure – in criticism as on the stage. By the end of Act I, the major themes of the play – commutative justice, usury, moderation, and equity – have all been set in motion.

Portia clearly is the pivotal figure in the action of the play, and in an interesting essay by Lord Norman, 'Portia's Judgment', in the *University of Edinburgh Journal* x (1939) 43–5, the argument is made that the court acted unfairly in leading him on, arguing against G.W. Keeton in *Shake-speare and His Legal Problems* (London, 1930), which had defended Portia as judge. The interpretation of Barbara Lewalski in 'Biblical Allu-sion and Allegory in *Merchant of Venice*', *Shakespeare Quarterly*, xiii (1962) 327–43 saw levels of meaning roughly analogous to Dante's four levels; but this interpretation ignores, or minimizes, the force of law and justice in the action of the play. For other discussions, see Sylvan Barnet, *Twentieth-Century Interpretations of Merchant of Venice* (1970).

It is patent that Shylock insists upon the letter of the law stipulated in his contract with Antonio, and it has become more accepted in recent scholarship that Portia's handling of the case in court invokes equitable principles and that these principles were well known in English law up to the time of the play. (Little attention has been given to analogous princi-ples in areas of the law other than equity.) But some recent Shakespearean criticism (and some lawyers) have given misleading views of equity in plays such as *Merchant of Venice* and *Measure for Measure*. In his essay on 'The Letter of the Law in *The Merchant of Venice*' in *Shakespeare Survey*, 29 (1976) 93–101, E.F.J. Tucker has moved discussion towards greater precision and clarity. Walter Cohen's focus on the development of equity in the Chancery, in '*The Merchant of Venice* and the Possibilities of Historical Criticism', *ELH* 49 (1982), is followed by William C. Jordan in *Shakespeare Quarterly*, 33 (1982) 49–50, and A.F. Kinney in *The Histori-cal Renaissance*, ed. Heather Dubrow and Richard Strier (Chicago, 1988).

The study of Joan Ozark Holmer, 'Miles Mosse's *The Arraignment and Conviction of Usurie* (1595): A New Source for *The Merchant of Venice*', *Shakespeare Studies*, xxi (1993) 11–54, is richly documented especially on usury and money-lending, together with the Jacob-Laban story from Gen-esis 30. *Pace* J.R. Brown in the *New Arden* ed (1955), p. 26, Miles Mosse twice refers specifically to the Jacob-Laban story, and Holmer concludes that 'almost all one can imagine Shakespeare would need to know about usury he could find in Mosse's book' (p. 46).

The ultimate source of equity (*epikeia*) was well-known: Book V of the *Ethica Nicomachea* of Aristotle, both directly (Aristotle was of course a prime author in the university curriculum) and indirectly (through Aquinas in his *Secunda Secundae*, Q.CXX; through Hooker in his *On the Laws of Ecclesiastical Polity*, 1595; and through Bodin, whose *Commonweale* was first published in French in 1576, in Latin in 1586, and in English in 1606). Thus it can be asserted that equity as a philosophical concept was well known to well-read Elizabethans, in law and philosophy, and much of the concept was in the air, especially of course around the Inns of Court.[23] So much was this so that there were popular views that equity mitigated the rigour of the law, and that Chancery was a 'court of conscience', with the Chancellor's jurisdiction 'supplying' the defects of the Common Law.[24] W. Nicholas Knight has usefully brought into play the existence of a copy of William Lambarde's *Archaionomia* of 1568 (an important treatise in the history of the common law) – in 'Law and Equity, the *Merchant of Venice*, and William Lambarde', in *Shakespeare Survey*, 27 (Cambridge: University Press, 1974) 93–104 – but as Tucker demonstrates he perpetuates the notion of conflicts between the Common Law courts and the Chancery. Slade's Case (1597–1602) has been used to develop the law of obligation, and analogies between that case and *Merchant of Venice* have been pressed too hard to argue for a conflict between a customary life and the practices of a contractual life; and the case of *Throckmorton* v *Finch* (1598) has been adduced, but it was a purely civil action, having nothing to do with the criminal law and the pardoning of capital offenses which is so central to *Merchant of Venice* and *Measure for Measure*. What must be stressed is that Portia's 'Quality of mercy' speech is not a Chancery action: rather it is a dramatic appeal to Shylock's conscience. Nothing remotely resembling the trial in *Merchant of Venice* ever 'took place at Westminster Hall', Tucker emphasizes (97); and other lines of legal action are too generally ignored (98). Further discussion is needed on the point implied in Tucker's citation bearing on the case of *Throckmorton* v *Tracy* (2, 3 Phil. & Mary), in which (in Plowden's commentary) Justice Stanford retorts to one argument as follow: 'to pursue the Words, is *summum ius*, which the judges ought to avoid, and rather pursue the Intent'. One of the most celebrated of the *Adagia* of Erasmus was on precisely the concept of *summum ius, summa iniuria* (*Adag.*, I.x.25): that is, the strictest law (may become) the greatest injury (or wrong).[25]

   Mark E. Andrews, *Law versus Equity in the Merchant of Venice: A Legalization of Act IV, Scene 1*, (Boulder, Colorado: University of Colorado Press, 1965), is filled with questionable law, poor history, and unsophisticated literary criticism; it is not recommended. Maxine McKay, 'The *Merchant of Venice*: A Reflection of the Early Conflicts between Courts of Law and Courts of Equity', *Shakespeare Quarterly*, 15 (1964), 371–5, is more substantial work, but it too presses too hard on the notions of conflicts between the common law courts and the courts of equity; there was less conflict of this kind than was for a number of years perceived.

Measure for Measure

Earlier critics had problems with this play, and as Ernest Schanzer has put
it, no other play called forth 'such violent, eccentric, and mutually opposed responses'. M.C. Bradbrook moved away from the excessive
discussions of the virginity of Isabella to examine 'Authority, Truth and
Justice in Measure for Measure', Review of English Studies, xviii (1961),
385–99. Ronald Berman's 'Shakespeare and the Law', Shakespeare Quarterly, xviii (1967) 141–50 is less focused on English law than the title
would suggest; instead he writes against what he saw as sentimentalized
Christianity persistently attributed to the play.

A number of studies have dealt with betrothals, marriage contracts and
bed-tricks in the play: D. Harding, 'Elizabethan Betrothals and Measure
for Measure', JEGP, xlix, (1950) 139–58; Ernest Schanzer, 'The Marriage-
Contracts in Measure for Measure', Shakespeare Studies, xiii (1960), 81–9;
Wilbur Dunkel, 'Law and Equity in Measure for Measure', Shakespeare
Quarterly, xiii, (1962) 275–85; J. Dickinson, 'Renaissance Equity and
Measure for Measure', ibid., 287–97; and S. Nagarajan, 'Measure for
Measure and Elizabethan Betrothals', Shakespeare Quarterly, xiv, (1963)
115–19. More recently, and more definitively, Margaret L. Ranald in her
Shakespeare Quarterly articles and in Shakespeare and His Social Context
(New York: AMS Press 1987). In her introduction to the Riverside Shakespeare (1972), Anne Barton takes a larger view, concluding that 'there is in
this play an unresolved conflict between absolutes and anarchy, between a
necessary but sterile order and a vigorous but suspect world of self-
gratification and individualism' As well as the overriding concern in the
play for justice there is the problem of authority, especially absent and
delegated when the de jure ruler is absent.

The conclusion of Schanzer in The Problem Plays of Shakespeare (New
York: Schoken Books, 1963) is a balanced one: there is a public concern
with the nature of justice, and a private concern in the nature of Isabella's
choice. J. Middleton Murry's earlier Shakespeare (London: Cape, 1936)
contains an analysis of the nature of justice in the play, but it must be
qualified and enlarged by later scholarly interpretation. One scholarly
monograph has been devoted to the issues here presented: Darryl F. Gless,
'Measure for Measure', the Law, and the Convent, (Princeton: University
Press, 1979), presses much too hard on the thesis of the convent, and there
is here a tendency to reduce meaning to theme – e.g., both the Sermon on
the Mount and Measure for Measure are seen as statements about law.
Much in Gless follows the general lines of the complex argument of G.
Wilson Knight on 'Measure for Measure and the Gospels', in The Wheel of
Fire (London: H. Milford, Oxford University Press, 1930) that the play is a
New Testament parable opposing love and mercy to justice. Marc Shell in
The End of Kinship: 'Measure for Measure', Incest, and the Ideal of Univer-
sal Sibling-hood (Stanford: Stanford University Press, 1988) has pursued a

line of investigation that is developed by McCabe, among others. Some of the ground traversed by Holmer and others, as discussed above, is re-examined by Alberto Cacicedo in '"She is fast my wife": Sex, Marriage, and Ducal Authority in *Measure for Measure*', *Shakespeare Studies*, xxiii (1995), 187–209.

The Tempest

In an interesting discussion of treason that places the play against a background of protest and revolt, Curt Breight in '"Treason doth never prosper": *The Tempest* and the Discourse of Treason,' *Shakespeare Quarterly*, 41 (1990) 1–28, digs into the Tudor law of treason and relates the examination to the law of proof, noting that failure to report treason was itself treason.

Troilus and Cressida

If it be true (as Anne Barton writes in the *Riverside Shakespeare*, 1974), that the play 'is a brilliant but scarifying vision of a world in pieces, all value and coherence gone', then one can more readily understand (and suspend disbelief for) many of the recent stage productions of the play. Central to the play's structure and to the concerns of this essay is Ulysses's celebrated speech on order and degree (I.iii): that it comes early in a play that subverts much in the speech, and that the speech is uttered by a master-rhetorician, are self-evident: see Herbert Howarth's corrective reading in *The Tiger's Heart* (London: Chatto and Windus, 1970). In her essay 'Discord in the Spheres' in *The Frontiers of Drama* (London: Methuen, 1945) Una Ellis-Fermor had argued that the play works out the 'discovery' that man cannot imagine absolute values, whether in imaginative or in objective terms.

In a recent article in *Journal of the History of Ideas* (April 1997) W.R. Elton has cogently argued the pertinence of Aristotle's *Nicomachean Ethics* to *Troilus and Cressida*. There is, Elton writes compellingly, a 'particular pattern of parallels with Aristotle's *Nicomachean Ethics* regarding ethical-legal questions surrounding an action: issues of the role of the voluntary or the involuntary, of volition and choice, of choice and virtue, and of virtue and habitual action' – all questions that have their place in determination of innocence or guilt. A close reading of the play also invokes Aristotelian concepts of equity (as with *Merchant of Venice*, as already seen). From the time of Erasmus scholars had been concerned with equity and intentionality – and here Hooker as elsewhere follows in the footsteps of his master, Erasmus – and Kathy Eden trenchantly quotes the following passage from Aristotle's *Rhetoric* (so much the curriculum-textbook at Oxford, especially in the magisterial exposition of John Reynolds), where Aristotle declares that equity bids us to be merciful to the weakness of human nature; to think less about the laws than about the man who framed them, and less about what he said than about what he meant; not to consider the actions of the accused so much as his intentions; nor this or that detail so much as the whole story.[26]

Viewed in this context of principles and ideas of intentionality, Ulysses' speech and the whole dramatic structure of *Troilus and Cressida* become both more complex and more meaningful. Yet a Shakespearean play is never simply 'an excuse for thought', as S.L. Bethell called the play in his *Shakespeare and the Popular Dramatic Tradition* (Durham, North Carolina: Duke University Press, 1944).

TRAGEDIES

Titus Andronicus

Titus Andronicus is printed among the tragedies in the First Folio, where it clearly belongs as doubtless the earliest of Shakespeare's tragedies and one that shows most clearly Shakespeare's heritage of revenge tragedy. From Dr Johnson to Mark Van Doren in his *Shakespeare* (New York: H. Holt, 1939) critics have been too much concerned with only the blood and brutality of the action. Beginning perhaps with Howard Baker's *Induction to Tragedy* (Louisiana: Louisiana University Press, 1939) and F. Bowers' *Elizabethan Revenge Tragedy 1587–1642* (Princeton, NJ: Princeton University Press, 1940), scholars have more acutely studied the place of *Titus* among revenge tragedies, which, again, project a primitive kind of justice: for the dictum of Francis Bacon (in 'Of Revenge') is apt indeed – revenge is a wild kind of justice. *Titus* is surely more than the burlesque of blood and bathos of previous drama that J. Dover Wilson saw in his Cambridge edition (Cambridge University Press, 1948), and one must look to Senecan models where the action that seems all too melodramatic reflects a marriage of Senecan rhetoric and revenge psychology.

Hamlet

There is a useful collection of criticism from the voluminous *Hamlet* literature in David Bevington, *Twentieth-Century Interpretations of Hamlet* (Englewood Cliffs, NJ: Prentice Hall, 1968). B. Joseph's *Conscience and the King* (London: Chatto and Windus, 1953) is a notable contribution, as is Fredson Bowers' much-cited article on 'Hamlet as Minister and Scourge', *PMLA*, lxx (1950), 740–47; the play demonstrably owes much to roots in revenge tragedy. *Hamlet*, as a number of critics have observed, is a most theatrical play, and it comments on appearance and reality as polarities of action. It is further a problematic play, with doubt projected and analysed; it yields 'a state of perplexity'. McCabe characterizes Hamlet himself as 'the Natural Law hero *par excellence*, the philosophy student from Faustus' university at Wittenberg which was also Luther's place of confrontation, and spending his play brooding on the fundamentals of reason and conscience in action' (*Natural Law in the Renaissance*, xii). John S. Wilks has written on discussions by Richard Hooker and other Elizabethan writers on conscience, and he focuses on the distinction sustained between synderesis and conscience, citing Philip the Chancellor in *Summa de Bono*: 'What was contributed by *synderesis* was unchangeable and dictated only good, but this conjoined with what was contributed by reason dictated sin. So, therefore, *synderesis* plus the reason for a free choice makes *conscientia* right or mistaken ... ' in 'The Discourse of Reason: Justice and the Erroneous Conscience in *Hamlet*', *Shakespeare Studies*, xviii (1986), 117–59. We are not to wonder that an Elizabethan Hamlet could cry out that 'conscience does make cowards of us all' (III.i).

Othello

Sister Jean Klene, CSC, argues that in the stress on honour in *Othello*, 'maintaining a good reputation made severe demands on the conscience of a Renaissance gentleman', leading to such extreme actions as defending that honour in a duel, or suicide – in Othello: 'A fixed figure for the time of scorn', in *Shakespeare Quarterly*, xxvi (1975) 139. See further W.M.T. Nowottny, 'Justice and Love in *Othello*', in *Casebook on Othello*, ed. L.F. Dean (New York: Crowell, 1961).

Frank Kermode sees the greatness of *Othello* in its beautiful complexity, rendering man as 'repository of truth, sink of uncertainty and error'. "Whence it appears clearly that, by means of grace, man is made like God and participates in his divinity; and that without grace, he resembles the beasts of the field'. So Pascal; and somewhere off the margins of the text the meaning of Shakespeare's Reputation touches that of Grace' (*Riverside Shakespeare*).

King Lear

Shakespeare repeatedly in the history plays emphasized the double nature of a king, and the historian E.H. Kantorowicz traced the concept of the king's two bodies (public and private) back to the Roman jurists: see Kantorowicz, *The King's Two Bodies* (1957), who then treats the appearance of this concept in legal writings of sixteenth-century England, especially in legal writers like Edmund Plowden. Lear's confusion about the nature and relationship of his two bodies is therefore rooted in legal thought, as is the sense of the three branches of justice – Distributive, Retributive, and Commutative – that are unfolded in the dramatic action, and especially in Act I, sc.i, and Act IV, sc.i. In a final looking-back upon the play we return to the words of Kantorowicz: 'The jurists discovered the immortality of the [King's] Dignity; but by this very discovery they made the ephemeral nature of the mortal incumbent all the more tangible'.

According to Justinian (and followed by Thomas Aquinas in *ST* 2a 2ae 58.1) justice is the basic intention – better, disposition – to give each his due. And as twentieth-century theologians like P. Tillich and B. Häring have expounded, love is more basic than justice. Shakespeare's Lear learns both teachings.

Writing on '"The Name and all th'addition": *King Lear*'s opening scene and the Common Law use', in *Shakespeare Studies*, xxiii (1995) 146–86, Charles Spinosa brings together a number of legal issues with a sense of personal identity. *Use* is explained as a form of trust, and the enfeoffment to Albany and Cornwall in I.i. 129–37 is discussed, and the dialogue of *Doctor and Student* by Christopher St. German (in the 1974 Selden Society edition by Plucknett and Barton) is adduced on enforceable duties of conscience.

THE HISTORY PLAYS

A helpful review of criticism of the histories is to be found in Harold Jenkins, 'Shakespeare's History Plays, 1900–1951', in *Shakespeare Survey* 6 (1953) 1–15. Among the problems that Shakespeare chose to explore in the histories is that of the title to the throne (where political theory and law run hand in hand), and George W. Keeton has studied this dimension of the background in his *Shakespeare's Legal and Political Background* (London: Pitman, 1967). Parts One, Two and Three of *Henry the Sixth* – these plays and their sequel, *Richard III*, constitute the first tetralogy – embraced scenes of battle and picture a kingdom torn by civil war. The keen awareness of the cost of struggles for lawless power background the history plays that follow. Legal and literary debates about the tyrant were caught up in the characterization of Richard, and the climactic scenes of retribution are a kind of legal fable, or *fictio*. M.M. Reese's *The Cease of Majesty* (London: Edward Arnold, 1961) reads *Richard III* as manifesting a formal, almost ritualistic structure, in which successive blows of fate constitute the fulfilment of a curse. R.S. White, in *Natural Law in English Renaissance Literature* (Cambridge: Cambridge University Press, 1996), implies the violation of natural law as an essential dimension of the play.

In the second tetralogy, *Richard II* is a splendid dramatization of a king who understands the emblems and symbols of royal power and is condemned, by his weakness, to abdicate sceptre and crown. The fullest exposition of the legal-political-theological symbolism is to be found in Kantorowicz, *The King's Two Bodies*. *Henry IV, Parts 1* and 2, are often read as the education of a prince: if Shallow and Silence provide comic material at the expense of a balanced view of the administration of local justice, the presence of the Lord Chief Justice in the oppositions and larger design of *Henry V* projects a fuller view of justice in the world of fifteenth-century England. W.F. Bolton in a far-reaching study of 'Ricardian Law Reports and *Richard II*', *Shakespeare Studies* xx (1988) 53–64 argued that the Yearbooks – 'the black-letter law books' being printed in sixteenth-century England – were of great interest to Renaissance readers; 'over 225 separate editions between 1553 and 1591' appeared; and these Yearbooks 'enable us to place the trial by combat in its correct context, to grasp some other legalisms scattered in the play, and to trace a central legal motif of plot and metaphor'.

War is ever-present in that world of Richard II, and Theodor Meron has studied *Henry's Wars and Shakespeare's Laws: Perspectives on the Law of War in the Later Middle Ages* (Oxford: Clarendon Press, 1993). The fourth act of *Henry V* is notable for its presentation of the idea of just war (much debated among theologians, legalists and political theorists). What Henry addresses in his response to Williams is the question of the state of an individual soldier's soul: for that, the individual is himself responsible, of course. But for his death in war – and on the question of whether or not the cause was just – the King has a unique responsibility. Donna B. Hamilton in 'The State of Law in *Richard II*', *Shakespeare Quarterly* 34 (1983) 5–17, intelligently discusses the king's prerogative and other aspects of kingship, and she emphasizes (as a few others have done) a 'law-centered kingship' as central to *Richard II*. E.A. Rauchut, 'Hotspur's Prisoners and the Laws of War in *1 Henry IV*', *Shakespeare Quarterly*, 45 (1994) is more narrowly focused; it builds upon M.H. Keen, *Laws of War in the Late* Middle Ages (London: Routledge, 1965) and other studies.

Henry A. Kelly has ably studied the role of Providence in *Divine Providence in the England of Shakespeare's Histories* (Cambridge, Mass: Harvard University Press, 1970); Kelly, one may conclude, sees that 'Shakespeare dramatizes the characters and thus eliminates all the purportedly objective providential arguments made by the histories on historical characters'. These concerns are pursued by C.G. Thayer in *Shakespearean Politics: Government and Misgovernment in the Great Histories* (Athens, Ohio: Ohio University Press, 1983), which deals with the death of the concept of divine kingship in Richard II and moves to discuss the growing strength of the sovereign in *Henry V*: this is, as he views it, a movement from injustice to justice. In a more complex analysis Robert R. Reed, Jr., in *Crime and God's Judgment in Shakespeare* (Lexington, KY: University Press of Kentucky, 1984) analyses questions of guilt, conscience and divine retribution in several of the history plays.

Through the two tetralogies there are deep concerns with order and chaos, proper authority and degree, justice, and the role of conscience in the due functioning of law. A full account of this dimension of Shakespeare has yet to be written, although many of the critics and historians cited have touched on parts of the larger whole.

Coriolanus

G.T. Tanselle and F.W. Dunbar (1962), 'Legal Language in *Coriolanus*', *Shakespeare Quarterly*, xiii, 231 ff. has as thesis that 'there is clearly a legal motif operative in *Coriolanus*, and that it plays a major role in the final effect of the play'. It is noted that there are at least 194 words and phrases of legal significance in *Coriolanus*, whereas Clarkson and Warren in their narrower study had noted only 64. Yet in the third scene of the play, with three women talking, there is no legal language.

THE POEMS

Sonnets

Aspects of the production and reading of the sonnets have legal interest, and these include (but are not limited to) the employments of legal language and metaphor, and the reasons for those employments; direct references to legal ideas, practices or terms (such as *will*); and the legal aspects of copyright, text, and liability. In her most impressive book on *The Art of Shakespeare's Sonnets* (Cambridge, Mass: Belknap Press, 1997), Helen Vendler writes of the speaker's mind as having 'a great number of compartments of discourse', of which the legal is but one of several (Introduction, 19). Then, interestingly, she continues: 'These compartments are semipervious to each other' and there is an osmosis between them. I would urge that there is a hierarchy among the compartments of Shakespeare's mind and that the legal occupies and energizes a higher place than the alchemical or medicinal. Vendler, to cite a single example, does not gloss *vassalage* in Sonnet 26 as she ably does the metaphor of the two lawsuits in Sonnet 35 and distributive justice in Sonnet 46. In both Sonnet 35 and 46 there is a complex world – one in which for Elizabethans the legal had a dominant role – and that world is both subsumed in the allusion and given life by means of it. See also Arthur F. Marotti, 'Shakespeare's Sonnets as Literary Property', in *Soliciting Interpretation: Literary Theory and Seventeenth-Century English Poetry*, ed. E.D. Harvey and K.E. Maus (University of Chicago Press, 1990).

These comments were not intended to be definitive, only heuristic: for it seemed worth concluding this survey of Shakespeare and the Law with a glance at his major achievement in lyric poetry.[27]

CONCLUSION

In the topic of Shakespeare and the Law we discover a field of thought that is immensely rich and also dynamic, adapting to the dramaturgical requirements of each new play and of changes in his theatre company and audience tastes over a long span of years, as well as to changes in the society. Shakespeare was neither doctrinaire nor static.

The hypothesis has been put forward (as noted above) that Shakespeare must have been a lawyer in order to handle the complexities of law that are incarnated in his plays; but complexities of law are also to be found in such contemporaries as John Webster, and complexities of theological thought are also found in his plays – yet no one has thought it necessary to invent theological training for William Shakespeare.

In addressing Shakespeare's use of ideas, one may profitably turn to W. Gordon Zeeveld's monographic study, *The Temper of Shakespeare's Thought* (New Haven, Ct: Yale University Press, 1974) for its finding that the notion of a static 'Elizabethan world picture' seriously misrepresents the tensions and general flux within sixteenth-century thought. However, if we find it heuristic to approve of Zeeveld's discussion of Shakespeare's 'deep-seated sense of tradition' to compare with that of Richard Hooker (adding that other comparisons between Shakespeare and Hooker may be drawn at least as fruitfully), we are allowed to demur from his viewing *Measure for Measure* as a reflection of 'the adjustment of the common law to the practice of equity in the Court of Chancery'. For, as D.J. Palmer observed in his summary in *Shakespeare Survey*, 29 (1976) 157–8, 'the historical evidence alone, for instance, does not compel us to regard the judgment passed on Shylock as "equitable" or the Christianity of Isabella as "irreproachable".'

To turn to a line often quoted out of context: 'The first thing we do, let's kill all the lawyers': we may observe the following. This line is not Shakespeare speaking *proprie persona*, of course; it is Dick, the butcher, in *1 Henry VI* (IV.ii.76), though the sentiment is echoed by Jack Cade, the rebel, who in a later scene (IV.vii) shouts directions to his company: 'So, sirs. Now go some and pull down the Savoy, others to the Inns of Court, down with them all', and, further, 'Away, burn all the records of the realm ... ' Yet the option of Dick and the directions shouted by Jack Cade are essential to the dramatic structure of the play, and Shakespeare's lines are faithful to the characterizations and historically faithful in representing the animus of the lower classes towards lawyers and their institutions, and to written legal documents as instruments and symbols of oppression.

The picture of Shakespeare and the law then is a great deal larger than seen by Dick the butcher or most twentieth-century readers: more dynamic, more nuanced, more metaphoric, than can be expressed by a single character in a single play. For Shakespeare, the law was not only useful, it was vital to an orderly society and not least to a Christian commonwealth. It was also fruitful, and from the responsible exercise of the law under the right persuasion good order and civility could emerge.

REFERENCES

1. Thus Arnaldo Momigliano in *The Classical Foundations of Modern Historiography*, The Sather Lectures at the University of California, Berkeley 1961–2, Berkeley: University of California Press, 1990, 78.

2. Ernst H. Kantorowicz, *The King's Two Bodies: A Study in Mediaeval Political Theology*, Princeton: Princeton University Press, 1957 – reviewed by R.J. Schoeck in 'Political Theology and Legal Fiction', in *Review of Politics*, xxii (April 1960), 281–4. Kantorowicz begins with Plowden's Reports (7–23) and then studies Shakespeare's *Richard II* (24–41) and the fusion of the public and the private bodies in this king portrayed by Shakespeare.

3. The French phrase *signifying before the word, or definition, was invented*, is used here to launch an awareness of the significance of technical language in any discussion of law and literature, whether Sophocles' Greek or Shakespeare's early modern English. Hundreds of technical terms in Law-French and Latin are imbedded in the English language, and twentieth-century readers have lost much understanding of their precise, original meaning (largely available to Shakespeare's generation, though less so than they were to Chaucer in the fourteenth century), not to speak of a knowledge of the roots of those technical words and phrases, a knowledge of which added resonance to spoken or written utterances. It is no accident that one of the bestsellers of the Elizabethan and Jacobean age was a little book called *Les Termes de la Ley*, published first as early as 1523 and reprinted some sixteen times in Shakespeare's lifetime (*STC*, 20701–20715). The fact of that book calls attention to an obvious need for readers (and writers) to arrive at a greater familiarity with the terms and concepts of the English common law without having gone through the rigors of legal education in the Inns of Court. (To be sure, many of the purchasers of *Les Termes de la Ley* were law students, and even practitioners; but that is another matter.)

  If *Les Termes* (and its English translation) served the need for exposition of the Law-French terms, there were other tools for the Latin: see R.J. Schoeck, 'Canon Law in England on the Eve of the Reformation', in *Mediaeval Studies* xxv (1963) 125–47, and 'Neo-Latin Legal Literature', in *Acta Conventus Neo-Latini Lovaniensis*, ed. J. IJsewijn and E. Kessler, Leuven and Munich: W. Fink, 1973, 577–88, noting especially the *Lexicon juridicum iuris romani . . .* of Johannes Calvinus.

  The legal maxim had a very considerable function not only in the Roman civil law but also in the English common law. For legal maxims in English legal language generally, see David Ogg, in *Johanni Seldeni 'Ad Fletam Dissertatio'*, Cambridge: Cambridge University Press, 1925, esp. xlii–xlvi. Peter Stein has addressed questions concerning the employment of the legal maxim (or *regula*) and its binding force in his analysis and history of *Regulae Iuris: From Juristic Rules to Legal Maxims* (Edinburgh: University Press, 1966); and on the invoking of legal maxims, see Kantorowicz, *The King's Two Bodies*, 10. There is an overlap of the legal maxim with the adage so richly explored by Erasmus in *Chiliades Adagiorum*; and one example of the maxim-adage is the *Summum ius, summa iniuria* briefly discussed below.

  An appended note is provided on the several significations of *law* still current in Shakespeare's time, so far as may be gleaned from an initiatory study of the *OED*.

4. On the interrelatedness of different legal systems in England earlier in the Middle Ages, see John A. Alford, 'Literature and the Law in Medieval England', *PMLA*, 92 (1977) 941–51. I have spoken briefly to this question in 'Canon Law in England', (cited above).

upon Shakespeare and others; and this edition will be a rich source for future studies of marriage and related concepts in the sixteenth century.

21. See David Bergeron, *Shakespeare: A Study and Research Guide*, 3d edn, (Lawrence, Kansas, Kansas University Press, 1995), for fuller description.

22. See Harold Brooks, 'Themes and Structure in *Comedy of Errors*', in *Early Shakespeare* (1961).

23. One finds equity discussed in Plowden's *Commentaries*, where much is due to St. Germain's *Doctor and Student*, which was much reprinted in the sixteenth century after its first printing in Latin (in 1528, if not earlier in 1523), then in English around 1530. *Doctor and Student* is a landmark for its grounding equity in common law cases rather than in the canon law.

24. Tucker characterizes these expressions as 'no more than pious commonplaces which any Elizabethan ostler may have known' (*Letter of the Law*, 93). Tucker 'serves writs of error upon several critics' who have suggested that *Merchant of Venice* is the playwright's personal commentary upon a supposed conflict between the exponents of equity and the supporters of the common law. There is not space here to reproduce the supporting details of Tucker's argument; but it might be added that late fifteenth-century common lawyers spoke of their recourse to conscience, and the judges of King's Bench and Common Pleas from time to time addressed their consciences, as I have observed elsewhere.

   Interpretation was a continuing concern of all lawyers in the Renaissance period, common lawyers as well as civilians and canonists on both sides of the Channel: see Ian Maclean, *Interpretation and Meaning in the Renaissance: the case of law*, Cambridge: Cambridge University Press, 1992, an important study. An untapped resource is the abundant literature of the *consilia*, those learned opinions of jurisprudents on the continent in many kinds of often complex cases: see Peter R. Pazzaglini and Catharine A. Hawks, *Consilia: A Bibliography of Holdings in the Library of Congress and Certain Other Collections in the United States*, Washington: Library of Congress, 1990. This is yet another dimension of the *Merchant of Venice*, for it highlights Portia's seeking the advice of Bellario in IV.i.

25. For a brief outlining of the signification and importance of the adage *summum ius, summa iniuria*, see Schoeck, *Erasmus of Europe*: vol. II, *The Prince of Humanists, 1501–1536*, Edinburgh: University Press, 1993, 80. For introduction to the critical question of the re-introduction and re-interpretation of Aristotle's 'Epieikeia' see Guido Kisch, *Erasmus und die Jurisprudenz seiner Zeit*, Basle: Helbing & Lichtenhahn, 1960, esp. 64–5.

26. Aristotle, *Rhetoric*, I.13, 1374b (q. by K. Eden in 'Equity and the Origins of Renaissance Historicism: The Case for Erasmus', in *Yale Journal of Law*, V (1993) 137–45. In the study by W.R. Elton on the *Nicomachean Ethics* already cited, there is an indication of the influence of Aristotle's key work during the Renaissance: see further, Eugenio Garin, 'La fortuna dell'etica Aristotelica nel Quattrocento', *La cultura filosofica del rinascimento italiano*, (Florence: Sansoni, 1979), 60–71; and C.B. Schmitt, 'Aristotle's Ethics in the Sixteenth Century: Some considerations', *Aristotle and Renaissance Universities*, Cambridge, Mass: Harvard University Press, 1983, 87–112. These last two studies, in addition to J.K. McConica's 'Humanism and Aristotle in Tudor Oxford', *EHR*, 94 (1979) 291–317, serve to emphasize the extent to which Aristotle was familiar to scholar readers in Elizabethan circles. There is more of Aristotle in Shakespeare than has met the average reader's eye.

27. A further reach of language is to be found in the rhetoric of sixteenth-century lawyers, on which I have commented in 'Rhetoric and Law in Sixteenth-Century England', *Studies in Philology*, 50 (1953) 110–27; to this

early study of the subject should be added the response of D.S. Bland, 'Rhetoric and the Law Student in Sixteenth-Century England', ibid. 54 (1957) 498–508. I have followed my earlier study with 'Lawyers and Rhetoric in Sixteenth-Century England', in *Renaissance Eloquence*, ed. J.J. Murphy (Berkeley: University of California Press, 1983), 274–91. To these (and several further studies on the constituent questions raised) should be added a study of Abraham Fraunce, in whose *The Lawiers Logike* (1588) and *The Arcadian Rhetorike* (also 1588) we may find examples of the kind of attention to grammar, logic and rhetoric that some common lawyers were capable of, together with samples of their close attention to contemporary poetry.

14   Shakespeare and the Italians

Frances K. Barasch

The recent decade has seen a growing appreciation of Italy's unique contribution to the production of early modern theatre in England, owing in large part to a cultural readiness among Shakespeare scholars to re-examine critical attitudes of the past. Since his death, Shakespeare has been regularized, nationalized, bowdlerized, and prioritized or, in Gary Taylor's (1989)[1] term, 'reinvented' by successive generations of critics who comprised the Shakespeare establishment. In the process of reinventing the Bard to suit the agenda of Victoria's England, Shakespeare's Italian affinities were minimized through a dialectical quest for differences that usually demonstrated how English genius had subdued foreign culture. Some recent critics attribute British (and American) neglect of Italian Renaissance drama to Elizabethan suspicion of foreigners, a bias registered in moral terms that persisted even to this century, although ambivalently the Italians also were credited for their humanist concerns and romantic sensibilities.[2]

Progressive critics like Manfred Pfister[3] now look for new ways to understand Shakespeare through Italian studies. Pfister faults 'positivist' research of the nineteenth and early-twentieth-century for its narrow biographical concern with what Shakespeare knew about Italy and how he knew it. Nor is Pfister content with the wider context of influence and reception theories provided in histories of ideas which focused on 'intercultural transactions such as travel writing, the mediating work of Italians in England, and translations and adaptation of . . . texts,' including scenarios for improvisation and scripted drama (296–97). He would prefer that current scholars generate new interpretations of Elizabethan constructions of Italy that reflect English 'interests, needs and anxieties' (299), a project already begun by culturally-oriented critics and 'new historicists'.

There is much more to be done, however, than Pfister proposes. Traditional source studies and histories need reworking to respond to new attitudes toward non-English cultures. One example of the problem is Geoffrey Bullough's[4] translation of Gl'Ingannati (1531), a source for *Twelfth*

Night, which omits a certain prurient character, as had the first English translation by Thomas L. Peacock.[5] The character is 'Capitan Giglio spanuolo' whose inclusion surely could have helped textual editors understand Shakespeare's enigmatic allusion to 'Castiliano vulgo' (1.3.58).[6] This Spanish captain, as Antonietta Cataldi[7] has shown, was a satirical figure, already available in *miles gloriosus*, who was given Spanish features as a protest to Spain's invasions of Italy in the early sixteenth century. Shakespeare's Don Armado and Falstaff are descendants of this Giglio, the first *Capitano* of New Italian Comedy.

Standard histories create other problems. Earlier this century, a number of important archival scholars – W.W. Greg,[8] E.K. Chambers[9] and Kathleen Lea[10] whose comprehensive research produced enduring information – looked for 'concrete' relationships between English and Italian performance. Finding only minimal archival evidence of foreign actors in England, however, they invariably concluded that there was insufficient 'direct' information to constitute significant Italian influence in Shakespeare's work. Given the nature of their discipline and their stature, their 'positivist' conclusions are understandable and have been widely respected in Shakespeare circles. Nevertheless, a good deal of work in this century, particularly within the last dozen years or so, has been devoted to the confirmation or refutation of their claims.

I

Passed from one generation of scholars to the next, British tradition dies hard. Kenneth Richards,[11] for instance, continues to resist the cumulative force of comparative analyses that have found strong links between English and Italian theatre. Echoing Kathleen Lea (1934), Richards declares that 'Elizabethan drama shows very little concrete evidence for its significant influence on English playwriting or performance' (209). Instead he suggests, in an essay on Inigo Jones, that 'if we are looking for some evidence of English interest in the Italian improvised comedy it is perhaps at the courts of James I and Charles I, rather than in the public theatres ... ' (210). As co-author of *The Commedia dell'Arte, A Documentary History*,[12] Richards should know: the 'documentary' evidence of *commedia*'s impact is essentially continental and his research cannot be faulted in this respect. However, in also dismissing the impressive work of Italian scholar Valentina Capocci in *Genio e Mestiere*,[13] he closes the door on other creditable views. Capocci had proposed, in view of the widespread impact of *commedia* on European theatre, that English actors saw and admired the improvisational work of their Italian colleagues and introduced their style to English plays.

While a good deal of recent work like Capocci's has established strong circumstantial evidence, other scholars, both European and American, tacitly confirm the traditional view by bypassing Italian New Comedy entirely and crediting Shakespeare with original adaptations of classical drama. Wolfgang Riehle[14] positions his recent study *Shakespeare, Plautus and the Humanist Tradition* at the centre of scholarly discourse concerned with native and classical influences. Although aware that perhaps he goes too far in suggesting that almost everything Shakespeare knew about comic characterization could be learned from Plautus directly, Riehle acknowledges the possiblity of indirect influence from Italy's *commedia erudita*. But once stated, the matter is no longer addressed. He believes that even the bittersweet love of Shakespearean comedies originated with Plautus and, without further consideration, dismisses the possibility of the transmission of plots and acting styles through *la commedia dell'arte*.

Some new projects in biography have revisited old issues and also confirm earlier findings. Murray J. Levith[15] does a full-scale review of the old biographical question: was Shakespeare 'an Italian traveller'? Re-examining conventional arguments such as the faulty allusion to sailmakers in Bergamo, or the accurate ones such as the 'Lady of Strachy', Levith weighs the evidence for a possible visit to Italy and finds it inconclusive. He ends his biographical quest with the declaration: 'It doesn't really matter ... ' (90) because, as has been the standard view, Shakespeare merely used Italy as a metaphor for England. Christopher Spencer[16] who does a source study to 'provide insight into the craft and meaning' of *The Merchant of Venice* (vii), briefly acknowledges Italian sources in the play. He may be the first to associate 'Graziano' with the figure of 'Gratiano' (the Doctor of *commedia dell'arte*), although he does not attempt to analyse the satirical meaning of this insight. And ultimately he repeats the apologist view of the Jewish question. Devoting considerable space to 'contemporary background material for Jews and usurers in Elizabethan England', he ignores Italian Jews and their economic history to argue that 'Shakespeare's presentation of Shylock is governed by the needs of the plot ... , rather than by a desire to say anything about Jews ... ' (5). In contrast to Spencer, Lisa Jardine[17] explores the commercial world of Venice, its mercantile exchange practices, its knowledge transactions, and Marlowe's historically precise treatment of these themes in *The Jew of Malta* compared with Shakespeare's construction of Shylock as the 'innate Jewish character'. Jardine refuses to apologize for Shakespeare: whether or not Shakespeare chose to demonize Shylock 'because that is dramatically the most effective strategy for engaging the audience against him,' she argues, the play 'dangerously persuades us that its prejudices are transhistorical or ahistorical' (113, 99).

For an even deeper analysis of *The Merchant of Venice* and other plays, one may turn to Walter Cohen[18] whose Marxist critique of Renaissance English and Spanish drama also examines the Italian historical background of *The Merchant*. Cohen finds the play 'a symptom of a problem in the life of the late-sixteenth-century England' (197): the fear of transition from late medieval feudalism to early modern capitalism embodied in the advanced commercial center of Venice where Jews participated 'as merchants involved in an international, trans-European economic network' (200). Contradictory forces in English and Italian economic history produce ahistorical results in the play where the 'procapitalist' resolution overcomes early modern fears through anti-Semitic scapegoating which exempts the 'charitable' merchant Antonio from the stigma of usury. With Shylock defeated, the Christian Antonio becomes 'the harbinger of modern capitalism' (202).

II

Not all scholarly activity on Italy has taken a traditional turn in the early half of this century. Many have countered Kathleen Lea's interpretation of what constitutes evidence and have turned up countless allusions and analogues of the Italian presence in Elizabethan texts to refute the notion that only instances supported by extant English documents can be accepted as credible signs of influence. Historical and critical studies in comparative drama and *commedia dell'arte* by Ferdinando Neri,[19] O.J. Campbell,[20] J.R. Moore,[21] followed by L.G. Clubb,[22] Leo Salingar,[23] Ninian Mellamphy[24] and others have persuaded many that the two great theatres of the Renaissance, England's and Italy's, shared common practices. The next step has been the examination of those practices through intertextual study.

In America, the substantial marks of Italian literary influence found in English texts has commanded primary attention, precluding extended engagement with *commedia* improvisation and other culturally prompted text formation until very recent years. The debate over 'evidence' needed closure before the neglected remains of Italian popular culture could be revitalized. Owing in a large part to *Italian Drama in Shakespeare's Time* by Louise George Clubb[25] whose own work on the Italian question began in the 1960s and continues in the 1990s (e.g., Clubb 1967;[26] 1995[27]), the narrow conclusions of traditional source studies have been overcome. Through the concept of 'theatregrams', Clubb has demonstrated unequivocally that 'there existed . . . a common system' for the construction of Renaissance plays and 'a broad kinship' in the theatrical texts of the two countries. 'Theatergrams' are dramatic elements derived from a 'contamination of sources, genres, and accumulated stage-structures' along with the 'interchange and transformation of units, figures, relationships, actions, *topoi*, and framing patterns.' Their combination served as a common principle of dramatic construction in England as in Italy, producing 'streamlined structures' with 'elements of high specific density, weighty with significance from previous incarnations'. This combinatory principle of construction precludes the identification of 'precise historical connections and attributions' that source hunters have demanded but offers access to layers of meaning within the cultural accretions of early modern drama.[28]

Clubb's analysis of the *giovane innamorata* (the young woman in love) of Italian New Comedy, created by Ariosto and developed over the next decades of the *Cinquecento* by Shakespeare's Italian and English predecessors, provides an example of the structural process. As a 'theatregram of person,' the young woman required a 'theatergram of association' to permit exposition and plot advancement toward the lovers' union and connections with other characters who might assist or block the union. As in Plautine comedy, the young woman in Ariosto's prose *Cassaria* (1508) is a slave awaiting purchase as her lover's mistress; her associate is another slave. Revised in the verse *Cassaria* (1508), the slaves become sisters. In Ariosto's later play *I suppositi* (1509), the young woman (Polimnesta) becomes an Italian girl intent on marriage and her associate, by way of contrast, becomes a bawdy nurse with intimations of the Roman *anus* and *La Celestina* (c.1499). Polimnesta and her nurse, Clubb explains,

> authorize the recombinations to come, of theatergrams of association (specific pairings in the *serva padrona* range) that would generate theatergrams of motion: actions and reactions with apposite speeches, kinds of encounters, use of props and parts of the set for hiding, meeting, attack, defense, seduction, deceit, and so forth. All these produce variations of plot and character united in theatergrams of design, patterns of meaning expressed by the disposition of material reciprocally organizing the whole comedy and the spectators' perception of its form (1989 pp.9–10).

Gascoygne's translation *The Supposes* (1556) introduced the '*serva padrona* theatergram' to England, and Shakespeare later recombined it with 'theatergrams of action' to produce the structural and generic variations of *Two Gentlemen of Verona, Romeo and Juliet* and *Merchant of Venice*, among other plays.

Similar recombinations are made of other Italian 'theatergrams'. The pastoral, a 'theatergram of genre' presented by Battista Guarini's *Il pastor fido, tragicomedia pastorale* (1589) as a fully developed example of the arcadian scenarios of magical romance, improvised and popularized by the *comici dell'arte*, included many of the 'theatergrams' also found in Shakespeare's later romances: 'exiled nobles, raucous peasants, and servants mingled . . . with shepherds, sorcerers, satyrs, tutelary deities, and other supernatural beings' (Clubb). The 'theatergram of woman as wonder', a more spiritual type of woman who functioned as a vehicle for counter-reformation ideas in Italy evolved from Alessandro Piccolomini's *L'amor costante* (1540), through interim plays, to Raffaello Borghini's *La donna costante* (1578), the latter a 'mosaic of dramatic commonplaces and novella situations' including those of *Romeo and Juliet*. Perceptively, Clubb points out that the 'woman as wonder theatergram' inspired the figures of Helena and Isabella of *All's Well that Ends Well* and *Measure for Measure*, respectively.

Clubb's unfaltering demonstration of 'the international nature of Renaissance drama and the scale on which Italian innovations infiltrated the English stage' (1989, 154) requires no proof of direct evidence of Italian 'influence' on Shakespeare, for the question of 'influence' is irrelevant when it is understood that early modern methods of play construction were common property. Whatever the London audience may have not known or liked about Italian theatre, English playwrights certainly knew and exploited their competition. Nor does this commonality detract from Shakespeare's distinctive use of the shared dramatic elements which placed him at the apex of early modern theatrical achievement.

In another progressive collection of essays, *Shakespeare's Italy*,[29] more than a dozen contributors set out to explore the staging of Italy in Elizabethan theatre and its purpose. Critical perceptions are varied. Angela Locatelli sides with tradition in finding the Italy of *Romeo and Juliet* a fictitious world that serves as a metaphor of London, while A.J. Hoenselaars argues that the stage-Italy of English plays is not merely a metaphor of England but an ideological site: an independent nation with its own identity-alterity construct. In a second contribution to the collection, Hoenselaars finds that the use of foreign languages in many English plays served to aggrandize English as 'a much-desired international language' (11). In other essays Veneto-located plays are viewed as a metatheatre, a stage, an idea, a divided identity . Leo Salingar reconstructs the Elizabethans' Venice as a splendid commercial and cosmopolitan city, governed by strict justice. Abraham Oz finds Venice an ideological construct in which racism and religious bigotry flourish. Other contributors deal with cross-cultural constructions of temptation and desire; historical and mythic themes in *Merchant of Venice*; and the function of language and ideology in Shakespeare's contemporaries.

Viviana Comensoli,[30] another contributor to *Shakespeare's Italy*, demonstrates that *commedia* sources can lead to recovered meanings in English plays. In her comparatist application of structural principles to Thomas Dekker's complex stagecraft and *commedia dell'arte*, she explains how:

> The Italian setting of the *Honest Whore* plays, together with Dekker's employment of characters and situations resembling those commonly found in Italian popular comedy, clarifies his satirical intent. The signal example of influence is the portrait of the self-satisfied merchant, suggesting that Candido is deliberately modelled after the comic mask of Pantalone, the old magnifico of the *commedia dell'arte* . . . . Dekker, like the Italian creators of Pantalone, satirises an unbridled mercantile ethic. (128)

As Comensoli apparently understands, the character types developed by the *comici dell'arte* and presented on tours across early modern Europe, once incorporated into Elizabethan criticism, add depth to cultural meanings of early modern English drama. Pantalone, for instance, is not only the greedy merchant familiar to modern readers; often he is an overwrought father, a widower, a lecherous old goat and frequent victim of his own vices. The values expressed in the dramatic conflicts between old and young, between arranged and companionate marriage and between mercenary and romantic ideals mark early modern Europe as a domestic, social and economic world in transition about to give birth to the modern era. Indeed, Shakespeare's 'Pantaloons' in *The Taming of the Shrew* (both Gremio and Baptista), old Capulet, Shylock, Polonius, 'the leane and slipper'd Pantaloone' and his younger cohorts in *As You Like It* (II.vii.139–66) need scrutiny as genre-constructions, layered with satirical meaning from *commedia erudita* and *all'improvviso*. In other words, Italian theatrical techniques and texts are essential background for Shakespeare studies.

III

A thorny issue from the start, Italian theatre practice has been better received in academic circles as a matter of 'common practice' than of 'influence'. As Harry Levin put it, Shakespeare

> was not less but more responsive than others to the currents of his age; and if his achievements turned out to be uniquely humane, he had achieved them by using the same materials and techniques that they [the Italians] did, and can be most fully understood in the light of conditions they shared. He himself recognised that he had been drawing upon the standard traditions of comedy when his stage directions referred to certain stock characters not by name but as Pantaloon, Pedant and Braggart – types, if not stereotypes, that had scarcely been novel with Aristophanes and were currently animating the *commedia dell'arte*.[31]

A revival of interest in *commedia dell'arte* on both sides of the Atlantic has produced important interdisciplinary research in the last two decades, made possible to a large extent by scholarly activity in Italy. At least until the early 1960s, British and American scholars were dependent on literary histories and translations that reflected the moral persuasions of their predecessors and the general appreciation of early Italian theatre was stymied by a dearth of Italian materials that might have encouraged intertextual and interdisciplinary work. However, a post-war boom in Italian research cultivated a widened curiosity about *commedia dell'arte* (the name now generally applied only to the Italian theatre of improvisation) resulting in modern editions, reprints, and translations of important Italian sources, including new Italian editions of performance accounts by actor-directors who flourished between 1560 and 1699: these are Leone De'Sommi,[32] Flaminio Scala,[33] Nicolò Barbieri[34] and Andreà Perrucci (1961;[35] tr. 1911–12).[36] The information they provide about Renaissance acting and stagecraft fills many gaps in Elizabethan as well as Jacobean and Restoration theatre practice: as in Hamlet's warning to the players, for example, Perucci advises Italian comics not to depart so much from the argument that the audience loses the thread of the main story.

Numerous collections of archival materials (supplementing those assembled by Vito Pandolfi, 1957)[37] and modern critical works have continued to appear: important among these are Ferdinando Taviani's *Il segreto della Commedia dell'Arte* (with Mirella Schino),[38] Roberto Tessari's *Commedia dell'arte: la maschera e l'ombra*[39] and his essay 'Sotto il segno di Giano: La Commedia dell'Arte di Francesco e Isabella Andreini' (Cairns, ed.).[40] Although bearing only indirectly on Shakespeare, new critical directions may be taken from Tessari's concern with cultural materialism in Renaissance Italy as expressed in the lives of actors, their aspirations, social status, profession and the tensions among them.

Complementing the Italian scholarship, primary research materials presented in English editions also appeared in the 1960s, including two books, which are still useful: *The Italian Comedy* by Pierre-Louis Duchartre (1929; repr. 1966 with a pictorial supplement)[41] and Flaminio Scala's *Scenarios of the Commedia dell'Arte* (1611), translated by Henry F. Salerno (1967; repr. 1989).[42] The first discusses Italian actors and masks, as well as *la comédie italienne*, organized in Paris by French and Italian actors about 1580. More important, Duchartre reproduces a selection of paintings and theatrical iconography printed on the Continent from the 1570s through the eighteenth century, representing characters and scenes from *commedia* plays that were widely distributed in early modern Europe. Duchartre's material should be studied in conjunction with new findings by art historian Peg Katritsky,[43] my own essays (Barasch 1993,[44] 1995[45]) and *The Oxford Illustrated History of Theatre* (Brown, ed.)[46] which includes the chapter 'Italian Renaissance Theatre' by Louise George Clubb. Scala's book is a memorial reconstruction of fifty scenarios or plot outlines performed *al'improvviso* by troupes like *I Gelosi*, one of the most famous acting companies of sixteenth-century Europe. While these performance materials do not provide 'concrete' evidence of Elizabethan theatre practice, they provide pictorial representations of contemporary scenes and outlines of plot structures that were part of shared theatrical conventions and performance conditions of the early modern stage. Another important contribution in recent years is the annotated bibliographical guide prepared by Thomas F. Heck.[47]

Fortunately also in recent years, an increasing number of international scholars have focused on the Italian theatre of improvisation to reconsider its shaping role in England and other European nations. Congresses and seminars entirely devoted to the subject of Italian origins of Renaissance theatre – its actors, playing conditions, staging, art, literature, scenarios, and cultural influence on the rest of Europe – have resulted in the publication of three valuable collections edited by Domenico Pietropaolo;[48] by Christopher Cairns[49] who includes essays by Roberto Tessari,[50] Kenneth Richards (see n. 11) and Peg Katritsky (see n. 43) already mentioned; and by M.B. Dixon and M.Y. Togami[51] who offer a general introduction to *commedia* then and now.

Although these volumes focus entirely on *commedia dell'arte*, they are packed with valuable information, including a reminder by Robert L. Erenstein (Dixon and Togami, eds. ibid.) that the term *commedia dell'arte* first appeared in eighteenth-century Italy 'to denote the acting style of professional' improvisators whose esteem was waning by that time (7). Another reminder comes from Domenico Pietropaolo (see n. 48) who formalizes the improvised dialogue that was 'far from the spontaneous sort of creation *ex nihilo* that amateurs and romantics have at times imagined it to be' (168). Described in theoretical terms as a 'stochastic composition process' (173), improvisational methods are charted by Pietropaolo who argues that the actors followed rhetorical conventions established in set pieces learned in advance and performed regularly as stimulus-response dialogues in concert with fellow actors of the company.

Shakespearan analogues, particularly with regard to shared sources, are implicit in many of the collected conference papers. In *The Science of Buffoonery* (Pietropaolo, ed. ibid.), Gabriele Erasmi traces *commedia* to Greek comic tradition; Douglas Radcliff-Umstead examines its relationship to the 'erudite' comic tradition; Guido Pugliese discusses *novelle* sources and Giulio Ferroni describes '*l'ossessione*' for doubling dramatic elements: lovers, masters and servants, comic scenes and plot situations. In Tim Fitzpatrick's[52] essay (Pietropaolo, ed. 1989), Flaminio Scala's prototypal scenarios are subjected to theoretical scrutiny that also suggests shared practices with Elizabethan theatre. In the play-building and staging of Italian scenarios, a sequential pattern is used to present both the main action and the diversions of secondary characters that sometimes amount to a sub-plot. These directions are divided by acts (usually three in the scenarios). The acts are then subdivided into numerous short scenes by diachronic segmentation, denoted by the entrance of new characters and directions for exits. Synchronic segmentation also occurs in the scenarios, i.e., the interaction that takes place within a given scene. It is a technique for grouping the characters onstage, usually in limited diadic or triadic arrangements at upper and lower levels, at the centre, aside, or in parallel actions. Speech-acts for the synchronic segments are also guided by directions in the scenario text with such verbals as: enter, is telling, continues . . . to say, greets . . . expressing his joy.

Fitzpatrick's analysis can be fruitfully compared with *commedia* iconography which graphically illustrates stage groupings and gestures for the speech acts. Comparison with the English 'platts' (stage directions guiding the performance of scripted plays such as the lost play *Dead Mans Fortune*) can be particularly illuminating. From such comparisons, the inference may be made that acting instructions, so detailed in the improvised scenarios, were embedded in the dialogues of English scripted plays which made specific mimetic instructions unnecessary. A further inference is that English actors used a universal system for blocking, movement and expression on the stage. It is not difficult to find verbal directions embedded in

Shakespeare's texts, as in Juliet's 'Good father, I beseech you on my knees' (3.5.158) or in Desdemona's anaphoric signs 'here' and 'here's' which mark her speech-act at the Senate:

> Des.   My noble father,
> I do perceive here a divided duty:
> To you I am bound for life and education,
> . . . . But here's my husband (1.3.180–83).

Shakespeare's Italian literary connections are specifically addressed (along with those of Ben Jonson and John Lyly) in a fourth collection of conference and commissioned papers edited by J.R Mulryne and Margaret Shewring.[53] This volume includes an entirely new approach to the issue of Italian improvisation vs. Shakespeare, a central theme in Capocci (mentioned above).[54] It is now possible to see that in rejecting connections and highlighting differences, earlier critics gave more credence than deserved to Thomas Nashe's famous defense of actors against Puritan attacks:

> Our Players are not as the players beyond the Sea – a sort of squirting baudie Comedians that haue whores and common Curtizens to playe womens partes, and forbeare no immodest speech or vnchast action that may procure laughter . . . (I: 215).[55]

The analysis of Italian professional improvisation by Richard Andrews in 'Scripted Theatre and the *Commedia dell'Arte*'[56] suggests a new way to understand Elizabethan performance through the improvising structure he terms the 'elastic gag'. Andrews examines structures found in 'Dialogues' (reprinted with his essay) used by the earliest *commedia* improvisators and demonstrates how they built dialogues out of small manageable units of 'elastic gags' (Clubb might call these 'theatergrams') that could be expanded or contracted as audience response might dictate. The gags were transported from play to play and interpolated as desired. After 1540, the 'elastic gag' was incorporated into the scripted plays of *commedia erudita* and may have entered Shakespeare's texts by that route. The question of transmission aside, Shakespeare's plays bear the mark of these improvised 'elastic' comic dialogues: e.g., the delayed reading of a document owing to repeated interruptions (Lance); the clown's delay in performing a service (Grumio); working through a list of suitors (Portia); or a delayed report like the Nurse's news of Tybalt's death which could be stretched or contracted by actorly improvisation. The imaginative reader will observe that the elasticity of improvised gags also pertains to monologues such as the Nurse's reflections on Juliet's childhood or Lance's account of his leave-taking in *Two Gentlemen of Verona*.

Improvisation is also central to the well-balanced discussion of 'Shakespeare and the actors of *commedia dell'arte*' by Andrew Grewar[57] which appears in yet another recent collection *Studies in the Commedia Dell'Arte* (George and Gossip, eds).[58] Grewar argues that, although circumstances and methods differed, Italian and English actors contributed significantly to the plays they performed. Shakespeare's allusions to extemporal performance prove he knew of the practice. His dialogues of witty lovers, which often close with couplets, reflect common improvisatory practice, as do his bawdy language, quibbling wordplay, servant parody of romantic lovers, deliberate repetition of a joke, phrase or action for comic effect. Grewar speculates that, as Shakespeare collaborated with other authors and actors willingly, he may have accepted their best *ad libs* for incorporation into his texts.

More important, Grewar has discovered significant evidence that the actors who later formed the Lord Chamberlain's Men with Shakespeare in 1594 performed in the English *commedia* play *Dead Mans Fortune* (?1590–92). The play survives only as an outline of stage directions, naming the actors Richard Burbage, Thomas Pope, George Bryan, Richard Cowley, John Duke, Augustine Phillips, John Sincler, and William Slye. With Pantalone a named character in the sub-plot of *Dead Mans Fortune*, it is beyond doubt that the directions given for the jealous husband, a disguised lover, cheating wife, and intriguing servants constitute a *commedia* play. Whether or not the play or its subplot was performed from a lost script or improvised from a scenario in the Italian manner seems a mere quibble in the face of the certain evidence that Shakespeare's colleagues presented an Italian Pantalone farce. A more useful undertaking would be an examination of Italian connections in the main plot of *Dead Mans Fortune* for its signs of pastoral lovers, imprisonment, magic, madness and faery dancers who help resolve the plot. Have we here an ur-version of *A Midsummer Night's Dream*?

The study of contemporary theatrical iconography is another new way to understand Elizabethan performance. Two of my recent essays perform dual functions in art and performance history: they identify, date and describe certain theatre art of the sixteenth century and interpret these 'graphic texts' in terms of Shakespeare's plays. In 'The Bayeux Painting and Shakespearean Improvisation',[59] I interpret the tableau represented in a French painting of 1571 as a scene from a romantic comedy of multiple lovers: as Catherine de'Medici watches from a far corner of the stage, simultaneous actions take place among a young woman in love, her disputing suitors, a father and his cronies who hold the centre stage. Behind them, two servants make bawdy love, another servant tattles, a rejected young woman in love tries to be noticed, and an unwanted suitor spies on all. The tableau shows us how a *commedia* troupe, including actresses, staged synchronic action and portrays the signifying gestures and costumes of conventional performance style. The inference that these conventions were used in Elizabethan performances with boys in leading romantic roles, as in *Two Gentlemen of Verona* and *Love's Labour's Lost*, is compelling. Stage history and Shakespearean intention are illuminated in '"He's for a Iigge, or tale of Baudry": Sixteenth-Century Images of the Stage-Jig'[60] where I reproduce woodcuts of French and Italian farces, including a scene in which the *commedia* Pantalone peeks through an arras to spy on a pair of lovers. The pictorial evidence is proposed as fair representations of the English Stage Jig, the popular bawdy genre Hamlet associates with Polonius. The Pantalone woodcut burlesques the romantic convention of lovers-spied-upon, revealing the farcical underpinnings of Polonius' character, the surveillance scenes between Ophelia and Hamlet and the bawdy/erotic suggestiveness of the Queen's closet encounter with Hamlet. That Shakespeare made the well-known comic 'theatergram' of the spying father culminate in the grotesque murder of Polonius surely surprised and deepened audience pleasure in the play.

The decade of new work on 'Shakespeare and the Italians' reviewed here ends appropriately, I think, with yet another area for exploration in Italian puppet theatres which were licensed to play in London as early as 1573. Susan Young[61] makes the tantalizing suggestion that Shakespeare's knowledge of Italy (or Italian plays) may have derived in some part from the *marionettisti*. Her evidence points to accessibility: several such theatres operated in Shakespeare's London at Stourbridge fair, Holborn Bridge, Fleet Steet and at Eltham; Thomas Dekker saw a marionette performance of *Julius Caesar* before 1599. She also notes that 'a version of *Hamlet* for *marionette* was performed' in Dresden, Hamburg, Gdansk and Frankfurt in 1626 (9). Young does no further investigation in this area, for the focus of her book *Shakespeare Manipulated* is not on Shakespeare's gleanings from Italian puppet theatre but on Italian adaptations of Shakespeare. For at least the past 170 years Shakespeare has served as inspiration for the popular *teatro di figura* in Italy. Young's work catalogues and preserves the extant record of these adaptations. Along with Verdi's operatic versions of Shakespeare, the circle of influence is completed: Shakespeare took inspiration from Italian innovations of the sixteenth century as the Italians have since taken inspiration from Shakespeare.

REFERENCES

1. Taylor, Gary (1989), *Reinventing Shakespeare, a Cultural History from the Restoration to the Present*, New York: Weidenfeld & Nicolson.
2. Levin, Harry (1993), 'Shakespeare's Italians' in Marrapodi, *op. cit.*, 16–19. Mahler, Andreas (1993), 'Italian vices: cross-cultural constructions of temptation and desire in English Renaissance drama' in Marrapodi, *op. cit.* (see n. 29), 49.
3. Pfister, Manfred (1993), 'Shakespeare and Italy, or, the law of diminishing returns' in Marrapodi, *op. cit.*
4. Bullough, Geoffrey (1959), *Narrative and Dramatic Sources of Shakespeare*, Vol. 2, London: Routledge and Kegan Paul.
5. Peacock, Thomas L. (1862), *Gl'Ingannati. The Deceived: a Comedy performed at Siena in 1531: and Aelia Laelia Crispis*, London: Chapman and Hall.
6. Barasch, Frances K. (1996), '"Castiliano vulgo" Revisited', *Shakespeare Newsletter*, 46 (21), 4 Winter.

7.   Cataldi, Antonietta (1989), *La Stirpe di Falstaff*, Firenze: Le Monnier.
8.   Greg, W.W. (1906), *Pastoral Poetry and Pastoral Drama: A Literary Inquiry, with Special Reference to the Pre-Restoration Stage in England*, London: A.H. Bullen.
9.   Chambers, E.K. (1923), *The Elizabethan Stage*, 4 vols. Oxford: Clarendon Press.
10. Lea, Kathleen (1934; repr.1962), *Italian Popular Comedy: a Study in the Commedia dell'arte, 1560–1620, with Special Reference to the English Stage*, 2 vols. Oxford and New York: Oxford University Press.
11. Richards, Kenneth (1989), 'Inigo Jones and the *Commedia Dell'Arte*', in Cairns, *op. cit.* (see n. 40).
12. Richards, Kenneth and Laura Richards (1990), *The Commedia dell'Arte, A Documentary History*, Oxford: Basil Blackwell.
13. Capocci, Valentina (1950), *Genio e Mestiere. Shakespeare e la Commedia dell'Arte*, Bari: G. Latenza.
14. Riehle, Wolfgang (1991), *Shakespeare, Plautus and the Humanist Tradition*, Cambridge: D.S. Brewer.
15. Levith, Murray J. (1989), *Shakespeare's Italian Settings and Plays*, New York: St. Martin's Press.
16. Spencer, Christopher (1988), *The Genesis of Shakespeare's 'Merchant of Venice'*, Lewiston, N.Y.: Edwin Mellen Press.
17. Jardine, Lisa (1996), *Reading Shakespeare Historically*, London and New York: Routledge.
18. Cohen, Walter (1985), *Drama of a Nation, Public Theater in Renaissance England and Spain*, Ithaca and London: Cornell University Press.
19. Neri, Ferdinando (1913), *Scenari delle Maschere in Arcadia*, Città di Castello: S. Lapi.
20. Campbell, O.J. (1925), '*Love's Labor's Lost* Re-studied' and '*The Two Gentlemen of Verona* and Italian Comedy', in *Studies in Shakespeare, Milton, and Donne*, New York: University of Michigan Publications.
21. Moore, John R.(1949), 'Pantaloon as Shylock', *Boston Public Library Quarterly*, 1 (1), July.
22. Clubb, Louise George (1967), 'Italian comedy and *The Comedy of Errors*', *Comparative Literature* (19).
23. Salingar, Leo (1974), *Shakespeare and the Traditions of Comedy*, Cambridge: Cambridge University Press.
24. Mellamphy, Ninian (1980), 'Pantaloons and Zanies: Shakespeare's "Apprenticeship" to Italian Professional Comedy Troupes', in Charney, Maurice (ed.), *Shakespearean Comedy*, New York: New York Forum.
25. Clubb, Louise George (1989), *Italian Drama in Shakespeare's Time*, New York and London: Yale University Press.
26. Clubb, Louise George (1967). See n. 22.
27. Clubb, Louise George (1995), 'Italian Renaissance Theatre' in Brown, *op. cit.* (see n. 46).
28. Clubb, Louise George (1989) 1, 5–6. See n. 25.
29. Marrapodi, Michele, A.J. Hoenselaars, Marcello Cappuzzo and L. Falzon Santucci, (eds) (1993), *Shakespeare's Italy. Functions of Italian locations in Renaissance drama*, Manchester and New York: Manchester University Press.
30. Comensoli, Viviana (1993), 'Merchants and madcaps: Dekker's *Honest Whore* plays and the commedia dell'arte', in Marrapodi, *op. cit.* (see n. 29).
31. Marrapodi, ed. (1993) 19. See n. 29.
32. Sommi, Leone De' (1968), *Quattro dialoghi in materia di rappresentazioni sceniche*, ed. Marotti, Ferruccio: Milan.

33. Scala, Flaminio (1976), *Il teatro della favole rappresentative*, 2 vols., ed. Marotti, Ferruccio: Milan.
34. Barbieri, Nicolò (1971), *La supplica, discorso famigliare ... a quelli che trattano de' comici*, ed. Taviani, Ferdinando: Milan.
35. Perrucci, Andreà (1961), *Dell'Arte Rappresentativa Premeditata ed all'improvviso* (1699), ed. Bragaglia, Giulio, Firenze: Sansoni.
36. Perrucci, Andreà (1911–12), *Arte Rappresentativa* in Craig, Edward Gordon (tr. and ed.), 'The Commedia dell'arte or Professional Comedy: Directions as to the Preparation of a Performance from a Scenario', *The Mask* 4.
37. Pandolfi, Vito (1957), *La Commedia dell'Arte*, 6 vols. Firenze: Sansoni.
38. Taviani, Ferdinando and Mirella Schino (1970), *Il segreto della Commedia dell'Arte, La memorie delle compagnie italiane del XVI, XVII, e XVIII secolo*, Firenze: La casa Usher.
39. Tessari, Roberto (1984), *Commedia dell'arte: la maschera e l'ombra*, Milan: Mursia.
40. Cairns, Christopher, (ed.) (1989), *The Commedia Dell'Arte, From the Renaissance to Dario Fo*. Lampeter, Dyfed, Wales: Edwin Mellen.
41. Duchartre, Pierre Louis (1929; repr. 1966), *The Italian Comedy*, tr. Randolph T. Weaver. New York: Dover Publications.
42. Scala, Flaminio (1967; repr.1989), *Scenarios of the Commedia dell'Arte: Flaminio Scala's Il Teatro Della Favole Rappresentative*, tr. Henry F. Salerno. New York: Limelight Editions.
43. Katritsky, Peg (1989), 'The Recueil Fossard 1928–88: a Review and Three Reconstructions' in Cairns, *op. cit.* (see n. 40).
44. Barasch, Frances K. (1993), 'Bayeux Painting and Shakespearean Improvisation, The', *Shakespeare Bulletin*, 2 (3), Summer.
45. Barasch, Frances K. (1995), '"He's for a Iigge, or tale of Baudry": Sixteenth-Century Images of the Stage-Jig', *Shakespeare Bulletin*, 13 (1), Winter.
46. Brown, John Russell, ed. (1995), *The Oxford Illustrated History of Theatre*, Oxford and New York: Oxford University Press.
47. Heck, Thomas F. (1988), *Commedia dell'arte: a Guide to the Primary and Secondary Literature*, New York: Garland.
48. Pietropaolo, Domenico, ed. (1989), *The Science of Buffoonery: Theory and History of the 'Commedia dell'Arte'*, (University of Toronto Italian Studies) Ottawa: Dovehouse Editions.
49. Cairns, Christopher (1989). See n. 40.
50. Tessari, Roberto (1989), 'Sotto il segno di Giano: La Commedia dell'Arte di Francesco e Isabella Andreini' in Cairns, *op. cit.* (see n. 40).
51. Dixon, Michael Bigelow and Michelle Y. Togami, (eds) (1990), *Commedia dell'Arte and the Comic Spirit*, Louisville (KY): Actors Theatre of Louisville.
52. Fitzpatrick, Tim (1989), 'Flaminio Scala's Prototypal Scenarios: Segmenting the Text/Performance' in Pietropaolo, *op. cit.* (see n. 48).
53. Mulryne, J.R. and Margaret Shewring, (eds) (1991), *Theatre of the English and Italian Renaissance*, New York: St. Martin's Press.
54. Capocci, Valentina (1950). See n. 13.
55. Nashe, Thomas (1592), *Pierce Penilesse his Supplication to the Diuell*, vol.1 in McKerrow, Ronald B. (ed.), *The Works of Thomas Nashe* (1958), 4 vols. Oxford: Basil Blackwell
56. Andrews, Richard (1991), 'Scripted Theatre and the *Commedia dell'Arte*' in Mulryne and Shewring, *op cit.* (see n. 53).
57. Grewar, Andrew (1993), 'Shakespeare and the actors of *commedia dell'arte*' in George and Gossip, *op.cit.* Revised from Grewar (1989), 'The Clowning Zanies: Shakespeare and the Actors of the *Commedia dell'Arte*', *Shakespeare in Southern Africa* 3.

58. George, David J. and Christopher J. Gossip, (eds) (1993), *Studies in the Commedia Dell'Arte*, Cardiff: University of Wales Press.
59. Barasch, Frances K. (1993). See n. 44.
60. Barasch, Frances K. (1995). See n. 45.
61. Young, Susan (1996), *Shakespeare Manipulated: The Use of the Dramatic Works of Shakespeare in 'teatro di figura' in Italy*, Madison, N.J.: Fairleigh Dickinson University Press.

PART 4

Plays and Poems

15 *Julius Caesar* 1937–1997: Where we are; How we got there

John W. Velz

Plays about major events in history are particularly subject to re-shaping by the biases of the later times in which they are read or seen in the theatre. *Julius Caesar*, which might well be read as a protagonist/antagonist play in the manner of *Othello* or *Richard II*, a clash between two temperaments, has in the past 200 years been seen in political, not just oppositional, terms. To the Romantics Brutus was an idealistic hero of the old Republic, dying with it, as Cato did. To the German Shakespeare critics of the Bismarck era and its aftermath, the play centres on Caesar (Kaiser), and makes a villain of Brutus (Velz 1994).[1] These two contrasting ways of thinking about the play in political terms lasted well into the second third of the twentieth century (for interpretations respectively pro-Caesar and pro-Brutus, see Brewer,[2] Breyer,[3] both from the early 1950s; for typical pro-Caesarian commentary late in the nineteenth century and early in the twentieth, see von Berger,[4] Gundolf[5]). During the Cold War the play was thought of in Marxist terms, especially in articles appearing in the *Jahrbuch der Deutschen Shakespeare Gesellschaft* (Weimar); predictably the Plebeians were often the collective protagonist.

One might say that in the decades 1937–57, when nearly every American high school student was exposed to *Julius Caesar* – its oratory, its high ideals of patriotism and public conscientiousness – there were two possible ways of presenting the play to students: if the teacher was a political conservative, the students were accorded an interpretation of the play in which Caesar was the heroic protagonist who returns as a ghost after his murder, tacitly to condemn and overtly to avenge the crime; if the teacher was a political liberal, the play was about Brutus, his principles and his heroic struggle against Caesarian tyranny, as his ancestor L. J. Brutus had struggled against Tarquinian tyranny before him – when he fails, something good goes out of the world with him. These mutually inverse senses of the play as a protagonist/antagonist play still can be found as the twentieth century wanes; but, for the most part, important changes have taken place in the conception of the action, changes that demand a more complex response than these simple alternatives of binary perception.

John Houseman, the theatrical and Hollywood producer, is at the starting point of the title above, 1937, as that is the year in which he staged *Julius Caesar* at an abandoned theatre just off Broadway which when refurbished the company named 'The Mercury Theatre'. Houseman in *Run-Through*[6] gives a very readable, nearly day-by-day account of the ordeals, financial, technical and artistic, that the company had to go through to get the production on the boards. The Federal Government (WPA) is sometimes spoken of as the sponsor of the production, but actually the bulk of the money came from private sources. Orson Welles directed, and played a Brutus 'high-minded, aristocratic [and] liberal-intellectual', the sort of man who is promptly done away with by dictators when they take power. This production unabashedly took an extreme political stance; Houseman and Welles advertised the play on handbills that read:

'JULIUS CAESAR
!!DEATH OF A DICTATOR!!'

and they made an overt reference to contemporary politics in Europe by dressing the principals in military uniforms dyed green with black belts to suggest German fascism. (It is commonly said that the uniforms suggested Mussolini's Black Shirts, but the off-green colour was clearly aimed at the German Nazis. Houseman speaks of the brass and percussion in the music written for the production by Marc Blitzstein as reflecting the marching Nazi troops so commonly seen in newsreels of the time.) At the time, the production was casually called by many 'the modern-dress *Caesar*', but Orson Welles's decision to use modern dress was not at all incidental, though Houseman acknowledges that it saved money in a tightly budgeted production. The dress (uniforms for aristocrats, second-hand street clothes for Plebeians) made a calculated political point.

This seemingly was the first production of *Julius Caesar* to use modern military uniforms to suggest the analogy between the fall of the Roman Republic and the fall of democracy to dictatorship in country after country in Europe in the 1930s. It had a huge éclat. We may justifiably attribute to the influence of this production the designers' convention of dressing Shakespeare's political figures in deliberately anachronistic costumes to make political points. In a sense the production (1976) of *Macbeth* in which Ian McKellen and Judi Dench starred in trench coats of gray-drab leather, and the currently popular film of *Richard III* in which McKellen plays the title role in fascist uniform can be traced ultimately back to the Mercury Theatre *Julius Caesar*. One must bear in mind, in reflecting on this fact, that using fascist costume was anything but a cliché in 1937, whatever it may have become by 1997.

Ecstatic reviewers made a legend of a production that we would not find so shocking as Americans did a year before the Nazis took the

Sudetenland of Czechoslovakia with the concurrence of Neville Chamberlain. What commentators on this production do not mention but which must have been on Welles's mind was the open war between the fascists and the leftists in Spain at this time (1936–1939).

The anti-fascist potential of *Julius Caesar* manifested itself in scholarship and criticism about the play during and after World War II. J. Dover Wilson's New Cambridge Edition of the play can speak for many other commentaries. Wilson asserts at the end of his 'Introduction' (dated 1948) that 'the Caesar who falls on Shakespeare's Capitol is the universal Dictator' (xxxiii).[7] The praise of Brutus in criticism from the World War II era also may be traced to the ambiance of the era it was written in. John Palmer's extended analysis of the characters in the play is pro-Brutus,[8] but it prefers Brutus' inner thoughts and the private philosophical dimension of his life to politics; this emphasis, however, may be not so much a reaction against the topicalities in contemporary response to the play as a legacy from A.C. Bradley[9] who insisted on seeing Shakespeare's characters as people with inner lives.

About the time that Brewer and Breyer were making opposed interpretations in the old manner – of *Julius Caesar* in political terms – John Houseman once again made a major statement in form of a production that would have long-term consequences, beginning only a few years after he made it. Working this time with Joseph Mankiewicz as director (Welles was trying and failing in Europe to get funding for a rival production), Houseman determined to make a major film for Metro Goldwyn Mayer. The film that emerged in June,1953, evoked response as enthusiastic as the response had been to the Houseman/Welles stage version 16 years earlier. But the Mankiewicz and Houseman film made quite a different statement from what the Mercury Theatre production had made; this film was not the ideological venture that Welles had directed. It scarcely could be, because no one actor was allowed to dominate the action and so to impose his ideology on the *Romanitas* of the play. In the 'fifties, 'sixties and 'seventies, American students showed more knowledge of this film than of most major Shakespeare films. And the reason for this familiarity is implicit in the nickname that the film carried/carries, 'The Marlon Brando *Julius Caesar*'.

These students, however, who made Brando's Antony a cult figure have been misguided, because the film is not Antony's except for two high points in the middle of the play; Houseman engaged an all-star cast. John Gielgud and James Mason came from England to play respectively a poetic and deprived Cassius and Brutus as 'a man of reason in a world of violence' and as 'Shakespeare's first draft for Hamlet' (*Front and Center* 401&n);[10] Louis Calhern played 'an ageing, tired, nervous dictator' (387) , and there are other well-known names in the cast, including Greer Garson (Calpurnia) and Deborah Kerr (Portia), both then under contract at MGM. Houseman confides that his intention was to balance the cast between

British and American actors and to forge a smooth ensemble in rehearsal. The rising Paul Scofield was considered for Antony, but Houseman gambled on Brando and won his bet. There are interesting anecdotes in *Front and Center* about Brando's and Gielgud's excellence on set. Gielgud worked generously with Brando, who had no classical experience, and came to admire the young and energetic actor so much that he offered him a contract to play with Scofield in a classical season that Gielgud was to direct in the winter of 1953–54. (Brando turned it down to go scuba diving [398n]; he never again attempted a classical role.)

Houseman's motives in this casting were to show that Americans could play in classics as well as British actors. But this is not the long-term effect that the film has had. People now look back at it as the first attempt to see *Julius Caesar* not as a doctrinaire political play or a protagonist/antagonist struggle, but as a play which is structured to permit each major character to rise in turn to prominence and then to recede from it, giving centre stage to another strong character played by a strong actor (Bevington).[11] According to this view, which Houseman did not intend to convey, the play is a mural-like succession of protagonists rather than any single character's play; no, not even Brando's.

Within five years after the 1953 film was screened, critics of the play began to emerge who saw in the action a multi-dimensional perspective instead of a face-off between two political figures. It can be argued that the Houseman/Mankiewicz film lies behind these critics' multiple perspectives. The film has remained in the art cinema repertoire for the 44 years since it was first screened, and it has had an ongoing influence on the view of the play in criticism and in classrooms. The ambiguity of the play was at first discussed as an irritant traceable to Shakespeare's determination to fit a tragedy of Caesar and a tragedy of Brutus into the same play (Bonjour).[12] Then other critics came forward with views of ambiguity as a calculated asset (Schanzer,[13] Traversi,[14] Hartsock,[15] Fortin[16]). We might describe as an aesthetics of uncertainty the efforts of these four critics to make sense of the inconsistencies and moral relativity of the play. For instance, René E. Fortin argued (without having seen Hartsock) that the play is 'An Experiment in Point of View' in which characters' responses to Caesar abound within the play from every band of the political and moral spectra; this reading has the advantage of widening scope without sacrificing focus, which remains on Caesar and Brutus. From this relativism it was a small step to an argument that the play portrays a series of sequential rises and falls, setting up possibilities for irony and suggesting that an ongoing process of history, not the moral worth of Caesar or of Brutus, is the real subject of the play (Velz, 1971).[17] The play which had in effect been seen as a pair of opposing statues was now, as it were, a frieze.

When the history of literary theory in the twentieth century is written, the work of Schanzer, Traversi, Hartsock and Fortin ought to be examined in search of evidence that the moral relativism that all recognized in the play in the 1960s prepared the way for more overtly and more generally deconstructive approaches to Shakespeare (other plays in his canon are similarly ambiguous, *Coriolanus*, for instance, and *Richard II*, and *Troilus and Cressida* and *Hamlet.*) One kind of interpretation of *Julius Caesar* to be fitted into a historical survey of post-modern criticism of Shakespeare is the combination of feminist criticism with psychoanalytic symbology that Coppélia Kahn published in 1997;[18] hers is the first book-length study of the Roman Plays from a feminist perspective. At the same time, 40 years earlier, as the first seeds of relativistic criticism of *Julius Caesar* were being sown, Gordon Ross Smith[19] published a fierce denigration of Brutus that in some ways resembles the cynical-cum-realist accounts of quondam sainted characters (Portia in *MV*, e.g.) who are sometimes subjected in our time to a severe critical lash wielded by post-modernists.

A major issue that is now more complicated than it once was is the place of *Julius Caesar* in the Shakespeare canon. Its central position, at the end of the sixteenth century, has caused critics of character to look closely at Brutus for evidence that he foreshadows Macbeth (Knight, 1930)[20] or Hamlet (see Houseman, 1979 discussed above). Moody Prior complicated the genre/canon question when he argued in 1969 that the play has affinities with the English histories, notably public morality as thematic and also interest hovering on many characters, not one, as in the Bradleian tragedies. In this latter point, Prior may be said to have made an advance over the relativists of the 1960s by providing a source for the troubling diffusion of focus in the play.

The complication of *Julius Caesar* as a function of ambivalence in the characters and varying perspectives in the design and genre was paralleled by a concurrent perception of complication in the style of the play. Samuel Johnson said in 1765[22] in his end-note to *Julius Caesar* that the play did not move him, perhaps because of Shakespeare's austere style, which he traced to Shakespeare's 'adherence to the real story, and to Roman manners.' The tradition has made much of Johnson's comment on the lean and undecorated style of the play and has seen this sparsity as Shakespeare's attempt to convey Stoic understatement, 'Roman manners'. (The relevance of Stoicism to Shakespeare is as lively an issue in the late twentieth century as the relevance of Senecanism was in the late nineteenth. See Vawter, 1974,[23] 1976,[24] Chew, 1988,[25] Monsarrat, 1984, for the terms of the argument.) The idea of a sparse play dominated criticism of *Julius Caesar* from Johnson's time into the twentieth century, until G. Wilson Knight first traced in two essays (1931)[26] some of the subtleties of language and theme that are now recognized to be there. Some have since said that the relatively unadorned style is traceable not to Stoicism but to Caesar's Commentaries, which Shakespeare (like modern schoolchildren) read, once his Latin was capable of Caesar's simple understated style. The illeism (references to the self in the third person) which dominate the play in the speeches – not just of Caesar as is often claimed, but as a characteristic language for aristocrats – is also from Caesar's *Gallic Wars*, where Caius Julius narrates the events of his Gallic campaigns with 'Caesar' as the frequent subject of sentences. In *Julius Caesar* Shakespeare certainly must have thought he was making his characters speak in a style of *Romanitas* (Velz, 1978).[27] This decision about personal style that makes *Julius Caesar* seem so public a play about heroism left its legacy in the heroic tragedies that followed: *Troilus and Cressida*, *Hamlet* and *Othello* (Viswanathan).[28] It remained to distinguish two styles in the play: the imperative style of the soldier turned politician and the oratorical style of persuasive public utterance. It is not only in the great orations of Act III ii that we should look for the conventions of oratory as Shakespeare understood them; we ought also to take note of speeches by lesser characters (e.g., Marullus in 1.1) and even talk in private settings, witness Portia's persuasion of Brutus to confide in her, a mini-oration. There are a number of other such orations in the play; if the style of the play seems oratorical, it is because the formal utterance and the manipulative devices of oratory (*ad hominem* argument and rhetorical questions) are in many scenes throughout (Velz, 1982).[29]

Another dimension of style (or should one say 'tone'?) that has added a colouring to the action is the recognition of rituals in the play, particularly Brutus' view of the assassins-to-be: 'Let's be sacrificers, but not butchers . . . ' Since Brents Stirling[30] showed the importance for the play of ceremonial moments and of attacks on them, the ritual dimension of the play has become so much a part of the critical tradition that it is easy to assume that it has always been observed. Among interpreters who have gone beyond Stirling's seminal essay, Naomi Liebler[31] can be singled out for her recognition that the ritual of the Lupercal, discussed in Plutarch's 'Life of Romulus', animates the play.

Source study of the play has been expanded since the mid-1950s to include both Renaissance commentators on ancient Rome (Spencer,[32] Ronan[33]) and previously neglected classical texts: Plato's *Republic* (Parker),[34] Seneca's 'De Clementia' (Velz 1969),[35] Virgil's *Aeneid* (Miola 1983),[36] and Caesar's *Commentaries*, the latter already mentioned above. The time (1910) when M.W. MacCallum could call his book *'Shakespeare's Roman Plays and Their Background'*[37] and deal only with Plutarch, was superseded in 1957 with Spencer's important study not just of source material, but of the temper of Roman life as Shakespeare and the educated in his audience understood it from the commentaries of their contemporaries. Ronan comments on a very large number of Tudor and Stuart Roman plays, placing Shakespeare's Rome in an illuminating context including morally charged concepts: *nobilitas, majestas, constantia, superbia* and *saevitia*. Plutarch's Greek bias and his Republican leanings had a major influence on Shakespeare, but they were not the only vision of Rome he encountered. Kermode offers a balanced view of Republic and Empire in Shakespeare's thought (1974, rpt. 1997).[38]

As for Plutarch, modern scholars are discovering that Shakespeare read more widely in the philosophical biographer than MacCallum's generation did; the Greek Lives that are paired with the Roman Lives were somewhat neglected until Homan[39] wrote about them; and Liebler, mentioned above, adds 'Romulus' to the sources of *Caesar*. The last word has not been said about the meaning of Plutarch in the Shakespeare canon. There is a refreshing openness in our time to new definitions of 'source' and 'influence'; see Miola (1988)[40] for a major commentary, focused on *Julius Caesar*. Energy expended on source study of *Julius Caesar* in our time is being rewarded.

It used to be universally said that *Julius Caesar* is the cleanest text in the First Folio, devoid of cruxes. The period 1937–97, especially the second half of that period, has complicated that oversimplification, as it has complicated such simplifications as interpretation of the characters and the moral themes, and likewise the putatively unadorned style of this subtle and rich play. A succession of scholars from the early 1950s through the '60s and '70s has resisted simple answers to textual questions in the play. The focus of such resistance is the alleged crux in 4.3 in which Brutus, who informs Cassius of Portia's death, learns from Messala a few minutes of stage time afterwards that she is dead 'by strange manner'. Some have defended the duplicate revelation on literary grounds; more have attacked it on those same grounds; some have labelled the Messala revelation a first version which Shakespeare intended to replace with Brutus's more dramatic revelation to Cassius. (More dramatic indeed; we may remember the profound remark of Lessing, 'Alles Stoische ist untheatralisch.' [Kannengiesser, who anticipates by fifty years or more much modern thought about the text in this scene[41]].) Among other hard knots is the 'just cause crux' in 3.1, where Caesar seemed to Ben Jonson to be 'ridiculous'. Though many scholars have spent ink on argument about what the passage should read, not many have seen that taking *wrong* as a verb, not a noun, relieves some of the ridiculousness. *To wrong* in Renaissance English is to injure. The offending sentence could then be paraphrased 'Caesar never wrongs [anyone] unless with the sort of reason that always permits sovereigns to abridge the rights of individual citizens in matters of state.' Another textual problem in the play is the loose ends between 1.3 and 2.1. Was there a scene here that was cut during rehearsal? The best single place to read about these matters and to find a postulated copytext for the play is in Bowers.[42]

The progression of production, criticism and scholarship of/on *Julius Caesar* has been in the past 60 years from easy answers to less easy ones. The richness of the play, in ambivalent plot and characterization, in language and genre, in its source pool and even in textual difficulties, has emerged after a long period of thinking of this as a 'simple' Play.

REFERENCES

No one should take this list of works cited as definitive; it is only indicative.
Choices were perforce arbitrary, though it is to be hoped not idiosyncratic.

1. Velz, John W. (1994), 'The Uses of Julius Caesar in the Nineteenth Century: Two Nationalist Responses', Shakespeare Association of America Convention (unpublished).
2. Brewer, D.S. (1952), 'Brutus' Crime: A Footnote to *Julius Caesar*', *Review of English Studies*, n.s. 3, 51–54.
3. Breyer, Bernard R. (1954), 'A New Look at *Julius Caesar*.' *Essays in Honor of Walter Clyde Curry*, Vanderbilt Studies in the Humanities, No. 2, Nashville: Vanderbilt University Press, 161–180.
4. Berger, [Alfred] Freiherrn von (1896), *Studien und Kritiken*, Wien: Literarische Gesellschaft [excerpted in translation in *JC* Variorum Edition of 1913].
5. Gundolf, Friedrich (1924), *Caesar: Geschichte seines Ruhms*, Berlin: G. Bondi, 273.
6. Houseman, John (1972), *Run-Through: A Memoir*, New York: Simon and Schuster, see Ch. VII, esp. 285–320.
7. Wilson, J. Dover (1949), ed., *Julius Caesar*, The New Shakespeare. London and New York: Cambridge University Press. See Part IV of Introduction 'Caesar and Caesarism', xix–xxxiii.
8. Palmer, John (1945), 'Marcus Brutus.' *Political Characters of Shakespeare*, London: Macmillan, 1–64.
9. Bradley, A.C. (1904). *Shakespearean Tragedy: Lectures on Hamlet, Othello, King Lear, Macbeth*, London and New York: Macmillan. See early chapters.
10. Houseman, John (1979), *Front and Center*, New York: Simon and Schuster, Part V, 'The Lion's Roar: 1951–53' esp. 382–409.
11. Bevington, David M. (1992), ed., Introduction to *Julius Caesar* in *The Complete Works of Shakespeare*. New York: HarperCollins.
12. Bonjour, Adrien (1958/1970), *The Structure of Julius Caesar*, Liverpool: Liverpool University Press. Rpt. n.p.: The Folcroft Press Inc.
13. Schanzer, Ernest (1963), *The Problem Plays of Shakespeare: A Study of Julius Caesar, Measure for Measure, Antony and Cleopatra*, New York: Schocken Books, see Ch. I.
14. Traversi, Derek (1963), *Shakespeare: The Roman Plays*, Stanford, Calif.: Stanford University Press, see Ch. 2.
15. Hartsock, Mildred E. (1966), 'The Complexity of *Julius Caesar*,' *PMLA*, 81, 56–62.
16. Fortin, René E. (1968), '*Julius Caesar*: An Experiment in Point of View,' *Shakespeare Quarterly*, 19, 341–347.
17. Velz, John W. (1971), 'Undular Structure in *Julius Caesar*', *The Modern Language Review*, 66, 21–30. (Rpt. *Shakespearean Criticism*, (ed.) Mark W. Scott. Detroit: Gale Research Corporation, 1988.)
18. Kahn, Coppélia (1997), *Roman Shakespeare: Warriors, Wounds, and Women*, London and New York: Routledge.
19. Smith, Gordon Ross (1959), 'Brutus, Virtue, and Will', *Shakespeare Quarterly*, 10: 367–379.
20. Knight, G. Wilson (1930), 'Brutus and Macbeth', *The Wheel of Fire: Essays in Interpretation of Shakespeare's Sombre Tragedies*, Oxford: Oxford University Press, 132–153.
21. Prior, Moody E. (1969), 'The Search for a Hero in *Julius Caesar*', *Renaissance Drama*, n.s. 2, 81–101.

22. Johnson, Samuel (1958), *Notes to Shakespeare Vol. III: Tragedies*, Arthur Sherbo (ed.), Los Angeles: Augustan Reprint Society,

23. Vawter, Marvin L. (1974), '"Division 'tween Our Souls": Shakespeare's Stoic Brutus', *Shakespeare Studies*, 7, 173–195.

24. Vawter, Marvin L. (1976), '"After Their Fashion": Cicero and Brutus in *Julius Caesar*', *Shakespeare Studies*, 9, 205–219.

25. Chew, Audrey (1988), *Stoicism in Renaissance English Literature: An Introduction*, (American University Studies Series 4: English Language and Literature 82.) New York, Bern, and Frankfurt am Main: Lang, 330.

26. Knight, G. Wilson (1931/1963), 'The Eroticism of *Julius Caesar*', *The Imperial Theme: Further Interpretations of Shakespeare's Tragedies, including the Roman Plays*, London: OUP (Rpt. 1963 from 3rd edn. (1951), London: Methuen): 63–95; Knight, G. Wilson (1931/1963), 'The Torch of Life: An Essay on *Julius Caesar*', ibid. 32–62.

27. Velz, John W. (1978), 'The Ancient World in Shakespeare: Authenticity or Anachronism? A Retrospect', *Shakespeare Survey*, 31, 1–12.

28. Viswanathan, S. (1969), '"Illeism With a Difference" in Certain Middle Plays of Shakespeare', *Shakespeare Quarterly*, 20, 407–415.

29. Velz, John W. (1982), 'Orator and Imperator in *Julius Caesar*: Style and the Process of Roman History', *Shakespeare Studies*, 15, 55–75.

30. Stirling, Brents (1951), '"Or Else This Were [sic] a Savage Spectacle"', *PMLA*, 66: 765–774.

31. Liebler, Naomi Conn. (1981), '"Thou Bleeding Piece of Earth": The Ritual Ground of *Julius Caesar*', *Shakespeare Studies*, 14, 175–96.

32. Spencer, T. J. B. (1957), 'Shakespeare and the Elizabethan Romans', *Shakespeare Survey*, 10, 27–38.

33. Ronan, Clifford (1995), *'Antike Roman': Power Symbology and the Roman Play in Early Modern England, 1585–1635*, Athens, Ga. and London: Univ. of Georgia Press. (Frequent references to *JC*. See Index.)

34. Parker, Barbara L. (1993), '"A Thing Unfirm": Plato's *Republic* and Shakespeare's *Julius Caesar*', *Shakespeare Quarterly*, 44, 30–43.

35. Velz, John W. (1969), 'Clemency, Will, and Just Cause in *Julius Cæsar*', *Shakespeare Survey*, 22, 109–18.

36. Miola, Robert, S. (1983), *Shakespeare's Rome*, Cambridge and New York: Cambridge University Press, 244.

37. MacCallum, M[ungo] W. (1910/1967), *Shakespeare's Roman Plays and Their Background*, London and Melbourne: Macmillan, *JC*, 168–299.

38. Kermode, Frank (1974), 'Introduction' to *Julius Caesar. The Riverside Shakespeare*, G. Blakemore Evans, et al. ed., Boston: Houghton Mifflin, Second edn. 1997.

39. Homan, Sidney (1975), 'Dion, Alexander, and Demetrius – Plutarch's Forgotten *Parallel Lives* – as Mirrors for Shakespeare's *Julius Caesar*', *Shakespeare Studies*, 8, 195–210.

40. Miola, Robert, S. (1988), 'Shakespeare and His Sources: Observations on the Critical History of *Julius Caesar*', *Shakespeare Survey*, 40, 69–76.

41. Kannengiesser, Paul (1908), 'Eine Doppelredaktion in Shakespeares "Julius Caesar"', *Shakespeare Jahrbuch*, 44, 51–64.

42. Bowers, Fredson (1978), 'The Copy for Shakespeare's *Julius Caesar*', *South Atlantic Bulletin* [now *South Atlantic Review*], 43, 23–36.

16   Merging the Kingdoms: *King Lear*

Richard Knowles

A decade and a half ago one began to hear declarations of a 'revolution' in Shakespearean textual studies – one of the editors of the Oxford Shakespeare once compared it even to the Copernican revolution in cosmology – and today one may still hear claims of a 'minor Kuhnian scientific revolution' or a 'major paradigm shift' in theories of editing texts. The centerpiece of evidence that a revolution was occurring was the confident assertion that the 1608 Quarto and 1623 Folio texts of *King Lear* represented two equally authentic Shakespearean versions of that play, and hence that they should be kept separate, not merged or 'conflated' as they had been in all critical texts since Lewis Theobald's edition of 1733. The idea that Folio *Lear* might embody Shakespearean revisions of the longer Quarto was in fact not a revolutionary idea but had been discussed by editors for more than two centuries and became dominant for part of the nineteenth century – a fact not usually mentioned. As G. Thomas Tanselle has recently remarked, 'One cannot help noticing how often theoretical discussions – in the field of textual scholarship as in other fields – proclaim as new insights what was taken for granted in earlier discussions'.[1]

From *Lear* the notion of possible multiple versions was quickly applied, often by the same critics who maintained that there were two *Lear*s, to other two-text plays – *Hamlet, Othello, Richard III, Troilus* – and to other Renaissance dramatists, notably Middleton, until there seemed to be, in the words of E.A.J. Honigmann, 'a gold-rush, with more and more speculators jostling or encouraging each other'.[2] Before long the theories of revision and multiple versions were further generalized and extended to other theories about textual instability, the 'politics' of editing, a putative 'crisis' in editing, hypertext and genetic editing, collaborative authorship, the materiality of the text and the immateriality of the author, the indeterminacy of meaning, the relation of literature to power and censorship, and other notions dear to recent critics, who have in one way or another found the ideas of revision and multiple versions of Shakespeare's plays, and particularly the exemplary disintegration of the standard version of his greatest tragedy, congenial to their own views. Whether or not one calls the shift in attention to revision and indeterminacy a revolution, it has certainly contributed to an active scholarly industry.

Yet while this industry has flourished like the palm tree, one of its major foundations, the root belief that there are two authorial *King Lear*s, has seemed increasingly to be questionable. Although it had its strong champions early on, and has since gained some relatively uncritical followers,[3] the revisionist faith in two *Lear*s seems not to have been warmly embraced by Shakespearean scholars and editors at large. Except for the recent Oxford and Cambridge editions by early enthusiasts of the two-*Lear* theory, and two special-purpose parallel-text editions, the texts in all of the many new editions and re-editions of *Lear* that I have seen have been critical, synthetic 'conflations' of the Quarto and Folio, indistinguishable from the conventional text of the past three centuries, except for a greater concern in a few of them to mark lines unique to Quarto or Folio. The new Norton Shakespeare, though using the Oxford texts and therefore Oxford's edited texts of both Q and F *Lear*s, has also included as a third alternative a conventional 'conflated' *Lear*; and even the editor of one of the recent parallel-text editions of *Lear*, René Weis, has privately expressed to me his opinion that it is time to return to a single text of that play. The two book-length arguments for two *Lear*s, Steven Urkowitz's *Shakespeare's Revision of* King Lear (Princeton, 1980) and Gary Taylor's and Michael Warren's *The Division of the Kingdoms* (Oxford, 1983), have received some very skeptical reviews[4] (in addition to more positive ones), and the whole revisionist argument has evoked a lengthy counter-response from R.A. Foakes, who in his Hamlet *versus* Lear (Cambridge, 1993) argues that the differences between Q and F reflect not two separate plays but only different states of the same play. More recently, of several substantial essays questioning various parts of the revisionist argument, one – Robert Clare's '"Who is it that can tell me who I am?": The Theory of Authorial Revision between the Quarto and Folio Texts of *King Lear*' – has won the Fredson Bowers prize for the best bibliographical essay of the past two years.[5]

Perhaps most remarkably indicating a growing doubt about the revisionist 'orthodoxy' is a partial recantation made recently by one of its early supporters. As long ago as 1965 E.A.J. Honigmann was arguing for the instability of Shakespeare's text, and his strong endorsement of the two-*Lear* point of view has been repeatedly cited by the *Lear* revisionists.[6] Having now reconsidered the issues while writing his new book on *Othello*, Honigmann has honorably and with characteristic independence of mind admitted to a change of opinion:

> Carried away by ... enthusiasm, I think that I went too far in 1982, comparing the revision of *Othello* with that of *King Lear*. Whatever the fate of *King*

Lear, Shakespeare seems not to have revised *Othello* by adding longer passages . . . [though] Q and F [may] reflect two authorial strains in some shorter
passages. . . .

Of late, the older practice of conflation has been dismissed as obsolete. . . .
[But] authorial revision is only a hypothesis, not a certainty, whereas widespread corruption in one or both texts is an undeniable fact. In *King Lear*, the
foremost candidate in the queue of Shakespeare's supposedly revised plays, the
relationship of revision to corruption, a crucial question, has not so far been
dealt with satisfactorily: it would not be too difficult to show that at least some
of the 'revision' could qualify no less readily as corruption. Yet even should one
accept *King Lear* as definitely revised, must conflation of the two texts therefore cease? . . . To retain either Q or F *King Lear* 'wherever we could make
defensible sense of it' is to invite disaster. . . .

As I see it, an editor who believes in the revision of *King Lear* must still come
to terms with Q and F corruption, and consequently will want to conflate now
and then, if not as much as in the past. Editors who argue for small-scale
revision in *Othello*, and who accept that misreading accounts for large-scale
corruption, cannot sensibly refuse to conflate.[7]

Behind this considered statement concerning *possible* kinds of revision in
Lear and *Othello*, and what to do about them, lies some degree of the
quiet agnosticism towards the revision hypothesis that many of its critics
have been urging since it first reappeared on the scene in the late 1970s
and early 1980s. Some of the textual variants between Q and F *Lear* and
Othello may be due to authorial revision; some may be due to corruption;
some may be authorial, some not; some may have been made simultaneously, others piecemeal at different times and for different reasons. The
posture that Q *Lear* is undoubtedly Shakespeare's first draft, F his holistic
later revision, datable within a few months – case closed! – still seems to
many students of that text to be premature, to say the least. Given the
present incompleteness of the facts, and the partiality of much of the
argument, the jury may well conclude, seems to be inclining to the conclusion, that no verdict should yet be given.

Doubtless there are many reasons why some scholars accepted so quickly
and easily the revived idea of authorial revision of *Lear*. A few champions
and promoters of the revision hypothesis were given to invoking a *Zeit-
geist*, as if acceptance of that hypothesis were part of an inevitable tide of
history. There is probably some truth in the notion: as Tanselle says,
'These ideas [textual instability, multiple versions, etc.] are obviously related to the anti-foundationalist tendencies of philosophy and literary
theory in the past generation'.[8] Paradoxically, the ideas were probably also
adopted on the opposite grounds of authority, issuing as they did from the
immensely prestigious and influential Oxford University Press and sanc-
tioned by as highly respected a scholar as Stanley Wells. The rapid decision
to print two *Lear*s in the Oxford Shakespeare not only reified the revision
theory but even seemed to institutionalize it overnight. Certainly high
visibility also furthered acceptance, as a few enthusiasts busily promoted
the revisionist views in several books, many essays, countless conference

papers, and even media appearances. The idea of revision seemed suddenly everywhere and inescapable.

By now, a decade and a half later, the case that F *Lear* is Shakespeare's second version has undergone more careful scrutiny, and many weaknesses have been found in it. Basic bibliographical arguments have collapsed: the claim that Shakespeare made his revision in a copy of Q1 shortly after its publication in 1608 was immediately undermined when Trevor Howard-Hill showed that all the readings in F supposedly deriving from Q1 could as well have been derived from Q2 (1619); and the claim that F1 was printed from an annotated copy of Q2 staggered under his demonstration that many unusual spellings in F probably derived from manuscript printer's copy.[9] In fact the relationship between Q1, Q2, playbook, possible transcript, and F1 is not yet understood. Linguistic arguments have likewise suffered: a few vocabulary coincidences with *Cymbeline* that supposedly showed the F revisions to be contemporary with that play may instead indicate only that *Lear* was given a revival while Shakespeare was writing *Cymbeline*, or that he had been reviewing Q1 at that time, astonished at what the printer Nicholas Okes had done to his play. In either case Shakespeare would have refamiliarized himself with the vocabulary of the old play as he wrote the new, without needing to revise *Lear* at all. The much-repeated claim that only Shakespeare had the dramatic genius to make the improvements found in F, when it comes up against strong counter-arguments that some of F's changes seem instead to be 'stupid and destructive',[10] often reverses itself: 'Well, Shakespeare can make mistakes too'. Arguments that F alterations of a few words or lines significantly change several characters, though the characters' actions throughout the play remain otherwise the same, have seemed to many to be subjective and exaggerated, especially since the motives for such purported changes of character are not clear, and the central character, Lear, remains virtually unchanged.

One kind of argument, however, still seems to command a certain respect and following, even from some who have doubts about the revision hypothesis. It is that differences between Q and F often imply underlying differences in the staging and conception of scenes, and perhaps even consequent differences in what happens offstage between these scenes. Because these arguments rely heavily on apparent evidence about what is actually seen on stage by an audience in a theatre, they may appear to be more factual, less subjective, less capable of exaggeration, than more literary interpretive arguments about character and theme. To test the apparently greater objectivity and reliability of this kind of argument, I wish to look at two significant examples of it, one from an early essay and the other from the latest major new edition of *Lear*.

II

I wish first to revisit one of the earliest of the recent essays reviving the revision hypothesis, Gary Taylor's 'The War in "King Lear"'.[11] This piece was a manifesto and a salvo, announcing at the outset, 'I wholly support the efforts of recent scholars to discredit the traditional conflated text' (28, n. 1). It has often been cited in support of the two-text case: for example, authors in *The Division of the Kingdoms* appeal to it repeatedly, Stephen Booth has called it one of three 'altogether persuasive demonstrations' of 'the integrity of the Quarto and Folio texts', and Stanley Wells has recommended it to anyone needing a persuasive argument for two *Lears*, pointing to it as cause sufficient for his decision not to conflate the Q and F texts. Evidently two-text theorists still consider it to be a fundamental, even classic statement of their case; as recently as last year it was anthologized by one of the original champions of the two-*Lear* hypothesis, Jay Halio.[12] To my knowledge, it has not been so intensively tested for validity as have the book-length studies of the two texts, and since some of its claims have been repeated or modified as recently as Jay Halio's Cambridge editions and R.A. Foakes's Arden edition,[13] its arguments should be worth reviewing.

The general thesis of the essay is that Shakespeare made revisions in the later, Folio version of *Lear*, changes deliberately designed to 'streamline' the play, to give the audience the impression 'that Cordelia seems to lead not an invasion [as in Q] but a rebellion, like Bolingbroke's or Richmond's', and to make Edmund simultaneously more dangerous, less predictable, and more sympathetic than he is in Q. Such basic general questions as how one can know whether Shakespeare (rather than his company, a censor, or another reviser) made such changes in F, and whether they were made all at once in interrelation with each other or piecemeal at different times, are simply dismissed as unworthy of discussion:

> It is hard to believe that such a succession of inter-related changes happened by accident, and it would be churlish (let alone unnecessary) to attribute them to anyone but Shakespeare. (34).

Possibly. Yet churlish doubts have persisted nonetheless, and it is not at all hard to conclude that the particular arguments supporting this essay's general claims are porous and uncompelling.

The first line of argument, that F's cuts 'streamline' (a metaphor from automobile design) and 'accelerate and clarify' and thereby 'strengthen the narrative line' has, I think, been sufficiently answered elsewhere by William C. Carroll, commenting on its many reappearances in *The Division of the Kingdoms*:

> To say that a deletion leads to faster playing time is merely a tautology. How could it not? . . . What is not effectively shown is why this acceleration and streamlining are really virtues. Indeed, the very metaphors used by these schol-

ars – positives like 'streamline' and 'accelerate' rather than, for example, 'abort' or 'truncate' – beg the question of the argument.

This kind of argument, in which a valorized terminology is substituted for logic and evidence, may be used to justify any deletion.[14]

It is hardly necessary to add that shortening of long plays, a common practice in the modern theatre, was also common in Shakespeare's. Such 'streamlining' of plays by cutting inessential speeches and scenes may have been done only to fit a long play like *Lear* into the three-hour playing limits agreed upon by the Lord Chamberlain and the Lord Mayor of London.[15] It is not necessary to assume that such cuts as occurred in *Lear* were authorial, or intended by the author, or even (in their particulars) approved or expected by him, though of course all of these are possibilities. The fact is that no one knows who made them, or when, or whether their purpose was anything but the practical one of shortening an overlong play. The fact that most of the F cuts in *Lear* occur towards the end of the play, especially late in Act III and early in the somewhat slow Act IV, and that the material cut is largely reflective rather than essential to advancing the action, may easily suggest that shortening was a major, if not the only, reason for F's cuts.[16] As Kenneth Muir has pointed out, such reflective passages are not inherently pointless or redundant, not initial mistakes that Shakespeare would later want to remedy, but part of his usual artistry:

> The various comments by the good characters on the deeds of the evil ones are felt by the audience to be a necessary expression of our sense of outrage. The multiple choric effects of the speeches of sympathetic characters are an essential part of Shakespeare's method. To cut them out will leave us feeling deprived, if not in a moral vacuum.[17]

Because they do not advance the plot, however, they might have been sacrificed to the exigencies of limited playing time. Any number of people besides the author could have marked such passages for omission.

The second line of argument, more germane to this investigation, is that the staging of certain scenes (IV.iv, V.ii, and V.iii) is so different in F from that in Q that the result is a 'radically' different impression of the background war, as a civil uprising rather than a foreign invasion. The discovery of this difference, which no one had ever detected previously, depends largely on the interpretation of the different stage directions provided in Q and F. Now if, as most scholars are now coming to agree, Q's text derives from a late stage of Shakespeare's rough draft, and F's text derives, in some way not yet fully understood, from the book of the play used by the company in production, then one would naturally expect to find that the F stage directions would be fuller and more precise than those in Q, reflecting more accurately the practical details of staging that would need to be attended to in performance. Many editors have thought that exactly such differences exist between Q and F *Lear*, reflecting their different provenance; Taylor, however, repeatedly interprets them to reveal 'radical' differences in staging due to revision.

In iv.iv, the first scene he discusses, there is in fact one real difference: for Q's Doctor, F substitutes an attendant Gentleman having considerable medical knowledge; later, in iv.vii, F also transfers the Doctor's lines to this same Gentleman, who otherwise would have only two lines and no essential function in that scene. F thereby merges a minor character, the Doctor, who in Q appears in only two scenes and has only eight speeches, with a larger and more essential character, the Gentleman who appears in iii.i, iv.iii, iv.vi, and iv.vii and is probably the same servant (called Gentleman in F, Knight in Q; knights are gentlemen) who attends on Lear in ii.iv. Many reasons have been offered for F's absorption of the Doctor's role in the Gentleman's – economy of personnel or costume, the Gentleman's previous role in caring for Lear, Cordelia's reliance on a familiar and trusted attendant, etc. Taylor's explanation is that

> though we easily associate surgeons with armies, Shakespeare and his contemporaries did not, usually restricting their doctors to attendance upon royalty. Perhaps partly or wholly for this reason, the Folio throughout [i.e., in two scenes] turns the Quarto's *Doctor* into the vaguer, less anomalous *Gentleman*. (30)

This rationale for the changes in F is almost certainly wrong: Cordelia and Lear are of course both royalty, and C.G. Cruickshank,[18] cited by Taylor, records that historically English armies travelled with both physicians (for the king) and surgeons (for the soldiers). As for contemporary theatrical practice, in *II Tamburlaine* ii.iv and v.iii Zenocrate and Tamburlaine are attended by several 'Physitians' (i.e., doctors, not surgeons), as is the title character in Fletcher's *The Humorous Lieutenant* (1619), iii.v.

The other difference in this scene is that Q's spare authorial stage direction has Cordelia enter with '*others*', whereas F's fuller playbook direction specifies '*Drum and Colours . . . and Souldiours*'. Taylor detects not simply a more specific direction in F but the indication of a radically different scene:

> Nothing in the Quarto text suggests that Cordelia's *others* are an army; the speeches decidedly suggest a more intimate scene . . . . The Quarto text thus seems to envision Cordelia in iv.iv in the company of several nondescript attendants; in the Folio she enters at the head of an army. (30)

But of course undescribed in Shakespeare's draft does not mean 'nondescript'. The 'others' attending Cordelia in or near the camp of her invading army would certainly be soldiers, officers, or other attendants suitable for military duty. Evidently at least one of them is an officer, since within a few lines Cordelia directs him to issue a military order that a hundred soldiers[19] be sent to search for Lear. Moreover, the Q and F scenes must be equally 'intimate,' since the number of speaking parts is identical and their spoken lines are substantially the same, and there is no indication anywhere that there are fewer of Q's 'others' on stage than of F's 'Souldiours'. Both texts could equally indicate 'an army', which on Shakespeare's stage would be represented by 'four or five most vile and ragged foils' (*H5* 4.Cho.50), or both may indicate merely a few military attendants (including, at least in F, but equally possibly in a performance of Q, a colour guard). There is no reason to think that the Q and F scenes are different in any essential way; Q's stage direction is simply that of an author's draft, F's is that of a theatrical prompt-book.

The most fundamental and 'radical' difference that Taylor detects between Q and F, however, is that in Q Cordelia leads a French army, whereas in F she *seems* to lead an English one. Like Madeleine Doran and a number of subsequent critics[20] he notes that a few references to France as invader of England are missing from F, and claims that F 'systematically remov[es] verbal and visual reminders of the French presence', thereby 'deliberately excising an extraneous political complication' and 'removing even the ghost of a reason for Cordelia's military defeat' (31). In fact, however, one may easily argue the contrary, that the omissions are incidental rather than systematic, and that F *adds* reminders of the French presence. Goneril's reference to French invasion in iv.ii.56 is omitted from F almost certainly because it is buried halfway through a series of some 34 lines cut from Albany and Goneril's lengthy altercation. Surely its loss is incidental to that larger omission; the presumed systematic deletion of a passing reference to France did not require the excision of 34 lines of dialogue. Similarly the reference to the King of France's landing in England and returning home is not the reason all 55 lines of iv.iii are cut, but is the incidental consequence of that larger omission of a whole scene. A better case can be made that Albany's reference to France's invasion in v.i.25, being part of only a six-line cut, might be the reason for that excision; but the lines might have been omitted simply because they seemed redundant. Albany, 'full of . . . selfe reprouing', announces his discovery that the king and some mistreated Britons have joined Cordelia, thereby intimating a moral scruple: he cannot attack Cordelia's invading forces without also attacking the old King and some of his own native countrymen. The next five lines may have been cut because they repeat the same scruple: he says that he can honestly fight against a foreign invasion, but is not 'touched' by [or moved to fight / against] the King and other Britons. Goneril's obscure reply may repeat the same idea a third time: 'Combine togither gainst the [invading] enemy, For these domestique dore particulars [F: 'domesticke and particurlar broiles'; i.e., the lesser complaints of Lear and some unhappy Britons] / Are not to question here' [not the main reason for our preparations for war, and hence not now worth considering].

On the other hand, F retains references to 'France' as spying on Britain (iii.i.24), to 'France' as owning or gaining 'aduantages' against Britain (iii.v.12), to the landing of the 'Army of France' (iii.vii.2–3), to the 'traitor' Gloucester's alleged 'Letters . . . late from France', to 'great France' as providing Cordelia's army against the 'Brittish Powres' (iv.iv.21–6), and to 'France' as Cordelia's realm (iv.vii.75); and F's stage directions twice add visual reminders of French presence by specifying that Cordelia's army displays '*Colours*' (IV.iv.0, v.ii.0) – that is, banners used to identify and rally troops in battle, which for an army led by a French queen would certainly feature a French flag or insignia. This obvious identification of the army possibly explains why when F added '*Colours*' in the entrance direction at v.ii.0 it dropped Q's '*powers of France*' as unnecessary, since the colors showed whose the powers were.[21] It is impossible to see in these many continual reminders of France an attempt to 'encourage the audience to forget' the French presence, and to transform the army led by Cordelia from French invaders into seemingly British rebels.

This claim – 'not an invasion but a rebellion' (31) – also ignores how often both Q and F repeatedly emphasize that Cordelia's forces are made up of *both* French invaders and British sympathizers; the latter include not only Lear's knights, who join her, and possibly sympathizers with Gloucester whose hearts are moved against Regan and Goneril (IV.v.11), but also the old king's 'well armed Friends' at Dover (III.vii.20), the 'Traitors, late footed [i.e., afoot]' (III.vii.44),[22] and 'others, whom the rigour of our State / Forc'd to cry out' (v.i.22–3). There is no reason whatever to believe that 'the Quarto and Folio treat the nationality of Cordelia's army in consistently different ways, and that any conflation of the two produces incoherence' (31). Clearly the forces are of mixed nationality in both texts, and essentially so, since the presence of British supporters in Cordelia's army allows the audience to sympathize with her efforts more than if she led only a French invasion.

As from the entrance directions for IV.iv, Taylor also infers very different scenes described by Q's authorial entrance to v.iii, '*Enter Edmund, with Lear and Cordelia prisoners*', and F's theatrical '*Enter in conquest with Drums and Colours, Edmund, Lear, and Cordelia, as prisoners, Souldiers, Captaine*'. He finds in Q 'a few guards, but no more', 'a deliberately secluded, secretive scene', and in F a 'crowded stage', a 'public scene', suggesting that 'Edmund here has reached the summit of his pyramid; by implication, he alone has won the battle' (32). But of course if Edmund has Lear and Cordelia as prisoners, he enters in conquest in both Q and F, and has reached the summit of his pyramid in both; and in neither is there any hint that he has done so single-handedly (even his soldiers, we are soon reminded, are levied in Albany's name, v.iii.103–4). And though Q's entrance direction does not specifically mention soldiers and captain, Edmund's guards on the battlefield would be soldiers, and his first order, 'Some officers take them away', and his subsequent conversation with a 'Captaine' make it clear that in both versions, the authorial draft and the playbook, he enters with a number of soldiers and officers. Whether or not 'Drums and Colours' formed part of the Q entrance (in performance it might well have), in all essential details the entrances in the two texts are the same.

Taylor goes to even greater lengths to differentiate the Duke and Duchesses' subsequent arrival in Q and F, whose directions are, respectively,

Enter Duke, the two Ladies, and others and Flourish. Enter Albany,
Gonerill, Regan, Soldiers. Again, except for the specification of a common
musical cue, the entrances are substantially the same, since the 'others' in
Q would be some kind of military personnel, whether officers or common
soldiers, who will soon arrest Edmund. Of the Q direction Taylor says,
'Albany's retinue does not include a drum, and need not include a trumpet', the latter being 'unnecessary to the Quarto staging' (32, 33 n. 2) –
claims impossible to reconcile with the fact that in Q Edmund says to
Albany 'Call by thy trumpet', v.iii.99, and Albany subsequently says 'let
the trumpet sound' (107). Then, though the F direction is essentially the
same, Taylor says, 'Albany, Goneril, and Regan enter, accompanied in the
Folio by trumpet and . . . perhaps a drum', which soon becomes 'probably
a drum' (33), though neither drum nor trumpet is any more called for in
F's direction or spoken lines than in Q's. This is not simply to discover
different stagings but to manufacture them.

Taylor's final line of argument is that Edmund is a significantly different
character in Q and F. He asserts that in Q, unlike in F, Edmund acts in
'overconfident bravado': 'For in the Quarto he, not Albany, calls the
Herald . . . ; he, not Regan, imperatively asserts his title'. The first claim is
simply false, since in Q (as in F) Albany does call the Herald – 'A Herald
ho' (v.iii.102) – just before Edmund does; the second claim is doubtful,
since whether or not line v.iii.81 was erroneously assigned in one of the
texts (rather than reassigned by revision) has been extensively debated by
editors without arrival at consensus. Furthermore, we are told, 'by making
Edmund the victim of a trick . . . the Folio makes him more sympathetic'
(34). However 'sympathetic' at this point a man might be who, among
other atrocities, has betrayed his father to blinding and later (IV.v.11–13)
sought to 'dispatch his nighted life' (IV.v.11–13), the 'tricks' arranged by
another potential victim, Albany – dismissing Edmund's army and having
an unknown champion challenge him – are the same in both texts, and so
must evoke the same 'sympathy' for Edmund in each. Though his argument is unsupported by evidence, Taylor yet concludes, 'I hope [critics]
would not dispute that there are two distinct treatments [of Edmund's
character], which it would be wrong to mix or confuse' (34). Prince Hal
responded to such another vain hope, 'I do, I will'.

One could at this point simply point out that the confident claims of
radical difference between Q and F in this much-cited essay, when they are
seen against the total evidence of those texts, prove in virtually every
instance to be without substance. They depend on over-literal interpretations of variant stage directions as if those directions told the whole story
of what happened in each text, when in fact the spoken lines supply
sufficient additional information to show that the action of the scenes is
virtually identical; and in some cases these claims even invoke false, non-
existent, or invented evidence. But one more kind of argument in this essay
needs to be looked at, one that purports to describe not simply what is

happening in the scenes, as all of the above do, but even what is going on offstage, and to claim that here too the Q and F texts differ significantly.

The locus of this argument is III.i.17–42, where F omits twelve-and-a-half lines from Q and prints eight new lines. Because the F lines omit necessary information originally in Q, and include a sentence fragment, a broken train of thought, and other obscurities, all editors since Theobald have treated the Q and F passages as supplementary and have retained both; and a number of editors have speculated how the new lines could have been mistakenly substituted in F for the Q passage rather than added to it.[23] In Q Kent informs the Gentleman of a French invasion, and sends him to Dover to report to Lear's sympathizers there of recent mistreatment of the king; a few lines later he adds that while on this errand the Gentleman should expect to meet Cordelia. Though the scene (IV.iii) in which the Gentleman describes this meeting near Dover is cut from F, in F the Gentleman is seen with Cordelia near Dover in both IV.iv and IV.vii, and Cordelia has clearly been informed by both him and later by Kent of Lear's mistreatment (see IV.vi.205–7; IV.vii.27–39). Since Kent's instructions in III.i, including news of any French landing, are cut from F, and yet the Gentleman leaves at the end of the scene expecting to meet Cordelia, Dr. Johnson objects, 'In the folio, the messenger is sent, he knows not why, he knows not whither', and Madeleine Doran adds, 'The dramatic reason for having the scene at all is gone'.[24]

For Taylor, however, the F text here is not a botch but an alternative version – in which case it would be the only instance in the whole play where a speech of any length was rewritten rather than merely cut or augmented. As he sees it,

> In fact Kent merely tells the Gentleman – and the audience – that he will see Cordelia, presumably soon, presumably nearby, presumably as she has made clear in her letter (II, ii). And when Cordelia does arrive, she enters in the presence of this Gentleman . . . in an unlocalized scene (IV, iv – traditionally, but unnecessarily, placed 'near Dover'). So, again, both texts offer coherent but incompatible alternatives, the Quarto beginning Act III with the imminence of a dubiously motivated French invasion, the Folio with the news that France knows what is happening, and that Cordelia – and Cordelia alone – is already on her way, somehow. (32)

There is no support anywhere in the text for this imagined version of Cordelia's travels in F – not surprisingly, since it is improbable in every detail. Since Goneril's rupture with Lear occurred only the previous day, and Regan's only some hour ago, there is no way possible that 'France knows what is happening' concerning 'the hard Reine which both of them hath borne / Against the old kinde King' (III.i.27–8, F only). Whatever Cordelia's letter to Kent (II.ii.165–70) says, and whoever (Cordelia or Kent) is going to remedy whose losses (Cordelia's or Kent's or Lear's), are quite unclear; quite possibly Kent has learned of an impending invasion not from Cordelia's letter but from the same informants at Gloucester's house who pass similar information to Gloucester (see III.iii.10, III.vii.47–8). In any case there is no reason given anywhere in the text to make an audience think, against all probability, that the Queen of France would have slipped into a hostile Goneril's duchy 'alone', without an armed escort, as 'sole representative of th[e] apocalyptic counter-movement', that she would be traveling unguarded all the way across Britain to Gloucester's house or 'nearby', that Kent would feel assured that the Gentleman would 'somehow' see her 'soon' by chance meeting, and that then without incident or notice to the audience she would return to Dover to meet Lear and fight the British forces. Against such fancies it may seem pedestrian to place inconvenient facts, such as that scene IV.iv must be located near Dover, since 'The Brittish Powres are marching hitherward' (IV.iv.21) for the final battle; or that Cordelia would not have had time for her imagined journey from Dover to Gloucester and back. Such a trip by Cordelia would cover almost four hundred miles and take several weeks, not the few days she has.[25] Surely such an extended absence of the French queen from the French army at Dover would require notice and explanation within the play; there is none. In short, there is no more reason to take seriously this theory of differences offstage in Q and F than the previous claims of differences onstage.

III

Of critics who have questioned the two-*Lear* hypothesis, R. A. Foakes holds a moderate position, believing that changes in F may be attributed to Shakespeare, but resisting the idea that these result in a second play. His new Arden edition of *Lear* is the richly informed work of a ripe scholar, a worthy successor to Kenneth Muir's enormously influential forerunner, and likely to be as influential in turn. For that reason it is important to recognize how some of the dubious ideas in Taylor's essay, though Foakes has repeatedly questioned them in their original form, continue to exert an unwarranted influence in his edition. In particular they lead him to produce a text for that troublesome scene III.i that differs from all previous texts. To his credit Foakes has tackled afresh the scene's problems, partly in response to an article of mine and correspondence between us, and he has justified his decisions both in an appendix to the edition and in a separate essay.[26] That his solution to the problems differs from mine is not surprising, but I think it has been influenced in regrettable ways by recent theories about the French invasion that, as I have suggested above, are without substance.

As has been described in the previous section, in the middle of III.i F substitutes eight lines for twelve and a half lines in Q. Because the F lines have seemed an inadequate substitution, all editors since Theobald have printed both Q and F lines. The important fact about the synthetic modern text is that it represents no more than Theobald's guess about how the Q and F lines might go together; Theobald simply printed the Q and F passages one after the other. Since the result has troubled many editors and commentators, I proposed an alternative way of combining the lines, first suggested by Peter Blayney, and an explanation of how the Q lines could have been accidentally omitted from F. Foakes has rejected this hypothesis as 'unnecessary', substituting instead his own selection and arrangement of Q and F lines. The result is the same as Theobald's, except that four and a half Q lines have been omitted. Now if Q derives from Shakespeare rough draft, these omitted lines are indubitably Shakespeare's; and since the substituted F lines have often been considered inauthentic in style and even vocabulary,[27] quite possibly in this case the Arden edition supplants Shakespearean lines by non-Shakespearean ones. The reason given for doing so, as we shall see, is yet another theory about a pattern of alterations concerning the French invasion. David Bevington has criticized the Oxford edition for being 'theory-driven', and recently Phebe Jensen has made the same point about Oxford's suppression of the F Epilogue to *Troilus and Cressida* to accommodate a critical theory about that play: 'The motto of the Shakespeare editor should perhaps be Hippocratan: above all, do no harm; above all, avoid amputating passages in the absence of solid bibliographical evidence'.[28] But that is exactly what has happened here in the Arden *Lear*.

Foakes claims that his arrangement makes the whole passage more 'consistent', but it solves none of the stylistic problems that have troubled many editors and commentators. It still preserves a faulty (here called 'indirect' [398]) apposition ('our state – what hath been seen'), and requires the emendation of a terminal period and sentence capital ('State. What') to create this apposition.[29] It still includes a clotted string of parentheses and relative clauses, and then causes Kent to abandon his long sentence ten lines later without finishing it (though Foakes half-disguises its incompleteness by ambiguous punctuation: 'furnishings. –'). Neither Kent nor anyone else in the play ever speaks this way.[30] Furthermore, Foakes's 'consistent' arrangement creates a metrically short line – 'Now to you' – where Q had metrical regularity.

Foakes's justifications for omitting Shakespeare's Quarto lines will by now sound familiar; not surprisingly, he cites Taylor's essay several times. Though he once again rejects Taylor's idea that F changes a foreign invasion into an apparent civil war, here he relies on altered forms of Taylor's arguments to sustain the idea of some kind of Shakespearean revision. The removal of a few references to France once again becomes highly significant, as it was to Taylor, though now it signifies someting different: a textual evolution that is supposed to have begun before Q was finished, and that is still ongoing in F:

> The changes in F in III.i, III.v, IV.ii, and V.i, and the omission of IV.iii, all may thus be seen as modifying an earlier conception of the action of the play that has left

its traces in Q. That earlier conception apparently included an invasion by French forces with the King of France at their head. . . . It would seem that in F Cordelia takes over the role of leader of the French invading army, which was originally to be commanded by the King of France.

As Taylor does, Foakes supposes that F's omissions of Q lines about a French invasion (III.i.30–4), France spreading his banners (IV.ii.56), and France invading the land (v.i.25) have a particular purpose (modifying an earlier conception of the war) rather than being incidental to the cuts of longer passages of which they are part. Like Taylor he also assumes the undemonstrable, that these longer cuts were made intentionally by Shakespeare. Before he is done he also, as Taylor does, describes events of the war that happen offstage, and even attempts to describe aspects of an imagined early draft of the play.

Foakes argues that the F reviser cut Q's lines in III.i concerning the beginning of a French invasion, thinking such an invasion premature, and replaced them with a reference to preliminary French spying only. This hypothesis is quite conceivable, as I have said elsewhere; but it is only a hypothesis, not a fact, and the evidence that Foakes adduces does not support it. For instance, he believes that F's change from 'landed' to 'footed' at III.iii.13 is part of the same intention of 'obscuring another reference to an invasion before III.vii; here [in F, as not in Q] 'footed' could refer to forces of Albany or Cornwall.' No previous editor has ever imagined such an unlikelihood. Gloucester says,

> I haue lock'd the Letter in my Closset, these iniuries the King now beares, will be reuenged home; ther is part of a Power already footed, we must incline to the King.

The context clearly implies that the Power is expected to revenge Lear's injuries, and certainly neither Albany nor Cornwall is planning that. References to the same letter in two subsequent scenes ('This is the Letter . . . aduantages of France', III.v.10–12; 'shew him this Letter, the Army of France is landed', III.vii.2–3) clearly indicate that the 'part of a Power' is the gathering army of France, not that of Albany or Cornwall.

As the quotation in the last paragraph shows, Foakes also pursues another of Taylor's claims, that Q and F give different impressions of who leads the invading army. Unlike Taylor, he traces the change back not just to Q but to an earlier draft of the play than Q represents. F, he believes, simply continues Q's imperfect attempt to erase traces of that early draft, in which the King of France led the invasion, and completes the impression that the French king has instead 'sent an army, apparently under [Cordelia's] command, to Britain' (401). But in fact, according to the evidence in the text, neither the King of France nor Cordelia acts as military commander of the invading forces, in either Q or F. Obviously the King of France has given his moral sanction to the invasion, as both Q and F make clear (IV.iv.25–6), and one would normally expect that as king he would lead the French army into Britain, as happens in Shakespeare's source, the old *King*

Leir play. A few lines in Q (IV.iii.1–8) explain his surprising absence, a useful bit of information that is sacrificed when F cuts the whole scene to shorten the play. In any case, in neither Q nor F does the King of France appear after I.i, and in both texts, though the French queen Cordelia remains as titular or political leader of the French forces, the army is commanded by a French general. The latter is identified in Q as General la Far, Marshall of France (IV.iii.8); though this information is cut from F, clearly there too Cordelia has her general (as Regan has Edmund), who leads her army towards the battle while she helps revive Lear (see IV.vi.215–16). All the textual evidence in the play makes it clear that the army supporting her is made up of both French soldiers and British sympathizers, and after her reunion with her father she may relinquish even titular leadership of her forces, for in v.ii.6 Edgar announces, 'King *Lear* [not Cordelia] hath lost.' Like Taylor, Foakes interprets over-literally the slightly different entrance directions of IV.iv and v.ii, finding that in Q Cordelia does not clearly lead the French army but that in F she (and Lear) do. The Q and F entrances for IV.iv – F's with its more theatrical specifics of *Drums and Colours* and *Souldiours* – have been discussed earlier; those for v.ii are, respectively, *Enter the powers of France ouer the stage, Cordelia with her father in her hand* and *Enter with Drumme and Colours, Lear, Cordelia, and Souldiers, ouer the Stage, and Exeunt*. The most that can be inferred from the entrance directions in IV.iv and v.ii is that Cordelia enters in the company of a very small part of the army; though she is presumably near the head of her forces in all of these entrance directions in both Q and F, she is not evidently the military commander in any of them.

Finally, in support of his theory of an evolving treatment of the war, Foakes argues that two references to France are omitted from F to avoid ambiguity and confusion between France the country (whose army is in Britain) and France the King (who is not present there). He insists that in Q's '*France* spreds his banners' (IV.ii.56) and '*France* inuades our land' (v.i.25) the King is referred to in both places as if he himself were in Britain, hence the lines containing these phrases were omitted from F. The lines were of course omitted as parts of larger cuts, and the phrases offer no likelihood of confusion. They clearly refer to the country's army, acting in their king's name and in the second case clearly not in his presence. Though he is at home in both Q and F, the King of France might still be said to 'invade our land,' since the French army was levied, mobilized, and embarked under his authority and with his approval. But there would be no reason for an audience of either a Q or F *Lear* to think that in v.i he himself was present in Britain and personally leading the combined French and British forces. He had not been seen since returning to his own country at the end of I.i, and no allusion after I.i in F (and only IV.iii.1–2 in Q) ever places him in Britain.

Foakes concedes that his theory about the evolution of *Lear* from early draft to Q to F 'must be speculative' (402), but on the grounds of such speculations alone, and on no bibliographical evidence, he is willing to cut lines surely by Shakespeare and replace them by other lines of more doubtful origin. He does not even attempt to explain how the marking of four and a half lines for deletion from F resulted in the deletion of twelve and a half lines – a basic question whose answer is hardly self-evident. The similarities of his overall argument with Taylor's – the focus on much of the same evidence, the drawing of similarly doubtful inferences from it, the forced interpretation of stage directions – are very evident. Unfortunately, a great deal of the case for Shakespearean revision of *Lear* has depended on such 'theatrical' arguments, which prove under scrutiny to be not necessarily any more objective and reliable than 'literary' ones.

IV

One great appeal of the two-text theory is its apparent simplicity: Q and F differ, we are assured, chiefly because Shakespeare made them differ. But to many familiar with the texts of *Lear*, this account of their differences seems to be an oversimplification. Almost 70 years ago my late colleague Madeleine Doran did ground-breaking work on the relationships of Q1, Q2, and F *Lear*, work which, because it was devalued by Walter Greg and others, has only recently been recognized as essentially right and has become the basis of much recent work on the play. Better than most people, she understood the complexities of the textual situation of *Lear*. I recall that when I first told her that the Oxford editors planned to issue two *Lears*, her reaction was high amusement: 'They've just given up!' What Honigmann's new book on *Othello* demonstrates is some of the kinds of things that still need to be done for *Lear* before the genesis and relationships of its texts and inferred manuscripts, and the sources and purposes of their variants, can be adequately understood. That is, it reminds us how much remains to be done before we can give up and declare the *Lear* puzzle solved.

Certainly the question of whether a scribal transcript was used for F printer's copy needs to be further explored, and what kinds of changes a scribe might have introduced. Besides the several transcripts provided to Jaggard by Ralph Crane, a number of others have been proposed in recent years as possible printer's copy for other plays such as *As You Like It*, *Julius Caesar*, *Twelfth Night*, and *Antony and Cleopatra*. Greg thought that the King's Men provided Jaggard with original playbook copy for a number of plays, but Fredson Bowers came to doubt that they ever did so for any play, lest the book be lost, defaced in the print shop by the casting-off of copy, etc. Peter Blayney has recently shown that the cost of preparing a fresh scribal transcript of a play could be only two or three shillings, a negligible fraction of a publisher's expenses.[31] Howard-Hill has detected signs of a manuscript behind F *Lear*. If it was a transcript freshly made for

Jaggard, did the scribe work on other plays as well, and can his working characteristics be discovered, as they have been for Ralph Crane? Might he independently have regularized features of the text in certain ways, or introduced certain recognizable kinds of error? Studying the thousand or so verbal variants, mostly indifferent, between Q and F *Lear*, I noticed that about 125 of them seemed to have no purpose except to smoothe the meter. Since in his later years, when he is imagined to have revised *Lear*, Shakespeare was given to increasingly free and irregular verse, such a form of revision as is found in these 125 lines would seem to be uncharacteristic of his writing at that time. Are these verbal variants instead the work of a scribe, making small adjustments in meter as he did in spelling and punctuation?

More work also needs to be done to test whether the author(s) of the revisions in this and other two-text plays can be identified. The Fool's Prophecy in III.ii has often been suspected of being spurious, and the clumsy lines added to III.i, with their endless parentheses and relative clauses, have seemed to Peter W. K. Stone[32] more like the work of Massinger than of Shakespeare. The latter lines are among three F additions (I.iv.322–33, III.i.22–9, IV.vi.165–70) having an unusually high incidence of words and usages found nowhere else in Shakespeare.[33] Their ratio of one unique word to every three lines is several times Shakespeare's usual rate, and so may suggest another authorial hand. Though the revisionists think that Shakespeare is the reviser in both *Hamlet* and *Lear*, Paul Werstine and Eric Rasmussen have noticed that the kinds of revision are quite different in these plays. In *Hamlet* the role of the title character is affected most by the revisions, in *Lear* it is affected hardly at all; in *Hamlet* passages are shortened by surgically removing lines from the middle of long speeches, in *Lear* they are usually shortened by lopping off the ends of speeches or scenes; and so on.[34] Do such different approaches to revision suggest different revisers? Were they Shakespeare, the bookkeeper, other actors or playwrights hired to vet the plays for revivals?

More also may yet be done on the adaptation of the texts of *Lear* for playing on different stages. As for many of Shakespeare's plays, we know virtually nothing of its early staging. We know only that it was performed at court in 1606 (and by another company in Yorkshire in 1610). It was certainly done at the Globe, and may have remained popular enough for later revivals at the Blackfriars Theatre; it was revived at least twice in the early Restoration before Nahum Tate rewrote it. Donald Foster thinks he can detect in F linguistic evidence of at least one revival, perhaps more; his work on this subject is yet unpublished and untested. Also, Andrew Gurr has now gleaned rich evidence from the REED files of how regularly the King's Men went on tour, including, in the years after *Lear* was written, records of several trips to Dover, a natural place for performing this play.[35] In IV.vii in Q the King is apparently discovered asleep and wakes to music; in F he is carried onstage apparently without music, and the roles of the

Doctor and Gentleman are merged. Could these different versions represent adaptation to different playing conditions rather than authorial first and second thoughts?

In short, much remains to be done before we can say with certainty why so much in Q *Lear* was changed in F, and when and by whom. In the meantime, to judge by recent experience, editors will remain cautious. Conflation may continue for some while to be a prudential expedient: the conflated text, after all, is conservative, preserving about 300 doubtlessly Shakespearean lines of Q and about 110 possibly Shakespearean lines of F. Perhaps eventually we will know enough to do things differently; but most editors seem reluctant to do so just yet.

REFERENCES

1. 'Textual Instability and Editorial Idealism', *SB*, 49 (1996), 4.
2. Honigmann, E.A.J., *The Texts of 'Othello' and Shakespearian Revision*, London & New York, 1996, 144.
3. Grace Ioppolo, *Revising Shakespeare*, Cambridge, Mass. & London, 1991; John Jones, *Shakespeare at Work*, Oxford, 1995.
4. Philip Edwards, [Review article], *Modern Language Review*, 77 (1982), 694–8; Trevor Howard-Hill, 'The Challenge of King Lear', 6 *The Library*, 7 (1985), 161–79; John Murphy, 'Sheep-Like Goats and Goat-Like Sheep: Did Shakespeare Divide *Lear's* Kingdom?' *Papers Bibliographical Soc. Am.*, 81 (1987), 53–63; David Bevington, 'Determining the Indeterminate: The Oxford Shakespeare', *Shakespeare Quarterly*, 38 (1987), 501–19; cf. my [review of Urkowitz], *Modern Philology*, 79 (1981), 197–200, and 'The Case for Two Lears', *Shakespeare Quarterly*, 36 (1985), 115–20.
5. Kenneth Muir, 'The Texts of *King Lear*: An Interim Assessment of the Controversy', *Aligarh Journal of English Studies*, 8.2 (1983), 99–113; Marion Trousdale, 'A Trip Through the Divided Kingdoms', *Shakespeare Quarterly*, 37 (1986), 218–23; W.R. Elton, *King Lear and the Gods*, 2nd edn., Lexington, Ky., 1988, 339–345; William C. Carroll, 'New Plays vs. Old Readings: The *Division of the Kingdoms* and Folio Deletions in *King Lear*', *Studies in Philology*, 85 (1988), 225–44; René Weis, 'Introduction', *King Lear: A Parallel Text Edition* (London & New York, 1993); Ann R. Meyer, 'Shakespeare's Art and the Texts of *King Lear*', *Studies in Bibliography*, 47 (1994), 128–46; Frank Kermode, 'Disintegraton Once More', *Proceedings of the British Academy*, 84 (Oxford, 1994), 93–111; see also my 'Revision Awry in Folio *Lear* 3.1', *Shakespeare Quarterly*, 46 (1995), 32–46, and 'Two Lears? By Shakespeare?' in *Lear from Study to Stage*, ed. James Ogden & Arthur H. Scouten, Madison & Teaneck, N. J., 1997, 57–68; Clare, 6 *The Library*, 17 (1995), 34–59.
6. Honigmann, E.A.J., 'Shakespeare's Revised Plays: *King Lear and Othello*', 6 *The Library*, 4 (1982), 142–73. For citations see, e.g., Stanley Wells and Gary Taylor, in *Division of the Kingdoms*, 22 n., 445 n.
7. *The Texts of 'Othello'*, 144–5.
8. Tanselle, 1.
9. 'Q1 and the Copy for Folio *Lear*', *Papers Bibliog. Soc. Am.*, 80 (1986), 419–35; 'The Problem of Manuscript Copy for Folio *King Lear*', 6, *The Library*, 4 (1982), 1–24. Cf. Jay L. Halio, ed., *The Tragedy of King Lear*, Cambridge,

1992, 65: 'Much of the . . . evidence Taylor uses to demonstrate the dependence of F upon annotated Q2 is subject to alternative interpretation or explanation. . . . Some kind of manuscript copy for F *King Lear* cannot be entirely ruled out'.

10. The phrase is from Honigmann's *Texts of 'Othello'*, p. 10; he is not referring to *Lear* in particular. Among the destructive changes commonly cited are the cutting of the brilliant 'mock trial' in III.vi and of the sympathetic reactions of the servants after Gloucester's blinding in III.vii; among the stupid, the addition of the 'Fool's Prophecy' at the end of III.ii, which besides interrupting dramatic illusion and tragic mood, consists of a list of petty pecadilloes (wordy sermons, watered beer, etc.) that have almost nothing to do with the tragic horrors of the play, despite eloquent arguments to the contrary.

11. *Shakespeare Survey*, 20 (1980), 27–34.

12. Booth, *King Lear, Macbeth, Indefinition, and Tragedy*, New Haven & London, 1983, 159; Wells, 'Revision in Shakespeare's Plays', *Editing and Editors: A Retrospect*, ed. Richard Landon, New York, 1988, 9; Halio, *Critical Essays on* King Lear, ed. Jay L. Halio, New York, 1996, 48–58.

13. Halio, *The Tragedy of King Lear*, 28, 71, 270; for Foakes, see below.

14. Carroll, 231.

15. Andrew Gurr, *The Shakespearean Stage 1574–1642*, 3rd ed., Cambridge, 1992, 32, 178; see also Eric Rasmussen, 'The Revision of Scripts', *A New History of Early English Drama*, ed. John D. Cox & David Scott Kastan, New York, 1997, 442–3.

16. See MacD.P. Jackson, 'Fluctuating Variation: Author, Annotator, or Actor?' *The Division of the Kingdoms*, ed. Gary Taylor & Michael Warren, Oxford, 1983, 329–31; Rasmussen, 'The Revision of Scripts', 444–5.

17. Muir, 104.

18. *Elizabeth's Army*, 2nd ed. (Oxford, 1966), 174.

19. Like virtually all modern editors but the recent Oxford editors, I take the true reading, mangled in both Q and F, to be 'a centurie send forth' (IV.iv.6). Line numbers in citations are those of *The Riverside Shakespeare*, ed. G.B. Evans (Boston, 1974), and of the Spevack concordances.

20. *The Text of 'King Lear'*, Stanford & Oxford, 1931, 73–6; George Ian Duthie, ed., *Shakespeare's* King Lear, Oxford, 1949, 8; R.A. Foakes, ed., *King Lear*, The Arden Shakespeare, Walton-on-Thames, 1997, 393–402.

21. Foakes (1993, 245–6): 'Taylor's arguments that the Folio changes a French invasion into a civil war . . . [are] not borne out either by the text, which in F, in spite of omissions, still emphasizes that Cordelia leads a French army, or by the stage directions calling for the "colours" of what must be a French army'. Like E.A.J. Honigmann ('Do-It-Yourself *Lear*', *New York Review of Books* [25 Oct. 1990], 59) earlier, Foakes says of these, 'The "Colours" shown . . . would presumably be those of France, perhaps echoing a display of a French coat of arms or banner when the King of France enters in the opening scene' (107).

22. Despite Ioppolo's (1991, 175) and Foakes's (ed. 1997, 298) unusual claims that these may be French, they must of course be British. *OED* (Traitor, *sb.* 2): 'One who is false to his allegiance to his sovereign or to the government of his country'. French invaders owe to British rulers no allegiance that they could betray. Cornwall and Regan first interrogate Gloucester about his connections with the French – 'What Letters had you late from France?' – and then, to plumb the depth of his supposed treachery, ask him also about his connection with British sympathizers at Dover, the 'well armed Friends' of Lear's knights – 'And [note the *And*] what confederacie haue you with the

Traitors, late footed in the Kingdome? *Reg.* To whose hands [at Dover] You haue sent the Lunaticke King'.

23. See 'Revision Awry in Folio *Lear* III.i', 41.

24. *The Plays of William Shakespeare*, ed. Samuel Johnson, 8 vols., London, 1765, 6:79; Doran, *The Text of 'King Lear'*, 75.

25. Only one night elapses between II.iv and IV.i. The next morning Lear and his knights, and later in the morning Gloucester and Edmund, all leave for Dover. Only a few days must intervene before Lear arrives in Dover in IV.iii and Gloucester arrives there in IV.vi; in that interval Oswald, Goneril, and a Messenger travel from Gloucester's house to Albany's house, and Oswald is sent back there, arriving in IV.v. In ordinary travel, on good modern roads, Elizabethans could expect to ride no more than twenty or thirty miles a day. See Charles Hughes, 'Land Travel', in *Shakespeare's England*, ed. W. Raleigh, Sidney Lee, & C.T. Onions, 2 vols. (Oxford, 1916), 1:201–2. The most that Portia or Imogen can hope to traverse is twenty miles (*MV* III.iv.84, *Cym.* III.ii.68–9), and Prince Hal can hope for only thirty by hard riding between breakfast and dinner (*1H4*, III.iii.198).

26. Arden *King Lear*, 393–402; 'French Leave, or Lear and the King of France', *Shakespeare Survey*, 49 (1996), 217–23. All quotations are from the edition.

27. For samples of such opinion, see my 'Revision Awry', 37–40. I add here one more example, from Edward Pechter, 'On the Blinding of Gloucester', *English Literary History*, 45 (1978), 191–2: 'We are made aware of a problem in this scene itself in the astonishingly clumsy writing that follows. First (22–25) we hear a stutter of interrupting and qualifying relative clauses, culminating in an awkward redundancy (is the abstract 'speculations | Intelligent' meant to gloss over the hard reality of 'spies'?). What follows (25–29) is a noun phrase (though for a moment we probably think we are hearing the beginning of a question), with an appositive range of three alternatives that is perplexing, to say the least, in the latter two (have *both* Dukes borne a hard rein against Lear? what could be deeper?). Before we can determine whether these alternatives are exclusive (the really crucial factor is …) or cumulative (all contribute to …), Kent breaks off altogether'. Pechter attempts to defend the clumsiness as 'willful contrivance' designed to create in the audience a sense of unclearness and doubt; he seems unaware that the stylistic difficulty may derive from a textual error in F and an imperfect patch by Theobald. For unShakespearean vocabulary in the F addition, see below, esp. n. 33.

28. 'The Textual Politics of *Troilus and Cressida*', *Shakespeare Quarterly*, 46 (1995), 423.

29. Of this emendation Foakes says, 'I also suppose that the punctuation is erratic, as so often in F, and that the full point after "State" is no more reliable than the semicolon after "set high", and that both should be commas' (p. 398). But F's punctuation is much more reliable than Q's, and its midline semicolon for a comma was quite usual: see Anthony Graham-White, *Punctuation and Its Dramatic Value in Shakespearean Drama* (Newark, Del., 1995), 34, 72.

30. Foakes says, 'I take it that Kent's message is meant to be mystifying, its hesitations and alternatives expressing his own uncertainties' (198). In fact the only uncertainty evident in the speech is whether ('perchance') 'something deeper' underlines the dukes' recent hostilities to Lear and each other. On the whole Kent sounds, as usual, downright, confident, and authoritative: 'dare', 'warrant', 'But true it is' (Q), 'my credit', 'will thanke', 'I am a Gentleman', 'From some knowledge and assurance' (no uncertainty there!),

and later 'confirmation', 'feare not but you shall', and 'Ile this way, you that'.

31. Blayney, 'The Publication of Playbooks', *A New History of Early English Drama*, ed. John D. Cox & David Scott Kastan, New York, 1997, 418.

32. Stone, *The Textual History of* King Lear (London, 1980), 127.

33. They are *buzz* [n.], *enguard, unfitness, speculations* (concretely, = spies), *furnishings, able* [v.], *hurtless*), as well as the unique usages of *snuffs* (= 'huffs', pl. and without *in*) and *packings* (= 'plottings', a usage that occurs once in *The Taming of the the Shrew*, in the singular).

34. Werstine, 'The Textual Mystery of *Hamlet*', *Shakespeare Quarterly*, 39 (1988), 11; Rasmussen, 445–6.

35. Gurr, *The Shakespearian Playing Companies*, Oxford, 1996, 305–6, 390–1.

17   A *Midsummer Night's Dream* in the 1990s

Judith M. Kennedy

A Midsummer Night's Dream continues to be fertile ground for Shakespeareans. The most prominent critical method in this as in other areas of 'early modern' English literature is still cultural materialism/new historicism, with various modifications in terms of gender, race and politics, but psychoanalytic and anthropological/sociological approaches remain popular. Aesthetic/humanist criticism is returning to favour, especially in terms of close attention to classical backgrounds and to language. Performance criticism is growing in importance, and various new editions seek to do more than merely capture part of a lucrative market. Anthologies and surveys of criticism, and bibliographies, provide guidance through the maze, but new vistas are still opening.

Perhaps the one article of the last 15 years that has had the most influence on criticism of *Dream* is Louis Adrian Montrose's 'Shaping fantasies'.[1] Recently he has returned to this play, still presenting the same view of its position in his Elizabethan world picture, but now with greater emphasis on its mythological content. *The Purpose of Playing*[2] 'addresses the complex, heterogeneous, and ubiquitous discourse in which the relationship between State and subject was constructed and contested' (xi), arguing that 'Shakespearean drama as enacted in the Elizabethan theatre *formally* contested the dominant ideological assertions of the Elizabethan state' (105). In Part Two of the book, 'The shaping fantasies of *A Midsummer Night's Dream*' (107) are used 'to give a local habitation and a name to the workings of ideology in cultural production,' the text being treated 'as a site of convergence of various and potentially contradictory cultural discourses' (xii). Readers who are undismayed by such an intention will be rewarded by some provocative explorations of the ways in which classical stories of the Amazons and of Hippolytus intersect with 'the gendered discourses of human physiology and domestic economy' (124), or how 'the conjuncture of the witch and the Virgin Queen is effected through mythological displacement, and activated through the trope of "the triple

287

Hecate"' (167). Some may be repelled by the pervasive jargon of the writing, but a downright ugly sentence such as 'it may also be the case that the appropriative potential of such subsequent acts of interpretation is enabled by Elizabethan cultural variations and contradictions that have been sedimented in the text of the play at its originary moment of production' is followed by an elegant couple of paragraphs which (with close attention to the play's text) clearly present the view of the play as affirming patriarchal ideology at the same time as it questions attitudes to marriage and procreation (144–145).

The ideas about politics, power, and accommodation voiced by Leonard Tennenhouse[3] and Theodore Leinwand[4] echo in Barbara Freedman's chapter 'Dis/Figuring Power: Censorship and Representation in *A Midsummer Night's Dream*'[5] and in Marcia McDonald.[6] Freedman is further interested in bringing the techniques of psychoanalysis to bear on the 'complex relationship among censorship, knowledge, and interpretation' (159), and in the operation of metaphor; McDonald places her discussion of the relative 'power' of Bottom and Theseus in the context of the Sidney/Gosson debate over the power of poetry. Montrose and Tennenhouse are also presences in Paul Yachnin's essay[7] concerning the 'mutually subversive effects of commerce and patronage' (64); despite a rather gloomy view of 'theatrical mirth,' he sees *Dream* as ending in 'the festive renewal of the social order' (62). Bruce Boehrer[8] paints a depressing picture of the *Dream*'s metaphoric intent: it might have been hoped that his essay was a jesting *ne plus ultra* of cultural criticism, but Laura Levine's feminist interpretation[9] of the play as revealing rape as a condition of existence in life and the theatre is entirely earnest and equally joyless. With serious intention but in a wittier style, Richard Wilson's exploration[10] of the social and political tensions in the play ties the historical unrest of the early 1590s both to Marx's references to Snug and the mechanicals in commenting on nineteenth-century British politics, and to current events, linking 1595 and 1992 through seeing each as an 'annus horribilis' for the two Queens Elizabeth. As his title suggests, Wilson is centrally concerned with the author's relationship to authority, and with the ways in which this 'is a play about poetry and power, and how they read each other' (204–5). Peter Holbrook[11] adopts a modified Marxist approach in arguing that 'the play's sensitivity about differences of rank is the basis for its consciousness of genre and the potential social uses of art' (109), but is less personally engaged with the modern English scene than the British Wilson.

Questions of authority and subversion, the place of the author, and the consciousness of his art, become involved with the construction of meaning, an idea most forcefully articulated by Terence Hawkes in his influential essay on Dream, 'Or'.[12] Starting from the premise that Nedar may as well be Helena's mother as her father, he ingeniously explores alternative meanings in various parts of the text. Hawkes's views of the indeterminacy of texts have provoked rebuttal; Laurence Lerner[13] instances this essay both in acknowledging his wit and in rejecting his theories. Michael Mangan[14] also seeks multiple meanings in Shakespeare's Elizabethan comedies, but is both more cautious and more inclusive in dealing with 'issues relating to staging, to gender, and to power'. His emphasis on laughter is welcome, and the chapter 'Twentieth-century reading of comedy' provides a useful overview of critical approaches, but perhaps because of his consciousness of other interpretations, his own chapter on *Dream* is somewhat tentative, finding that the ending of the play gives 'the experience of being suspended between conflicting realities,' and asking 'How *are* we to find a concord of this discord?' (176).

The play is often read in its historical context to yield parallels with and insights into our late twentieth-century preoccupations, or to promote a particular political agenda. Class struggle frequently colours writing of British cultural materialists, and issues of race, gender, and colonialism often engage North American writers. *The Tempest* has been most thoroughly adopted into the post-colonial sensibility, but Margo Hendricks[15] appeals to some of the same attitudes in her musings on the changeling boy. Kim F. Hall[16] links race and gender, finding that in *Dream* 'threatening female sexuality and power are located in the space of the foreign: male, Grecian order is opposed to the dark, feminine world of the forest, which is also replete with Indians, Tartars, and "Ethiops"' (22). Early in this decade the contemporary need to oppose destructive patriarchal dominance, and find feminine archetypes, explicitly (and at this date it seems somewhat sentimentally) colours such readings of *Dream* as Tom Absher's;[17] nowadays discussions of patriarchy are more likely to be interwoven with other themes such as the influence of carnival, the exploration of the psyche, rites and rituals, the nature of poetry, etc. Diana E. Henderson's focus[18] on lyric poetry in the drama does not result in her succumbing, as Swinburne[19] does, to the appeal of 'sweetness and springtide of fairy fancy crossed with light laughter and light trouble that end in perfect music' (25), but in her finding (with evident antipathy) that 'Shakespeare ... turns a conquered Amazon and a surrogate for his Tudor Fairy Queen into willing advocates for his own fantasy of a benign, male-ruled patriarchal state' (223). Today's critics are unapologetic about their heavily politicized interpretations; indeed, when Jonathan Hall[20] sees 'crisis management of sexual politics at the centre of national concerns' in Elizabethan England, and hence *Dream* addressing 'the desires and fears that a carnivalesque inversion at the heart of a patriarchal order sets up' (98), it is not hard to understand why this play engages the attention of those troubled by the implications of the Million Man March and the rise of Promise Keepers.

Some historical, rather than historicist, readings use the play more to explore past attitudes than as a forum for discussing their own feelings about what is happening today. Penry Williams[21] believes that it 'enables us to enter the social world of the late Elizabethan court' (56–57), and Matthew Wikander[22] takes it as a starting point in his study of the ways in which the monarchy and the stage interacted over more than two centuries.

Three book-length critical studies are devoted to *Dream*. James Calderwood[23] joyously revels in the opportunities afforded by the multiplicity of contemporary theories for approaching this many-faceted play from different perspectives. He admires Montrose's 1983 essay[24] but the exuberance of his engagement with the play and its critics is not contained by any one school of thought. There is an introductory sketch of the history of the play's publishing, performance, and reception, including a good condensed survey of criticism since the 1980s, and then in seven short, packed chapters he explores familiar aspects of the play such as patriarchal authority, love and marriage, seeing and perspective, illusion, the discovery of the self, liminality, metamorphosis, metadrama, dreams and more, drawing on psychoanalysts, anthropologists, art historians, classical writers and so on, to make the familiar seem fresh and exciting. The abundance of his ideas spills over into lengthy notes, or rather mini-essays, that take up a fifth of the book. Out of context such flat statements as 'In psychoanalytic terms Hippolyta suffers castration in having to renounce her desire for the masculine phallus and resign herself to her "proper" gender' (10) may provoke an impatient reaction, but as a whole Calderwood's delighted response to the play is exhilarating. Calderwood's study is one of the *New Critical Introductions to Shakespeare* published in North America by Twayne and in Britain by Harvester Wheatsheaf, which according to its general editor is a series 'designed to offer a challenge to all students of Shakespeare'. Peter Hollindale's book[25] appears in the series *Penguin Critical Studies*, 'intended for students who are studying the play in senior forms at school and in universities and colleges'. It provides an interesting contrast with Calderwood's volume. Hollindale ignores modern theoretical approaches, referring mostly to critics writing between the latter 1950s and early 1970s. The book is valuable in its insistence on letting 'the play's theatrical life invade the whole discussion' (vii), and probably helpful to newer readers in closely following the text in examining such topics as structure, characters, and language. David Wiles[26] returns to an ancient topic that shows it still has life: the question of the occasion of the play, and what it might suggest both about Shakespeare's relations with his aristocratic patrons and the themes of the play.

The psychoanalytic approach which Calderwood finds fruitful continues to inform commentary on *Dream*, for example in Meredith Skura,[27] particularly in her treatment of Bottom. Gail Paster[28] similarly presents Bottom as childlike and narcissistic; in her reading, 'the central scenes between Titania and Bottom take on the aspect of an elaborately encoded scatological joke' (125), and the substitution of Bottom for the changeling 'constructs a parodic image of adult female sexuality in which the differences between heterosexual intercourse and the anal cathexes of maternal nurture become blurred' (128). She confesses to being 'aware that so desublimated a reading of the scenes between Titania and Bottom may provoke repugnance' (143). Bruce Clarke's concern[29] with 'the mode of allegory and the trope of metamorphosis' leads him through myth to find that 'Titania is a Jocasta who has arrogated to herself a phallic son-consort' (131). Catherine Belsey[30] uses psychoanalytic theory subtly and interestingly to explore the meaning of Bottom's desire to have Peter Quince write a ballad of his dream.

Anthropological studies, especially of rites of passage and of the social uses of carnival, have also provided an attractive path to exploration of *Dream*. Calderwood draws particularly on Van Gennep and Turner; the suppressed hilarity of a sentence such as 'Critics have been slow to recognize the influence of the Tzotzil Indians on Shakespeare' (85) does not detract from his seriousness in arguing that the play's appeal comes partly from its engagement with the recurring patterns of liminality and rites of passage. F. Nicholas Clary[31] is also indebted to Turner in discussing the Pyramus and Thisbe interlude as 'the threshold moment' (155) when 'no one was his own' (163). René Girard[32] is most entirely committed to anthropological approaches: after 30 years of preoccupation with his theories of mimetic desire, he is so convinced of the interdependence of the literary and the anthropological that he would make *Dream* 'compulsory reading for all anthropologists,' because 'Magical religion is the most pervasive and perfect mask of mimetic interaction, the original mask, human culture itself. In *A Midsummer Night's Dream* the mask is lifted' (31). Like Calderwood's, Girard's writing is attractive in its energy, but he sometimes distorts the play in pursuing his theories; for example, in arguing that the plots of the young lovers and of the mechanicals are similar because both are involved in supernatural experience, he implies that the fairies are visible to the lovers and to Bottom's companions, as well as to Bottom himself (57). Hanna Scolnicov[33] is also interested in masks, myths, and rituals, claiming that 'Shakespeare's masks are, strictly speaking, not merely zoomorphic but theriomorphic. *Zoon* is any animal, whereas *ther* or *therion* is a beast, or, sometimes, more specifically, a monster, a hybrid creature such as a centaur or satyr' (64), and adopting the approaches of Eliade and Lévi-Strauss in her examinaion of *Dream* and *The Merry Wives of Windsor*. Jeanne Addison Roberts's studies of wilderness, forests, and birth rites[34, 35] also interpret aspects of *Dream* from an anthropological perspective.

C.L. Barber,[36] without benefit of Bakhtin, brought carnival and popular festivities to the forefront of critical interpretation of the comedies, and these elements continue to be an important part of contemporary studies. Inversion of social order in riotous holiday play supports arguments about the subversion of authority, and about the ways in which Shakespeare's dramas may be seen to question or to uphold the political status quo, as well as allowing for meditations on the nature of aristocratic and popular entertainment. The books of Michael Bristol,[37] François Laroque (1988, translated 1991)[38] and Annabel Patterson[39] consolidated the place of these ideas in discussions of the comedies, including *Dream*, so that Thomas Healy[40] can take *Dream* as an example of the drama's function in examining the relationship between high and low culture, and Michael Mangan,[41] though tentative in his conclusions about the meanings of *Dream*, is in no doubt of its 'oppositional and carnival aspects' (177). In an interesting offshoot of such cultural studies, Skiles Howard[42] explores the social implications of courtly and popular dancing in *Dream*.

Two substantial books, while still attentive to questions of culture and context, shift the focus of attention to language, and to patterns of structure and meaning derived from close study of the language. Mark Stavig[43] analyses *Romeo and Juliet* and *Dream* in conjunction with a series of circular charts that indicate humours and astrological connections, and patterns of metaphor in various acts of the plays; he contends that 'Instead of privileging rulers, fathers, and males in general by identifying them with reason and God, Shakespeare relates the structures of the self, love, the family, society, and the cosmos to both the shifting cycles of nature and the longer lasting but still mutable values of hierarchy' (3). Patricia Parker,[44] in her rich and subtle study, devotes a chapter to '"Rude Mechanicals": *A Midsummer Night's Dream* and Shakespearean joinery,' in which through close examination of meanings of 'rude,' 'mechanical,' 'joining,' 'walls,' 'parts,' 'partitions,' 'mispointings,' etc., she works towards explorations of the play's world of language and ideas. The chapter demonstrates the value of her methodological presupposition 'that Shakespearean wordplay – the very feature relegated by the subsequent influence of neoclassicism to the rude and deformed as well as ornamental or trivial – provides a way into networks whose linkages expose the very orthodoxies and ideologies the plays themselves often appear simply to rehearse' (114). In smaller-scale studies, David Hillman[45] uses something of Parker's method in examining the ideological implications of the word 'discretion' in *Dream*, in the context of the ideas of Foucault, Raymond Williams, Hoskyns and Puttenham. Maurice Hunt[46] deals sensitively with the sounds of words and the varied music of the play: the Orphic voice, finally, is Shakespeare's. Douglas Peterson[47] and John Baxter[48] find insights through concentrating on structure, Peterson especialy concerned with closure, and Baxter with mimesis, or the representation of tragic action in the mechanicals' play.

Aesthetic concern with form and the pleasure afforded by the beautiful, and humanist engagement with language and classical literature, are prominent in a number of recent studies. The importance of classical mythology in *Dream* is of course recognized in many types of criticism, whether historicist, psychoanalytical, anthropological, feminist or linguistic, but those I would call more obviously humanist deal most directly with the ways in which the treatment of myth in classical literature and the Renaissance affects our understanding of its function in the play. Charles and

Michelle Martindale,[49] and Jonathan Bate,[50] provide good basic surveys of the use of Ovidian myth in *Dream*. Mihoko Suzuki,[51] partly building on the suggestions of Harold Brooks,[52] explores the Senecan subtext of the myth of Hippolytus; Peter Holland[53] also engages closely with Brooks's claims for Senecan influence, but ranges more widely in the myths of Theseus, in ancient and early modern literature. Maurice Hunt's study[54] of the 'intertextual nexus' between *Dream* and Sidney's *Arcadia* leads to drawing a 'rationale for a harmonic solution' in *Dream* 'to the problem posed by the disruptive results of romantic love' from neoplatonized myths of Venus and Urania. Pierre Brunel's study[55] of baroque elements in drama focusses on *Dream* and on Calderón's *La vida es sueño*, examining not only the use of myth but also providing a richly allusive context of European literature, art and music from the sixteenth to the twentieth century.

Neoplatonism combines with astrology, cosmology, modern scientific theory and a myriad of other ideas in an extraordinary voice from the grave, the posthumous publication of the draft of a long essay on *Dream* by William Empson,[56] expanding the views first adumbrated in his review of Harold Brooks's edition.[57]

Some studies in the aesthetic/humanist tradition either ignore or repudiate many contemporary approaches. Stuart M. Tave[58] asserts that comedy 'is not about psychology, or philosophy, or anthropology, or theology. It is not even interdisciplinary,' and that *Dream* 'is a beautiful play, in design and detail,' with 'a symmetry in the development of the story it works out, a clarity of distinction among the characters it presents, a happy command of the languages they speak at every level of their varied abilities' (xii–xiii). Gunnar Sorelius[59] studies *Dream* and the other early comedies 'against their aesthetic, literary and cultural background with particular attention to Petrarchan, Ovidian, mythological and neoplatonic aspects. Special emphasis is given to the enrichment of the dramatic language made possible by the taking over of verse forms and language usage from tragedy and epic, particularly the mythological metaphor' (abstract). Sorelius's placing of Shakespeare's plays in the context of the writings of his contemporaries rather than those of twentieth-century social scientists leads to the unusual conclusion that *Dream* is 'arguably a more conventional and perhaps a more old-fashioned play' than the four earlier ones, because of its greater concern with 'the proper ordering of the relationship between human beings as members of larger wholes' than as individuals (168), and that it is 'the most chaotic of Shakespeare's early comedies' (184). John K. Hale[60] wishes to treat the comedies 'diversely; to bring interpretation nearer than before to the unique multiplicity of the subject' (14). However, he omits such approaches as performance criticism, feminist criticism, New Historicism, and deconstructionism, although his reasons for doing so are more gently expressed than Brian Vickers's denunciation[61] of the deficiencies of these and other schools. Hale relies mainly on the theory that the function of comedy is to please, and on assessing the play's design through source-criticism. His theoretical stance does not cast new light on his discussion of *Dream*, but his close reading of style and image yields good results.

Hale's book 'aims to help *teach* the comedies'; he believes that students 'need to be eclectic and indeed doctrinally uncommitted' in interpreting the comedies, and wishes to bring them closer to 'the constitutive pleasure' of plays that 'remain less accessible to [them] than tragedies and histories' (9). Maurice Charney[62] clearly shows his didactic purpose in hoping to produce 'a user-friendly and self-teaching book' (xi–xii) for students in large classes, an update of Mark Van Doren's 1939 general introduction to Shakespeare. His treatment of *Dream* embraces attitudes of the earlier part of the century in comments on the endearing mechanicals and the celebratory character of the play, but his conclusion sees 'aspects of nightmare' in the 'symbolic locale' of the wood, which 'is the place of the Id, the amoral, perturbations of the unconscious, darkness, lawlessness, and uncontrollable impulse. All these baleful assumptions lie behind Shakespeare's seemingly placid *Midsummer Night's Dream*' (40).

Pedagogical concerns have also contributed to an increase in the quantity and variety of performance criticism. Having students act scenes is hardly a new teaching method, but it is becoming increasingly popular in college as well as school settings, and is allied to exploration of critical approaches. The trend is put to practical test in *Shakespeare Set Free*;[63] a product of the Teaching Institute of the Folger Shakespeare Library; it is designed to be used with the reliable New Folger texts, edited by Barbara A. Mowat and Paul Werstine.[64] The widespread use of videos of filmed and televised performances in the classroom is matched by the many publications listing and assessing them. The confluence of performance review and critical interpretation can be seen in books such as those by H.R. Coursen[65] and Samuel Crowl,[66] and in Jay L. Halio's volume on *A Midsummer Night's Dream* in the *Shakespeare in Performance* series.[67] An interesting example of the interaction of performance and criticism is Barbara Hodgdon's response (1996,[68] expanded from 1993[69]) to Robert Lepage's 1992 production for the National Theatre: she 'aims to illuminate the cultural meanings of Lepage's *Dream* to particular spectators in a specific socio-historical moment and so to contribute to discussions about the spect[at]orial effects of performed Shakespeare' (70). The long-awaited and now sumptuously produced history of *Dream* in the theatre by Gary Jay Williams[70] is alert to the importance of the cross-fertilization of critical theory and performing practice.

More material for performance criticism is provided in a series for Cambridge University Press, *Shakespeare in Production*, in which Trevor Griffiths' edition of *Dream*[71] is the first to appear. An introductory essay surveys the stage history and major productions (in the case of this volume, contrary to the preface of the Series Editors, almost exclusively in Britain), and a running commentary on the text gives information about how details were presented in various productions. The series should prove valuable, but the problem of what to include from the wealth of available information perhaps cannot be solved to everyone's satisfaction. Another recent series of editions is related to performance somewhat differently: in an attempt to help readers understand the 'theatrical life' of the play each volume provides 'a continuous commentary on the text by a professional director or a leading actor,' in the case of *Dream* by the director John Hirsch (Brown ed.[72]). Performers' suspicions of centuries of editorial accretions to the texts and desire for an authentic text may be part of the impetus for the series *Shakespeare Originals: First Editions*; T. O. Treadwell's *Dream*[73] is faithful to the principles enunciated by the general editors in presenting an original-spelling diplomatic text of the First Quarto 'with a minimum of editorial mediation' (9), but his introductory essay on the implications of features of the printing of the 1600 text is more enthusiastic than authoritative. He does not refer to Homer Swander's excellent article[74] demonstrating how even the editorial substitution of a period for a comma alters local meaning and wider significance.

The most important scholarly edition of *Dream* to appear in this decade is Peter Holland's[75] for the Oxford Shakespeare (also called World's Classics). His extensive introduction focuses mainly on dreams and dreaming, turning attention back from modern psychoanalytic and physio-psychological theories to ancient tradition from the *Oneirocritica* of Artemidorus to the Renaissance, then exploring 'the play by setting out . . . the sources which fed this particular dream': throughout he succeeds in keeping 'in the foreground the pleasure of watching or reading the play' (3). The older editions in the competing series, by R.A. Foakes for Cambridge[76] and by Harold Brooks for the New Arden,[77] continue to be influential; however, the Third Arden is now in progress, and the forthcoming edition of *Dream* by Patricia Parker promises to be exciting.

Three anthologies of *Dream* criticism give something of an overview of trends. The volume in the *Longman Critical Essays* series[78] presents commissioned essays; keywords in the titles suggest the preoccupations of the time: transformation, appearance and reality, film and fantasy, illusion, the translation of Bottom. A limitation of the volume is that the essays are virtually undocumented, not helping students find the source of the critical ideas being disseminated. More scholarly in presentation, though less accessible in English-speaking countries, is an Italian collection[79] covering such topics as the transformation of Theseus, metatheatricality, *discordia concors*, failures of sense/senses and classical ideals of physical perfection. Both collections include contributions from theatrical practitioners, the title of the Italian text emphasizing the connection between text and stage. The volume on *Dream* in the *New Casebook* series[80] presents a judicious selection of the most important articles from 1975 to 1993, with an excellent introduction explaining their place and significance. There is a good categorized and annotated section on further reading (which nevertheless has some oddities, not least the omission of the World Shakespeare

Bibliography from the first section). Clifford Huffman's selected and annotated bibliography[81] is also excellent. As Huffman points out, the survey and bibliography for this play by David J. Palmer[82] actually refers to criticism before 1973, and even then is a little misleading in not mentioning Jan Kott,[83] already by 1973 a major influence on critics and directors. Kott is prominent, however, in Stanley Wells's survey[84] of criticism since 1967; more recent trends are sketched in various general works, such as those by Calderwood[85] and Mangan[86] already mentioned, and Camille Slights.[87]

Undoubtedly the best guide to what is going on in Shakespeare studies and performance is the World Shakespeare Bibliography, published by *Shakespeare Quarterly*, and now available on CD-ROM. Through its descriptive entries it is possible to have some idea of what is being thought and written about *Dream* in languages inaccessible to many anglophones, and in books not readily available in many British or North American libraries. European critics, especially in French, German, and Italian, continue to provide fresh perspectives by setting the play in different performance or literary or cultural contexts. Critics in India, Japan, and Korea open new areas in comparative studies.

Exploration of the ways in which the responses of musicians and graphic artists illuminate the *Dream* has been a less crowded field, although Gary Schmidgall[88] gives some attention to operatic connections, especially Britten, whose entrancing version of the play has been the focus of most of the recent scholarly work in this area (e.g. Godsalve[89] and Guest[90]). Perhaps the *Shakespeare Music Catalogue*[91] will inspire more efforts. In criticism related to graphic art, except for two sections on eighteenth and early-nineteenth-century illustrations and paintings in an article not widely available in British and North American libraries,[92] and a narrowly focused note on representations of Bottom by the early nineteenth-century Chalon Sketching Society,[93] there has been little to set beside the articles of W. Moelwyn Merchant[94] or Kenneth Garlick,[95] but the excellent volume produced in conjunction with the Royal Academy of Arts 1998 exhibition of Victorian fairy painting[96] may stimulate further study. Meanwhile, introductions to scholarly editions are increasingly well illustrated by realizations of characters and scenes from *Dream* drawn from books, productions, and art galleries. Cover illustrations for two paperback editions project images of two extremes of critical response: for the Folger edition,[97] Kinuko Y. Craft has provided a sleeping Titania embowered by flowers and fairies in the best neo-romantic tradition; while the selection for the World's Classics[98] is the aggressively phallic seventeenth-century woodcut of Robin Goodfellow. Which best represents how we see this play after four hundred years?

REFERENCES

1. Montrose, Adrian (1983), '"Shaping Fantasies": Figurations of Gender and Power in Elizabethan Culture', *Representations*, 1 (2).
2. Montrose, Adrian (1996), *The Purpose of Playing: Shakespeare and the Cultural Politics of the Elizabethan Theatre*, Chicago: The University of Chicago Press.
3. Tennenhouse, Leonard (1985), 'Strategies of State and Political Plays: *A Midsummer Night's Dream, Henry IV, Henry V, Henry VIII*' in Dollimore, J. and A. Sinfield (eds.), *Political Shakespeare: New Essays in Cultural Materialism*, Manchester: Manchester University Press.
4. Leinwand, Theodore (1986), '"I Believe We Must Leave The Killing Out": Deference and Accommodation in *A Midsummer Night's Dream*', *Renaissance Papers*.
5. Freedman, Barbara (1991), *Staging the Gaze: Postmodernism, Psychoanalysis, and Shakespearean Comedy*, Ithaca: Cornell University Press.
6. McDonald, Marcia (1994), 'Bottom's Space: Historicizing Comic Theory and Practice in *A Midsummer Night's Dream*' in Teague, Frances (ed.), *Acting Funny: Comic Theory and Practice in Shakespeare's Plays*, Rutherford: Fairleigh Dickinson University Press.
7. Yachnin, Paul (1992), 'The Politics of Theatrical Mirth: *A Midsummer Night's Dream, A Mad World My Masters*, and *Measure for Measure*', *Shakespeare Quarterly*, 43 (1).
8. Boehrer, Bruce (1994), 'Bestial Buggery in *A Midsummer Night's Dream*' in Miller, David et al. (eds.), *The Production of English Renaissance Culture*, Ithaca: Cornell University Press.
9. Levine, Laura (1996), 'Rape, repetition, and the politics of closure in *A Midsummer Night's Dream*' in Traub, Valerie, M. Lindsay Kaplan and Dympna Callaghan (eds), *Feminist Readings of Early Modern Culture*, Cambridge: Cambridge University Press.
10. Wilson, Richard (1993), 'The Kindly Ones: The Death of the Author in Shakespearean Athens' in Smith, Nigel (ed.), *Essays and Studies 1993*, Cambridge: D. S. Brewer.
11. Holbrook, Peter (1994), *Literature and Degree in Renaissance England: Nashe, Bourgeois Tragedy, Shakespeare*, Newark: University of Delaware Press.
12. Hawkes, Terence (1992), *Meaning by Shakespeare*, London: Routledge.
13. Lerner, Laurence (1995), 'Wilhelm S and Shylock', *Shakespeare Survey*, 48.
14. Mangan, Michael (1996), *A Preface to Shakespeare's Comedies: 1594–1603*, London: Longman.
15. Hendricks, Margo (1996), '"Obscured by dreams": Race, Empire, and Shakespeare's *A Midsummer Night's Dream*', *Shakespeare Quarterly*, 47 (1).
16. Hall, Kim F. (1995), *Things of Darkness: Economies of Race and Gender in Early Modern England*, Ithaca and London: Cornell University Press.
17. Absher, Tom (1990), *Men and the Goddess: Feminine Archetypes in Western Literature*, Rochester, Vermont: Park Street.
18. Henderson, Diana E. (1995), *Passion Made Public: Elizabethan Lyric, Gender, and Performance*, Urbana and Chicago: University of Illinois Press.
19. Swinburne, Algernon (1876), 'The Three Stages of Shakespeare', *Fortnightly Review*, January.
20. Hall, Jonathan (1995), *Anxious Pleasures: Shakespearean Comedy and the Nation-state*, Cranbury, NJ: Associated University Presses.
21. Williams, Penry (1995), 'Shakespeare's *A Midsummer Night's Dream*: Social Tensions Contained' in Smith, David et al. (eds.), *The Theatrical City: Cul-*

ture, Theatre and Politics in London, 1576–1649, Cambridge: Cambridge University Press.

22. Wikander, Matthew (1993), *Princes to Act: Royal Audience and Royal Performance, 1578–1792*, Baltimore: The Johns Hopkins University Press.

23. Calderwood, James (1992), *A Midsummer Night's Dream*, New Critical Introductions to Shakespeare, London: Harvester Wheatsheaf, New York: Twayne.

24. Montrose, Adrian (1983). See n. 1.

25. Hollindale, Peter (1992), *A Midsummer Night's Dream*, Penguin Critical Studies, London: Penguin Books.

26. Wiles, David (1993), *Shakespeare's Almanac: A Midsummer Night's Dream, Marriage and the Elizabethan Calendar*, Cambridge: D.S. Brewer.

27. Skura, Meredith (1993), *Shakespeare the Actor and the Purposes of Playing*, Chicago: The University of Chicago Press.

28. Paster, Gail (1993), *The Body Embarrassed: Drama and the Disciplines of Shame in Early Modern England*, Ithaca: Cornell University Press.

29. Clarke, Bruce (1995), *Allegories of Writing: The Subject of Metamorphosis*, Albany: SUNY Press.

30. Belsey, Catherine (1994), 'Peter Quince's Ballad: Shakespeare, Psychoanalysis, History', *Deutsche Shakespeare-Gesellschaft/Deutsche Shakespeare-Gesellschaft West Jahrbuch*.

31. Clary, F. Nicholas (1996), '"Imagine No Worse of Them": Hippolyta on the Ritual Threshold in Shakespeare's *A Midsummer Night's Dream*' in Rutledge, Douglas F. (ed.), *Ceremony and Text in the Renaissance*, Newark: University of Delaware Press.

32. Girard, René (1991), *A Theater of Envy*, New York: Oxford University Press.

33. Scolnicov, Hanna (1993), 'The Zoomorphic Mask in Shakespeare', *Assaph Section C: Studies in the Theatre*, 9.

34. Roberts, Jeanne (1991), *The Shakespearean Wild: Geography, Genus, and Gender*, Lincoln and London: University of Nebraska Press.

35. Roberts, Jeanne (1992), 'Shakespeare's Maimed Birth Rites', in Woodbridge, L. and E. Berry (eds.), *True Rites and Maimed Rites: Ritual and Anti-ritual in Shakespeare and His Age*, Urbana and Chicago: University of Illinois Press.

36. Barber, C.L. (1959), *Shakespeare's Festive Comedy: A Study of Dramatic Form in its Relation to Social Custom*, Princeton: Princeton University Press.

37. Bristol, Michael (1985), *Carnival and Theater: Plebeian Culture and the Structure of Authority in Renaissance England*, New York: Methuen.

38. Laroque, François (1991), *Shakespeare's Festive World: Elizabethan Seasonal Entertainment and the Professional Stage*, translated by Janet Lloyd, Cambridge: Cambridge University Press.

39. Patterson, Annabel (1989), *Shakespeare and the Popular Voice*, Oxford: Basil Blackwell.

40. Healy, Thomas (1992), *New Latitudes: Theory and English Renaissance Literature*, London: Arnold.

41. Mangan, Michael (1996). See n. 14.

42. Howard, Skiles (1993), 'Hands, Feet and Bottoms: Decentering the Cosmic Dance in *A Midsummer Night's Dream*', *Shakespeare Quarterly*, 44 (3).

43. Stavig, Mark (1995), *The Forms of Things Unknown: Renaissance Metaphor in* Romeo and Juliet *and* A Midsummer Night's Dream, Pittsburgh: Duquesne University Press.

44. Parker, Patricia (1996), *Shakespeare from the Margins: Language, Culture, Context*, Chicago: The University of Chicago Press.

45. Hillman, David (1996), 'Puttenham, Shakespeare, and the Abuse of Rhetoric', *Studies in English Literature 1500–1900*, 36 (1).
46. Hunt, Maurice (1992), 'The Voices of *A Midsummer Night's Dream*', *Texas Studies in Literature and Language*, 34 (2).
47. Peterson, Douglas (1995), 'Beginnings and Endings: Structure and Mimesis in Shakespeare's Comedies' in Willson, R. (ed.), *Entering the Maze: Shakespeare's Art of Beginning*, New York: Peter Lang.
48. Baxter, John (1996), 'Growing to a Point: Mimesis in *A Midsummer Night's Dream*', *English Studies in Canada*, 22.
49. Martindale, Charles and Michelle (1990), *Shakespeare and the Uses of Antiquity: An Introductory Essay*, London and New York: Routledge.
50. Bate, Jonathan (1993), *Shakespeare and Ovid*, Oxford: Clarendon Press.
51. Suzuki, Mihoko (1990), 'The Dismemberment of Hippolytus: Humanist Imitation, Shakespearean Translation', *Classical and Modern Literature*, 10.
52. Brooks, Harold (ed.) (1979), *A Midsummer Night's Dream*, London: Methuen.
53. Holland, Peter (1994), 'Theseus' Shadows in *A Midsummer Night's Dream*', *Shakespeare Survey*, 47.
54. Hunt, Maurice (1996), '*The Countess of Pembroke's Arcadia*, Shakespeare's *A Midsummer Night's Dream*, and the School of Night: An Intertextual Nexus', *Essays in Literature, Macomb, Illinois*, 23 (1).
55. Brunel, Pierre (1996), *Formes baroques au théâtre*, Paris: Klincksieck.
56. Empson, William (1994), *Essays on Renaissance Literature*, Haffenden, John (ed.), Cambridge: Cambridge University Press.
57. Empson, William (1979), 'Fairy Flight in *A Midsummer Night's Dream*', *London Review of Books*, 25 October. Reprinted in Pirie, David (ed.), *Essays on Shakespeare*, Cambridge: Cambridge University Press.
58. Tave, Stuart (1993), *Lovers, Clowns, and Fairies: An Essay on the Comedies*, Chicago: The University of Chicago Press.
59. Sorelius, Gunnar (1993), *Shakespeare's Early Comedies: Myth, Metamorphosis, Mannerism*, Uppsala: Acta Universitatis Upsaliensis.
60. Hale, John K. (1996), *The Shakespeare of the Comedies: A Multiple Approach*, Bern: Peter Lang.
61. Vickers, Brian (1993), *Appropriating Shakespeare: Contemporary Critical Quarrels*, New Haven: Yale University Press.
62. Charney, Maurice (1993), *All of Shakespeare*, New York: Columbia University Press.
63. O'Brien, Peggy (ed.) (1993), *Shakespeare Set Free: Teaching Romeo and Juliet. Macbeth. A Midsummer Night's Dream*, New York: Washington Square Press.
64. Mowat, Barbara and P. Werstine (eds.) (1993), *A Midsummer Night's Dream*, The New Folger Library Shakespeare, New York: Washington Square Press.
65. Coursen, H. R. (1992), *Shakespearean Performance as Interpretation*, Newark: University of Delaware Press.
66. Crowl, Samuel (1992), *Shakespeare Observed: Studies in Performance on Stage and Screen*, Athens, Ohio: Ohio University Press.
67. Halio, Jay (1994), *A Midsummer Night's Dream*, Shakespeare in Performance, Manchester and New York: Manchester University Press.
68. Hodgdon, Barbara (1996), 'Looking for Mr. Shakespeare after "The Revolution": Robert Lepage's intercultural *Dream* machine' in Bulman, James (ed.), *Shakespeare, Theory, and Performance*, London and New York: Routledge.
69. Hodgdon, Barbara (1993), 'Splish Splash and the Other: Lepage's Intercultural *Dream* Machine', *Essays in Theatre/Études Théatrales*, 12 (1).
70. Williams, Gary Jay (1997), *Our Moonlight Revels: A Midsummer Night's Dream in the Theatre*, Iowa City: University of Iowa Press.

71. Griffiths, Trevor (1996), *A Midsummer Night's Dream*, Shakespeare in Production, Cambridge: Cambridge University Press.
72. Brown, John Russell (ed.) (1996), *A Midsummer Night's Dream*, New York: Applause.
73. Treadwell, T.O. (ed.) (1996), *A Midsommer Nights Dreame*, Shakespearean Originals: First Editions, London and New York: Prentice Hall/ Harvester Wheatsheaf.
74. Swander, Homer (1990), 'Editors Vs. a Text: The Scripted Geography of *A Midsummer Night's Dream*', *Studies in Philology*, 87.
75. Holland, Peter (ed.) (1994), *A Midsummer Night's Dream*, Oxford: Clarendon Press.
76. Foakes, R.A. (ed.) (1984), *A Midsummer Night's Dream*, Cambridge: Cambridge University Press.
77. Brooks, Harold (1979). See n. 52.
78. Cookson, Linda and B. Loughrey (eds.) (1991), *A Midsummer Night's Dream*, Longman Critical Essays, London: Longman.
79. Tempera, Mariangela (ed.) (1991), *A Midsummer Night's Dream dal testo alla scena*, Bologna: Cooperativa Libraria Universitaria Editrice.
80. Dutton, Richard (ed.) (1996), *A Midsummer Night's Dream*, New Casebooks, London: Macmillan.
81. Huffman, Clifford (1995), '*Love's Labor's Lost*', '*A Midsummer Night's Dream*', and '*The Merchant of Venice*': *An Annotated Bibliography of Shakespeare Studies 1888–1994*, Pegasus Shakespeare Bibliographies, Binghampton, NY: Medieval & Renaissance Texts & Studies.
82. Palmer, D.J. (1990), 'The Early Comedies' in Wells, S. (ed.), *Shakespeare: A Bibliographical Guide*, Oxford: Oxford University Press.
83. Kott, Jan (1964), *Shakespeare Our Contemporary*, translated by B. Taborski, Garden City: Anchor.
84. Wells, Stanley (1991), '*A Midsummer Night's Dream* Revisited', *Critical Survey*, 3 (1).
85. Calderwood (1992). See n. 23.
86. Mangan, (1946). See n. 14.
87. Slights, Camille (1993), *Shakespeare's Comic Commonwealths*, Toronto: University of Toronto Press.
88. Schmidgall, Gary (1990), *Shakespeare and Opera*, Oxford: Oxford University Press.
89. Godsalve, William (1995), *Britten's A Midsummer Night's Dream: Making an Opera from Shakespeare's Comedy*, London and Toronto: Associated University Presses.
90. Guest, Harry (1994), 'Aspects of the *Dream*: Shakespeare, Purcell and Britten' in Klein, H. and C. Smith (eds.), *Shakespeare Yearbook 4: The Opera and Shakespeare*.
91. Gooch, Bryan and D. Thatcher (1991), *A Shakespeare Music Catalogue*, Oxford: Oxford University Press.
92. Holland, Peter (1994), '"A Midsummer Nights' Dream"', 1660–1800: Culture and the Canon' in Faini, Paola and Viloa Papetti (eds), *Le forme del teatro; Saggi sul teatro elisabettiano e della Restaurazione*, Rome: Pubblicazione del Departimento di letteratura comparata della Terza università degli studi di Roma.
93. Kennedy, Judith (1996), 'Bottom Transformed by the Sketching Society', *Shakespeare Quarterly*, 47 (3).
94. Merchant, W.M. (1961), '*A Midsummer Night's Dream*: A Visual Re-Creation' in Brown, J.R. and B. Harris (eds), *Early Shakespeare*, Stratford-Upon-Avon Studies 3, London: Arnold.

95. Garlick, Kenneth (1984), 'Illustrations to *A Midsummer Night's Dream* before 1920', *Shakespeare Survey*, 37.
96. Maas, Jeremy, Pamela White Trimpe, Charlotte Gere, and others (1997), *Victorian Fairy Painting*, edited by Jane Martineau, London: Royal Academy of Arts, Iowa: The University of Iowa Museum of Art, Toronto: The Art Gallery of Toronto, in association with Merrell Holberton Publishers London.
97. Mowat and Werstine (eds.) (1993). See n. 64.
98. Holland (ed.) (1994). See n. 75.

18   Criticism on the *Sonnets*, 1994–7

Heather Dubrow

I

The critical reception of Shakespeare's sonnets has long been as paradoxical and inconsistent as the poems themselves. While the quality of the scholarly inquiry in question has varied strikingly at any given moment, the degree of interest excited by these poems has differed equally sharply from one period to another. One might, of course, assert similar claims about responses to many of the plays and the other non-dramatic poems; one of the most reliable barometers to changes in the academic climate is the shift in which texts attract scrutiny. But erratic variations in both quality and quantity have been exceptionally marked, and exceptionally revealing, in the instance of work on the sonnets. With her usual trenchancy, Helen Vendler describes the history of their reception as 'highly diverting, if appalling'.[1]

On the one hand, then, these lyrics have attracted intense interest both in our own and earlier centuries, in part, of course, because of their tantalizing hints of biographical revelations. On the other hand, Shakespeareans who are deeply engaged with even the most minor of the plays in the canon often bestow on the sonnets only cursory attention; undergraduates and postgraduates studying Shakespeare are often permitted, even encouraged, to ignore them completely. Moreover, though some connections between their author's dramatic and non-dramatic works, such as the references to blackness that at once unite and distinguish *Love's Labour's Lost* and the sonnets, have long been recognized, many other potential links have been virtually ignored. Marble and gilded monuments of princes do indeed sometimes seem more powerful than these rhymes.

Equally paradoxical, as I suggested, is the quality of the books and articles these lyrics have inspired. Some analyses can hold their own against the most impressive studies of the plays; for example, although they can be faulted on certain grounds, Stephen Booth's *Essay on Shakespeare's Son-*

302

nets[2] and Joel Fineman's *Shakespeare's Perjured Eye: The Invention of Poetic Subjectivity in the Sonnets*[3] aptly represent some of the most stimulating work of their respective critical moments. Yet, while Brents Stirling's[4] contributions to the subject are refreshingly sane, most attempts to reorder the collection could most charitably be described by adducing Johnson's adage about the triumph of hope over experience. Similarly, A. L. Rowse's confident identification of the Dark Lady in his edition, *The Poems of Shakespeare's Dark Lady*,[5] was the culmination of centuries of equally irresponsible biographical speculation. And in *Shakespeare Verbatim: The Reproduction of Authenticity and the 1790 Apparatus*[6] Margreta de Grazia has demonstrated the distortions created by scholars' anxieties about the sexualities manifest in these poems. The sonnets, a wise observer noted, affect otherwise sane critics the way catnip affects otherwise sane cats.

II

This chapter focuses on the years between 1994 and 1997, though it occasionally encompasses earlier publications in the interest of tracing developments in critical practice. Even that span of three years has witnessed so much work on the sonnets that my overview is necessarily selective, pivoting on exemplary instances at the necessary cost of omitting other worthy critical texts. However one delimits it, though, that period can best be understood in the context of the critical and methodological developments that demarcate the decades after about 1970. Again, paradoxes abound. The critical approaches and questions that flourished in the wake of post-structuralism offer renewed reasons for studying the sonnets and new ways of studying them acutely. Thus, for example, Fineman's *Shakespeare's Perjured Eye* draws on Lacanian and other post-structuralist approaches. Another instance of the influence of newer approaches during the 1990's is Peter Stallybrass's 'Editing as Cultural Formation: The Sexing of Shakespeare's *Sonnets*'.[7] Participating in the project of tracing cultural values and shifts through the scrutiny of editorial practices, Stallybrass finds in the reception of Shakespeare's lyrics the development of modern ideas of sexuality and of character.

Yet from another perspective the critical climate since 1970, especially in the United States, also encourages the longstanding tendency to marginalize Shakespeare's non-dramatic poems. In particular, during both the 1980s and 1990s critics in the United States specializing in early modern studies typically privileged drama over lyric poetry. The association of lyric with the creation and celebration of the individual, with private emotions, and with elite writers all rendered its study suspect in an academic environment emphasizing historical and political inquiry. And the new historicist interest in theatricality and performance in both the narrow and the broad senses encouraged the study of drama.

Transgressive in so many respects, in the years since 1970 these poems have inspired numerous analyses focusing on what has been termed the holy trinity of race, class, and gender. Many, though not all, earlier students of the sonnets had interpreted the Dark Lady's blackness in terms of a hair colour manifesting the moral blackness within. In contrast, contemporary analyses of race inform the reading of the sonnets in Kim F. Hall's book, *Things of Darkness: Economies of Race and Gender in Early Modern England*.[8] Spurred by nationalistic and imperialist ventures, this study maintains, the early modern period witnessed a discourse of race based on clearly demarcated, insistently bifurcated, and morally charged distinctions between black and white (other recent critics have instead emphasized the amorphousness of such categories, especially in a period when conceptions of race were in the process of development). Though Hall's wide-ranging analysis of references to color in sonnet sequences focuses more on Sidney than Shakespeare, the study comments explicitly and acutely on the latter at certain key points and refers implicitly to his Dark Lady throughout. Hall's argument could be enriched and nuanced by more attention to Continental developments and to the tone of some of the passages she cites (for example, I find less anxiety in Sidney's references to black eyes than she does); but the book is, deservedly, already an influential contribution to one of the most central topics in contemporary early modern studies.

An essay by Jonathan Crewe[9] incisively engages with the complexities of discussing race. While recognizing the amorphousness and changeableness of its construction in early modern England, he argues that developing attitudes are 'ubiquitously prophesied' (13) throughout Shakespeare's canon. In discussing how those responses relate to other socio-political categories, he deploys a cinematic analogue, 'The Crying Game'. Offering astute readings of race in Sonnets 20 and 127, Crewe maintains that the latter poem 'holds both racialized "truth" and its momentous undoing in prophetic suspension' (25). Crewe's reading, like Fineman's, tends to underplay the ways the ideal of fairness represented by the young man is problematized and criticized, and his emphasis on the sonnets' anticipation of later racial attitudes finesses central questions about race in early modern England; but his article is exemplary in its subtlety.

The second member of this critical triumvirate, class, was addressed immediately before the period on which this article concentrates, in one of the several important articles Margreta de Grazia has published on these poems, 'The Scandal of Shakespeare's Sonnets'.[10] Demonstrating that Benson did not in fact make as concerted an attempt to disguise the gender of the beloved as most critics have assumed, this essay opens by providing a revisionist perspective on common generalizations about the history of Shakespeare criticism. De Grazia's central argument, however, is that the principal scandal of the sonnets involves not gender but class: 'In praising the youth's fair lineaments, social distinction had been maintained; in praising the mistress's dark colours, social distinction is confounded' (46).

'"Thou maist have thy *Will*": The Sonnets of Shakespeare and His Stepsisters', an essay by the late Josephine A. Roberts,[11] advocates approaching problems of gender by teaching Shakespeare's sonnets in relation to those of women writers; in the course of her argument Roberts also comments intelligently about the central interpretive questions that plague studies of Shakespeare's poems. Above all, however, the issue of homoeroticism has dominated discussions of gender in those sonnets, inspiring work that is always provocative, frequently illuminating, yet sometimes at best strained. Deploying Eve Kosfosky Sedgwick's groundbreaking contributions to gay and lesbian studies and queer theory, as well as the pioneering if problematical arguments in Joseph Pequigney's *Such Is My Love: A Study of Shakespeare's Sonnets*,[12] Bruce R. Smith addresses the issue of sexualities in *Homosexual Desire in Shakespeare's England: A Cultural Poetics*.[13] Informed and judicious, this book locates the sexual politics of the poem in relation to both the conditions of manuscript publication and the models of courtly love and Christian marriage. Studies like the work of Sedgwick, Smith, and Pequigney have spurred the interest in the homoeroticism of the sonnets that is apparent in a number of books and articles published during 1994-7. During those years many critics assumed as a given the name of the love that previous critics of the sonnets dared not speak and discussed its manifestations in fresh ways. For example, in *Impersonations: The Performance of Gender in Shakespeare's England* Stephen Orgel[14] insists that, for all its denials of same-sex love, Sonnet 20 presupposes that form of eroticism. Building on suggestions from other critics, he proceeds to offer a novel reading of the couplet of that vexed and vexing lyric: 'But since she prick/d thee out for women's pleasure, / Mine be thy love, and thy love's use their treasure'.[15] In the absence of twentieth-century editorial interventions, these lines could, he persuasively maintains, suggest that men are indeed physically equipped for homoerotic relationships; with 'loves' interpreted as a plural noun rather than a possessive and 'use' as a verb, the couplet might emphasize the mutability and variability of desire, one of the principal arguments of queer theorists. In the edition cited below, Katherine Duncan-Jones[16] also assumes and reinterprets the homoeroticism of these poems.

Though some of the most influential criticism during the years encompassed by this essay focuses on race, class, and above all gender, equally important studies have variously addressed the post-structuralist implications of Shakespeare's sequence, the longstanding questions about form, sources, and style posed by these poems, and the connections among all those concerns. Timothy Bahti's *Ends of the Lyric: Direction and Consequence in Western Poetry*[17] provides a sophisticated reexamination of closure, demonstrating that lyric often effects it through chiasmic structures that work by 'inverting their ends into non-ends, and their readings into rebeginnings or not yet readings' (13). Bahti sometimes adapts and sometimes challenges Fineman's assumptions about the poems, finding that chiasmus operates throughout the sequence and does so in ways quite different from those Fineman ascribes to the figure; the author of *Ends of the Lyric* is particularly interested in how and why sonnets deploy that trope to return to their beginnings and draw attention to their *modus operandi*. In exploring those points in relation to Shakespeare, he offers impressively subtle readings of a number of the lyrics. David Schalkwyk's '"She never told her love":[18] Embodiment, Textuality and Silence in Shakespeare's Sonnets and Plays', incisively questions longstanding assumptions about the workings of the sonnet form. Variously adducing and criticizing post-structuralist assumptions about textuality. he emphasizes the embodiment of the lyrics in social situations. In another important revisionist move, Schalwyk questions the recent refusal to entertain biographical hypotheses about the Dark Lady and reconsiders issues about silence and speech.

In the years on which this essay concentrates, many other critics have also addressed problems of sources, form, and meaning in the sonnets. Two recent articles explore from quite different perspectives the ways the sequence undercuts its apparent emphasis on the power of verse to immortalize. Both *Venus and Adonis* and the sonnets, Pauline Kiernan[19] contends in 'Death by Rhetorical Trope: Poetry Metamorphosed in *Venus and Adonis* and the Sonnets', investigate the dangers of turning the material and corporeal into lifeless tropes. Appearing in *The Review of English Studies* in 1995 and subsequently incorporated into *Shakespeare's Theory of Drama,* this essay maintains that Shakespeare's use of the terms 'shadow', 'shade', and 'substance' demonstrates his engagement with Ovid's treatment of similar concepts; Shakespeare deploys this vocabulary precisely, not loosely as others have claimed, and does so to express the dangers of rhetorical and other bodiless illusions. Werner Habicht's ' "My tongue-tied Muse": Inexpressibility in Shakespeare's Sonnets',[20] argues that Shakespeare emphasizes the inexpressibility conceit more than most other sonneteers. His description of the workings of speech and silence in the sonnets could contribute fruitfully to feminist discussions of those apparent poles; and his essay, like Kiernan's, is also valuable because it locates the sonnets among other texts, whether by their author or other poets, rather than interpreting as *sui generis,* a common tendency. Style and language are approached from a different perspective in Jane Hedley's 'Since First Your Eye I Eyed: Shakespeare's *Sonnets'*.[21] Hedley argues convincingly that the narcissism of the sonnets is expressed in certain stylistic mannerisms of the lyrics, being, as it were, troped in its tropes. In particular, she offers incisive analyses of patterns of punning.

In the sonnets even more than other texts, editorial and critical debates are inextricably connected, and the period on which this essay focuses has also seen continuing attention to longstanding debates about such questions as the order and direction of address of the poems. In ' "Incertainties now crown themselves assured": The Politics of Plotting Shakespeare's

Sonnets',[22] I advocate a re-examination of the widespread assumption that the first one hundred twenty-six poems involve the Friend and the subsequent ones the Dark Lady. Once we acknowledge how unstable the evidence about direction of address is, I suggest, widespread and longstanding assumptions about plot and character are revealed as unstable as well; I proceed to offer revisionist interpretations of those issues and to explore the reasons so many critics have been attracted to the possibility of a radical break after Sonnet 126. (These arguments are briefly foreshadowed in my 1995 study, *Echoes of Desire: English Petrarchism and Its Counterdiscourses*,[23] where I also attempt to redefine the relationship between Shakespeare's poems and the traditions in my title, arguing that Shakespeare's often neglected debts to Petrarchism illuminate in particular his approaches to narrativity and to agency.)

The period 1994–97 has witnessed as well significant new editions of the sonnets. Given the centrality of the editorial issues to which I referred and the complexity of the cruxes in these poems, it is not surprising that scholarly editions have played so crucial a role in their critical history. Stephen Booth's *Shakespeare's Sonnets*[24] remains one of the major sources for any student of these poems, as well as a monument to the growing influence of post-structuralism at the moment it appeared. Published in the New Cambridge Shakespeare series, G. Blakemore Evans's *Sonnets*[25] demonstrates the thoroughness and care that have established Evans among the leading editors of his generation. His textual analysis, building on the compositor analysis of Macdonald P. Jackson, addresses a number of controversial issues; Evans argues persuasively, for example, that the punctuation is not authorial though the italicization may well be. The notes accompanying the poems occupy some one hundred and fifty double columned pages, and they encompass a number of original arguments about meaning and about sources and analogues. Evans finds in the final line of Sonnet 130 a negative undertow virtually neglected by other Shakespeareans; he notes and traces the noteworthy interpretive implications of the ambiguous punctuation of 6.7–11; and he offers emendations for a number of cruxes, speculating that 12.4 should read 'o'er-silvered are' and 35.8 'Accusing their sins more than their sins are'. Anthony Hecht's introduction to the volume treats some contemporary debates, notably the issue of homoeroticism, too glancingly. It provides, however, valuable perspectives drawing on Hecht's own work as a poet; his close reading of Sonnet 35, a poem too often neglected by critics, is particularly acute.

III

Two consequential books appeared just as I was completing this essay: too late to provide the comprehensive reviews both of them clearly merit and are likely to receive here and elsewhere, but in time to gesture towards their significance. Katherine Duncan-Jones's Arden edition[26] propounds a number of important arguments: she assigns the poems to later dates than most critics have assumed, for example, and maintains that previous scholars' nervousness about the homoeroticism of these texts has generated undue attention to the Dark Lady, as well as other distortions. Above all, her edition is rooted in her tenet that Thorpe's edition was not pirated. Thus finding authorial intent in the current order of the poems, Duncan-Jones posits links between them and stresses their connections with 'A Lover's Complaint'; that poem appears in this volume, as it did in John Kerrigan's Penguin edition.[27] An essay Duncan-Jones published in *Essays in Criticism* in 1995, 'Filling the Unforgiving Minute: Modernizing SHAKESPEARES SONNETS (1609)',[28] anticipates the edition, demonstrates how modernized spellings of 'filed' and 'mynuit' risk curtailing meanings; in particular, her points about puns on 'minuit', the French term for midnight, enrich already complex passages in the sonnets. In addition, some of Duncan-Jones's broader arguments about Thorpe's reliability were outlined in her earlier article, 'Was the 1609 *Shake-speare's Sonnets* Really Unauthorized?'[29] Although I take issue with her on some key issues, notably the order of the poems (see '"Incertainties now crown themselves assured"', discussed above), certainly the quality of her previous work on the sonnets and on other Renaissance poetry will assure her edition the attention it deserves.

Helen Vendler, probably our leading critic of lyric poetry, offers in *The Art of Shakespeare's Sonnets*[30] poem-by-poem commentaries on the sonnets, providing subtle analyses of such issues as the workings of their couplets. Her approach to the poems, adumbrated in essays published earlier in the 1990s[31, 32] in collections such as Russ McDonald's *Shakespeare Reread: The Texts in New Contexts* and Bruce McIver and Ruth Stevenson's *Teaching with Shakespeare: Critics in the Classroom,* emphasizes the successful resolution of aesthetic challenges through linguistic strategies. Vendler, who maintains that recent critics have neglected 'the art of seeing drama in linguistic action' (4), takes issue with assumptions that have pervaded many other studies of these and other poems; for example, she firmly distinguishes the poet from the speaker, finding in the latter a fully realized character, argues that lyric is fundamentally private meditation rather than social interaction, and emphasizes artistic control and achievement. Though I question certain of these assumptions (for example, the multiple diegetic audiences of pastoral stage, the ways early modern lyric in general typically moves between the public and private), they result in brilliant interpretations that remind us that formal analysis is hardly an exhausted mode of inquiry. It is fitting that the final years of this century thus witness the appearance of a study likely at once to provoke the contentious debates that have long characterized the reception of these poems, to intensify the types of critical interest and inquiry that they have frequently but not consistently received, and to exemplify the rigorous intelligence that has graced their critical history at its best.

REFERENCES

1. Vendler, Helen (1994), 'Reading, Stage by Stage: Shakespeare's Sonnets', in Russ Mcdonald, (ed.), *Shakespeare Reread: The Texts in New Contexts*, Ithaca: Cornell University Press, 29.
2. Booth, Stephen (1969), *An Essay on Shakespeare's Sonnets*, New Haven: Yale University Press.
3. Fineman, Joel (1986), *Shakespeare's Perjured Eye: The Invention of Poetic Subjectivity in the Sonnets*, Berkeley: University of California Press.
4. Stirling, Brents (1968), *The Shakespeare Sonnet Order: Poems and Groups*, Berkeley: University of California Press.
5. Lanier, Emilia (1978), *The Poems of Shakespeare's Dark Lady*, A.L. Rowse (ed.), London: Cape.
6. de Grazia, Margreta (1991), *Shakespeare Verbatim: The Reproduction of Authenticity and the 1790 Apparatus*, Oxford: Clarendon Press.
7. Stallybrass, Peter (1995), 'Editing as Cultural Formation: The Sexing of Shakespeare's Sonnets', in *The Uses of Literary History*, Marshall Brown (ed.), Durham, NC: Duke University Press. Reprinted from *Modern Language Quarterly*, 54 (1993), 91–103.
8. Hall, Kim F. (1995), *Things of Darkness: Economies of Race and Gender in Early Modern England*, Ithaca: Cornell University Press.
9. Crewe, Jonathan (1995), 'Out of the Matrix: Shakespeare and Race-Writing', *Yale Journal of Criticism*, 8, 13–29.
10. de Grazia, Margreta (1993), 'The Scandal of Shakespeare's Sonnets', *Shakespeare Survey*, 46, 35–49.
11. Roberts, Josephine A. (1996), ' "Thou maist have thy *Will*": The Sonnets of Shakespeare and His Stepsisters', *Shakespeare Quarterly*, 47, 407–423.
12. Pequigney, Joseph (1985), *Such Is My Love: A Study of Shakespeare's Sonnets*, Chicago: University of Chicago Press.
13. Smith, Bruce R. (1991), *Homosexual Desire in Shakespeare's England: A Cultural Poetics*, Chicago: University of Chicago Press.
14. Orgel, Stephen (1996), *Impersonations: The Performance of Gender in Shakespeare's England*, Cambridge: Cambridge University Press.
15. Evans, G. Blakemore (ed.) (1997), *The Riverside Shakespeare,* 2nd edn, Boston: Houghton Mifflin.
16. Duncan-Jones, Katherine, in *Shakespeare's Sonnets* (see n. 25).
17. Bahti, Timothy (1996), *Ends of the Lyric: Direction and Consequence in Western Poetry*, Baltimore: Johns Hopkins Press.
18. Schalwyk, David (1994), ' "She never told her love': Embodiment, Textuality, and Silence in Shakespeare's Sonnets and Plays', *Shakespeare Quarterly*, 45, 381–407.
19. Kiernan, Pauline (1995), 'Death by Rhetorical Trope: Poetry Metamorphosed in *Venus and Adonis* and the Sonnets', *Review of English Studies*, 46, 475–501. Kiernan, Pauline (1996), *Shakespeare's Theory of Drama*, Cambridge: Cambridge University Press.
20. Habicht, Werner (1996), ' "My tongue-tied Muse": Inexpressibility in Shakespeare's Sonnets', in *Shakespeare's Universe: Renaissance Ideas and Conventions, Essays in Honour of W.R. Elton*. John M. Mucciolo et al. (eds), Aldershot: Scolar Press.

21. Hedley, Jane (1994), 'Since First Your Eye I Eyed: Shakespeare's *Sonnets* and the Poetics of Narcissism', *Style*, 28, 1–30.
22. Dubrow, Heather (1996), ' "Incertainties now crown themselves assured": The Politics of Plotting Shakespeare's Sonnets', *Shakespeare Quarterly*, 47, 291–305.
23. Dubrow, Heather (1995), *Echoes of Desire: English Petrarchism and Its Counterdiscourses*, Ithaca: Cornell University Press.
24. Shakespeare, William (1977), *Shakespeare's Sonnets*, Stephen Booth (ed.), New Haven: Yale University Press.
25. Evans, G. Blakemore (1996) (ed.), *Sonnets*, with an introduction by Anthony Hecht, Cambridge: Cambridge University Press.
26. Duncan-Jones, Katherine (1997) (ed.), *Shakespeare's Sonnets*, The Arden Shakespeare, Nashville, Tennessee: Thomas Nelson.
27. Kerrigan, John (1986) (ed.), The Sonnets and 'A Lover's Complaint', Harmondsworth: Penguin.
28. Duncan-Jones, Katherine (1995), 'Filling the Unforgiving Minute: Modernizing SHAKE-SPEARES SONNETS (1609)', *Essays in Criticism*, 45, 199–207.
29. Duncan-Jones, Katherine (1983), 'Was the 1609 Shake-speare's Sonnets Really Unauthorized?', *Review of English Studies*, 34, 151–71.
30. Vendler, Helen (1997), *The Art of Shakespeare's Sonnets*, Cambridge: Harvard University Press.
31. Vendler, Helen (1994), 'Poems Posing Questions', 'Reading for Differnce: *The Sonnets*', 'Sonnets 33, 60, *Romeo and Juliet* 1. 5. 93–106, Sonnets 94, 105, 116, 129'. *Teaching with Shakespeare: Critics in the Classroom*, Bruce McIver and Ruth Stevenson (eds), Newark and London: University of Delaware Press and Associated University Presses.
32. Vendler, Helen (1994), 'Reading, Stage by Stage: Shakespeare's Sonnets', in *Shakespeare Reread: The Texts in New Contexts*, Russ Mcdonald (ed.), Ithaca: Cornell University Press.
Sedgwick, Eve Kosofsky (1985), *Between Men: English Literature and Male Homosocial Desire*, New York: Columbia University Press.

19   Shakespeare's 'Colonialist' *Tempest*, 1975 to the present day

John M. Mucciolo

There is not a word in *The Tempest* about America or Virginia, colonies or colonising, Indians or tomahawks, maize, mocking birds or tobacco. Nothing but the Bermudas, once barely mentioned as a far-away place, like Tokio [sic] or Mandalay. This interest and sympathy Shakespeare keeps to himself.[1]

Seventy years ago, in these terms, E.E. Stoll cautioned critics against transforming Shakespeare's *Tempest*[2] into a New World play. But Stoll's admonition, decades later, still goes unheeded. Colonialist critics still argue that Shakespeare's play reflects not only New World explorations but also 'brutal British colonialism'.[3]

Colonialist perspectives on Shakespeare's play include such notions as:

1   *Source*: William Strachey's unpublished account (c. 1610) of a 1609 shipwreck is the source for the play's opening scene;
2   *Caliban*: Actual hero of the play – sympathetic and 'disenfranchised' – Caliban is held to be not only legal inheritor of the island but also a suitable match for Prospero's Miranda.[4]

THE STRACHEY SOURCE-CLAIM

Critics asserting *The Tempest* as a play concerning colonial conquest believe that 'Strachey's account . . . helped shape *The Tempest*'.[5] Although they concede that 'the play was performed long before Strachey's narrative was printed', they claim that Shakespeare 'read a manuscript version of the work [Strachey's letter]'.[6] But what was earlier claimed to be merely a 'conjunction' of Strachey's unpublished letter and Shakespeare's play now becomes an unqualified fact of Shakespeare's indebtedness: 'Such then were the narrative materials that passed from Strachey to Shakespeare, from the Virginia Company to the King's Men'.[7] This colonialist hypothesis concerning 'presumed sources' slips into accepted fact – '*The Tempest* conflates the Bermuda and Virginia materials'.[8] Despite the claim that Strachey knew members of the Virginia Company, the circulation of Strachey's manuscript among its members does not in itself prove Shakespeare read it.

Further, among parallels between Strachey and Shakespeare, these colonialist critics cite a reference to St. Elmo's fire.[9] Strachey's description of St. Elmo's fire in the ship's rigging, colonialists believe, inspired Ariel's lines: 'sometimes I'd divide / And burn in many places' (I.ii.198–99). But St. Elmo's fire recurs in other Renaissance voyage narratives.[10] Richard Eden's account of Magellan's voyage (1572), for example, tells of a St. Elmo's fire in ship's rigging.[11] Another St. Elmo's fire is also found in Erasmus's account of a ship in a storm, 'Naufragium'.[12] These parallels between Strachey and Shakespeare, as E.E. Stoll pointed out years ago, may be little more than a commonplace.

Despite such inconclusive links between Strachey and Shakespeare, the critical notion of a colonialist *Tempest* has become widespread: in fact, it is held 'inarguable ... that Shakespeare intended a contribution to a philosophical debate on colonialism and race relations'.[13] Similarly, another critic concludes: it is 'an axiom of contemporary criticism that *The Tempest* is a play about the European colonial experience in America'.[14]

As these critics strain to assert Strachey is the play's source, so such critics insist that Caliban is the play's hero.

CALIBAN, SYMPATHETIC HERO

Caliban's claim to possession of the island

> Caliban 'knows something of the laws of inheritance'.[15]
> Caliban's claim to the legitimate possession of the island (I.ii.331) is never really answered by Prospero.[16]
> I think, to the Jacobean playgoer, and perhaps especially one who saw his interests reflected by the Commons, the plight of Caliban as the New World native who had been subjected to a tyrant might have appeared structurally comparable to his own condition.[17]

Citing Caliban's 'This island's mine by Sycorax my mother' (I.ii.331), colonialist critics confirm Caliban's assertion of ownership: 'the island is rightly his ... and Prospero is an invader and a usurper.[18]

One such critic argues for Caliban's 'double claim' to the island: 'both through inheritance from his mother, Sycorax, the first settler, and through prior possession'.[19] In addition, to reinforce Caliban's claim, this critic holds Caliban a bastard – as in Prospero's 'Thou poisonous slave, got by the devil himself / Upon a wicked dam' (I.ii.319–20). Regarding this notion, it is supposed that the play's audiences would have linked Caliban to 'numerous royal precedents, including the two previous queens of England, Elizabeth and her half-sister, Mary Tudor, both of whom were technically illegitimate'.[20]

Caliban: poet and singer

Colonialist commentators insist that Caliban is not only legally right in possession of the island, they also claim he is 'the other great poet of the play'.[21] Because he is a native, Caliban has an 'eloquent appreciation of the island's mysterious sounds'.[22] Caliban, moreover, speaks with a 'rich, irreducible concreteness'.[23] His language – e.g., 'the isle is full of noises' (III.ii.140–148) – 'compels us to acknowledge the independence and integrity of Caliban's construction of reality'.[24]

With critics who argue for the 'integrity' of Caliban's speech, one such critic agrees that Caliban's 'loud assertions *sound* alien, but only to [European] intruders, who regard as [Caliban's] "crude hooting" what is ... really "racial poetry" '.[25] Caliban's sound, moreover, is 'a sound of protest and resistance, asserting "a potent force ... that cannot be comprehended or controlled by Western philosophy" '.[26] Caliban's 'words and their sounds are both deformational and transformational, creating a song of protest and of freedom',[27] as in Caliban's:

> No more dams I'll make for fish;
>   Nor fetch in firing
>   At requiring;
> Nor scrape trenchering, nor wash dish.
>   'Ban, 'Ban, Ca: Caliban
> Has a new master: get a new man.
> (II.ii.188–193)

These critics argue that Caliban's speech is noble – he 'loves music, has learned good English, speaks good poetry'.[28] They agree in claiming that Caliban's speech is 'the first representation of a "vernacular" voice in Western literature'.[29] Through such assertions, these commentators justify naming Caliban 'the other great poet of the play'.[30]

Caliban: 'Free love in the New World'[31]

'The issue is not whether Caliban is actually a rapist or not, since Caliban accepts the charge'.[32]

As colonialist critics uphold Caliban's legal claim to the island, and praise his 'noble' and 'poetic' language, they also exonerate him from blame for his attempted rape. They excuse this attempt on Miranda (I.ii.349–350) as his 'ignorance of all cultural refinements and sexual mores',[33] or his 'failure in European sexual ethics'.[34] Caliban's 'lust' for Miranda is, according to one colonialist critic, merely a Renaissance New World *topos*: 'free love in the New World is regularly treated [in Renaissance travel narratives] not as an instance of the lust of savages, but of their edenic innocence'.[35] This critic, moreover, perceives Caliban's 'assault upon Miranda ... not as destructive and uncivilized but as an act of political economy, dictated by the same impulse that prompted Romulus to promote the rape of the Sabine women'.[36] As an 'edenic savage' or an 'empire-building Romulus', Caliban is cleared of blame for his attempted rape of Miranda.

While some critics would absolve Caliban as would-be rapist, others would diminish his culpability. Caliban's attempt on Miranda, such critics insist, is no worse than similar attempts that Prospero, were he in Milan, could expect from his own townsmen: 'many men in Prospero's home of Milan might also have attempted to violate the honor of his child, but such behavior would not necessarily have stigmatized them as incapable of civility or wholly irredeemable'.[37] Paradoxically, a recent *Tempest* study excuses Caliban: 'Caliban's assault upon Prospero's daughter once more genders the colonizing impulse; here it is the defense of the European woman that justifies repression of the non-European'.[38] These exculpatory critics even condemn Prospero for defending his daughter against a rapist.[39]

This study has examined a major critical perspective on *The Tempest* which holds, 'it is very difficult to argue that *The Tempest* is *not* about imperialism'.[40] E.E. Stoll, quoted above, would have found such critical views extraordinary: e.g., the play 'demonstrates the crucial nexus of civil power and sexuality in colonial discourse'.[41] About such colonialist notions, Stoll remarked some seven decades ago, 'their proof rests upon a few slight parallels, most precariously'; indeed, Stoll notes, among other excesses,

> they take 'great pains to endeavor to prove acquaintance on Shakespeare's part with the promoters of colonizing in Virginia, and sympathy with their motives and aspirations – only, Shakespeare himself says not a word to that effect'.[42]

REFERENCES

1. Stoll, 487. Here Stoll questions the relevance of early twentieth century claims that Strachey is the play's source.
2. All quotations from Shakespeare's *The Tempest* are taken from Kermode's Arden edition.
3. Cartelli in Daniell, links the play to 'British colonialism in Africa' (81). In the present paper, 'colonialist' indicates those critics who hold that *The Tempest* reflects English exploitation of 'natives' during the early seventeenth century. Such colonialist readings cite terms in the play which occur also in early seventeenth-century travel narratives – e.g., 'plantation' (*Temp.*, II.i.147), 'Indian' (II.ii.35), 'still-vexed Bermoothes' (I.ii.229). In addition, these commentators derive the play's opening storm scene from William Strachey's account of a shipwreck off the Bermudas in July 1609. These selective citations lead to such claims as, e.g., Shakespeare 'anticipated remarkably well the future language of English–speaking colonialism' (John S. Hunt, 280).

4. Hirst 22.
5. Greenblatt, *Negotiations*, 147: Passages from Strachey's account of the wreck of Sir Thomas Gates's ship claimed to be relevant to the play may be found in Kermode's edition. Like Stracheyans before him, Greenblatt holds that the play is 'full of conspicuous allusions to contemporary debates over the project of colonialization: The Virginia Company's official report on the state of its New World colony and the account by Wiliam Strachey, secretary of the settlement at Jamestown, of a violent storm and shipwreck off the coast of Bermuda, are examples' (*Chronicle*, B1). In particular, Greenblatt alleges that Strachey's 'unmerciful tempest' is reflected in the play's violent shipwreck. In addition, he holds that Strachey's depiction of the governor's 'heartening every man unto his labour' mirrors the Boatswain's exhortation to the mariners, 'Heigh, my hearts!' and 'You mar our labour' (I.i.5 and 13) (*Negotiations*, 149). This alleged 'conjunction' of Strachey and Shakespeare has been the object of Greenblatt's 'most sustained and passionate attention' (*Representations*, 26).
6. Greenblatt, *Negotiations*, 147–54; 197.
7. Greenblatt, *Negotiations*, 147–54; 197.
8. Greenblatt, *Negotiations*, 147–54; 197.
9. Hirst, 11.
10. Daniell, 74–75.
11. Frey 31.
12. Baldwin, 742 and Rea, 281.
13. Patterson, 156.
14. Fuchs, 45.
15. Patterson, 155.
16. Greenblatt, *Negotiations*, 157.
17. Jordan, 197.
18. Orgel, *Cannibals*, 54.
19. Orgel, *Cannibals*, 54.
20. Speculation upon Caliban's legal right to the island has resulted in a substantial questioning response to this claim. Brian Vickers, for example, points out: 'Whether Sycorax as an exiled aggressor has more right to the island than Prospero as an injured victim, is a moot point, but it is in any case not one raised by the play' (246). Caliban's claim, Anne Barton agrees, 'sounds less like the cry of an oppressed native than the frustration of a second-generation inhabitant of the island displaced by later arrivals' (54). Similarly, the 'only figures who can be said to have some natural claim to priority', according to David Norbrook, are 'Ariel and his fellow spirits' and they 'do not seem to think of land as something to be possessed' (2). If Caliban neither inherited the island nor first possessed it – 'even prefers to leave with Prospero' (Vickers 246) – colonialist assertions seem questionable.
21. Orgel, *Cannibal*, 57.
22. Hunt, 287.
23. Greenblatt, 'Learning to Curse', 31.
24. Greenblatt, 'Learning to Curse,' 31.
25. Fox-Good, 262.
26. Fox-Good, 261–62.
27. Fox-Good, 262.
28. Patterson, 159.
29. Fox-Good, 261.
30. Orgel, *Cannibals*, 57.
31. Orgel, Oxford edn., 34.
32. Brown, 62.

33. Hunt, 278.
34. Sharp, 273.
35. Orgel, Oxford edn., 34.
36. Orgel, *Cannibals*, 55.
37. Hamlin, 20.
38. Fuchs, 61.
39. Ironically, the critics justify Caliban's attempt to rape Miranda in a play celebrating legitimate marriage. When Caliban is prevented from his sexual assault and 'peopling the isle' (I.ii.352), he offers Miranda to the drunken clown Trinculo: 'She will become thy bed, I warrant,/And bring thee forth brave brood' (III.ii.102–03). Contrast Ferdinand: 'the strong'st suggestion . . . shall never melt/Mine honor into lust' (IV.i.26–28).
40. Greenblatt, *Chronicle*, B1.
41. Paul Brown, 62.
42. Stoll, 487.

SELECTIVE BIBLIOGRAPHY (MAINLY 1975 TO PRESENT)

Adams, Robert M. (1988), *The Four Romances*, New York: Norton.

Baker, Houston (1986), 'Caliban's Triple Play' in *'Race,' Writing and Difference*, ed. Henry Louis Gates, Jr., Chicago: University of Chicago Press.

———— (1987), *Modernism and the Harlem Renaissance*, Chicago: University of Chicago Press.

Barker, Francis and Peter Hulme (1985), 'Nymphs and Reapers Heavily Vanish: The Discursive Contexts of *The Tempest*', in John Drakakis, (ed.), *Alternative Shakespeares*: 191–205.

Barton, Anne (1991), 'Perils of Historicism', *New York Review of Books*, March, 28, 53–54.

———— (1993), *Essays Mainly Shakespearean*, Cambridge: Cambridge, University Press.

Berger, Harry Jr. (1969), 'Miraculous Harp: A Reading of Shakespeare's *Tempest*', *Shakespeare Survey*, 5, 253–283.

Bristol, Frank, M. (1898), *Shakespeare and America*, Chicago: W.C Hollister.

Brockbank, Philip (1966), '"The Tempest": Conventions of Art and Empire', in John Russell Brown and Bernard Harris, (eds.), *Later Shakespeare*, Stratford-upon-Avon Studies, 8, London: Edward Arnold, 183–201.

Brown, Paul (1985), '"This Thing of Darkness I Acknowledge Mine": *The Tempest* and the Discourse of Colonialism', in Jonathan Dollimore and Alan Sinfield (eds.), *Political Shakespeare: New Essays in Cultural Materialism*, Ithaca, NY: Cornell University Press, 48–71.

Bullough, Geoffrey (1957–75), *Narrative and Dramatic Sources of Shakespeare*, 8 vols., London: Routledge & Kegan Paul.

Cartelli, Thomas (1987), 'Prospero in Africa: *The Tempest* as Colonialist Text and Pretext', in Jean E. Howard and Marion F. O'Connor (eds.),

Shakespeare Reproduced: The Text in History and Ideology, London: Methuen.

Cawley, Robert Ralston (1926), 'Shakespeare's Use of the Voyagers in *The Tempest*', *Pub. Modern Languages Assoc.*, XLI, no. 3, Sept., 688–726.

Cheyfitz, Eric (1991), *The Poetics of Imperialism: Translation and Colonialization from the Tempest to Tarzan*, New York: Oxford University Press.

Chiappelli, Fredi et al., eds. (1986), *First Images of America: The Impact of the New World on the Old*, 2 vols., Berkeley: University of California Press.

Clark, Sandra (1986), *The Tempest: Penguin Critical Edition*, London: Penguin Books.

Cohen, Walter (1987), 'Political Criticism of Shakespeare', in Jean E. Howard and Marion F. O'Connor (eds.), *Shakespeare Reproduced: The Text in History and Ideology*, London: Methuen.

Daniell, David (1989), *The Tempest: An Introduction to the Variety of Criticism*, Atlantic Highlands, NJ: Humanities Press International, Inc.

Davidson, Frank (1963), '*The Tempest*: An Interpretation', *Journal of English and Germanic Philology*, July, 62, (3), 501–517.

Dawson, Anthony, B. (1988), '*Tempest* in a Teapot: Critics, Evaluation, Ideology', in *Bad Shakespeare: Revaluations of the Shakespeare Canon*, Maurice Charney (ed.), Rutherford, N.J.: Fairleigh Dickinson University Press, 61–73.

Dollimore, Jonathan and Alan Sinfield (eds.) (1985), *Political Shakespeare: New Essays in Cultural Materialism*, Ithaca, N.Y.: Cornell University Press.

Drakakis, John (1985), *Alternative Shakespeares*, London: Methuen.

Dryden, John (1962), *Of Dramatic Poesy and Other Critical Essays*, George Watson (ed.), Vol. 1, London: J.M. Dent & Sons, 252–53.

Eagleton, Terry (1986), *William Shakespeare*, Oxford: Basil Blackwell.

Erlich, Bruce (1977), 'Shakespeare's Colonial Metaphor: On the Social Function of the Theatre in *The Tempest*', *Science and Society*, XLI, 43–65.

Evans, Gareth Lloyd (1973), *Shakespeare, V: 1606–1616*, Edinburgh: Oliver & Boyd.

Evans, Malcolm (1986), 'Master and Slave' in *Signifying Nothing: Truth's True Content in Shakespeare's Text*, University of Georgia Press.

Felperin, Howard (1987), 'Making It "Neo": The New Historicism and Renaissance Literature', *Textual Practice*, I, 262–77.

Fernandez Retamar, Roberto (1989), *Caliban and Other Essays*, Trans. Edward Baker, Minneapolis: University of Minnesota Press.

Fiedler, Leslie, A. (1972), *The Stranger in Shakespeare*, New York: Stein & Day.

Fox-Good, Jacquelyn (1996), 'Other Voices: The Sweet, Dangerous Air(s) of Shakespeare's *Tempest*', *Shakespeare Studies*, Leeds Barroll, (ed.), XXIV, Madison: Fairleigh Dickinson Press, 241–274.

Frey, Charles (1979), 'The Tempest and the New World', Shakespeare Quarterly, XXX, 31–41.

Fuchs, Barbara (1997), 'Conquering Islands: Contextualizing The Tempest,' Shakespeare Quarterly, 48, (1), 45–62, Spring.

Fulton, Robert C., III (1978), 'The Tempest and the Bermuda Pamphlets: Source and Thematic Intention', Interpretations: Studies in Language and Literature, 10, (1), 1–10.

Gayley, Charles Mills (1917), Shakespeare and the Founders of Liberty in America, New York: Macmillan.

Greenblatt, Stephen (1986), 'Learning to Curse: Aspects of Linguisitic Colonialism in the Sixteenth Century', in Chiappelli, Vol. II, 561–80.

——— (1988), Shakespearean Negotiations: The Circulation of Social Energy in Renaissance England, Oxford: Oxford University Press.

——— (1991), 'The Best Way to Kill Our Literary Inheritance Is to Turn It Into a Decorous Celebration of the New World Order', The Chronicle of Higher Education, June 12, xxxvii, (39), B1–B3.

——— (1991), Marvellous Possessions: The Wonder of the New World, Chicago: The University of Chicago Press.

——— (1997), 'The Touch of the Real', Representations, Summer, (59), 14–29.

Griffiths, Trevor R. (1983), ' "This island's mine": Caliban and colonialism', The Yearbook of English Studies, 13, 159–80.

Halpern, Richard (1994), ' "The Picture of Nobody": White Cannibalism in The Tempest', in David Lee Miller, Sharon O'Dair and Harold Weber, (eds.), The Production of English Renaissance Culture, Ithaca: Cornell University Press, 262–92.

Hamilton, Donna B. (1990), Virgil and The Tempest: The Politics of Imitation, Columbus: Ohio State University Press.

Hamlin, William M. (1995), The Image of America in Montaigne, Spenser, and Shakespeare: Renaissance Ethnography and Literary Reflections, New York: St. Martin's Press.

——— (1994), 'Men of Inde: Renaissance Ethnography and The Tempest', Shakespeare Studies, Leeds Barroll, (ed.), Vol. XXII, Madison: Fairleigh Dickinson University Press, 15–37.

Hankins, J.E. (1947), 'Caliban the Bestial Man', Pub. Modern Languages Assoc., LXII, 793.

Hawkes, Terence (1985), 'Swisser-Swatter: Making a Man of English Letters', in John Drakakis, (ed.), Alternative Shakespeares, London: Methuen.

——— (1986), That Shakespearian Rag: essays on a critical process, New York: Methuen.

Hirst, David L. (1984), The Tempest: Text & Performance, New York: Macmillan.

Hodgen, Margaret T. (1964), Early Anthropology in the Sixteenth Centuries, Philadelphia: University of Pennsylvania Press.

Honour, Hugh (1975), *The New Golden Land: European Images of America from the Discoveries to the Present*, New York: Random House.

Howard, Jean, E. (1986), 'The New Historicism in Renaissance Studies', *English Literary Renaissance*, XVI, 13–43.

Howard, Jean E. and Marion F. O'Connor, (eds.) (1987), *Shakespeare Reproduced: The Text in History and Ideology*, London: Methuen.

Hulme, Peter (1981), 'Hurricanes in the Caribees: The Constitution of the Discourse of English Colonialism', in Francis Barker et al., (eds.), *1642: Literature and Power in the Seventeenth Century* (Proceedings of the Essex Conference on the Sociology of Literature, July 1980), University of Essex, 55–83.

Hulme, Peter (1986), *'Colonial Encounters': Europe and the Native Caribbean, 1492–1797*, London: Methuen.

Hunt, John S. (1994), 'Prospero's Empty Grasp', *Shakespeare Studies*, Leeds Barroll, (ed.), 22, 277–313.

James, D.G. (1967), *The Dream of Prospero*, Oxford: Clarendon Press.

Jordan, Constance (1997), *Shakespeare's Monarchies: Ruler and Subject in the Romances*, Ithaca: Cornell University Press.

Jorgensen, Paul, A. (1986), 'Shakespeare's Brave New World', in Chiappelli, Vol. I.

Kastan, David Scott (1988), 'Review: Shakespeare in History', *College English*, 50 (6), 694–699, October.

Kermode, Frank, ed. (1958), *The Tempest* 'The Arden Edition of the Works of William Shakespeare', 6th edn, London: Methuen, reprinted 1977.

Knudson, Roslyn L. (1994), 'A Caliban in St. Mildred Poultry' in *Shakespeare and Cultural Traditions: The Selected Proceedings of the International Shakespeare Association World Congress, Tokyo, 1991*, Tetsuo Kishi, Roger Pringle and Stanley Wells (eds.), Newark: University of Delaware Press, 110–126.

Kott, Jan. (1967), *Shakespeare Our Contemporary*, 2nd edn, London: Methuen.

——— (1977), '*The Tempest*, or Repetition', *Mosaic*, X, 9–36.

Knight, G. Wilson (1980), 'Caliban as a Red Man', in Philip Edwards, Igna-Stina Ewbank, and G.K. Hunter, (eds.), *Shakespeare's Styles: Essays in Honour of Kenneth Muir*, Cambridge University Press; reprinted in G. Wilson Knight, *Shakespearean Dimensions*, Sussex, U.K.: Harvester Press, 1984.

Kuhl, E.P. (1962), 'Shakespeare and the Foundations of America: Topical *The Tempest*', *Philological Quarterly*, 41, (1), 123–146, January.

Lee, Sidney (1907), '*The Call of the West: America and Elizabethan England*', Part 3: 'The American Indian in Elizabethan England', *Scribner's Magazine*, 42, 313–30.

Levin, Harry (1976), *Shakespeare and the Revolution of the Times*, Oxford: Oxford University Press.

Loomba, Ania (1989), *Gender, Race, Renaissance Drama*, Manchester: Manchester University Press.

Malone, Edmond (1808), *An Account of the Incidents, from Which the Title and Part of the Story of Shakespeare's Tempest Were Derived; and Its True Date Ascertained*, London: C.&R. Baldwin.

Mannoni, O. (1964), *Prospero and Caliban: The Psychology of Colonization*, 2nd edn, Pamela Powesland, (trans.) New York: Praeger.

Marcus, Leah S. (1988), *Puzzling Shakespeare: Local Reading and Its Discontents*, Berkeley: University of California Press, 1988.

Marx, Leo. (1960), 'Shakespeare's American Fable', *The Massachusettes Review*, II, , 40–71.

Masaki, Tsuneo. (1960), 'Shakespeare's *Use* of the New World in *The Tempest*', *Studies in English Literature*, (Japan) English number, 3–13.

McDonald, Russ (1991), 'Reading *The Tempest*', *Shakespeare* Survey, 43, 15–28.

Mucciolo, John M. (1993), 'Shakespeare's *The Tempest* and Jacobean Political Contexts', *DAI* 54, 101, 182, July, New York: City University of New York.

Nixon, Rob. (1987), 'Caribbean and African Appropriations of *The Tempest*', *Critical Inquiry*, 13, (3), 557–578, Spring.

Norbrook, David (1992), ' "What Cares these Roarers for the Name of King?" Language and Utopia in *The Tempest*', in Gordon McMullan and Jonathan Hope, eds, *The Politics of Tragicomedy: Shakespeare and After*, New York: Routledge, 21–54.

Nuzumi, David, G. (1959), 'The London Company and *The Tempest*', *West Virginia Philological Papers*, XII, 12–23.

Orgel, Stephen (1985), 'Prospero's Wife', *Representations*, 8 1–13.

—— (ed.) (1987), Shakespeare's *The Tempest*, New York: Oxford University Press.

—— (1987), 'Shakespeare and the Cannibals' in *Cannibals, Witches, and Divorce: Estranging the Renaissance*, Marjorie Garber, (ed.) (Selected Papers from the English Institute, 1985) New Series, no. 11, Baltimore: The Johns Hopkins University Press.

Pagden, Anthony (1993), *European Encounters with the New World*, New Haven: Yale University Press.

Patterson, Annabel (1984), *Censorship and Interpretation: The Conditions of Writing and Reading in Early Modern England*, Madison: University of Wisconsin Press.

Pechter, Edward (1987), 'The New Historicism and Its Discontents: Politicizing Renaissance Drama', *Pub. Modern Languages Assoc.*, CII, 3, May, 292–303.

Peterson, Dale, and Jane Goodall (1993), *Visions of Caliban: On Chimpanzees and People*, Boston: Houghton Mifflin.

Pinciss, G.M. (1979), 'The Savage Man in Spenser, Shakespeare and Renaissance English Drama', in G.R. Hibbard, (ed.), *The Elizabethan Theatre*

VIII, Papers Given at the English International Conference on Eliza-bethan Theatre . . . 1979, Port Credit, Ontario: P.D. Meany.

Porter, H.C. (1979), *The Inconstant Savage: England and the North American Indian, 1500–1660*, London: Gerald Duckworth.

Retamar, Roberto Fernandez (1974), 'Caliban: Notes toward a Discussion of Culture in Our America', *The Massachusettes Review*, XV, 11–16.

Rawson, Claude (1997), 'The Horror, the holy horror,' *TLS* October 31, 1997: 3–4.

Rowse, A.L. (1959), *The Elizabethans and America*, London: Macmillan.

Schmidgall, Gary (1981), *Shakespeare and the Courtly Aesthetic*, Berkeley: University of California Press.

Schneider, Ben Ross, Jr. (1994), '"Are We Being Historical Yet?": Colonialist Interpretations of Shakespeare's *Tempest*', *Shakespeare Studies*, Leeds Barroll, (ed.), Vol. XXIII, Madison: Fairleigh Dickinson University Press, 120–145.

Siegel, Paul N. (1983), 'Historical Ironies in "The Tempest"', *The Shakespeare Jahrbuch*, CXIX, 104–111.

Sharp, Corona (1981), 'Caliban: The Primitive Man's Evolution, *Shakespeare Studies*, XIV, 267–283.

Sheehan, Bernard (1980), *Savagism and Civility: Indians and Englishmen in Colonial Virginia*, Cambridge University Press.

Spreaight, Robert (1970), 'Shakespeare in Britain' in *Shakespeare Quarterly*, **XXI**, (4), 439–49, Autumn.

Stoll, Elmer Edgar (1927), 'Certain Fallacies and Irrelevancies in the Literary Scholarship of the Day', *Studies in Philology*, XXIV, 486–87.

Takaki, Ronald (1992), '*The Tempest* in the Wilderness: The Radicalization of Savagery', *Journal of American History*, 79, 892–912.

Taylor, Gary (1988), *Reinventing Shakespeare: A cultural history from the Restoration to the Present*, London: Hogarth.

Vaughan, Alden, T. and Virginia Mason Vaughan (1991), *Shakespeare's Caliban: A Cultural History*, New York: Cambridge University Press.

Vickers, Brian (1993), *Appropriating Shakespeare: Contemporary Critical Quarrels*, New Haven: Yale University Press.

———— (1988), 'Bard-watching', *TLS* 26 August–1 September, 933–935.

Walsh, Martin W. (1993), '"Get a new Man": Caliban's Song and Autumnal Hiring Customs', *CahiersE* 43, 57–60.

Zeeveld, W. Gordon (1974), *The Temper of Shakespeare's Thought*, New Haven, Conn.: Yale University Press.

20   *Twelfth Night*

Elizabeth S. Donno

Twelfth Night (performed 1602, together with *Much Ado About Nothing* (1599) and *As You Like It* (1600) were in the mid-1920s frequently linked together under the rubric of Shakespeare's 'joyous' or 'festive' comedies. Of the latest of the three, *Twelfth Night*, in particular, has been described as 'bittersweet', in anticipation, it seems, of Shakespeare's techniques in the three plays that were to follow, once called 'problem comedies' because of the intrusion of 'dark' and enigmatic elements into plays with happy endings.[1]

Though criticism of the last fifteen years, which is what this short essay focuses on, has largely been directed to such elements, it is noteworthy that in his 1709 Preface the first critical editor of Shakespeare's plays, Nicholas Rowe, acknowledged that *Twelfth Night* should be called a 'tragicomedy'. This in despite of the fact that the play, as its title is intended to recall, is keyed to a saturnalian holiday represented by Sir Toby Belch, Sir Andrew Aguecheek – the would-be wooer of the Lady Olivia – and the clown Feste who wears his motley, one critic observed long ago, as a 'badge of knowledge'.[2]

Yet on the basis of three seventeenth-century allusions, it is the strait-laced steward Malvolio who was best remembered. These include that of the barrister John Manningham, who having seen a performance at the Middle Temple in 1602 comments in his *Diary* on the 'good practice' of its author's prescribing his smiling and his garb in the wooing of Olivia; secondly, the fact that King Charles in his copy of the Folio wrote Malvolio against the title, the play having been performed under that title in 1621, and, thirdly, that Leonard Digges, who, having written a commendatory poem for the First Folio, also provided verses for the 1640 edition of the *Poems* in which he signalled out for comment on *Twelfth Night* the 'cross-gartered gull' Malvolio.

The appeal of the comic scenes continued in the eighteenth century, evidenced according to Lois Potter, by the use of John Bull's popular edition for performances both at Drury Lane and Convent Garden,[3] while a survey of performances from 1791 to 1883 reveals the urge to retain a festive mood through the interpolation of a speech for Orsino pardoning the 'notorious pirate' and 'salt-water thief' Antonio.[4] With the nineteenth century, producers turned to elaborate spectacles and musical insertions, one such production, for example, at Convent Garden in 1820 offering no fewer than fifteen songs, the words drawn from Shakespeare's texts with Feste's last song serving as the finale. By the last quarter of the century there came a radical shift from the comic emphasis on the projection of Malvolio to his pitiable, even tragical, ending; this was highlighted by Henry Irving in 1884 and was followed in America by E.H. Sothern who imbued the character with a 'pitiful and comic dignity', that, according to one of his reviewers, indeed offered a novel interpretation of the character.[5]

A volume out of Manchester, part of its 'Cultural Politics' series avowedly attempting to transform the social order in terms of race, gender, and class, is called *The Shakespeare Myth*. It is, as the above aims suggest, a somewhat mixed bag of goods. There is the to-be-expected piece of Ann Thompson on feminism; a second, too clever by half, by Simon Shepherd plays on a variety of spellings of the dramatist's name – Shackspaire, Shagspair, Shackespiere – and concludes that the Renaissance distinguished homosexuality from friendship or 'disinterested love'.[6]

In 1996 another collection of essays on *Twelfth Night*, all but one previously published, purports to ascertain how the 'new' critical theories have changed the interpretation of a text and its author. The point of Geoffrey Hartman's 'Shakespeare's Poetical Character in *Twelfth Night*' seems to be that the 'dramatic and linguistic action' is to turn away the 'evil eye', equated here with the malevolent interpretation that Malvolio presents. The following piece, Elliot Krieger's '*Twelfth Night*: The Morality of Indulgence', with a patent Marxist bias, asserts that Malvolio's fantasy is to 'jump' class while Maria's and Feste' manipulation of him demonstrates the implicit limitations of the ruling-class attitude that 'all is fortune'. The third essay, Michael Bristol's 'Shakespeare's Festive Agon: the Politics of Carnival' briefly discusses theatre as a social institution, consequently creating the possibilities for social action and initiative. A reprint of Stephen Greenblatt's 'Fiction and Friction,' is largely a recounting of medical doctrines, but in the pages devoted to *Twelfth Night* he finds that the centre of the play exemplifies 'erotic chafing'; since this could not be presented on the stage, Shakespeare employed 'witty, erotic sparring' to present it figuratively. Two pages later, he explains: 'Dallying with words is the principal Shakespeare representation of erotic heat; hence his plots go out of their way to create not only obstacles in the lovers' path but occasions for friction between them'. Edging over from the social–political into the matter of gender, Dympna Callahan historicizes the play by discussing contemporary ideas about transvestism and sexuality: 'And all is semblative a woman's part: Body Politics in *Twelfth Night*'. She finds that the play serves for the 'maintenance and reproduction of patriarchy' and that class transvestism proves more threatening than gender, while Christine

Malcolmson concludes in 'What You Will: Social Mobility and Gender in 'Twelfth Night' that the play links gender and status to make marriage the model of all social bonds.[7]

In a blending of social–political and gender approaches, Lisa Jardine asserts that in the Renaissance household, male and female youths were expected to 'submit' to those above them; as a desired dependent of Orsino, Viola-Cesario would thus have been available for his sexual pleasure, with such potential service, she observes, being contained within the admissible boundaries of the patriarchal household.[8]

In this same vein, Lorna Hutson, while acknowledging that Shakespeare's texts have helped to construct the moral characteristics appropriate to a biology of sexual difference, declares that discussions of the subversive erotics 'trivialize' the economic and social stakes in Twelfth Night.[9]

Extending the issues of gender and disguise into the social realm, Susie Campbell finds the central question of Twelfth Night to be 'What is proper masculinity?' Her conclusion is that if all behaviour is an act, then gender becomes part of the performance.[10]

In contrast to Jardine's somewhat tentative explanation above, Stevie Davies believes that the homoerotic resonances – pederastic and sapphic – would have been understood by the auditors and that that design was intended to appeal to the 'latent homosexual or bisexual in each member of the audience'; this suffusion of sexuality becomes permissible and licit, however, because confined to the realm of the imagination. In commenting on the differences between the Elizabethan stage and that of today, she also notes that the transvestism (a boy actor playing a girl playing a boy) would have been nearer to a pederastic dream than modern convention allows.[11] Apropos of this chronological difference, Lois Potter pertinently observes of the stage action when Maria says to Sir Andrew 'bring your hand to th' buttery bar' and places his hand on her breast as in many productions, that had the original boy actor done this, it would have been a different kind of joke.[12]

Focusing only on the Viola-Cesario character, David Schalwyk in 'She never told her love: Embodiment, Textuality in Shakespeare's Sonnets and Plays' concludes (not surprisingly) that in the allowed relationship with Orsino, Viola remains embodied in all senses as 'Orsino's mistress and his fancy's queen'.[13]

Equally not surprising is that in many of the current discussions of the play the greatest emphasis has been placed on its resolution, with variant responses to its dramatic effect. Earlier mention was made of the late nineteenth-century interpretation introduced by Henry Irving with its projection of Malvolio as a pitiful, if not victimized, figure. This has been picked up in two essays published in 1990: Cedric Watts in 'The Problem of Malvolio' describes his humiliation as 'severe and protracted', while Bill Alexander in 'Why we shall make him mad in deed', terms it monstrously unfair.[14] Roger Warren and Stanley Wells, on the other hand, assign the 'potential heartbreak' to Act III, Scene iv, when Sir Toby, Fabian, and Maria bait Malvolio as if he were possessed, and Fabian observes, 'Why, we shall make him mad indeed'. The editors later comment that even in a 'quasi-tragic reading' Malvolio is not mad, adding that if Malvolio has a tragedy, 'it is that he remains irremediably sane'.[15]

Attempting to ascertain the 'when' of spectators' response, Ralph Berry determines that the 'unease' begins in III.iv, where Malvolio makes his prescribed appearance in yellow stockings and broadly smiling: here the activities of Sir Toby, Fabian, and Maria begin to look like 'open sadism'. By the time of the cell scene (IV.ii), 'the audience is now conscious that the affair is much less funny than it was', observing parenthetically that 'one cannot point to a precise moment in Act III or even IV when the audience becomes aware of its own queasiness; yet, he affirms, 'it must surely happen'.[16]

On the other hand, in the same issue of *Shakespeare Survey*, Karen Greif concludes that 'Malvolio remains isolated and egotistical to the end'. What is more, 'the mockers' – Sir Toby, Maria, and Fabian – 'are no more altered by the experience than he is'. She also observes that 'fittingly' they are absent from the recognition scene and that Shakespeare shrugs off any would-be illumination with 'delightful finesse'.[17]

While the range of interpretation of Malvolio's treatment in the action of the play has been as varied (and as extreme) as its chronological limits – from an object of sport to a victimized creature of the ruling class – the resolution has also been variably interpreted. This is perhaps surprising for a play once deemed as 'festive' or 'joyous,' an alteration of interpretation perhaps stemming from the recent emphasis on the socio-political and gender approaches rather than on the play's esthetic and dramatic merits. An ironic point made as long ago as 1962 (by John Dover Wilson and recalled by Herschel Baker three years later) generally overlooked by readers and spectators alike is that Shakespeare makes Olivia plight her troth with Viola's twin in the very chantry that she has erected to the memory of her brother (IV.iii.22 ff).[18]

Two essays, both originally published in 1972, offer a somewhat more malleable view of the conclusion. Anne Barton in '*As You Like It* and *Twelfth Night*: Shakespeare's Sense of an Ending'[19] observes that Sir Andrew vanishes and Sir Toby leaves the stage but that the four main characters have no need to leave Illyria, though their pairing off is 'perfunctory'. It is Feste as mediator among all the characters who keeps us – spectators and readers – aware of the realities of life and death. R.A. Foakes more or less leaves the concluding mood up to the director and actor, noting that because of his lack of humour, solemnity, and hostile response to festivity, Malvolio can be seen as a scapegoat: his expulsion either enhancing the joy of the ending or as being punished beyond his deserts. Feste's song can then provide a long perspective.[19]

Stevie Davies also admits to a director's latitude in handling the minor Antonio–Sebastian action; some directors integrate the silent Antonio with the joyous patrician lovers with 'darker readings' suggesting exclusion and alienation.[20]

The reliance on the impact of Feste's song to 'shrug off' would-be ambiguities if the resolution is followed by a number of the commentators – Belsey, Greif, and Dickey. Ralph Berry, on the other hand, who holds that Sir Toby's actions are sadistic and that Feste's reveal a 'sustained animosity', 'surmises' that the ultimate effect of Malvolio's last entrance and exit is to make the audience 'ashamed' of itself.[21] Here Feste's song apparently offers no palliative or perspective.

Catherine Belsey in an essay accompanying the 'New Folger Library Shakespeare' posits that Viola represents the figure of 'desire' which in the other characters keep moving – from Olivia to Cesario and on to Sebastian; from Orsino to Olivia and then on to Viola. If there is a 'fixed place' in Act V, she concludes, it is only that the play must end and in comedies traditionally it ends in marriage.[22]

Stephen Dickey in 'Shakespeare's Mastiff Comedy' finds that the ending is a 'stalemate', with the characters testing their pleasures against their pains only to find them indistinguishable.[23] Joost Dalder, taking somewhat the same view in 'Perspectives of Madness in *Twelfth Night*', feels that while Malvolio's self-absorption provides something of a tragic note and that his exit should be seen as fitting in with Feste's final song about painful realities; 'the comedy', i.e. Shakespeare the dramatist, 'deliberately does not resolve these into harmony'.[24]

In her comment on the ending, Stevie Davis blends the social–political with gender emphasis by noting 'not only does Jack get his Jill but Jack shall have his 'Jack' and (in the marriage of Olivia with Viola's double) Jill her '"Jill" under cover of social orthodoxy'.[25]

In an extreme reversal of 'joyous' or 'festive', Bill Alexander concludes that the play presents a 'bleak picture' of the human condition, the characters being shallow, foolish, and capable of extreme cruelty: as for any resolution, they have gone nowhere – it is a 'full circle' to where the action began.[26]

In a brief but wide-ranging survey of gender in the period, Stephen Orgel explores the significance of the employing of boys to enact female roles in the drama. His thesis in respect to *Twelfth Night* is that 'clothes make the woman, clothes make the man: the costume is of the essence'. He finds proof of this in the 'flummery of the conclusion': the impossibility of proceeding with the marriage of Orsino and Viola (and therefore the impossibility of concluding the plot) until Viola's clothes have been found declares in the clearest possible way that, whatever Viola says about the erotic realities of her inner life, she is not a woman unless she is dressed as one.[27]

As indicated above, a number of commentators rely on Feste's final song to supplement the resolution, or, sometimes, the irresolution, of the play. In the words of Anne Barton, his song restores the audience (or reader) to a bridge between the 'golden world' and the 'age of iron,' or what R.A. Foakes, as cited earlier, terms 'a long perspective.'[28] Thad Jenkins Logan, on the other hand, accepts Feste's final song as a synecdoche for society, protecting the privileged within, citing the buffeting of the wind and the rain as the fortune that the unprotected experience.[29] Describing love in *Twelfth Night* as by turns lyrical, sad, and ridiculous, and as elusive as the crossed-dress protagonist, Catherine Belsey questions the meaning in the Fool's concluding song, 'Is it more or less real than the realm of desire identified as Illyria?'[30]

What is the predominant characteristic of these twenty-odd pieces written, in general, over the last fifteen years? I suppose that the most apt term would be 'tendentious' because of their deriving, or imposing, ideological concepts from or on to the text. The scant concern evidenced of its artistic or dramatic elements indicates either that these have received sufficient earlier discussion or that other factors have more current appeal. A reader may well take to heart Feste's view (III.i) that an opinion or a judgement is only a 'cheveril glove to a good wit – how quickly the wrong side may be turned outward!'

REFERENCES

1. The term 'problem comedies' has been reintroduced by Jean-Pierre Maquerlot in a volume published in 1997, *Shakespeare and the Mannerist Tradition* (CUP); to this group he also adds *Hamlet* and *Julius Caesar*.
2. Herschel Baker in his edition for the Signet Classic Shakespeare (c. 1965; later editions in 1977 and 1987), p.xxx.
3. Lois Potter (1985), *Twelfth Night*. Text and Performance', 37.
4. Laurie E. Osborne (1994), 'Antonio's Pardon', *Shakespeare Quarterly*, 45, 108–114.
5. For instances of the variant ways in which producers (and actors) have handled the text, see my edition, Cambridge University Press (1985), 26–40.
6. Graham Holderness (Ed.) (1988), *The Shakespear Myth*, Manchester University Press.
7. *New Casebooks*, (1996) R.S. White, (ed.) St. Martin's Press. The quotation from Greenblatt appears on p. 90 of his *Shakespeare Negotiations*, University of California Press, 1988.
8. Jardine, Lisa (1992), 'Twins and Travesties: Gender dependency and sexual availability in *Twelfth Night* in *Erotic Politics: Desire on the Renaissance Stage*, Susan Zimmerman (ed.), 27–38.
9. Hutson, Lorna (1996), 'On Not Being Deceived: Rhetoric and the Body in *Twelfth Night*, *Texas Studies on Literature and Language*, 38 (2), Summer, 140–174. She also fancifully remarks that 'the drunken and inept or irresponsible Toby and Aguecheek ... are finally banished ... beyond Olivia's gates' (163). Fanciful, indeed, since on seeing Sir Toby, Olivia simply says, 'Get him to bed and let his hurt be looked to'.
10. Campbell, Susie (1990), 'The knave counterfeits well: a good knave': gender

and disguise in *Twelfth Night*', *Critical Essays on Twelfth Night*, Linda Cookson, Bryan Loughey (ed.), Longman Literature Guides, 62–81.

11. Davies, Stevie (1993), *Twelfth Night, Penguin Critical Studies*, 10.
12. Potter, 64.
13. Schalwyk, David (1994), *Shakespeare Quarterly* 45, 381–407, Winter.
14. Watte, Cedric (1990), 'The Problem of Malvolio', and Alexander, Bill (1990), 'Why we shall make him mad indeed', *Critical Essays on Twelfth Night*, 19; 84; cited in n. 10.
15. *Twelfth Night or What You Will*, Roger Warren and Stanley Wells (eds), 59.
16. Berry, Ralph (1981), '*Twelfth Night*': The Experience of the Audience', *Shakespeare Survey* 34, 111–119.
17. Greif, Karen (1981), 'Plays and Playing in *Twelfth Night*, 34, 121–130.
18. Citing Wilson, John Dover (1962), *Shakespeare's Happy Comedies*, 19. *Stratford Upon Avon Studies*, (1972) (121–141). 18.
19. Barton, Anne (1986), 'Shakespeare's Sense of an Ending in *Twelfth Night; Critical Essays*, Stanley Wells, (ed.), 160–180, reprinted from *Shakespeare Comedy*, Stratford upon Avon Studies 14 (1972); Foakes, 'The Owl and the Cuckoo: Voices of Maturity in Shakespeare Comedy,' *Stratford upon Avon Studies*, 1972 (121–141).
20. Ed. *Twelfth Night, Penguin Critical Studies*, 1993.
21. '*Twelfth Night*': The Experience of the Audience', *Shakespeare Survey*, 34 (1981), 111–119.
22. '*Twelfth Night: A Modern Perspective*', (1993), 197–207.
23. 'Shakespeare's Mastiff Comedy', *Shakespeare Quarterly*, 42 (3), 255–275, Fall 1991.
24. Dalder, Joost (1997), *English Studies*, 78, March, 105–110.
25. Davies, Stevie (1993), *Twelfth Night, Penguin Critical Studies*, 32.
26. Alexander, cited in n. 14, 97, 98.
27. *Impersonations: The Performance of Gender in Shakespeare's England*, Cambridge University Press (1996), 104.
28. Barton, 310; Foakes, 139; See n. 19.
29. '*Twelfth Night*': the Limits of Festivity', *Studies in English Literature*, 22 (1982), 163.
30. '*Twelfth Night*': *A Modern Perspective*, 206.

Appendix 1
Kenneth Muir (1907–96):
An appreciation

Philip Edwards

I first met Kenneth Muir in the late 1940s at one of the early Shakespeare Conferences at Stratford-upon-Avon. These conferences had been started by Allardyce Nicoll as part of his bold programme when he came to the University of Birmingham in 1945 to found a Shakespeare centre at Stratford, together with a new journal and an annual international conference. The Shakespeare Institute, *Shakespeare Survey*, and the Conference (now biennial) were all set up within three years. To begin with, the Conference was a small, almost family, affair, and Kenneth was one of the first of the younger generation to be invited to join the senior founding members. I was acting as Secretary, and I well remember – after 50 years – an afternoon discussion in which someone (it might have been Una Ellis-Fermor) wanted to cite a line from Sonnet 94 ('They that have power to hurt and will do none'). But she couldn't immediately get the right phrase. 'How *does* it go?' she asked. Without warning or hesitation, Kenneth recited the entire sonnet from memory. He had a wonderful voice, and spoke poetry beautifully. At that time, the late 1940s, he was a lecturer in English at the University of Leeds, and high among his many activities was acting in plays of Shakespeare which he himself directed. He played Gloucester to Wilson Knight's Lear. Many years later, when he retired from Liverpool, his colleagues staged *The Tempest* in his honour and gave him the part of Prospero which he rendered *con amore*.

Kenneth was born in London in 1907, the son of a doctor who died when Kenneth was seven. He was educated, on a free place, at Epsom College (a boarding school), and although he was not much in sympathy with the school's outlook, and later wrote to the Headmaster: 'I am one of your failures', he became a prefect and won numerous prizes. He abandoned his medical studies in London and read English at Oxford (St Edmund Hall). He blamed his lack of interest in the linguistic approach to

Old English for his not getting a First. In 1931 Kenneth was appointed to a lectureship at St John's College, York, largely on the strength of a recommendation from the Poet Laureate, John Masefield, who, mistaking him for another Muir, had given him a leading part in *The Comedy of Errors*. He was sacked on three separate occasions for opposing compulsory chapel and being too familiar with the students, but on each occasion was reinstated by the governors, whose chairman, the Archbishop of York, William Temple, was on his side (he thought) because he liked the Shakespeare productions which Kenneth had been doing for the York settlement.

Kenneth's first volume of poems, *The Nettle and the Flower*, came out in 1933,[1] followed by *Jonah and the Whale* in 1935.[2] In 1937 *The Voyage to Illyria: a New Study of Shakespeare*,[3] written in collaboration with Sean O'Loughlin, was published. This was the year he was appointed at Leeds, and Kenneth claimed that one of the reasons for his appointment was that *The Voyage to Illyria* had not yet appeared. What is interesting about the book is its close attention to Shakespeare's imagery, and its sensitivity to the inter-relationship between passages of verse in different plays. Otherwise it is a conventional book, Dowdenesque in its determination to infer the developing inner life of the author from the sequence of plays and poems. The supposed breach with Southampton, the youth of the Sonnets, is regarded as the source of the bitterness about treachery and betrayal in the tragedies.

In a checklist of his writings which Kenneth submitted for *Shakespeare's Styles*, a book of essays in his honour edited by Inga-Stina Ewbank, George Hunter and myself, published in 1980,[4] Kenneth said that he was omitting verse and fiction, as well as 'articles on educational topics, articles on politics, pseudonymous and anonymous articles'. He had contributed 'hundreds of articles' (his own words) to the *Leeds Weekly Citizen* in his years in the city, a great many of them under various pseudonyms and a great many of them political. His political engagement was not confined to articles in the press. He was a very active member of the Labour Party and the Fabian Society, and served as a Labour member of Leeds City Council. In those years he found a convenient outlet for literary comment in *Proceedings of the Leeds Philosophical and Literary Society*, which was generous with offprints. Some quite important Shakespeare essays – one called 'The Future of Shakespeare' – were written for *Penguin New Writing*[5] at the invitation of the editor, John Lehmann. But his major work of the Leeds years was the Muses Library edition of the *Collected Poems of Sir Thomas Wyatt*,[6] published in 1949. We think of Kenneth Muir as a Shakespearean, but his publications ranged widely and Wyatt was one of the many authors who engaged him deeply. When he was acting as External Examiner in Trinity College, Dublin, in the late Fifties he came across the Blage manuscript, and he brought out *Unpublished Poems*,[7] by Wyatt and his circle, in 1961. Wyatt's *Life and Letters*[8] followed in 1963, and a revised *Collected Poems*, in collaboration with Patricia Thomson, in 1969.

Kenneth had married Mary Ewen in 1936. She died in 1975; Kenneth was a widower for over twenty years. They had two children: Katherine, who was born in 1943 and who died of leukemia (as her mother had done) in 1981, and David, born in 1951. In that year the family moved to Birkenhead, on Kenneth's appointment as King Alfred Professor of English Literature at Liverpool University, the post in which he remained until his retirement twenty-three years later. In those years Kenneth built up one of the best English Departments in the country. He had a talent for discerning talent. In the Shakespeare field, he saw the potential of young scholars such as Inga-Stina Ewbank, Ernest Schanzer, G.K. Hunter and Ann Thompson and in other areas Kenneth and Miriam Allott, Hermione Lee, Brian Nellist and many others.

The 1960s were the years of diversification and expansion in universities in England. Departments grew in size, centres for this and that were set up, second, third and fourth chairs were established. In particular, the convention of the patriarch-professor as head of his (not her) department until he retired gave way to chairmen serving a limited term of years. Not in the Department of English Literature at Liverpool. The Department remained compact, and it remained under Kenneth's benevolent control. And it remained traditional in its syllabus, declining to branch out into the new areas and new schemes being developed elsewhere. What Kenneth maintained and developed were standards of teaching and scholarship. G. K. Hunter, who was a colleague of his as I was not, wrote in an obituary for The Times:[9] 'At Liverpool he was able to show to the full his talents as chairman, administrator and collaborative scholar, clear in what he demanded of himself and of others, but unsurprised by challenge and compromise. He was 'a model of industry and fair-mindedness to all his younger colleagues, a commanding figure, but a fiercely egalitarian one'.

After the war, Methuen the publishers had given Una Ellis-Fermor the task of organising a completely new Arden Shakespeare, and, before his Liverpool appointment, Kenneth accepted the invitation to undertake both King Lear and Macbeth. It is characteristic of him that his editions of these plays should be the first volumes to appear in that famous series. They made his name. They were constantly reprinted, and remained standard texts for decades. He was commissioned to write a 'retrospect' of Shakespeare criticism from 1900 to 1950 for Shakespeare Survey 4 (1951), and the mammoth essay which he submitted, 15,000 words, is a good indication of the breadth of his reading and the quality of his judgement, tolerant common-sense being more apparent than hard-edged ideology. My own links with Kenneth in the early Fifties were partly in connection with a summer school on Shakespeare at Stratford-upon-Avon (for the University of Birmingham) that I directed for a time. Kenneth lectured at that summer school for many years. (He enjoyed the opportunity of the theatre visits as much as anything.) When I was in charge or was a fellow-lecturer we were at close quarters for weeks at a time. He was always an equable and easy-going companion, but he was reserved and had little small talk. I was sixteen years younger, but he wanted me to tell him why a joke in a lecture had failed to get across. He listened carefully to my embarrassed suggestion that it needed a rather different projection, and, to my astonishment, he put the joke back into his next day's lecture. I don't remember its succeeeding any better. I learned a great deal from him in those Stratford summers. I had been working on *Pericles*, and he was at that time much interested in Shakespeare's collaborative plays (resulting in *Shakespeare as Collaborator* in 1960).[10] We had long arguments about George Wilkins without much agreement. We were also both working on books in a little series being run by Longmans. He wrote on Milton, I on Ralegh. Kenneth showed more respect for my early work than it deserved, and he backed me strongly in a number of important applications But I remember being a little dashed when I gave him a lecture I had written on *Julius Caesar* which I thought broke new ground. He was a very fast reader, and he handed it back to me after a few minutes. 'I concur,' he said, and that was that.

What was intended to be the first part of a two volume work, *Shakespeare's Sources: Comedies and Tragedies*, appeared in 1957.[11] But the first instalment of Geoffrey Bullough's monumental collection of the texts of Shakespeare's sources was published in the same year, and Kenneth turned to other things. In 1977, however, he brought out a one-volume *Sources of Shakespeare's Plays*,[12] revising his earlier volume and adding material on the remaining plays. Kenneth's work on the sources is a complement to Bullough's, and I think it shows his critical methods at their best. The plays come alive as he shows us Shakespeare creating them from the materials at hand.

Kenneth's interest in European drama centred on the work of Racine, Calderón, and Ibsen. He spent a great amount of time on his translations of the first two. His *Five Plays of Racine* appeared in 1960.[13] He could be rather fierce about the merits of rival translators. In his later years he worked in collaboration with Ann Mackenzie on his translations of Calderón. He freely admitted his French was better than his Spanish: he complained to me once that at a Calderón conference in Canada the proceedings were in Spanish. He was content that the task of bringing out new translations of Ibsen should be in the hands of his friend Inga-Stina Ewbank, whose work he greatly admired. But he wrote on Ibsen in *Last Periods of Shakespeare, Racine and Ibsen* in 1961.[14]

In 1965 Kenneth became the editor of *Shakespeare Survey*. Allardyce Nicoll had been editor since he founded the annual journal, the first issue appearing in 1948. Given the close link between *Survey* and the Shakespeare Conference, it would have been desirable, other things being equal, to continue the editing from the Shakespeare Institute at Stratford, but T.J.B. Spencer, Nicoll's successor, was not available because of his commitment to *Modern Language Review*, and the Advisory Board preferred the man to the place. Kenneth edited *Survey* for fifteen years, and this is the period of his dominance in the English academic scene and the international Shakespeare scene. As regards the former, he was continuously in demand as External Examiner up and down the country, and served as assessor or member of the appointing committee for university chairs almost whenever they came up. He had great influence but he was not a kingmaker in the manner of some, ensuring professorships for their own nominees. He was elected as a Fellow of the British Academy in 1970. As regards the world of Shakespeare, he became the first chairman of the International Shakespeare Association in 1976 and presided over more than one of the triennial Conferences. He cemented his friendships with Shakespearians all over the world at the Shakespeare Conferences, and of course was invited to lecture in a great many countries.

Since, as well as all this, Kenneth was active in administration at Liverpool – as Public Orator, Dean of the Arts Faculty, Chairman of the Library Committee and so on – it is astounding that he kept up his prodigious output of books, editions and articles. There were editions of *Richard II* in the Signet series (1963)[15] and of *Othello* for the Penguin New Shakespeare (1968);[16] both of these very widely used by students throughout the world. He collaborated with Michael Allen in the major facsimile edition of Shakespeare's Quartos in 1981.[17] Outside Shakespeare there was his book on Restoration comedy in 1970[18] and an edition of Middleton in 1975.[19]

I have not said enough about Kenneth's interest in the Romantics. I cannot now find, alas, the typescript of a radio play he wrote for the BBC about Wordsworth, broadcast in the early Fifties. He knew his Blake intimately and collected the very expensive Trianon Press reproductions of the prophetic books. He edited a book of essays on Keats in 1958.[20] On his retirement from Liverpool, Bernard Beatty and R.T. Davies dedicated to him a book of essays by colleagues in his department, *Literature of the Romantic Period 1750–1850*.[21] The conclusion of the preface runs as follows.

> The inspiration behind this volume is Kenneth Muir, one of whose particular interests is the literature of the Romantic period. Our enterprise will be more than justly rewarded if this volume succeeds in taking its place among the writings of a period to which Kenneth Muir has himself contributed with such distinction.

Many of Kenneth's publications were undertaken in response to invitations or commissions from publishers or series-editors. In his eighties he began to complain that such invitations were drying up. He started on his autobiography in compensation. But he never stopped writing. Invitations to contribute to a volume of essays or to a Festschrift kept coming and so did invitations to lecture. And there was always Calderón.

In his final years he was less mobile, and as he had never owned or driven a car he became more dependent on others to travel about, especially to the theatre. But he was remarkably healthy. He distrusted doctors and attributed the ailments of others to hanging about in doctors' waiting rooms. He was once knocked down in the road near his house and amazed us by being out of hospital and on his feet again in a matter of days. In the summer of 1996 my wife and I arranged that we should as usual pick him up in Birkenhead on our way south from Cumbria to the Shakespeare Conference at Stratford. At the age of 89, he was once more due to give a paper, this time on Shakespeare's verse. I telephoned him a day or two beforehand, and was shocked to find his voice so faint and distorted as to be scarcely audible. I thought he must have had a stroke and assumed he would not be going to the Conference. Had he seen a doctor? He brushed this aside. Of course he was going. Would I please read his paper for him? When we reached Birkenhead we thought he was far too ill to travel, but we got him to Stratford, and to his hotel – and he had a triumphant week, attending the lectures and going to the theatre, delighted to meet his friends though he could scarcely converse with them.

Back in Birkenhead, he was in hospital within a week, with bronchial pneumonia and the possibility of cancer. I visited him twice. I knew he was not an easy patient, and I was relieved that his list of complaints was short. He didn't like the nurses calling him Ken. The second time my wife was with me. He was asleep, but when he woke he recognised us both immediately and smiled. Then, quite cheerfully, he said, 'I'm dying.' He was quite extraordinarily content, and had a good word for everyone, especially the nurses. It was not always easy to follow what he was saying. There was something on his mind; an occasion forty years or more earlier when he felt that of two candidates for a post he had made the wrong choice and done someone an injustice. He couldn't get the names but I knew whom he was talking about. It was moving that this should be worrying him now. Apart from that, he was serenity itself. He died two days later.

Kenneth always saw himself as a rebel and a radical. There were contradictions. In spite of his socialism, he travelled First Class when he could in order to get on with his work while travelling. He was less of a democrat than he perhaps realised in matters of organisation and administration. Departmental meetings scarcely existed. The revolution in literary studies in the Eighties pained him deeply, and it wounded him that in the eyes of some of the young he had come to seem a conservative establishment figure.

Friendship, he said himself, was a priority in his life. In spite of his reserve, he was deeply affectionate, and a great many people, students, colleagues, and fellow-scholars remember with gratitude what he did to help them. He was generous in all sorts of ways, from lending books from his formidable library to campaigning for those who he thought were victims of injustice. If it sometimes seemed that he lived for his work, yet his work was a passion. He loved literature. He loved it as he loved the theatre, for its human values, its accord with truth as he saw it. He did his best in a lifetime of extraordinary industry to interpret that truth, and share it with his readers and his students.[22]

REFERENCES

1. Muir, Kenneth (1933), *The Nettle and the Flower*, London: Oxford University Press.
2. Muir, Kenneth (1935), *Jonah and the Whale*, London: Samson Press.
3. Muir, Kenneth and O'Loughlin, Sean (1937), *The Voyage to Illyria: a New Study of Shakespeare*, London: Methuen.
4. Ewbank, Inga-Stina, Hunter, George and Edwards, Philip (eds.) (1980), *Shakespeare's Styles*, Cambridge: Cambridge University Press.
5. Muir, Kenneth (1985), 'The Future of Shakespeare', in Lehmann, John (ed.) *Penguin New Writing*, Harmondsworth: Penguin.
6. Muir, Kenneth (1949), *Collected Poems of Sir Thomas Wyatt*, London: Routledge. Revised 1969.
7. Muir, Kenneth (1961), *Unpublished Poems*, Liverpool: Liverpool University Press.
8. Muir, Kenneth (1963), *Life and Letters*, Liverpool: Liverpool University Press.
9. *The Times*, 16 October 1996.
10. Muir, Kenneth (1960) *Shakespeare as Collaborator*, London: Methuen.
11. Muir, Kenneth (1957), *Shakespeare's Sources: Comedies and Tragedies*, London: Methuen.
12. Muir, Kenneth (1977), *Sources of Shakespeare's Plays*, London: Methuen.
13. Muir, Kenneth (1960), *Five Plays of Racine*, London: Methuen.
14. Muir, Kenneth (1961), *Last Periods of Shakespeare, Racine and Ibsen*, Liverpool: Liverpool University Press.
15. Muir, Kenneth (1963), *Richard III*, New York and London: Signet.
16. Muir, Kenneth (1968), *Othello*, New Penguin Shakespeare Series, Harmondsworth: Penguin.
17. Allen, M.J.B. and K. Muir (eds) (1981), *Shakespeare's Plays in Quarto*, Berkeley and London: California University Press.
18. Muir, Kenneth (1970), *Comedy of Manners*, London: Hutchinson.
19. Muir, Kenneth (1975), *Three Plays of Thomas Middleton*, London: Dent.
20. Muir, Kenneth (1958), *John Keats: a Reassessment*, Liverpool: Liverpool University Press.
21. Beatty, B. and Davies, R.T. (eds) (1976), *Literature of the Romantic Period 1750–1850*, Liverpool: Liverpool University Press.
22. In this essay I have drawn on an obituary which I wrote for the *Independent* newspaper on 2 October 1996.

Appendix 2
Key Reference Works:
Some suggestions

W.R. Elton

Some recent ancillary tools for Shakespearean research are here listed. These concern conventional Renaissance uses, and include works which deserve to be more regularly consulted and cited by editors.[1]

Proverbs

R.W. Dent, (ed.) (1991), *Shakespeare's Proverbial Language; an index*, Berkeley, University of California Press. Cf. xi: 'primarily a revision and expansion of Tilley's "Shakespeare Index"'. [See Morris Palmer Tilley's *A Dictionary of the Proverbs in England in the Sixteenth and Seventeenth Centuries*, Ann Arbor, Michigan: University of Michigan Press, 1950.] Tilley's index, Dent notes (xi), 'has been ignored or badly misused in a surprising number of recent major editions. Two decades after Tilley, two additional proverb collections of major importance appeared: *Proverbs, Sentences, and Proverbial Phrases from English Writings Mainly before 1500*, edited by B.J. and H.W. Whiting, Cambridge, Massachusetts: The Belknap Press of Harvard University Press, 1968; and F.P. Wilson's Shakespeare-and-Tilley-minded revision of *The Oxford Dictionary of English Proverbs*, Oxford University Press, 1970. Both have been largely ignored by Shakespeare scholarship'. Dent's diagnosis is still applicable today.

See also R.W. Dent, (ed.) (1984), *Proverbial Language in English Drama Exclusive of Shakespeare, 1495–1616*, Berkeley: University of California Press.

P. 11: indexes 'extant English drama from Medwall to the year of Shakespeare's death'. It aims 'to be used without recourse to the proverb dictionaries of M.P. Tilley, B.J. Whiting, and F.P. Wilson which are the principal sources . . .'

Detlev Liebs, (ed.) (1998), *Lateinische Rechtsregeln und Rechtssprichwörter*, 6th ed., München, C.H. Beck. Latin and German indices. A valuable lexicon of legal maxims; some of these lie buried and unannotated in Shakespeare's legally allusive works.

Rhetoric

Heinrich Lausberg, *Handbook of Literary Rhetoric. A Foundation for Literary Study*. Ed. David E. Orton and R. Dean Anderson, Leiden: Brill, 1998.
Newly translated into English; an invaluable central dictionary of rhetorical terms. Indices in Latin, Greek, and French. (Lausberg was a student of E.R. Curtius.) Faults include omission of an Index Nominum; and, bibliographically, of names such as Sister Miriam Joseph and Brian Vickers. P.xxviii: 'A separate "Handbook of Literary Dialectics" is in preparation'.

Stanley E. Porter, ed., *Handbook of Classical Rhetoric in the Hellenistic Period, 330 BC–AD 400*, Leiden: Brill, 1997. Collection of essays by various hands on rhetoric and its history: e.g., Wilhelm Wuellner, 'Arrangement', including rhetorical order. Index of Ancient Authors; Index of Modern Authors.

Gert Ueding, (ed.), *Historisches Wörterbuch der Rhetorik*. 3 vols. of 8 thus far published: A-Hör (1992–1996), Tübingen: Max Niemeyer.
Valuable rhetorical reference tool. Bibliographies. Analogous to the invaluable *Historisches Wörterbuch der Philosophie*, ed. Günther Bien and Joachim Ritter; based on work by Rudolf Eisler, Basle: Schwabe. Vols. 1–9 (A-Sp: 1971–1995).

Heinrich F. Platt, (ed.) (1995), *English Renaissance Rhetoric and Poetics: A Systematic Bibliography of Primary and Secondary Sources*, Leiden: Brill. Shakespeare on pp. 448–65.

Language

Marvin Spevack, (1993), *A Shakespeare Thesaurus*, Hildesheim: Georg Olms. First conceptual classification of the entire Shakespearean vocabulary: 37 main groups, and 897 subgroups.
See also his *Harvard Concordance to Shakespeare* (1973), Hildesheim: Georg Olms; and his *Complete and Systematic Concordance to the Works of Shakespeare*. 9 vols, Hildesheim: Georg Olms, 1968–1980.

Gordon Williams, (ed.) (1994), *A Dictionary of Sexual Language and Imagery in Shakespearean and Stuart Literature*, 3 vols, London: Athlone Press.

Most expansive of such lexicons since the effort by Eric Partridge and subsequent such dictionaries; nevertheless, has significant omissions.

– *A Glossary of Shakespeare's Sexual Language* (London, Athlone Press, 1997). Draws on his larger dictionary.

EMBLEMS, ICONOGRAPHY, AND 'TOPOI'

Emblems

Arthur Henkel and Albrecht Schöne, (eds.) (1967), *Handbuch zur Sinnbildkunst des XVI. und XVII. Jahrhunderts*, Stuttgart: J.B. Metzler. (Far from complete. Cf. review by William S. Heckscher, *Renaissance Quarterly*, 23 (1970), 59–80.)

———— (1975), *Emblemata. Supplement der Erstausgabe*, Stuttgart, J.B. Metzler.

See emblem subject-index, ed. José Manuel Díaz de Bustamente, *Instrumentum Emblematicum*. 2 vols, Hildesheim: George Olms, 1992.

See editions with concordances and indices in Peter M. Daly (1988), *Index Emblematicus: The English Emblem Tradition*, 5 vols: University of Toronto Press. See Daly, 'Directions in Emblem Research – Past and Present', *Emblematica*, 1 (1986), 154–74; and Daly, 'The Bibliographic Basis for Emblem Studies', *Emblematica*, 8 (1994), 151–75.

Iconography

Guy de Tervarent, ed., *Attributs et Symboles dans l'Art Profane, 1450–1600*. 2nd edn, Geneva: Droz, 1997.

Peggy Muñoz Simonds, *Iconographic Research in English Renaissance Literature. A Critical Guide*, New York: Garland, 1985.

'Topoi'

Ernst R. Curtius (1967), *European Literature and the Latin Middle Ages*, Princeton University Press. Bible of *topos* studies. Urgently needs continuation through Renaissance.

Addenda

Bibliography

Bruce T. Sajdak, (ed.) (1991), *Shakespeare Index. An Annotated Bibliography of critical articles on the plays, 1959–1983.* 2 vols, Millwood: New York, Kraus International Publications. Includes very full index volume to a useful compilation.

Characters

Thomas L. Berger, S.L. Sondergard and William C. Bradford, Jr., (eds.) (1975), *An Index of Characters in Early Modern English Drama. Printed Plays, 1500–1660,* 2nd edn, Cambridge University Press, 1998.

Chronology

Yoshiko Kawachi, (ed.) (1986), *Calendar of English Renaissance Drama, 1558–1642,* New York: Garland. Includes day-to-day record of performances and tours.

Dedications

Franklin B. Williams, Jr., (ed.) (1962), *Index of Dedications and Commendatory Verses in English Books before 1641,* London, Bibliographical Society. Valuable and still untapped research tool; e.g., for study of patterns of dedications to a particular nobleman, such as Southampton. *STC* numbers.

Folk-motifs

Stith Thompson, (ed.) (1955–58), *Motif-index of folk literature; a classification of narrative elements in folk-tales, ballads, myths, fables, mediaeval romances, exempla, fabliaux, jest-books, and local legends,* Rev. edn, 6 vols, Bloomington, Indiana: Indiana University Press. Vol. 6, Index.

Here, again, Dent (*Shakespeare's Proverbial Language,* p. xvi) is apropos: 'A Tilley-like *Dictionary* devoted to folklore and superstition would be a useful tool'.

Renaissance Philosophy

Wilhelm Risse, *Bibliographia Philosophica Vetus. Repertorium generale systematicum operum philosophicorum usque ad MDCCC,* Hildesheim: George Olms, 1997. Invaluable 11–volume chronological listing including

Renaissance works: a year-by-year philosophical subject-index useful to Shakespeareans. (Proof of existing copies from over 450 libraries.)

Pars I.   Philosophia generalis.
Pars II.   Logica.
Pars III.   Metaphysica.
Pars IV.   Ethica et Politica.
Pars V.   De Anima
Pars VI.   Philosophia naturalis.
Pars VII.   Doxoscopia. (Geschichte der Philosophie)
Pars VIII.   Theses academicae. (Disputationem; Programme und aka-
             demische Reden). In 3 Teilbänden.
Pars IX.   Syllabus Auctorum.

For similar chronological listing of Renaissance logical works, see Risse (1965), *Bibliographia Logica*, Band I (1492–1800), Hildesheim, Olms. Contains also Index Auctorum, Index Commentatorium, Index Systematicus (by topics).

Renaissance Psychology

Hermann Schüling (1967), *Bibliographie der psychologischen Literatur des 16. Jahrhunderts*, Hildesheim, Olms.

Renaissance Theology

Hans J. Hillerbrand, (ed.) (1996), *Encyclopedia of the Reformation*, 4 vols, New York: Oxford University Press.

Peter Milward, (ed.) (1977), *Religious Controversies of the Elizabethan Age*, London: Scolar Press. Potentially very useful: has indices of authors and titles, but lacks subject index.
——— (1978), *Religious Controversies of the Jacobean Age*, London: Scolar Press; Lincoln, Nebraska: University of Nebraska Press. Annotated. Author and title indices; lacks subject index.

NOTE

1. For other such reference tools, see my *Shakespeare's World* (1979) New York, Garland, 419–40; see also, *ibid.*, 'Topoi, Themes, Emblems, etc.', 291–419. The present list is merely suggestive; further references are invited.

Notes on contributors

Frances K. Barasch ('Shakespeare and the Italians', pp. 240–54) is Professor of English at Baruch College of The City University of New York. She is the author and editor of numerous studies in art and literature, including 'The Grotesque', the Bauchun Chapel bosses at Norwich Cathedral (England), and Renaissance theatrical art and performance (*Commedia dell'Arte*) and Shakespeare).

Norman Blake ('Studies on Shakespeare's Language: An Overview', pp. 168–86) is Research Professor in English Language at the University of Sheffield, where he has been since 1973. He is the author of *Shakespeare's Language: An Introduction* (Macmillan, 1983) (re-issued as *The Language of Shakespeare*) and *Essays on Shakespeare's Language 1st Series* (Language Press, 1996), as well as numerous articles on Shakespeare's language. He is currently writing a new grammar of Shakespeare's language.

Graham Bradshaw ('State of Play', pp. 3–25) is Professor of English at Chuo University, Tokyo. He is the author of *Shakespeare's Scepticism* and *Misrepresentations: Shakespeare and the Materialists*.

John Russell Brown ('Shakespeare in Performance', pp. 108–17) is Consultant in Drama and Theatre at Middlesex University. He is a former Associate of the Royal National Theatre, London, and Professor of Theatre at the University of Michigan. His publications include *New Sites for Shakespeare: Theatre, the Audience and Asia* (Routledge, 1999), *William Shakespeare: Writing for Performance* (Macmillan, 1996), *Theatre Language* (Allen Lane, the Penguin Press, 1972) and *Shakespeare's Plays in Performance* (Arnold, 1966; Penguin Books, 1969; Applause, 1993). He is also the editor of *The Oxford Illustrated History of the Theatre* (Oxford University Press, 1996).

John G. Demaray ('The Still-Elusive Globe: Archaeological remains and scholarly speculations', pp. 142–51) is Abraham Pierson Professor of English and Renaissance Studies at Rutgers University. His books include the recently-published *Shakespeare and the Spectacles of Strangeness* (Duquesne University Press, 1998); *The Inventions of Dante's 'Commedia'* (Yale University Press, 1987); and *Milton's Theatrical Epic: The Invention and Design of* 'Paradise Lost' (Harvard University Press, 1980).

Elizabeth Story Donno ('Twelfth Night', pp. 322–8) is Senior Research Associate at The Huntington Library. Her publications include *An Elizabethan in 1582: The Diary of Richard Madox* (Hakluyt Society, 1976), *Complete Poetry of Andrew Marvell* (Penguin Books, 1972; St Martin's Press, 1974), *Elizabethan Minor Epics* (Columbia University Press and Routledge Kegan Paul, 1963) and *Sir John Harington's Metamorphosis of Ajax* (Columbia University Press and Routledge Kegan Paul, 1962).

Heather Dubrow ('Criticism on the *Sonnets*', 1994–7, pp. 302–10) is Tighe-Evans Professor (and also John Bascom Professor) at the University of Wisconsin–Madison. She is the author of four books and co-editor of a collection of essays. Her new book, *Shakespeare and Domestic Loss: Forms of Deprivation, Mourning, and Recuperation*, is forthcoming from Cambridge University Press. She has also published a chapbook of poetry and numerous articles on Renaissance literature and on pedagogy.

Philip Edwards ('Kenneth Muir (1907–96): An appreciation', pp. 329–35) has been professor of English Literature at Trinity College, Dublin, Essex University and Liverpool University, as well as visiting professor at the University of Michigan and Williams College. He is a Fellow of the British Academy. He has written widely on Shakespeare and the literature of his time, including *Shakespeare and the Confines of Art*, 1968; *Threshold of a Nation*, 1979; *Shakespeare: A Writer's Progress*, 1986; *Sea-Mark: The Metaphorical Voyage, Spenser to Milton*, 1997.

W.R. Elton ('Key Reference Works: Some Suggestions', pp. 336–40), founder and co-editor of the *Shakespearean International Yearbook*, is Professor of English literature at the Graduate School, City University of New York. His books include *'King Lear' and the Gods* (Huntington Library Press, 1966, University Press of Kentucky, 1988), *Shakespeare's World: Renaissance Intellectual Contexts* (Garland, 1979); (co-ed.) *Shakespeare and Dramatic Tradition* (Delaware, 1989); and (co-ed.) *A Selective, Annotated Bibliography of Shakespeare's 'Timon of Athens'* (Mellen, 1991). He is author of the forthcoming Ashgate monograph, *Shakespeare's 'Troilus and Cressida' and the Inns of Court Revels*. He was first Visiting Mellon Professor at the Institute for Advanced Study, Princeton, New Jersey.

Donna B. Hamilton ('Shakespeare and Religion', pp. 187–202) is Professor of English at the University of Maryland, College Park. Her publications include *Shakespeare and the Politics of Protestant England* (Harvester-Wheatsheaf, 1992; University Press of Kentucky, 1992); *Virgil and 'The Tempest': The Politics of Imitation* (Ohio State University Press, 1990); an edition of The Puritan, in *The Complete Works of Thomas Middleton*. Ed. Gary Taylor (Oxford University Press, forthcoming); and *Religion, Literature and Politics in Post-Reformation England, 1580–1680*, co-edited with Richard Strier (Cambridge University Press, 1996).

John Jowett ('After Oxford: Recent developments in textual studies', pp. 65–86) is a Fellow of the Shakespeare Institute, University of Birmingham. He is an Associate General Editor of the forthcoming Oxford University Press edition of Thomas Middleton's *Collected Works*, and is editing *Richard III* for the Oxford World's Classics series. He was an editor of the Oxford Shakespeare *Complete Works*, and has published various articles on textual studies.

Judith M. Kennedy ('*A Midsummer Night's Dream* in the 1990s', pp. 287–301) is former Professor of English at St Thomas University, Fredericton, New Brunswick, and has edited works by Montemayor, Googe and Ford, and published articles on Spenser and Shakespeare. She is co-author with Richard F. Kennedy of the volume on *A Midsummer Night's Dream* for the series 'Shakespeare: The Critical Tradition' (General Editor Brian Vickers, Athlone Press, Spring 1999), and co-ordinating editor of the New Variorum edition of the same play (in progress).

Ros King ('Staging the Globe', pp. 121–41) lectures in the School of English and Drama, Queen Mary and Westfield College, University of London. She serves on the Academic Committee at the Globe and on the Board of Directors of the English Shakespeare Company, and has worked as a dramaturge with both organisations: *Damon and Pythias* by Richard Edwards (Globe, 1996) and *As You Like it* and *Antony and Cleopatra* (ESC, 1998). She is currently finishing a collected edition of Richard Edwards's plays, poems and music for Manchester University Press.

Richard Knowles ('Merging the Kingdoms: *King Lear*', pp. 266–87) is Dickson-Bascom Professor in the Humanities at the University of Wisconsin–Madison. He is one of two general editors of the Modern Language Association's New Variorum Edition of Shakespeare. He edited the Variorum *As You Like It* and is completing the Variorum *King Lear*.

Richard Levin ('The Old and New Materialising of Shakespeare', pp. 87–107), Professor Emeritus of English at the State University of New York at Stony Book, is the author of *The Multiple Plot in English Renaissance Drama* and *New Readings vs. Old Plays: Recent Trends in the Reinterpretation of English Renaissance Drama*. His current project is a systematic critique of some of the newer approaches to Shakespeare and his contemporaries.

John M. Mucciolo ('Shakespeare's 'Colonialist' *Tempest*, 1975 to the present day', pp. 311–21), co-editor of *The Shakespearean International Yearbook*, is editor of *Shakespeare's Universe: Essays in Honour of W.R. Elton* (Ashgate, 1996). He is currently working on Shakespeare's *The Tempest* and Renaissance emblems.

R.J. Schoeck ('Shakespeare and the Law: An overview', pp. 219–39) is Emeritus Professor of English and Humanities at the University of Colorado. He was editor of the *Shakespeare Quarterly* while Director of Research Activities at the Folger Shakespeare Library. His publications include *More's Confutation of Tyndale*, (general editor), 3 vols, and *Erasmus of Europe*, 2 vols (Edinburgh University Press, 1990–93).

Bruce R. Smith ('What! *You* Will? Shakespeare and Homoeroticism', pp. 45–64) is Professor of English at Georgetown University, and is author of *Homosexual Desire in Shakespeare's England: A Cultural Poetics* (1991; revised edition 1994), as well as of a series of articles on gender and sexuality in early modern England. His most recent book is *The Acoustic World of Early Modern England: Attending to the O-Factor* (1999). Forthcoming are a volume on *Shakespeare and Masculinity* for the Oxford University Press series 'Shakespeare Topics' and an edition of *Twelfth Night* for the Bedford Books series 'Texts and Contexts'.

Johann P. Sommerville ('The Reign of James VI: A survey of recent writings', pp. 155–67) is Professor of History at the University of Wisconsin–Madison. His publications include *Royalists and Patriots. Politics and Ideology in England 1603–1640*, Addison Wesley/Longman, 1999, *Thomas Hobbes: Political Ideas in Historical Context*, Macmillan/St Martin's, 1992, and an edition of the *Political Writings* of King James VI and I, Cambridge University Press, 1994.

John M. Steadman ('Magnanimity and the Image of Heroic Character in Shakespeare's Plays: A Reappraisal', pp. 203–18) is Senior Research Associate at the Henry E. Huntington Library in San Marino, California, and a Professor of English Emeritus at the University of California. He is the author of numerous books, articles and reviews. His publications include *Milton and the Renaissance Hero* (Clarendon Press: Oxford 1967), *Milton's Epic Characters: Image and Idol* (Chapel Hill, N.C. 1968), and *The Myth of Asia* (New York: Simon and Schuster, 1969, and London: Macmillan, 1970).

Claus Uhlig ('Shakespeare between Politics and Aesthetics', pp. 26–44) teaches in the Institute for English and American Studies at Philipps-Universität Marburg. His research interests include Renaissance literature, Shakespeare studies, literary theory, literature and philosophy, aesthetics and comparative literature. Professor Uhlig has written and edited numerous books and articles, including *Klio und Natio: Studien zu Spenser und der englischen Renaissance* (1995).

John W. Velz ('*Julius Caesar* 1939–97: Where we are; How we got there', pp. 257–65), Professor Emeritus at the University of Texas, has published more than a dozen articles on various aspects of *Julius Caesar*. His special interest is in the classical and medieval backgrounds to Shakespeare. He is currently working on a monograph on Shakespeare and Plutarch and an article on 'Shakespeare's Ovid in the Twentieth Century', an ongoing project supplementing his *Shakespeare and the Classical Tradition* (1968).

Index